Julie Paschkis art—Uncle Sam on bike

This book is one of fifteen awarded as part of

the 2007 **We the People Bookshelf** on the **Pursuit of Happiness**

Presented by the National Endowment for the Humanities (NEH) in cooperation with the American Library Association (ALA). NEH and ALA gratefully acknowledge support from Scholastic Inc. for the 2007 Bookshelf.

www.neh.gov **www.ala.org**

COMMON SENSE
AND OTHER WRITINGS

Thomas Paine

Common Sense

and Other Writings

Edited and with an Introduction
by Gordon S. Wood

Notes by George W. Boudreau

THE MODERN LIBRARY

NEW YORK

2003 Modern Library Paperback Edition

Grateful acknowledgment is made to *The New York Review of Books* for permission to reprint
an essay from the June 8, 1995, issue of *The New York Review of Books* by Gordon S. Wood, as
revised by the author, as the Introduction to this volume. Copyright © 1995 by NYREV, Inc.
Revised and reprinted by permission of *The New York Review of Books*.

LIBRARY OF CONGRESS CATALOGING-IN-PUBLICATION DATA
Paine, Thomas, 1737–1809.
Common sense and other writings / Thomas Paine; with an introduction by
Gordon S. Wood; notes by George W. Boudreau.
p. cm.
Contents: Common sense—Four letters on interesting subjects—The American crisis,
number 1—The American crisis, number 13—Letter to Abbé Raynal—
The rights of man, part the second—The age of reason, part one.
ISBN 0-375-76011-3
1. Political science—Early works to 1800. I. Title.
JC177 .A3 2002   320.973—dc21   2002070279

Modern Library website address: www.modernlibrary.com

Printed in the United States of America

6 8 9 7 5

THOMAS PAINE

Thomas Paine, the political pamphleteer whose impassioned democratic voice played a pivotal role in the struggle for American independence and in the egalitarian revolution that swept the Western world in the late eighteenth century, was born in the English village of Thetford, Norfolk, on January 29, 1737. His father was a Quaker and a middle-class tradesman who made stays for women's corsets. Paine received a rudimentary education in history, mathematics, and science, but quit Thetford Grammar School at the age of thirteen to begin an apprenticeship as a corsetmaker in his father's shop. In 1757 he left home in search of adventure, spending time at sea aboard the privateer ship *King of Prussia*, a vessel engaged in England's latest war with France. Afterward he found employment in London as a journeyman staymaker, but failed to make a success of his own business in the seaside town of Sandwich. All the while Paine pursued a disciplined regimen of self-education: He kept abreast of current ideas and was particularly influenced by the work of two leading figures of the Enlightenment, Isaac Newton and John Locke. In 1761 Paine embarked on a new career as an exciseman in the coastal district of Lincolnshire, eventually settling in Lewes, Sussex. In *The Case of the Officers of Excise* (1772), his first political pamphlet, he argued that customs officers deserved higher wages. Subsequently dismissed from his post and living destitute in London, he became acquainted with Benjamin Franklin, who encouraged him to emigrate to the British colonies in North America.

Bearing a letter of introduction from Franklin praising him as "an ingenious, worthy young man," Paine arrived in Philadelphia on November 30, 1774, and was soon hired as an editor by *The Pennsylvania Magazine*. In 1775 he wrote *African Slavery in America*, an early abolitionist tract that endures as a scathing denunciation of the African slave trade. With the publication in 1776 of *Common Sense*, a stirring pamphlet calling for America's absolute political freedom from England, Paine emerged overnight as a leading figure in the struggle for independence. In assessing the work's impact, Woodrow Wilson stated: "*Common Sense* came from the press in Philadelphia early in January, 1776, the year the Congress uttered its Declaration of Independence, and no writing ever more instantly swung men to its humor. It was hard to resist its quick, incisive sentences, which cut so unhesitatingly to the heart of every matter they touched; which spoke, not the arguments of the lawyer or the calculations of the statesman, but the absolute spirit of revolt, and were as direct and vivid in their appeal as any sentences Mr. Swift himself could have written. They were cast, every one, not according to the canons of taste, but according to the canons of force, and declared, every one, without qualification, for independence."

At the outbreak of the Revolutionary War, Paine began distributing *The American Crisis* (1776–83), a series of pamphlets aimed at rallying American morale. "These are the times that try men's souls," wrote Paine in the first issue, published on December 19, 1776: "The summer soldier and the sunshine patriot will, in this crisis, shrink from the service of his country; but he that stands it NOW, deserves the love and thanks of man and woman. Tyranny, like hell, is not easily conquered; yet we have this consolation with us, that the harder the conflict, the more glorious the triumph." So moved was George Washington by these words that he ordered the pamphlet read to his troops at Valley Forge. *Public Good* (1780), another work from this period, appeals to the separate states to cooperate for the well-being of the entire nation and calls for a strengthened centralized government. By the end of the Revolution, however, Paine's influence as a philosopher and propagandist had run its course, and he fell out of political favor.

"Where liberty is not, there is my country," Paine once quipped. In 1787 he returned to Europe as a self-appointed "statesman for humanity" and soon became involved in the turmoil of the French Revolution. Enraged by Edmund Burke's attack on the uprising in *Reflections on the Revolution in France* (1790), Paine responded with *Rights of Man* (1791–92). The enormously popular two-part treatise, which both vindicates the revolution and boldly incites Englishmen to replace their own monarchy with a constitutional democracy, led to a warrant for his arrest on charges of high treason. Taking sanctuary in France, Paine was awarded French citizenship and elected a delegate to the National Convention, but he was imprisoned during the Reign of Terror for opposing the execution of Louis XVI. Upon his release he completed *The Age of Reason* (1794–96), a penetrating critique of organized religion that struck many readers as blasphemous. Paine further alienated the public with *Letter to George Washington* (1796), a stinging attack on his former compatriot. *Agrarian Justice* (1797), Paine's last significant pamphlet and the clearest articulation of his economic views, criticizes the accumulation of landed property in the hands of a wealthy few as the major cause of poverty in Europe.

"I wish most anxiously to see my much loved America," Paine wrote to a friend while still in France. "It is the Country from whence all reformations must originally spring." Increasingly disillusioned with life abroad, Paine accepted an invitation from President Thomas Jefferson to return to the United States. Yet he arrived back in his adopted land in 1802, after an absence of fifteen years, only to find himself vilified as an agitator and atheist. Having lost virtually all of his political influence, Thomas Paine died in relative obscurity in New York City on June 8, 1809, and was buried in New Rochelle on the farm given to him by the state of New York in recognition of his revolutionary writings. A decade later British journalist William Cobbett exhumed Paine's coffin and shipped it to England. But plans to erect a monument to Paine at a burial site in his homeland never materialized, and Paine's remains were eventually lost to posterity.

"I know not whether any man in the world has had more influence on its inhabitants or affairs for the last thirty years than Tom Paine," wrote John Adams in 1805. "Without the pen of Paine the sword of Washington would have been wielded in vain." Thomas Jefferson agreed: "[An] advocate for human liberty, Paine wrote for a country which permitted him to push his reasoning to whatever length it would go. . . . No writer has exceeded Paine in ease and familiarity of style; in perspicuity of expression, happiness of elucidation, and in simple and unassuming language." And Abraham Lincoln reflected: "I never tire of reading Paine."

"Paine was born a century before the world was prepared to accept and cherish his conception of human freedom and the rights of mankind," observed his biographer W. E. Woodward. "He was a forerunner of Abraham Lincoln [and] the most potent advocate during the whole of the eighteenth century for human freedom, equality of men, free education, universal suffrage, and rights of women." British politician and literary biographer Michael Foot commented: "Paine developed and was the first master of democratic prose, which is as important in explaining his appeal to a mass readership as is the content of his arguments. . . . All American presidents speak the language of Thomas Paine, although few of them know it." Philosopher Sidney Hook concluded: "Paine was a true cosmopolitan who felt that he was personally engaged wherever injustice was committed. . . . His passion for human freedom shines through everything he wrote."

CONTENTS

INTRODUCTION

Gordon S. Wood

In 1805 cantankerous old John Adams pondered what to call the wild and tumultuous age he had lived through. Perhaps, he said, it might be called "the Age of Folly, Vice, Frenzy, Brutality, Daemons, Buonaparte, . . . or the Age of the Burning Brand from the Bottomless Pit." Call it "anything," he said, but don't call it "the Age of Reason." It couldn't be "the Age of Reason" because it had been dominated by Thomas Paine. Adams doubted "whether any man in the world has had more influence on its inhabitants or affairs for the last thirty years than Tom Paine." But this influence was far from a good thing. Indeed, said Adams, "there can be no severer satyr on the age. For such a mongrel between pig and puppy, begotten by a wild boar on a bitch wolf, never before in any age of the world was suffered by the poltroonery of mankind, to run through such a career of mischief. Call it then the Age of Paine."

Despite Adams's bitter sarcasm, Paine would have loved the title: He was nothing if not vain. Why shouldn't the age be named after him? Who deserved it more? "With all the inconveniences of early life against me," Paine once wrote, "I am proud to say that with a perseverance undismayed by difficulties, a disinterestedness that compelled respect, I have not only contributed to raise a new empire in the world, founded on a new system of government, but I have arrived at an eminence in political literature, the most difficult of all lines to succeed and excel in, which aristocracy, with all its aids, has not been able to reach or to rival." Paine thought he had as much claim to being a Founder of the United States as Franklin, Adams, or Jefferson.

Can we honestly say he was wrong in this view? Did not Jefferson say in 1801 that Paine had labored on behalf of liberty and the American Revolution "with as much effort as any man living"? We can imagine "the age of Jefferson," but despite Adams's quirky comment, it is unlikely that we Americans will ever call the period of our Revolution "the age of Paine." Most Americans have never been able to make Paine a central figure in even the American Revolution, never mind the age as a whole. Indeed, for most of our history we have tended to ignore him. We let him die in obscurity in 1809 and ten years later even allowed William Cobbett to take his bones away to England. Even the Revolutionary leaders eventually came to ignore him. Although they all knew him, none of them publicly eulogized him upon his death. Most who had known him were embarrassed by the connection and wanted only to forget him. His papers were scattered and destroyed and memory of him was allowed to fade.

To this day Americans have never mounted any serious campaign to publish a complete and authoritative collection of all his writings, a collection that would match in aim if not in size those monumental multivolume editions of the Revolutionary leaders that are presently being published. The early biographies Americans wrote were muckraking diatribes that pictured Paine as an arrogant, drunken atheist. Despite a few feeble attempts in the nineteenth century to refute this image of Paine, not until the end of that century, with Moncure D. Conway's two-volume *The Life of Thomas Paine* (1892), was an authoritative laudatory treatment of Paine finally written. The place of Paine in the American pantheon of Revolutionaries has improved considerably since then, of course. But it was not until the 1970s that modern historians, as distinct from literary scholars, attempted a biography. Even with all the studies of Paine we have had over the past several decades, the man still does not quite fit in. Paine ranked himself "among the founders of a new Independent World," but most Americans have not agreed. Everyone senses that he is not like the other Revolutionaries, not like Franklin, Washington, Adams, or Jefferson. We cannot quite bring ourselves to treat him as one of America's founding fathers.

This neglect is actually quite astonishing, especially when we consider the breadth of his influence. His most thorough and recent biographer, Englishman John Keane, in his *Tom Paine: A Political Life* (1995), calls Paine "the greatest public figure of his generation." Paine, writes Keane, "made more noise in the world and excited more attention than such well-known European contemporaries as Adam Smith, Jean-Jacques Rousseau, Voltaire, Immanuel Kant, Madame de Stael, Edmund Burke, and Pietro Verri." His important works—*Common Sense, Rights of Man,* and *The Age of Reason*—"became the three most widely read political tracts of the eighteenth century." Paine's vision of a decent and happy life for ordinary people in this world, writes Keane, is still "alive and universally relevant, . . . undoubtedly more relevant than that of Marx, the figure most commonly identified with the nineteenth- and twentieth-century political project of bringing dignity and power to the wretched of the earth." In fact, says Keane, "not only is Paine's bold rejection of tyranny and injustice as far-reaching as that of his nineteenth-century successor, but his practical proposals . . . are actually more radical than Marx's, mainly because they managed to combine breathtaking vision, a humble respect for ordinary folk, and a sober recognition of the complexity of human affairs."

For Americans, Paine's most important work was *Common Sense,* the most influential and widely read pamphlet of the American Revolution and one of the most brilliant pamphlets ever written in the English language. It went through dozens of editions and sold at least 150,000 copies, at a time when most pamphlets sold in the hundreds or a few thousand at best. Although the pamphlet, published in January 1776, probably did not cause Americans to think of declaring independence, it did express more boldly and eloquently than any other writing what many of them had come to feel about America's tie to the British crown. Paine dismissed the king as the "Royal Brute" and called for American independence immediately. "For God's sake, let us come to a final separation . . . ," he implored. "The birthday of a new world is at hand." There is no doubt that, as his friend Benjamin Rush said, "its effects were sudden and extensive upon the American mind."

Nearly everyone knew it was a work of genius, and it immediately made Paine an American celebrity.

Paine may not have been an original thinker, but he did have the uncanny ability to put into readable form what others had conceived of. In *Common Sense* Paine may not have uttered new thoughts, but he did set forth much of what constituted radical, enlightened Anglo-American thinking during the last quarter of the eighteenth century. Like fellow radical Thomas Jefferson, Paine optimistically believed that every person had a natural or moral sense that compelled them to reach out to others. Indeed, both he and Jefferson thought that the natural sociability of people might even replace much of governmental authority. If only the natural moral tendencies of people to love and care for one another were allowed to flow freely, unclogged by the artificial interference of government, particularly monarchical government, Paine and other optimistic republicans believed, then society would hold itself together and prosper.

Unlike liberals of the twenty-first century, Paine and other liberal-minded thinkers in the eighteenth century tended to see society as beneficent and government as malevolent. Social honors, social distinctions, perquisites of office, business contracts, legal privileges and monopolies, even excessive property and wealth of various sorts—indeed, all social inequities and deprivations—seemed to flow from connections to government, in the end from connections to monarchical government. "Society," said Paine in a brilliant summary of this liberal view in the opening paragraph of *Common Sense,* "is produced by our wants and government by our wickedness." Society "promotes our happiness *positively* by uniting our affections," government "*negatively* by restraining our vices." Society "encourages intercourse," government "creates distinctions." The emerging liberal Jeffersonian view that the least government was the best was based on just such a hopeful belief in the natural harmony of society.

But Paine and other liberals went further in their radicalism. In that new and better world that Paine and other Revolutionaries envisioned, war itself might be abolished. Just as enlightened liberal Americans sought a new kind of republican domestic politics that would end tyranny, so too did many of them seek a new kind of international republican politics that would promote peace among nations. Paine very much held out this kind of enlightened vision.

Throughout the eighteenth century, liberal intellectuals had looked forward to a new republican world in which corrupt monarchical diplomacy, secret alliances, dynastic rivalries, and balances of power would be abolished. Since the dynastic ambitions, the bloated bureaucracies, and the standing armies of monarchies were what promoted the waging of war, the elimination of monarchy promised the elimination of war. A world of republican states would encourage a peace-loving diplomacy—one based on the natural concert of international commerce. If the people of the various nations were left alone to exchange goods freely among themselves—without the corrupting interference of selfish war-mongering monarchical courts, irrational dynastic rivalries, and the secret double-dealing diplomacy of the past—then, it was hoped, international politics would become republicanized and pacified.

"Our plan is commerce," Thomas Paine told Americans in *Common Sense,* "and that, well attended to, will secure us the peace and friendship of all Europe; because it is the interest of all Europe to have America a free port." America had no need to form traditional military alliances. Trade between peoples alone would be enough. Indeed, for Paine and other liberals, peaceful trade among the people of the various nations became the counterpart in the international sphere to the sociability of people in the domestic sphere. Just as enlightened thinkers like Paine and Jefferson foresaw a republican society held together solely by the natural affection of people, so too did they envision a world held together by the natural interests of peoples in commerce. In both the national and international spheres, monarchy and its intrusive institutions and monopolistic ways were what prevented a natural harmony of people's feelings and interests.

After *Common Sense* established his reputation, Paine came to know nearly all of the political leaders of the United States, including Washington, Jefferson, and Franklin, and he continued to write on politics and on behalf of the American cause. If the distinguished literary scholar A. Owen Aldridge is correct in his well-argued attribution made nearly two decades ago, Paine also wrote in 1776 *Four Letters on Interesting Subjects,* one of the most significant pamphlets on American constitutional thinking published during the Revolution. It is a brilliant radical piece, and Paine seems as likely an author as anyone, for few other Americans in Pennsylvania in 1776 could have written it.

Perhaps because *Four Letters* was so radical and so controversial, Paine never claimed authorship of it. But he did claim his important and popular *American Crisis* series, thirteen essays that appeared throughout the war with Britain. The most famous was the first, published on December 19, 1776, that opens with the memorable lines:

> These are the times that try men's souls: The summer soldier and the sunshine patriot will, in this crisis, shrink from the service of his country; but he that stands it NOW, deserves the love and thanks of man and woman.

Washington had this essay read to his troops at Christmas 1776 on the eve of their first victory at Trenton.

When during the Revolutionary War the French *philosophe* the Abbé Raynal criticized the French monarchy for allying itself with a republic and the new United States for not having a justifiable cause to revolt, it was left to Paine to formulate a powerful reply. In his *Letter to the Abbé Raynal on the Affairs of North America* (1782), he turned the American Revolution into a world-historical event and the harbinger of world citizenship and world peace. Other Americans conceived of the Revolution in these terms, but no one was able to say it as he did.

If these important contributions were not sufficient to immortalize Paine as one of the founders of the United States, then we have his extraordinary book *Rights of Man* (1791–92), which one of his recent biographers says became "the best-selling book in the history of publishing." Although the book was written after Paine had left the United States in 1787 and was intended as a refutation of Edmund Burke's *Reflections on the Revolution in France* (1790), it actually sums up what he had learned about constitutionalism and political theory during his years in America. In fact, *Rights of Man*, especially Part II, is the best and most succinct expression of American Revolutionary political thinking ever written.

Paine himself noted how "American" were his reactions to events in Europe. In *Rights of Man* Paine laid out with great clarity the new assumptions about politics and society that the American Revolution had recently made manifest: that the age of hereditary monarchy and aristocracy was over; that people were citizens, not subjects, and were born with equal natural rights; that the people created written constitutions that defined and limited their governments; that these written constitutions could not be changed by the governments but only by the sovereign people themselves; that the rulers had no rights of their own but were only temporary agents of the people, who must continually watch and empower them through electoral consent; that because people are naturally sociable, society is practically autonomous and self-regulating; and that people were free and independent to pursue happiness in their own way. Indeed, if Jefferson had ever written out in any systematic way what he believed about politics, it would have resembled much of *Rights of Man.*

Despite these great intellectual contributions, however, Paine apparently has never quite had what it takes to get admitted to the sacred temple of American Founders. Perhaps it is because Paine never became president of the United States as most of the other Founders did. But neither did Franklin, and his credentials as a Founder seem solid. There seems to be something else at work to account for America's relative neglect of Paine and its inability to think of him as one of its Founders.

Maybe his religious views account for his relative neglect. Everyone seems to recall that Theodore Roosevelt called him that "filthy little atheist," a label that summed up the nineteenth-century fear of the man. Paine did publish *The Age of Reason* in 1793. The work was a vehement attack on Christianity, the Bible, and orthodox religion, but it was in no way atheistic; indeed, Paine went out of his way to set forth his deistic belief in God the creator and harmonizer of the world. But in the fearful times of the French Revolution most Americans could see only infidelity, and the label of atheist stuck.

Yet important as Paine's religious views were in shaping America's response to him, by themselves they do not seem to be what really distinguishes him from the other founding fathers. In fact, one would be hard put to demonstrate the ways his rationalistic religion, his deism, differed from the religious views of his contemporaries Franklin or Jefferson. Paine's religious opinions were common among liberal thinking gentlemen of the era. Yet no one calls the other founding fathers "atheists." It is not just his religious views that account for Paine's peculiar place in our Revolutionary tradition.

Perhaps it is because Paine was a recent immigrant to America. He came to America in late 1774, only fourteen months before he burst upon the American mind with publication of *Common Sense*. Yet, of course, other important Revolutionary leaders were also recent immigrants. James Wilson arrived from Scotland in 1765, just at the beginning of the imperial crisis, and Alexander Hamilton came from the West Indies to New York only in 1772. As Paine himself said in 1778, "In a country where all men were once adventurers, the difference of a few years in their arrival" could not make them less American.

Maybe the explanation of Paine's peculiarity lies in the fact that he was not born a gentleman. But of course most of the founding fathers were not born gentlemen either. They had to achieve that important eighteenth-century status, usually by getting a liberal arts education at Harvard, Princeton, or some such college. Of the Revolutionary leaders, Franklin's origins were most similar to Paine's. Both were born of obscure parents, both were apprenticed as artisans, and both received only a few years of education; neither attended college. But Franklin became a very different person from Paine. Franklin became a very wealthy man, and long before the Revolution he had become fully acculturated and assimilated to gentlemanly status. Because of Franklin's great literary legacy to us, his autobiography (which was never published in his lifetime), we actually have a very misleading image of Franklin. We are too apt to think of Franklin as "Poor Richard," the hardworking printer who made it. But after ostentatiously retiring from his printing business at the age of forty-two, Franklin never again worked a day in his life. He became a full-fledged leisured gentleman with all his time and energy devoted to science, philanthropy, and public service. Although Franklin never achieved his hopes of becoming a member of the upper levels of the English government, he moved at ease in the highest aristocratic circles. Franklin in fact played the social game of courtier as well as anyone in Anglo-American society, and until the Revolution, built his career on cultivating the right people. While no doubt many in London and in Philadelphia could never hide their contempt for Franklin as a parvenu, he seldom let his origins show. He was a man superbly of the eighteenth century, wearing masks as that century taught men to do. So he always "appeared" the gentleman.

In this respect Paine was different from Franklin and all the other founding fathers. He never really shed his lowly origins. Paine was born in Thetford, England, in 1737. For a while he followed the trade of his father as a corsetmaker. He went to sea for several years, tried his hand at running a tobacco shop, and was twice dismissed as an excise officer collecting taxes for the British government. His first wife died after a year of marriage, and he separated from his second wife after three years of marriage and never married again. During all this time in England he mingled in radical circles and picked up from lectures and pamphlets a substantial understanding of the most liberal thinking in the English-speaking world. Only in 1774, deeply in debt, did he arrive in the colonies filled with rage at the society that had denied him what he believed was his rightful place.

Not only was he unable to shed his humble origins, but, unlike Franklin, he could never entirely throw off the effects of all those years living in poverty and obscurity pressed close to the bottom of English society. Paine never really became a gentleman in the way Franklin did. To be sure, he moved in aristocratic and gentry circles, especially after his fame was established in 1776. His writings became an entrée into liberal gentry society and enabled him to mingle with Washington, Jefferson, or Lafayette. Yet as much as he joined in their conversations, Paine was never fully accepted as a gentleman.

Something about Paine bothered members of the America's gentry, particularly the aristocratic likes of William Smith of Philadelphia and Gouverneur Morris of New York. These sorts of gentlemen called Paine many things, but one of the most common and opprobrious terms they could think of to abuse him with was to say that he lacked connections. Smith charged Paine in 1776 with having neither "character nor connections." And Morris in 1779 called him a "mere adventurer from England, without fortune, without family or connections, ignorant even of grammar."

To be "without connections" hardly strikes us today as much of an insult, but for the vertically organized and patronage-dominated social world of the eighteenth century it said a lot. Paine seemed to be someone floating loose in this hierarchical world, coming out of nowhere and tied to no one, a man without a home and even without a country. Paine's initial response to this sort of criticism was defensive. In his debate in the press with Smith in 1776 he felt compelled to deny that he was a mere piece of debris that had washed up on America's shores.

The culture's emphasis on connections forced Paine to emphasize that when he sailed from England to America in 1774 he had possessed a letter of introduction from Franklin, whom he had met in London.

But after the explosive success of *Common Sense* Paine had no further need for such letters of introduction in America. Paine's reputation was made at once, and no one needed to be told who he was. Of course, he continued to rely on patronage of one sort or another. In 1777 friends got him a position as secretary to the Committee of Foreign Affairs of the Continental Congress, which only drew him into one political dispute after another, culminating in his forced resignation in 1779. Increasingly, he seemed at odds with everyone and complained endlessly of his poverty and America's neglect of him. Franklin's daughter said in 1781 that Paine should have died "the instant he had finished his *Common Sense,* for he never again will have it in his power to leave the world with so much credit."

Although friends eventually secured for him a 300-acre farm in New Rochelle and a 3,000-dollar congressional grant, Paine's complaints of poverty and neglect continued. He felt unwanted, unattached, but soon he began to turn the criticism of himself as a person "without connections" into a positive attribute. As early as 1778, in No. 7 of *The American Crisis,* he declared that he wrote for no personal advantage, not even for America. "My principle is universal. My attachment is to all the world, and not to any particular part, and if what I advance is right, it is right no matter where or who it comes from."

He became obsessed with his lack of connections. He boasted that he owned no property, had no residence, had never voted, and could "view the matter rather than the parties, and having no interests, connections with, or personal dislike to either, shall endeavor to serve all." He talked of being "a citizen of the world," one who "never had nor ever would have anything to do in private affairs." Of course, much of this was conventional eighteenth-century liberal rhetoric. Most of the founding fathers at one time or another talked of being citizens of the world. All enlightened gentlemen were supposed to be members of the cosmopolitan "republic of letters" that transcended all national boundaries. But Paine gave this traditional notion a special emphasis. The other Revolutionary leaders may have considered themselves citizens of the world, but America was still home to them. But for

Paine this was always much in doubt. Perhaps Americans did not know, he wrote in 1779 with some bitterness, "that it was neither the place nor the people but the Cause itself that irresistibly engaged me in its support; for I should have acted the same part in any other country could the same circumstances have arisen there which have happened here." He saw himself as little better than a "refugee, and that of the most extraordinary kind, a refugee from the Country I have befriended." He became a man without a home, without a country, and quite literally a citizen of the world.

Thus it was inevitable that sooner or later he would return to Europe. By 1787, when he returned, he had come to see himself as the intellectual progenitor of revolutions. After being hounded out of England for writing *Rights of Man,* Paine fled to France and was granted French citizenship and a seat in the National Convention, where he pled for the life of Louis XVI and was shouted down by Marat. During the Terror he was held for ten months in prison, where he continued work on his *Age of Reason.* Even after these harrowing experiences in France and his persistent inability to learn to speak French, he hesitated to leave France for the United States, whose citizenship he had claimed while in prison. The United States was not home, but just a symbol for him; and from the time he returned to America in 1802 until his death in 1807, he was not happy.

By then it was clear how Paine's status differed from the founders. He was exclusively a writer, not a political leader. He stood in an adversarial relationship to the dominant political culture, having spent most of his adult life as an opposition political writer. In 1802 Paine described himself as having achieved "an established fame in the literary world," which is why he merits a collection of his writings. Today we might more accurately describe him as a "public intellectual," as someone who spent his life writing and criticizing his society. He was not simply someone who wrote for money, a hired pen. Although he did sometimes write on commission, he was not really like those Grub Street scribblers hired by English officials to turn out political propaganda. But as a "public intellectual" neither was he a man of letters involved in the belletristic tradition. Paine was not a literary figure in the sense that the novelist Charles Brockden Brown or the poet John Trumbull wanted to be. He was a modern intellectual, America's first modern intellectual, an unconnected social critic, who, as he said in 1779, knew "but one kind of life . . . and that is a thinking one, and of course, a writing one."

This goes to the heart of the important differences separating Paine from the other Revolutionary luminaries. As much as Jefferson, Madison, Adams and others wrote, they do not resemble modern critical intellectuals in the way that Paine does. They were gentlemen attached in various ways to their society, and their writing was very different from Paine's. They were not social critics; in fact, they were amateurs at writing—meaning that their writing was only a by-product of their careers as lawyers, planters, or political leaders. Writing was only one of their many duties or accomplishments as gentlemen. They were amateur writers in the same way they were amateur politicians. For all the time and energy the Revolutionary leaders devoted to politics, most of them cannot accurately be described as professional politicians, at least not in any modern sense of that term. Their relationship to public life and their conception of public service were very different from those of today. Their political careers, like their literary careers, did not create but rather followed from their previously established social positions as important gentlemen. Paine's status was very different from any of them.

Some of this difference between Paine and the other Revolutionary leaders is revealed in the different kinds of audiences they wrote for and in the different tone of their writings. Most of the Revolutionary leaders—Adams, Jefferson, John Dickinson—spoke and wrote for one another, for rational, enlightened, restricted audiences of educated men like themselves. Their speeches and writings were generally reasonable affairs that aimed to persuade or explain. Their works were often highly stylized by rhetorical rules and were usually very erudite, filled with Latin quotations and classical and esoteric citations to the literature of Western culture.

Paine's writing was very different. Much of the consternation and awe aroused by Paine's writings came from his deliberate rejection of the traditional apparatus of persuasion in his determined effort to reach a wide audience and to express feelings—revulsions and visions—that the existing conventions of writing would not allow. Paine looked for readers everywhere, but especially in the tavern- and artisan-centered worlds of the cities. So he used simple, direct—some critics said coarse, barnyard—metaphors and relied on his readers knowing only the Bible and the Book of Common Prayer. "As it is my design to make those that can scarcely read understand," he wrote, "I shall therefore avoid every literary ornament and put it in language as plain as the alphabet." He aimed to break through the usual niceties and forms of rhetoric and to reach people with what Keane calls "a thoroughly plebeian style." What was frightening to authorities about Paine's writings was not so much what he said but how he said it and to whom. He spoke to common ordinary people about issues of government and religion as no one in history ever had. He sought to make political and religious criticism accessible to the common reader.

But, more important, he spoke with a rage and a fury that none of the founding fathers ever expressed. He spoke out of a deep anger shared by many common people in these years—artisans, shopkeepers, traders, petty merchants—people who were at long last tired of being scorned and held in contempt by a monarchical and aristocratic world. The American Revolutionary gentry-leaders, liberally educated graduates of Harvard or Princeton, could not really represent the indignation and rage of these ordinary people, but Paine could. He spoke out of a tradition of radical republicanism that ran deeper and was more bitter and yet more modern than the balanced and reasonable classical republicanism of most of the founders. Some of the Revolutionary leaders were uneasy over the anger that Paine was stirring up among ordinary folk, but because they themselves spoke in the name of the people, they were in no position to resist his fiery language. Only in the 1790s, when American artisans and small farmers like Matthew Lyon and William Manning began voicing their own resentments and rage against the leisured aristocracy, did many of the founders come to realize what the Revolution and Paine's rhetoric had released—a democratic revolution of common ordinary folk that went well beyond what the Revolutionary leaders of 1776 had anticipated.

Unfortunately for Paine's reputation, most of the common people that he emotionally represented brought with their democratic revolution and their anti-aristocratic attitudes an intense religiosity and an evangelical Christianity that Paine never shared. Upon his return to America, Paine was attacked as a "lying, drunken, brutal infidel," and sympathizers like aged Samuel Adams grieved over what they took to be Paine's efforts to "unchristianize the mass of our citizens." Paine denied truthfully that he was ever an atheist, but it was to no avail. Every defense he made only made matters worse. He had lived by the pen, and in the end he died by the pen. He became, in his biographer's words, one of "the first modern public figures to suffer firsthand" from a scurrilous and powerful press. He was always a man out of joint with his times, and he has remained so ever since.

———

GORDON S. WOOD received his B.A. from Tufts University and his Ph.D. from Harvard University. Since 1969 he has been at Brown University, where he is a professor of history. In 1993 he won the Pulitzer Prize for *The Radicalism of the American Revolution.* He lives in Providence, Rhode Island.

A NOTE ON THE TEXT

All of Thomas Paine's pamphlets, letters, and essays were reprinted countless times. For accuracy, the earliest text of each piece was used wherever possible for this edition, or the most reliable text based on current scholarship. Save for several small errors, we have preserved the texts intact.

The various editions used are:

Common Sense—Styner and Cist, February 1776

Four Letters—Styner and Cist, 1776

American Crisis I—Styner and Cist, December 1776

American Crisis XIII—*Pennsylvania Packet*, April 19, 1783

Excerpts from *Letter to the Abbé Raynal*—Philip Foner's *Complete Writings of Thomas Paine*

Rights of Man, Part Two—J. S. Jordan, February 1792, third printing

The Age of Reason—Barrois, February 1794, third printing.

Manuscripts for *Common Sense, Four Letters on Interesting Subjects, The American Crisis I,* and *The Age of Reason, Part the First* were provided by the American Philosophical Society. *The American Crisis XIII* manuscript was provided by the Library Company of Philadelphia and the *Rights of Man, Part Two* manuscript was provided by the New York Public Library.

The American Crisis is a group of articles Paine wrote over a seven-year period. They were numbered I–XI; he titled the tenth *The Crisis*

Extraordinaire. He continued with *The American Crisis, Number XII* and finished the series with the article *The Last Crisis, Number XIII,* although some editors label it *The American Crisis, Number XIII.* This article was printed in both the *Pennsylvania Packet* and *The Pennsylvania Journal* on April 19, 1783 (it appeared in two other papers a week later). Scholarship has pointed to the *Pennsylvania Packet* as the more accurate of the two printings.

After Thomas Paine's arrest in December 1793, he added a final section to *The Age of Reason.* This revised, complete edition was printed only once, in Paris by Barrois in February 1794, and is extremely rare. The text of the final section included here comes from Moncure Conway's edition *The Writings of Thomas Paine,* volume 3.

Please note that this edition presents both footnotes and endnotes. The footnotes are Paine's own and are preserved in full. The endnotes were compiled by a modern scholar.

COMMON SENSE
AND OTHER WRITINGS

COMMON SENSE

ADDRESSED TO THE
INHABITANTS OF AMERICA
1776

Just six months and a few city blocks separated the publication of Common Sense *by Philadelphia printer Robert Bell on January 10, 1776, at his Third Street shop and the Continental Congress's approval of the Declaration of Independence in the Pennsylvania State House on July 4. The pamphlet that Thomas Paine anonymously presented to the public that January day played a crucial role in gaining public support for American independence. In words they could understand, using references they knew, the British-born writer told them why they no longer needed their king.*

Thomas Pain (he did not begin using the "e" at the end of his name until 1776, name spelling being like spelling in general somewhat fluid in the eighteenth century) was a recent immigrant to Philadelphia, arriving from Britain late in 1774 with letters of reference from Benjamin Franklin, who was then colonial agent at London representing Pennsylvania and three other colonies, and a career record that was strewn with failures. His first days in the city—the largest in Britain's American colonies—were devoted to finding work, and eventually he was hired to write for, then edit, The Pennsylvania Magazine. *Like those of many residents of the city, his thoughts were often filled with the conflict going on between England and the colonies. The British attack on Lexington and Concord on April 19, 1775, led Paine to write, "Surely the ministry are all mad; they never will be able to conquer America." In the months that followed, Paine's friendships with leaders of the American cause deepened, as did his interest in writing about that cause.*

The public's reaction to Common Sense was overwhelming. All copies of the two-shilling pamphlet sold in one week. New editions were immediately rushed to press by both Bell—with whom Paine had already had a falling-out over the proceeds for the publication—and Philadelphia printer Thomas Bradford, whose volume included an appendix and Paine's "Address to the Quakers." By March, a report in Britain stated that Common Sense "is read to all ranks; and as many as read, so many become converted; tho' perhaps an hour before were most violent against the least idea of independence." Paine himself estimated that over 150,000 copies were soon in print, and we know that many of these were read publicly or shared by several readers. Paine prided himself that he made no profits from the pamphlet; he gave the money he did receive to buy mittens for the American troops in Quebec.

INTRODUCTION

Perhaps the sentiments contained in the following pages, are not *yet* sufficiently fashionable to procure them general favor; a long habit of not thinking a thing *wrong*, gives it a superficial appearance of being *right*, and raises at first a formidable outcry in defence of custom. But the tumult soon subsides. Time makes more converts than reason.

As a long and violent abuse of power, is generally the Means of calling the right of it in question (and in Matters too which might never have been thought of, had not the Sufferers been aggravated into the inquiry) and as the King of England hath undertaken in his *own Right*, to support the Parliament in what he calls *Theirs*, and as the good people of this country are grievously oppressed by the combination, they have an undoubted privilege to inquire into the pretensions of both, and equally to reject the usurpation of either.

In the following sheets, the author hath studiously avoided every thing which is personal among ourselves. Compliments as well as censure to individuals make no part thereof. The wise, and the worthy, need not the triumph of a pamphlet; and those whose sentiments are injudicious, or unfriendly, will cease of themselves unless too much pains are bestowed upon their conversion.

The cause of America is in a great measure the cause of all mankind. Many circumstances hath, and will arise, which are not local, but universal, and through which the principles of all Lovers of Mankind are affected, and in the Event of which, their Affections are interested. The laying a Country desolate with Fire and Sword, declaring War against the natural rights of all Mankind, and extirpating the Defenders thereof from the Face of the Earth, is the Concern of every Man to whom Nature hath given the Power of feeling; of which Class, regardless of Party Censure, is the

AUTHOR.

P. S. The Publication of this new Edition hath been delayed, with a View of taking notice (had it been necessary) of any Attempt to refute the Doctrine of Independance: As no Answer hath yet appeared, it is now presumed that none will, the Time needful for getting such a Performance ready for the Public being considerably past.

Who the Author of this Production is, is wholly unnecessary to the Public, as the Object for Attention is the *Doctrine itself,* not the *Man.* Yet it may not be unnecessary to say, That he is unconnected with any Party, and under no sort of Influence public or private, but the influence of reason and principle.

Philadelphia, February 14, 1776

OF THE ORIGIN AND DESIGN OF GOVERNMENT IN GENERAL. WITH CONCISE REMARKS ON THE ENGLISH CONSTITUTION.

Some writers have so confounded society with government, as to leave little or no distinction between them; whereas they are not only different, but have different origins. Society is produced by our wants, and government by our wickedness; the former promotes our happiness *positively* by uniting our affections, the latter *negatively* by restraining our vices. The one encourages intercourse, the other creates distinctions. The first is a patron, the last a punisher.

Society in every state is a blessing, but government even in its best state is but a necessary evil; in its worst state an intolerable one; for when we suffer, or are exposed to the same miseries *by a government,* which we might expect in a country *without government,* our calamity is heightened by reflecting that we furnish the means by which we suffer. Government, like dress, is the badge of lost innocence;[1] the palaces of kings are built on the ruins of the bowers of paradise. For were the impulses of conscience clear, uniform, and irresistably obeyed, man would need no other lawgiver; but that not being the case, he finds it necessary to surrender up a part of his property to furnish means for the protection of the rest; and this he is induced to do by the same prudence which in every other case advises him out of two evils to choose the least. *Wherefore,* security being the true design and end of government, it unanswerably follows that whatever *form* thereof appears most likely to ensure it to us, with the least expence and greatest benefit, is preferable to all others.

In order to gain a clear and just idea of the design and end of government, let us suppose a small number of persons settled in some sequestered part of the earth, unconnected with the rest, they will then represent the first peopling of any country, or of the world. In this state of natural liberty, society will be their first thought. A thousand motives will excite them thereto, the strength of one man is so unequal to his wants, and his mind so unfitted for perpetual solitude, that he is soon obliged to seek assistance and relief of another, who in his turn requires the same. Four or five united would be able to raise a tolerable dwelling in the midst of a wilderness, but *one* man might labour out the common period of life without accomplishing any thing; when he had felled his timber he could not remove it, nor erect it after it was removed; hunger in the mean time would urge him from his work, and every different want call him a different way. Disease, nay even misfortune would be death, for though neither might be mortal, yet either would disable him from living, and reduce him to a state in which he might rather be said to perish than to die.

Thus necessity, like a gravitating power, would soon form our newly arrived emigrants into society, the reciprocal blessings of which, would supersede, and render the obligations of law and government unnecessary while they remained perfectly just to each other; but as nothing but heaven is impregnable to vice, it will unavoidably happen, that in proportion as they surmount the first difficulties of emigration, which bound them together in a common cause, they will begin to relax in their duty and attachment to each other; and this remissness, will point out the necessity, of establishing some form of government to supply the defect of moral virtue.

Some convenient tree will afford them a State-House, under the branches of which, the whole colony may assemble to deliberate on public matters. It is more than probable that their first laws will have the title only of REGULATIONS, and be enforced by no other penalty than public disesteem. In this first parliament every man, by natural right, will have a seat.

But as the colony increases, the public concerns will increase likewise, and the distance at which the members may be separated, will render it too inconvenient for all of them to meet on every occasion as at first, when their number was small, their habitations near, and the public concerns few and trifling. This will point out the convenience of their consenting to leave the legislative part to be managed by a select number chosen from the whole body, who are supposed to have the same concerns at stake which those have who appointed them, and who will act in the same manner as the whole body would act were they present. If the colony continue increasing, it will become necessary to augment the number of the representatives, and that the interest of every part of the colony may be attended to, it will be found best to divide the whole into convenient parts, each part sending its proper number; and that the *elected* might never form to themselves an interest separate from the *electors,* prudence will point out the propriety of having elections often; because as the *elected* might by that means return and mix again with the general body of the *electors* in a few months, their fidelity to the public will be secured by the prudent reflexion of not making a rod for themselves. And as this frequent interchange will establish a common interest with every part of the community, they will mutually and naturally support each other, and on this (not on the unmeaning name of king) depends the *strength of government, and the happiness of the governed.*

Here then is the origin and rise of government; namely, a mode rendered necessary by the inability of moral virtue to govern the world; here too is the design and end of government, viz. freedom and security. And however our eyes may be dazzled with show, or our ears deceived by sound; however prejudice may warp our wills, or interest darken our understanding, the simple voice of nature and of reason will say, it is right.

I draw my idea of the form of government from a principle in nature, which no art can overturn, viz. that the more simple any thing is, the less liable it is to be disordered, and the easier repaired when disordered; and with this maxim in view, I offer a few remarks on the so much boasted constitution of England.[2] That it was noble for the dark and slavish times in which it was erected, is granted. When the world was over-run with tyranny the least remove therefrom was a glorious rescue. But that it is imperfect, subject to convulsions, and incapable of producing what it seems to promise, is easily demonstrated.

Absolute governments (tho' the disgrace of human nature) have this advantage with them, that they are simple; if the people suffer, they know the head from which their suffering springs, know likewise the remedy, and are not bewildered by a variety of causes and cures. But the constitution of England is so exceedingly complex, that the nation may suffer for years together without being able to discover in which part the fault lies, some will say in one and some in another, and every political physician will advise a different medicine.

I know it is difficult to get over local or long standing prejudices, yet if we will suffer ourselves to examine the component parts of the English constitution, we shall find them to be the base remains of two ancient tyrannies, compounded with some new republican materials.

First.—The remains of monarchical tyranny in the person of the king.

Secondly.—The remains of aristocratical tyranny in the persons of the peers.

Thirdly.—The new republican materials, in the persons of the commons, on whose virtue depends the freedom of England.

The two first, by being hereditary, are independent of the people; wherefore in a *constitutional sense* they contribute nothing towards the freedom of the state.

To say that the constitution of England is a *union* of three powers reciprocally *checking* each other, is farcical, either the words have no meaning, or they are flat contradictions.

To say that the commons is a check upon the king, presupposes two things.

First.—That the king is not to be trusted without being looked after, or in other words, that a thirst for absolute power is the natural disease of monarchy.

Secondly.—That the commons, by being appointed for that purpose, are either wiser or more worthy of confidence than the crown.

But as the same constitution which gives the commons a power to check the king by withholding the supplies, gives afterwards the king a power to check the commons, by empowering him to reject their other bills; it again supposes that the king is wiser than those whom it has already supposed to be wiser than him. A mere absurdity!

There is something exceedingly ridiculous in the composition of monarchy; it first excludes a man from the means of information, yet empowers him to act in cases where the highest judgment is required.

The state of a king shuts him from the world, yet the business of a king requires him to know it thoroughly; wherefore the different parts, by unnaturally opposing and destroying each other, prove the whole character to be absurd and useless.

Some writers have explained the English constitution thus; the king, say they, is one, the people another; the peers are an house in behalf of the king; the commons in behalf of the people; but this hath all the distinctions of an house divided against itself; and though the expressions be pleasantly arranged, yet when examined they appear idle and ambiguous; and it will always happen, that the nicest construction that words are capable of, when applied to the description of some thing which either cannot exist, or is too incomprehensible to be within the compass of description, will be words of sound only, and though they may amuse the ear, they cannot inform the mind, for this explanation includes a previous question, viz. *How came the king by a power which the people are afraid to trust, and always obliged to check?* Such a power could not be the gift of a wise people, neither can any power, *which needs checking,* be from God; yet the provision, which the constitution makes, supposes such a power to exist.

But the provision is unequal to the task; the means either cannot or will not accomplish the end, and the whole affair is a felo de se;[3] for as the greater weight will always carry up the less, and as all the wheels of a machine are put in motion by one, it only remains to know which power in the constitution has the most weight, for that will govern; and though the others, or a part of them, may clog, or, as the phrase is, check the rapidity of its motion, yet so long as they cannot stop it, their endeavors will be ineffectual; the first moving power will at last have its way, and what it wants in speed is supplied by time.

That the crown is this overbearing part in the English constitution needs not be mentioned, and that it derives its whole consequence merely from being the giver of places and pensions[4] is self-evident, wherefore, though we have been wise enough to shut and lock a door against absolute monarchy, we at the same time have been foolish enough to put the crown in possession of the key.

The prejudice of Englishmen, in favour of their own government by king, lords and commons, arises as much or more from national pride than reason. Individuals are undoubtedly safer in England than in some other countries, but the *will* of the king is as much the *law* of the land in Britain as in France, with this difference, that instead of proceeding directly from his mouth, it is handed to the people under the more formidable shape of an act of parliament. For the fate of Charles the First,[5] hath only made kings more subtle—not more just.

Wherefore, laying aside all national pride and prejudice in favour of modes and forms, the plain truth is, that *it is wholly owing to the constitution of the people, and not to the constitution of the government* that the crown is not as oppressive in England as in Turkey.[6]

An inquiry into the *constitutional errors* in the English form of government is at this time highly necessary; for as we are never in a proper condition of doing justice to others, while we continue under the influence of some leading partiality, so neither are we capable of doing it to ourselves while we remain fettered by any obstinate prejudice. And as a man, who is attached to a prostitute, is unfitted to choose or judge of a wife, so any prepossession in favour of a rotten constitution of government will disable us from discerning a good one.

Of monarchy and hereditary succession.

Mankind being originally equals in the order of creation, the equality could only be destroyed by some subsequent circumstance; the distinctions of rich, and poor, may in a great measure be accounted for, and that without having recourse to the harsh ill sounding names of oppression and avarice. Oppression is often the *consequence,* but seldom or never the *means* of riches; and though avarice will preserve a man from being necessitiously poor, it generally makes him too timorous to be wealthy.

But there is another and greater distinction for which no truly natural or religious reason can be assigned, and that is, the distinction of men into KINGS and SUBJECTS. Male and female are the distinctions of nature, good and bad the distinctions of heaven; but how a race of men came into the world so exalted above the rest, and distinguished like some new species, is worth enquiring into, and whether they are the means of happiness or of misery to mankind.

In the early ages of the world, according to the scripture chronology, there were no kings; the consequence of which was there were no wars; it is the pride of kings which throw mankind into confusion. Holland without a king[7] hath enjoyed more peace for this last century than any of the monarchical governments in Europe. Antiquity favors the same remark; for the quiet and rural lives of the first patriarchs hath a happy something in them, which vanishes away when we come to the history of Jewish royalty.

Government by kings was first introduced into the world by the Heathens, from whom the children of Israel copied the custom. It was the most prosperous invention the Devil ever set on foot for the promotion of idolatry. The Heathens paid divine honors to their deceased kings, and the christian world hath improved on the plan by doing the same to their living ones. How impious is the title of sacred majesty applied to a worm, who in the midst of his splendor is crumbling into dust!

As the exalting one man so greatly above the rest cannot be justified on the equal rights of nature, so neither can it be defended on the authority of scripture; for the will of the Almighty, as declared by Gideon and the prophet Samuel, expressly disapproves of government by kings. All anti-monarchical parts of scripture have been very smoothly glossed over in monarchical governments, but they undoubtedly merit the attention of countries which have their governments yet to form. "*Render unto Cæsar the things which are Cæsar's*" is the scripture doctrine of courts, yet it is no support of monarchical government, for the Jews at that time were without a king, and in a state of vassalage to the Romans.

Near three thousand years passed away from the Mosaic account of the creation, till the Jews under a national delusion requested a king. Till then their form of government (except in extraordinary cases, where the Almighty interposed) was a kind of republic administered by a judge and the elders of the tribes. Kings they had none, and it was held sinful to acknowledge any being under that title but the Lord of Hosts. And when a man seriously reflects on the idolatrous homage which is paid to the persons of Kings, he need not wonder, that the Almighty ever jealous of his honor, should disapprove of a form of government which so impiously invades the prerogative of heaven.

Monarchy is ranked in scripture as one of the sins of the Jews, for which a curse in reserve is denounced against them. The history of that transaction is worth attending to.

The children of Israel being oppressed by the Midianites, Gideon marched against them with a small army, and victory, thro' the divine interposition, decided in his favour. The Jews elate with success, and attributing it to the generalship of Gideon, proposed making him a king, saying, *Rule thou over us, thou and thy son and thy son's son.* Here was temptation in its fullest extent; not a kingdom only, but an hereditary one, but Gideon in the piety of his soul replied, *I will not rule over you, neither shall my son rule over you,* THE LORD SHALL RULE OVER YOU. Words need not be more explicit; Gideon doth not *decline* the honor, but denieth their right to give it; neither doth he compliment them with invented declarations of his thanks, but in the positive stile of a prophet charges them with disaffection to their proper Sovereign, the King of heaven.

About one hundred and thirty years after this, they fell again into the same error. The hankering which the Jews had for the idolatrous customs of the Heathens, is something exceedingly unaccountable; but so it was, that laying hold of the misconduct of Samuel's two sons, who were entrusted with some secular concerns, they came in an abrupt and clamorous manner to Samuel, saying, *Behold thou art old, and thy sons walk not in thy ways, now make us a king to judge us like all the other nations.* And here we cannot but observe that their motives were bad, viz. that they might be *like* unto other nations, i. e. the Heathens, whereas their true glory laid in being as much *unlike* them as possible. *But the thing displeased Samuel when they said, Give us a king to judge us; and Samuel prayed unto the Lord, and the Lord said unto Samuel, Hearken unto the voice of the people in all that they say unto thee, for they have not rejected thee, but they have rejected me,* THAT I SHOULD NOT REIGN OVER THEM. *According to all the works which they have done since the day that I brought them up out of Egypt, even unto this day; wherewith they have forsaken me and served other Gods; so do they also unto thee. Now therefore hearken unto their voice, howbeit, protest solemnly unto them and show them the manner of the king that shall reign over them,* i. e. not of any particular king, but the general manner of the kings of the earth, whom Israel was so eagerly copying after. And notwithstanding the great distance of time and difference of manners, the character is still in fashion, *And Samuel told all the words of the Lord unto the people, that asked of him a king. And he said, "This shall be the manner of the king that shall reign over you; he will take your sons and appoint them for himself, for his chariots, and to be his horsemen, and some shall run before his chariots* (this description agrees with the present mode of impressing men) *and he will appoint him captains over thousands and captains over fifties, and will set them to ear his ground and to reap his harvest, and to make his instruments of war, and instruments of his chariots; and he will take your daughters to be confectionaries, and to be cooks and to be bakers* (this describes the expence and luxury as well as the oppression of kings) *and he will take your fields and your olive yards, even the best of them, and give them to his servants; and he will take the tenth of your seed, and of your vineyards, and give them to his officers and to his servants* (by which we see that bribery, corruption and favoritism are the standing vices of kings) *and he will take the tenth of your men servants, and your maid servants, and your goodliest young men and your asses, and put them to his work; and he will take the tenth of your sheep, and ye shall be his servants, and ye shall cry out in that day because of your king which ye shall have chosen,* AND THE LORD WILL NOT HEAR YOU IN THAT DAY." This accounts for the continuation of monarchy; neither do the characters of the few good kings which have lived since, either sanctify the title, or blot out the sinfulness of the origin; the high encomium given of David takes no notice of him *officially as a king,* but only as a *man* after God's own heart. *Nevertheless the People refused to obey the voice of Samuel, and they said, Nay, but we will have a king over us, that we may be like all the nations, and that our king may judge us, and go out before us, and fight our battles.* Samuel continued to reason with them, but to no purpose; he set before them their ingratitude, but all would not avail; and seeing them fully bent on their folly, he cried out, *I will call unto the Lord, and he shall send thunder and rain* (which then was a punishment, being in the time of wheat harvest) *that ye may perceive and see that your wickedness is great which ye have done in the sight of the Lord,* IN ASKING YOU A KING. *So Samuel called unto the Lord, and the Lord sent thunder and rain that day, and all the people greatly feared the Lord and Samuel. And all the people said unto Samuel, Pray for thy servants unto the Lord thy God that we die not, for* WE HAVE ADDED UNTO OUR SINS THIS EVIL, TO ASK A KING. These portions of scripture are direct and positive. They admit of no equivocal construction. That the Almighty hath here entered his protest against monarchical government is true, or the scripture is false. And a man hath good reason to believe that there is as much of king-craft, as priest-craft, in withholding the scripture from the public in Popish countries. For monarchy in every instance is the Popery of government.[8]

To the evil of monarchy we have added that of hereditary succession; and as the first is a degradation and lessening of ourselves, so the second, claimed as a matter of right, is an insult and an imposition on posterity. For all men being originally equals, no *one* by *birth* could have a right to set up his own family in perpetual preference to all others for ever, and though himself might deserve *some* decent degree of honors of his cotemporaries, yet his descendants might be far too unworthy to inherit them. One of the strongest *natural* proofs of the folly of hereditary right in kings, is, that nature disapproves it, otherwise she would not so frequently turn it into ridicule by giving mankind an *ass for a lion.*

Secondly, as no man at first could possess any other public honors than were bestowed upon him, so the givers of those honors could have no power to give away the right of posterity, and though they might say "We choose you for *our* head," they could not, without manifest injustice to their children, say "that your children and your childrens children shall reign over *ours* for ever." Because such an unwise, unjust, unnatural compact might (perhaps) in the next succession put them under the government of a rogue or a fool. Most wise men, in their private sentiments, have ever treated hereditary right with contempt; yet it is one of those evils, which when once established is not easily removed; many submit from fear, others from superstition, and the more powerful part shares with the king the plunder of the rest.

This is supposing the present race of kings in the world to have had an honorable origin; whereas it is more than probable, that could we take off the dark covering of antiquity, and trace them to their first rise, that we should find the first of them nothing better than the principal ruffian of some restless gang, whose savage manners or pre-eminence in subtility obtained him the title of chief among plunderers; and who by increasing in power, and extending his depredations, overawed the quiet and defenceless to purchase their safety by frequent contributions. Yet his electors could have no idea of giving hereditary right to his descendants, because such a perpetual exclusion of themselves was incompatible with the free and unrestrained principles they professed to live by. Wherefore, hereditary succession in the early ages of monarchy could not take place as a matter of claim, but as something casual or complimental; but as few or no records were extant in those days, and traditionary history stuffed with fables, it was very easy, after the lapse of a few generations, to trump up some superstitious tale, conveniently timed, Mahomet like, to cram hereditary right down the throats of the vulgar. Perhaps the disorders which threatened, or seemed to threaten, on the decease of a leader and the choice of a new one (for elections among ruffians could not be very orderly) induced many at first to favor hereditary pretensions; by which means it happened, as it hath happened since, that what at first was submitted to as a convenience, was afterwards claimed as a right.

England, since the conquest, hath known some few good monarchs, but groaned beneath a much larger number of bad ones; yet no man in his senses can say that their claim under William the Conqueror[9] is a very honorable one. A French bastard landing with an armed banditti, and establishing himself king of England against the consent of the natives, is in plain terms a very paltry rascally original.—It certainly hath no divinity in it. However, it is needless to spend much time in exposing the folly of hereditary right, if there are any so weak as to believe it, let them promiscuously worship the ass and lion, and welcome. I shall neither copy their humility, nor disturb their devotion.

Yet I should be glad to ask how they suppose kings came at first? The question admits but of three answers, viz. either by lot, by election, or by usurpation. If the first king was taken by lot, it establishes a precedent for the next, which excludes hereditary succession. Saul was by lot, yet the succession was not hereditary, neither does it appear from the transaction there was any intention it ever should. If the first king of any country was by election, that likewise establishes a precedent for the next; for to say, that the *right* of all future generations is taken away, by the act of the first electors, in their choice not only of a king, but of a family of kings for ever, hath no parrallel in or out of scripture but the doctrine of original sin, which supposes the free will of all men lost in Adam; and from such comparison, and it will admit of no other, hereditary succession can derive no glory. For as in Adam all sinned, and as in the first electors all men obeyed; as in the one all mankind were subjected to Satan, and in the other to Sovereignty; as our innocence was lost in the first, and our authority in the last; and as both disable us from reassuming some former state and privilege, it unanswerably follows that original sin and hereditary succession are parellels. Dishonorable rank! Inglorious connexion! Yet the most subtile sophist cannot produce a juster simile.

As to usurpation, no man will be so hardy as to defend it; and that William the Conqueror was an usurper is a fact not to be contradicted.

The plain truth is, that the antiquity of English monarchy will not bear looking into.

But it is not so much the absurdity as the evil of hereditary succession which concerns mankind. Did it ensure a race of good and wise men it would have the seal of divine authority, but as it opens a door to the *foolish,* the *wicked,* and the *improper,* it hath in it the nature of oppression. Men who look upon themselves born to reign, and others to obey, soon grow insolent; selected from the rest of mankind their minds are early poisoned by importance; and the world they act in differs so materially from the world at large, that they have but little opportunity of knowing its true interests, and when they succeed to the government are frequently the most ignorant and unfit of any throughout the dominions.

Another evil which attends hereditary succession is, that the throne is subject to be possessed by a minor at any age; all which time the regency, acting under the cover of a king, have every opportunity and inducement to betray their trust. The same national misfortune happens, when a king worn out with age and infirmity, enters the last stage of human weakness. In both these cases the public becomes a prey to every miscreant, who can tamper successfully with the follies either of age or infancy.

The most plausible plea, which hath ever been offered in favour of hereditary succession, is, that it preserves a nation from civil wars; and were this true, it would be weighty; whereas, it is the most barefaced falsity ever imposed upon mankind. The whole history of England disowns the fact. Thirty kings and two minors have reigned in that distracted kingdom since the conquest, in which time there have been (including the Revolution) no less than eight civil wars and nineteen rebellions. Wherefore instead of making for peace, it makes against it, and destroys the very foundation it seems to stand on.

The contest for monarchy and succession, between the houses of York and Lancaster,[10] laid England in a scene of blood for many years. Twelve pitched battles, besides skirmishes and sieges, were fought between Henry and Edward. Twice was Henry prisoner to Edward, who in his turn was prisoner to Henry. And so uncertain is the fate of war and the temper of a nation, when nothing but personal matters are the ground of a quarrel, that Henry was taken in triumph from a prison to a palace, and Edward obliged to fly from a palace to a foreign land; yet, as sudden transitions of temper are seldom lasting, Henry in his turn was driven from the throne, and Edward recalled to succeed him. The parliament always following the strongest side.

This contest began in the reign of Henry the Sixth, and was not entirely extinguished till Henry the Seventh, in whom the families were united. Including a period of 67 years, viz. from 1422 to 1489.

In short, monarchy and succession have laid (not this or that kingdom only) but the world in blood and ashes. 'Tis a form of government which the word of God bears testimony against, and blood will attend it.

If we inquire into the business of a king, we shall find that in some countries they have none; and after sauntering away their lives without pleasure to themselves or advantage to the nation, withdraw from the scene, and leave their successors to tread the same idle round. In absolute monarchies the whole weight of business, civil and military, lies on the king; the children of Israel in their request for a king, urged this plea "that he may judge us, and go out before us and fight our battles." But in countries where he is neither a judge nor a general, as in England, a man would be puzzled to know what *is* his business.

The nearer any government approaches to a republic the less business there is for a king. It is somewhat difficult to find a proper name for the government of England. Sir William Meredith[11] calls it a republic; but in its present state it is unworthy of the name, because the corrupt influence of the crown, by having all the places in its disposal, hath so effectually swallowed up the power, and eaten out the virtue of the house of commons (the republican part in the constitution) that the government of England is nearly as monarchical as that of France or Spain. Men fall out with names without understanding them. For it is the republican and not the monarchical part of the constitution of England which Englishmen glory in, viz. the liberty of choosing an house of commons from out of their own body—and it is easy to see that when republican virtue fails, slavery ensues. Why is the constitution of England sickly, but because monarchy hath poisoned the republic, the crown hath engrossed the commons?

In England a king hath little more to do than to make war and give away places; which in plain terms, is to impoverish the nation and set it together by the ears. A pretty business indeed for a man to be allowed eight hundred thousand sterling a year for, and worshipped into the bargain! Of more worth is one honest man to society and in the sight of God, than all the crowned ruffians that ever lived.

THOUGHTS ON THE PRESENT STATE OF AMERICAN AFFAIRS.

In the following pages I offer nothing more than simple facts, plain arguments, and common sense; and have no other preliminaries to settle with the reader, than that he will divest himself of prejudice and prepossession, and suffer his reason and his feelings to determine for themselves; that he will put *on,* or rather that he will not put *off,* the true character of a man, and generously enlarge his views beyond the present day.

Volumes have been written on the subject of the struggle between England and America. Men of all ranks have embarked in the controversy, from different motives, and with various designs; but all have been ineffectual, and the period of debate is closed. Arms, as the last resource, decide the contest; the appeal was the choice of the king, and the continent hath accepted the challenge.

It hath been reported of the late Mr. Pelham[12] (who tho' an able minister was not without his faults) that on his being attacked in the house of commons, on the score, that his measures were only of a temporary kind, replied "*they will last my time.*" Should a thought so fatal and unmanly possess the colonies in the present contest, the name of ancestors will be remembered by future generations with detestation.

The sun never shined on a cause of greater worth. 'Tis not the affair of a city, a county, a province, or a kingdom, but of a continent—of at least one eighth part of the habitable globe. 'Tis not the concern of a day, a year, or an age; posterity are virtually involved in the contest, and will be more or less affected, even to the end of time, by the proceedings now. Now is the seed time of continental union, faith and honor. The least fracture now will be like a name engraved with the point of a pin on the tender rind of a young oak; the wound will enlarge with the tree, and posterity read it in full grown characters.

By referring the matter from argument to arms, a new æra for politics is struck; a new method of thinking hath arisen. All plans, proposals, &c. prior to the nineteenth of April,[13] *i. e.* to the commencement of hostilities, are like the almanacks of the last year; which, though proper then, are superceded and useless now. Whatever was advanced by the advocates on either side of the question then, terminated in one and the same point, viz. a union with Great-Britain; the only difference between the parties was the method of effecting it; the one proposing force, the other friendship; but it hath so far happened that the first hath failed, and the second hath withdrawn her influence.

As much hath been said of the advantages of reconciliation, which, like an agreeable dream, hath passed away and left us as we were, it is but right, that we should examine the contrary side of the argument, and inquire into some of the many material injuries which these colonies sustain, and always will sustain, by being connected with, and dependant on Great Britain. To examine that connexion and dependance, on the principles of nature and common sense, to see what we have to trust to, if separated, and what we are to expect, if dependant.

I have heard it asserted by some, that as America hath flourished under her former connexion with Great-Britain, that the same connexion is necessary towards her future happiness, and will always have the same effect. Nothing can be more fallacious than this kind of argument. We may as well assert that because a child has thrived upon milk, that it is never to have meat, or that the first twenty years of our lives is to become a precedent for the next twenty. But even this is admitting more than is true, for I answer roundly, that America would have flourished as much, and probably much more, had no European power had any thing to do with her. The commerce, by which she hath enriched herself are the necessaries of life, and will always have a market while eating is the custom of Europe.

But she has protected us, say some. That she hath engrossed us is true, and defended the continent at our expence as well as her own is admitted, and she would have defended Turkey from the same motive, viz. the sake of trade and dominion.

Alas, we have been long led away by ancient prejudices, and made large sacrifices to superstition. We have boasted the protection of Great-Britain, without considering, that her motive was *interest* not *attachment*; that she did not protect us from *our enemies* on *our account*, but from *her enemies* on *her own account*, from those who had no quarrel with us on any *other account*, and who will always be our enemies on the *same account*. Let Britain wave her pretensions to the continent, or the continent throw off the dependance, and we should be at peace with France and Spain were they at war with Britain. The miseries of Hanover last war[14] ought to warn us against connexions.

It hath lately been asserted in parliament, that the colonies have no relation to each other but through the parent country, *i. e.* that Pennsylvania and the Jerseys, and so on for the rest, are sister colonies by the way of England; this is certainly a very round-about way of proving relationship, but it is the nearest and only true way of proving enemyship, if I may so call it. France and Spain never were, nor perhaps ever will be our enemies as *Americans*, but as our being the *subjects of Great-Britain*.

But Britain is the parent country, say some. Then the more shame upon her conduct. Even brutes do not devour their young, nor savages make war upon their families; wherefore the assertion, if true, turns to her reproach; but it happens not to be true, or only partly so, and the phrase *parent* or *mother country* hath been jesuitically adopted by the king and his parasites, with a low papistical design of gaining an unfair bias on the credulous weakness of our minds. Europe, and not England, is the parent country of America. This new world hath been the asylum for the persecuted lovers of civil and religious liberty from *every part* of Europe. Hither have they fled, not from the tender embraces of the mother, but from the cruelty of the monster; and it is so far true of England, that the same tyranny which drove the first emigrants from home, pursues their descendants still.

In this extensive quarter of the globe, we forget the narrow limits of three hundred and sixty miles (the extent of England) and carry out friendship on a larger scale; we claim brotherhood with every European christian, and triumph in the generosity of the sentiment.

It is pleasant to observe by what regular gradations we surmount the force of local prejudice, as we enlarge our acquaintance with the world. A man born in any town in England divided into parishes, will naturally associate most with his fellow parishioners (because their interests in many cases will be common) and distinguish him by the name of *neighbour;* if he meet him but a few miles from home, he drops the narrow idea of a street, and salutes him by the name of *townsman;* if he travel out of the county, and meet him in any other, he forgets the minor divisions of street and town, and calls him *countryman,* i. e. *county-man;* but if in their foreign excursions they should associate in France or any other part of *Europe,* their local remembrance would be enlarged into that of *Englishmen.* And by a just parity of reasoning, all Europeans meeting in America, or any other quarter of the globe, are *countrymen;* for England, Holland, Germany, or Sweden, when compared with the whole, stand in the same places on the larger scale, which the divisions of street, town, and county do on the smaller ones; distinctions too limited for continental minds. Not one third of the inhabitants, even of this province, are of English descent.[15] Wherefore I reprobate the phrase of parent or mother country applied to England only, as being false, selfish, narrow and ungenerous.

But admitting, that we were all of English descent, what does it amount to? Nothing. Britain, being now an open enemy, extinguishes every other name and title: And to say that reconciliation is our duty, is truly farcical. The first king of England, of the present line (William the Conqueror) was a Frenchman, and half the Peers of England are descendants from the same country; wherefore, by the same method of reasoning, England ought to be governed by France.

Much hath been said of the united strength of Britain and the colonies, that in conjunction they might bid defiance to the world. But this is mere presumption; the fate of war is uncertain, neither do the expressions mean any thing; for this continent would never suffer itself to be drained of inhabitants, to support the British arms in either Asia, Africa, or Europe.

Besides, what have we to do with setting the world at defiance? Our plan is commerce, and that, well attended to, will secure us the peace and friendship of all Europe; because, it is the interest of all Europe to have America a *free port.* Her trade will always be a protection, and her barrenness of gold and silver secure her from invaders.

I challenge the warmest advocate for reconciliation, to shew, a single advantage that this continent can reap, by being connected with Great Britain. I repeat the challenge, not a single advantage is derived. Our corn will fetch its price in any market in Europe, and our imported goods must be paid for buy them where we will.

But the injuries and disadvantages we sustain by that connection, are without number; and our duty to mankind at large, as well as to ourselves, instruct us to renounce the alliance: Because, any submission to, or dependance on Great-Britain, tends directly to involve this continent in European wars and quarrels; and sets us at variance with nations, who would otherwise seek our friendship, and against whom, we have neither anger nor complaint. As Europe is our market for trade, we ought to form no partial connection with any part of it. It is the true interest of America to steer clear of European contentions, which she never can do, while by her dependance on Britain, she is made the make-weight in the scale of British politics.

Europe is too thickly planted with kingdoms to be long at peace, and whenever a war breaks out between England and any foreign power, the trade of America goes to ruin, *because of her connection with Britain*.[16] The next war may not turn out like the last, and should it not, the advocates for reconciliation now will be wishing for separation then, because, neutrality in that case, would be a safer convoy than a man of war. Every thing that is right or natural pleads for separation. The blood of the slain, the weeping voice of nature cries, 'TIS TIME TO PART. Even the distance at which the Almighty hath placed England and America, is a strong and natural proof, that the authority of the one, over the other, was never the design of Heaven. The time likewise at which the continent was discovered, adds weight to the argument, and the manner in which it was peopled encreases the force of it. The reformation[17] was preceded by the discovery of America, as if the Almighty graciously meant to open a sanctuary to the persecuted in future years, when home should afford neither friendship nor safety.

The authority of Great-Britain over this continent, is a form of government, which sooner or later must have an end: And a serious mind can draw no true pleasure by looking forward, under the painful and positive conviction, that what he calls "the present constitution" is merely temporary. As parents, we can have no joy, knowing that *this government* is not sufficiently lasting to ensure any thing which we may bequeath to posterity: And by a plain method of argument, as we are running the next generation into debt, we ought to do the work of it, otherwise we use them meanly and pitifully. In order to discover the line of our duty rightly, we should take our children in our hand, and fix our station a few years farther into life; that eminence will present a prospect, which a few present fears and prejudices conceal from our sight.

Though I would carefully avoid giving unnecessary offence, yet I

am inclined to believe, that all those who espouse the doctrine of reconciliation, may be included within the following descriptions. Interested men,[18] who are not to be trusted; weak men, who *cannot* see;
prejudiced men, who *will not* see; and a certain set of moderate men,
who think better of the European world than it deserves; and this last
class, by an ill-judged deliberation, will be the cause of more calamities to this continent, than all the other three.

It is the good fortune of many to live distant from the scene of sorrow; the evil is not sufficiently brought to *their* doors to make *them* feel
the precariousness with which all American property is possessed. But
let our imaginations transport us for a few moments to Boston, that
seat of wretchedness will teach us wisdom, and instruct us for ever to
renounce a power in whom we can have no trust. The inhabitants of
that unfortunate city, who but a few months ago were in ease and affluence, have now, no other alternative than to stay and starve, or turn
out to beg. Endangered by the fire of their friends if they continue
within the city, and plundered by the soldiery if they leave it. In their
present condition they are prisoners without the hope of redemption,[19] and in a general attack for their relief, they would be exposed to
the fury of both armies.

Men of passive tempers look somewhat lightly over the offences of
Britain, and, still hoping for the best, are apt to call out, "*Come, come, we
shall be friends again, for all this.*" But examine the passions and feelings
of mankind, Bring the doctrine of reconciliation to the touchstone of
nature, and then tell me, whether you can hereafter love, honour, and
faithfully serve the power that hath carried fire and sword into your
land? If you cannot do all these, then are you only deceiving yourselves, and by your delay bringing ruin upon posterity. Your future
connection with Britain, whom you can neither love nor honour, will
be forced and unnatural, and being formed only on the plan of present
convenience, will in a little time fall into a relapse more wretched than
the first. But if you say, you can still pass the violations over, then I ask,
Hath your house been burnt? Hath your property been destroyed before your face? Are your wife and children destitute of a bed to lie on,
or bread to live on? Have you lost a parent or a child by their hands,
and yourself the ruined and wretched survivor? If you have not, then
are you not a judge of those who have. But if you have, and still can
shake hands with the murderers, then are you unworthy the name of

husband, father, friend, or lover, and whatever may be your rank or
title in life, you have the heart of a coward, and the spirit of a syco-
phant.

This is not inflaming or exaggerating matters, but trying them by
those feelings and affections which nature justifies, and without which,
we should be incapable of discharging the social duties of life, or enjoying the felicities of it. I mean not to exhibit horror for the purpose
of provoking revenge, but to awaken us from fatal and unmanly slum-
bers, that we may pursue determinately some fixed object. It is not in
the power of Britain or of Europe to conquer America, if she do not
conquer herself by *delay* and *timidity*. The present winter is worth an
age if rightly employed, but if lost or neglected, the whole continent
will partake of the misfortune; and there is no punishment which that
man will not deserve, be he who, or what, or where he will, that may be
the means of sacrificing a season so precious and useful.

It is repugnant to reason, to the universal order of things to all examples from former ages, to suppose, that this continent can longer remain subject to any external power. The most sanguine in Britain does
not think so. The utmost stretch of human wisdom cannot, at this time,
compass a plan short of separation, which can promise the continent
even a year's security. Reconciliation is *now* a falacious dream. Nature
hath deserted the connexion, and Art cannot supply her place. For, as
Milton wisely expresses, "never can true reconcilement grow where
wounds of deadly hate have pierced so deep."[20]

Every quiet method for peace hath been ineffectual. Our prayers
have been rejected with disdain; and only tended to convince us, that
nothing flatters vanity, or confirms obstinacy in Kings more than repeated petitioning—and nothing hath contributed more than that very
measure to make the Kings of Europe absolute: Witness Denmark and
Sweden.[21] Wherefore, since nothing but blows will do, for God's sake,
let us come to a final separation, and not leave the next generation to
be cutting throats, under the violated unmeaning names of parent and
child.

To say, they will never attempt it again is idle and visionary, we
thought so at the repeal of the stamp-act,[22] yet a year or two unde-
ceived us; as well may we suppose that nations, which have been once
defeated, will never renew the quarrel.

As to government matters, it is not in the power of Britain to do this continent justice: The business of it will soon be too weighty, and intricate, to be managed with any tolerable degree of convenience, by a power, so distant from us, and so very ignorant of us; for if they cannot conquer us, they cannot govern us. To be always running three or four thousand miles with a tale or a petition, waiting four or five months for an answer, which when obtained requires five or six more to explain it in, will in a few years be looked upon as folly and childishness—There was a time when it was proper, and there is a proper time for it to cease.

Small islands not capable of protecting themselves, are the proper objects for kingdoms to take under their care; but there is something very absurd, in supposing a continent to be perpetually governed by an island. In no instance hath nature made the satellite larger than its primary planet, and as England and America, with respect to each other, reverses the common order of nature, it is evident they belong to different systems: England to Europe, America to itself.

I am not induced by motives of pride, party, or resentment to espouse the doctrine of separation and independance; I am clearly, positively, and conscientiously persuaded that it is the true interest of this continent to be so; that every thing short of *that* is mere patchwork, that it can afford no lasting felicity,—that it is leaving the sword to our children, and shrinking back at a time, when, a little more, a little farther, would have rendered this continent the glory of the earth.

As Britain hath not manifested the least inclination towards a compromise, we may be assured that no terms can be obtained worthy the acceptance of the continent, or any ways equal to the expence of blood and treasure we have been already put to.

The object, contended for, ought always to bear some just proportion to the expence. The removal of North, or the whole detestable junto, is a matter unworthy the millions we have expended. A temporary stoppage of trade, was an inconvenience, which would have sufficiently ballanced the repeal of all the acts complained of, had such repeals been obtained; but if the whole continent must take up arms, if every man must be a soldier, it is scarcely worth our while to fight against a contemptible ministry only. Dearly, dearly, do we pay for the repeal of the acts, if that is all we fight for; for in a just estimation, it is as great a folly to pay a Bunker-hill price[23] for law, as for land. As I have always considered the independancy of this continent, as an event, which sooner or later must arrive, so from the late rapid progress of the continent to maturity, the event could not be far off. Wherefore, on the breaking out of hostilities, it was not worth the while to have disputed a matter, which time would have finally redressed, unless we meant to be in earnest; otherwise, it is like wasting an estate on a suit at law, to regulate the trespasses of a tenant, whose lease is just expiring. No man was a warmer wisher for reconciliation than myself, before the fatal nineteenth of April 1775*, but the moment the event of that day was made known, I rejected the hardened, sullen tempered Pharoah of England for ever; and disdain the wretch, that with the pretended title of FATHER OF HIS PEOPLE can unfeelingly hear of their slaughter, and composedly sleep with their blood upon his soul.

But admitting that matters were now made up, what would be the event? I answer, the ruin of the continent. And that for several reasons.

First. The powers of governing still remaining in the hands of the king, he will have a negative over the whole legislation of this continent. And as he hath shewn himself such an inveterate enemy to liberty, and discovered such a thirst for arbitrary power; is he, or is he not, a proper man to say to these colonies, *"You shall make no laws but what I please."* And is there any inhabitant in America so ignorant, as not to know, that according to what is called the *present constitution,* that this continent can make no laws but what the king gives leave to; and is there any man so unwise, as not to see, that (considering what has happened) he will suffer no law to be made here, but such as suit *his* purpose. We may be as effectually enslaved by the want of laws in America, as by submitting to laws made for us in England. After matters are made up (as it is called) can there be any doubt, but the whole power of the crown will be exerted, to keep this continent as low and humble as possible? Instead of going forward we shall go backward, or be perpetually quarrelling or ridiculously petitioning.—We are already greater than the king wishes us to be, and will he not hereafter endeavour to make us less? To bring the matter to one point. Is the power who is jealous of our prosperity, a proper power to govern us? Whoever says *No* to this question is an *independant,* for independancy means no more, than, whether we shall make our own laws, or, whether the king, the greatest enemy this continent hath, or can have, shall tell us *"there shall be no laws but such as I like."*

* Massacre at Lexington.

But the king you will say has a negative in England; the people there can make no laws without his consent. In point of right and good order, there is something very ridiculous, that a youth of twenty-one[24] (which hath often happened) shall say to several millions of people, older and wiser than himself, I forbid this or that act of yours to be law. But in this place I decline this sort of reply, though I will never cease to expose the absurdity of it, and only answer, that England being the King's residence, and America not so, makes quite another case. The king's negative *here* is ten times more dangerous and fatal than it can be in England, for *there* he will scarcely refuse his consent to a bill for putting England into as strong a state of defence as possible, and in America he would never suffer such a bill to be passed.

America is only a secondary object in the system of British politics, England consults the good of *this* country, no farther than it answers her *own* purpose. Wherefore, her own interest leads her to suppress the growth of *ours* in every case which doth not promote her advantage, or in the least interferes with it. A pretty state we should soon be in under such a second-hand government, considering what has happened! Men do not change from enemies to friends by the alteration of a name: And in order to shew that reconciliation *now* is a dangerous doctrine, I affirm, *that it would be policy in the king at this time, to repeal the acts for the sake of reinstating himself in the government of the provinces;* in order, that HE MAY ACCOMPLISH BY CRAFT AND SUBTILTY, IN THE LONG RUN, WHAT HE CANNOT DO BY FORCE AND VIOLENCE IN THE SHORT ONE. Reconciliation and ruin are nearly related.

Secondly. That as even the best terms, which we can expect to obtain, can amount to no more than a temporary expedient, or a kind of government by guardianship, which can last no longer than till the colonies come of age, so the general face and state of things, in the interim, will be unsettled and unpromising. Emigrants of property will not choose to come to a country whose form of government hangs but by a thread, and who is every day tottering on the brink of commotion and disturbance; and numbers of the present inhabitants would lay hold of the interval, to dispose of their effects, and quit the continent.

But the most powerful of all arguments, is, that nothing but independence, i. e. a continental form of government, can keep the peace of the continent and preserve it inviolate from civil wars. I dread the event of a reconciliation with Britain now, as it is more than probable, that it will be followed by a revolt somewhere or other, the consequences of which may be far more fatal than all the malice of Britain.

Thousands are already ruined by British barbarity; (thousands more will probably suffer the same fate) Those men have other feelings than us who have nothing suffered. All they *now* possess is liberty, what they before enjoyed is sacrificed to its service, and having nothing more to lose, they disdain submission. Besides, the general temper of the colonies, towards a British government, will be like that of a youth, who is nearly out of his time; they will care very little about her. And a government which cannot preserve the peace, is no government at all, and in that case we pay our money for nothing; and pray what is it that Britain can do, whose power will be wholly on paper, should a civil tumult break out the very day after reconciliation? I have heard some men say, many of whom I believe spoke without thinking, that they dreaded an independance, fearing that it would produce civil wars. It is but seldom that our first thoughts are truly correct, and that is the case here; for there are ten times more to dread from a patched up connexion than from independance. I make the sufferers case my own, and I protest, that were I driven from house and home, my property destroyed, and my circumstances ruined, that as man, sensible of injuries, I could never relish the doctrine of reconciliation, or consider myself bound thereby.

The colonies have manifested such a spirit of good order and obedience to continental government, as is sufficient to make every reasonable person easy and happy on that head. No man can assign the least pretence for his fears, on any other grounds, than such as are truly childish and ridiculous, viz. that one colony will be striving for superiority over another.

Where there are no distinctions there can be no superiority, perfect equality affords no temptation. The republics of Europe are all (and we may say always) in peace. Holland and Swisserland are without wars, foreign or domestic: Monarchical governments, it is true, are never long at rest; the crown itself is a temptation to enterprizing ruffians at *home;* and that degree of pride and insolence ever attendant on regal authority, swells into a rupture with foreign powers, in instances, where a republican government, by being formed on more natural principles, would negociate the mistake.

If there is any true cause of fear respecting independance, it is because no plan is yet laid down. Men do not see their way out—Wherefore, as an opening into that business, I offer the following hints; at the same time modestly affirming, that I have no other opinion of them myself, than that they may be the means of giving rise to something better. Could the straggling thoughts of individuals be collected, they would frequently form materials for wise and able men to improve into useful matter.

———

Let the assemblies be annual, with a President only. The representation more equal. Their business wholly domestic, and subject to the authority of a Continental Congress.

Let each colony be divided into six, eight, or ten, convenient districts, each district to send a proper number of delegates to Congress, so that each colony send at least thirty. The whole number in Congress will be at least 390. Each Congress to fit and to choose a president by the following method. When the delegates are met, let a colony be taken from the whole thirteen colonies by lot, after which, let the whole Congress choose (by ballot) a president from out of the delegates of *that* province. In the next Congress, let a colony be taken by lot from twelve only, omitting that colony from which the president was taken in the former Congress, and so proceeding on till the whole thirteen shall have had their proper rotation. And in order that nothing may pass into a law but what is satisfactorily just, not less than three fifths of the Congress to be called a majority.—He that will promote discord, under a government so equally formed as this, would have joined Lucifer in his revolt.

But as there is a peculiar delicacy, from whom, or in what manner, this business must first arise, and as it seems most agreeable and consistent, that it should come from some intermediate body between the governed and the governors, that is, between the Congress and the people, let a CONTINENTAL CONFERENCE be held, in the following manner, and for the following purpose.

A committee of twenty-six members of Congress, viz. two for each colony. Two members from each House of Assembly, or Provincial Convention; and five representatives of the people at large, to be chosen in the capital city or town of each province, for, and in behalf of the whole province, by as many qualified voters as shall think proper to attend from all parts of the province for that purpose; or, if more convenient, the representatives may be chosen in two or three of the most populous parts thereof. In this conference, thus assembled, will be united, the two grand principles of business, *knowledge* and *power*. The members of Congress, Assemblies, or Conventions, by having had experience in national concerns, will be able and useful counsellors, and the whole, being impowered by the people, will have a truly legal authority.

The conferring members being met, let their business be to frame a CONTINENTAL CHARTER, or Charter of the United Colonies; (answering to what is called the Magna Charta of England) fixing the number and manner of choosing members of Congress, members of Assembly, with their date of sitting, and drawing the line of business and jurisdiction between them: (Always remembering, that our strength is continental, not provincial:) Securing freedom and property to all men, and above all things, the free exercise of religion, according to the dictates of conscience; with such other matter as is necessary for a charter to contain. Immediately after which, the said Conference to dissolve, and the bodies which shall be chosen conformable to the said charter, to be the legislators and governors of this continent for the time being: Whose peace and happiness, may God preserve, Amen.

Should any body of men be hereafter delegated for this or some similar purpose, I offer them the following extracts from that wise observer on governments *Dragonetti*. "The science" says he "of the politician consists in fixing the true point of happiness and freedom. Those men would deserve the gratitude of ages, who should discover a mode of government that contained the greatest sum of individual happiness, with the least national expence.

DRAGONETTI ON VIRTUE AND REWARDS."[25]

But where says some is the King of America? I'll tell you Friend, he reigns above, and doth not make havoc of mankind like the Royal Brute of Britain. Yet that we may not appear to be defective even in earthly honors, let a day be solemnly set apart for proclaiming the charter; let it be brought forth placed on the divine law, the word of God; let a crown be placed thereon, by which the world may know, that so far as we approve of monarchy, that in America THE LAW IS KING. For as in absolute governments the King is law, so in free countries the law *ought* to be King; and there ought to be no other. But lest any ill use should afterwards arise, let the crown at the conclusion of the ceremony be demolished, and scattered among the people whose right it is.

A government of our own is our natural right: And when a man seriously reflects on the precariousness of human affairs, he will become convinced, that it is infinitely wiser and safer, to form a constitution of our own in a cool deliberate manner, while we have it in our power, than to trust such an interesting event to time and chance. If we omit it now, some * Massanello may hereafter arise, who laying hold of popular disquietudes, may collect together the desperate and the discontented, and by assuming to themselves the powers of government, may sweep away the liberties of the continent like a deluge. Should the government of America return again into the hands of Britain, the tottering situation of things, will be a temptation for some desperate adventurer to try his fortune; and in such a case, what relief can Britain give? Ere she could hear the news, the fatal business might be done; and ourselves suffering like the wretched Britons under the oppression of the Conqueror. Ye that oppose independance now, ye know not what ye do; ye are opening a door to eternal tyranny, by keeping vacant the seat of government. There are thousands, and tens of thousands, who would think it glorious to expel from the continent, that barbarous and hellish power, which hath stirred up the Indians and Negroes to destroy us,[26] the cruelty hath a double guilt, it is dealing brutally by us, and treacherously by them.

To talk of friendship with those in whom our reason forbids us to have faith, and our affections wounded through a thousand pores instruct us to detest, is madness and folly. Every day wears out the little remains of kindred between us and them, and can there be any reason to hope, that as the relationship expires, the affection will increase, or that we shall agree better, when we have ten times more and greater concerns to quarrel over than ever?

Ye that tell us of harmony and reconciliation, can ye restore to us the time that is past? Can ye give to prostitution its former innocence? Neither can ye reconcile Britain and America. The last cord now is broken, the people of England are presenting addresses against us.

---

* Thomas Anello, otherwise Massanello, a fisherman of Naples, who after spiriting up his countrymen in the public market place, against the oppression of the Spaniards, to whom the place was then subject, prompted them to revolt, and in the space of a day became King.

There are injuries which nature cannot forgive; she would cease to be nature if she did. As well can the lover forgive the ravisher of his mistress, as the continent forgive the murders of Britain. The Almighty hath implanted in us these unextinguishable feelings for good and wise purposes. They are the guardians of his image in our hearts. They distinguish us from the herd of common animals. The social compact would dissolve, and justice be extirpated the earth, or have only a casual existence were we callous to the touches of affection. The robber, and the murderer, would often escape unpunished, did not the injuries which our tempers sustain, provoke us into justice.

O ye that love mankind! Ye that dare oppose, not only the tyranny, but the tyrant, stand forth! Every spot of the old world is overrun with oppression. Freedom hath been hunted round the globe. Asia, and Africa, have long expelled her.—Europe regards her like a stranger, and England hath given her warning to depart. O! receive the fugitive, and prepare in time an asylum for mankind.

Of the present ABILITY of AMERICA, with some miscellaneous REFLEXIONS.

I have never met with a man, either in England or America, who hath not confessed his opinion, that a separation between the countries, would take place one time or other: And there is no instance, in which we have shewn less judgment, than in endeavouring to describe, what we call, the ripeness or fitness of the Continent for independance.

As all men allow the measure, and vary only in their opinion of the time, let us, in order to remove mistakes, take a general survey of things, and endeavour, if possible, to find out the *very* time. But we need not go far, the inquiry ceases at once, for, the *time hath found us*. The general concurrence, the glorious union of all things prove the fact.

It is not in numbers, but in unity, that our great strength lies; yet our present numbers are sufficient to repel the force of all the world. The Continent hath, at this time, the largest body of armed and disciplined men of any power under Heaven; and is just arrived at that pitch of strength, in which, no single colony is able to support itself, and the whole, when united, can accomplish the matter, and either more, or, less than this, might be fatal in its effects. Our land force is already sufficient, and as to naval affairs, we cannot be insensible, that Britain would never suffer an American man of war to be built, while the continent remained in her hands. Wherefore, we should be no forwarder an hundred years hence in that branch, than we are now; but the truth is, we should be less so, because the timber of the country is every day diminishing, and that, which will remain at last, will be far off and difficult to procure.

Were the continent crowded with inhabitants, her sufferings under the present circumstances would be intolerable. The more sea port towns we had, the more should we have both to defend and to loose. Our present numbers are so happily proportioned to our wants, that no man need be idle. The diminution of trade affords an army, and the necessities of an army create a new trade.

Debts we have none; and whatever we may contract on this account will serve as a glorious memento of our virtue. Can we but leave posterity with a settled form of government, an independant constitution of it's own, the purchase at any price will be cheap. But to expend millions for the sake of getting a few vile acts repealed, and routing the present ministry only, is unworthy the charge, and is using posterity with the utmost cruelty; because it is leaving them the great work to do, and a debt upon their backs, from which, they derive no advantage. Such a thought is unworthy a man of honor, and is the true characteristic of a narrow heart and a pedling politician.

The debt we may contract doth not deserve our regard if the work be but accomplished. No nation ought to be without a debt. A national debt is a national bond;[27] and when it bears no interest, is in no case a grievance. Britain is oppressed with a debt of upwards of one hundred and forty millions sterling, for which she pays upwards of four millions interest. And as a compensation for her debt, she has a large navy; America is without a debt, and without a navy; yet for the twentieth part of the English national debt, could have a navy as large again. The navy of England is not worth, at this time, more than three millions and an half sterling.

The first and second editions of this pamphlet were published without the following calculations, which are now given as a proof that the above estimation of the navy is a just one. *See Entic's naval history,*[28] *intro.* page 56.

The charge of building a ship of each rate, and furnishing her with masts, yards, sails and rigging, together with a proportion of eight months boatswain's and carpenter's sea-stores, as calculated by Mr. Burchett, Secretary to the navy.

			£.
For a ship of a	100 guns	——	35,553
	90	— —	29,886
	80	— —	23,638
	70	— —	17,785
	60	— —	14,197
	50	— —	10,606
	40	— —	7,558
	30	— —	5,846
	20	— —	3,710

And from hence it is easy to sum up the value, or cost rather, of the whole British navy, which in the year 1757, when it was at its greatest glory consisted of the following ships and guns.

Ships.	Guns.	Cost of one.		Cost of all.
6	— 100	— 35,553*l*	——	213,318*l*
12	— 90	— 29,886	——	358,632
12	— 80	— 23,638	——	283,656
43	— 70	— 17,785	——	764,755
35	— 60	— 14,197	——	496,895
40	— 50	— 10,606	——	424,240
45	— 40	— 7,558	——	340,110
58	— 20	— 3,710	——	215,180
85	Sloops, bombs, and fireships, one with another, at	2,000		170,000
		Cost		3,266,786
	Remains for guns,	——		233,214
				3,500,000

No country on the globe is so happily situated, or so internally capable of raising a fleet as America. Tar, timber, iron, and cordage are her natural produce. We need go abroad for nothing. Whereas the Dutch, who make large profits by hiring out their ships of war to the Spaniards and Portuguese, are obliged to import most of the materials they use. We ought to view the building a fleet as an article of commerce, it being the natural manufactory of this country. It is the best money we can lay out. A navy when finished is worth more than it cost. And is that nice point in national policy, in which commerce and protection are united. Let us build; if we want them not, we can sell; and by that means replace our paper currency with ready gold and silver.

In point of manning a fleet, people in general run into great errors; it is not necessary that one fourth part should be sailors. The Terrible privateer, Captain Death,[29] stood the hottest engagement of any ship last war, yet had not twenty sailors on board, though her complement of men was upwards of two hundred. A few able and social sailors will soon instruct a sufficient number of active landmen in the common work of a ship. Wherefore, we never can be more capable to begin on maritime matters than now, while our timber is standing, our fisheries blocked up, and our sailors and shipwrights out of employ. Men of war, of seventy and eighty guns were built forty years ago in New-England, and why not the same now? Ship-building is America's greatest pride, and in which, she will in time excel the whole world. The great empires of the east are mostly inland, and consequently excluded from the possibility of rivalling her. Africa is in a state of barbarism; and no power in Europe, hath either such an extent of coast, or such an internal supply of materials. Where nature hath given the one, she has withheld the other; to America only hath she been liberal of both. The vast empire of Russia is almost shut out from the sea; wherefore, her boundless forests, her tar, iron, and cordage are only articles of commerce.

In point of safety, ought we to be without a fleet? We are not the little people now, which we were sixty years ago; at that time we might have trusted our property in the streets, or fields rather; and slept securely without locks or bolts to our doors or windows. The case now is altered, and our methods of defence, ought to improve with our increase of property. A common pirate, twelve months ago, might have come up the Delaware, and laid the city of Philadelphia under instant contribution, for what sum he pleased; and the same might have happened to other places. Nay, any daring fellow, in a brig of fourteen or sixteen guns, might have robbed the whole Continent, and carried off half a million of money. These are circumstances which demand our attention, and point out the necessity of naval protection.

Some, perhaps, will say, that after we have made it up with Britain, she will protect us. Can we be so unwise as to mean, that she shall keep a navy in our harbours for that purpose? Common sense will tell us, that the power which hath endeavoured to subdue us, is of all others, the most improper to defend us. Conquest may be effected under the pretence of friendship; and ourselves, after a long and brave resistance, be at last cheated into slavery. And if her ships are not to be admitted into our harbours, I would ask, how is she to protect us? A navy three or four thousand miles off can be of little use, and on sudden emergencies, none at all. Wherefore, if we must hereafter protect ourselves, why not do it for ourselves? Why do it for another?

The English list of ships of war, is long and formidable, but not a tenth part of them are at any one time fit for service, numbers of them not in being; yet their names are pompously continued in the list, if only a plank be left of the ship: and not a fifth part, of such as are fit for service, can be spared on any one station at one time. The East, and West Indies, Mediterranean, Africa, and other parts over which Britain extends her claim, make large demands upon her navy. From a mixture of prejudice and inattention, we have contracted a false notion respecting the navy of England, and have talked as if we should have the whole of it to encounter at once, and for that reason, supposed, that we must have one as large; which not being instantly practicable, have been made use of by a set of disguised Tories to discourage our beginning thereon. Nothing can be farther from truth than this; for if America had only a twentieth part of the naval force of Britain, she would be by far an over match for her; because, as we neither have, nor claim any foreign dominion, our whole force would be employed on our own coast, where we should, in the long run, have two to one the advantage of those who had three or four thousand miles to sail over, before they could attack us, and the same distance to return in order to refit and recruit. And although Britain by her fleet, hath a check over our trade to Europe, we have as large a one over her trade to the West Indies, which, by laying in the neighbourhood of the Continent, is entirely at its mercy.

Some method might be fallen on to keep up a naval force in time of peace, if we should not judge it necessary to support a constant navy. If premiums were to be given to merchants, to build and employ in their service, ships mounted with twenty, thirty, forty, or fifty guns, (the premiums to be in proportion to the loss of bulk to the merchants) fifty or sixty of those ships, with a few guard ships on constant duty, would keep up a sufficient navy, and that without burdening ourselves with the evil so loudly complained of in England, of suffering their fleet, in time of peace to lie rotting in the docks. To unite the sinews of commerce and defence is sound policy; for when our strength and our riches, play into each other's hand, we need fear no external enemy.

In almost every article of defence we abound. Hemp flourishes even to rankness, so that we need not want cordage. Our iron is superior to that of other countries. Our small arms equal to any in the world. Cannon we can cast at pleasure. Saltpetre and gunpowder we are every day producing. Our knowledge is hourly improving. Resolution is our inherent character, and courage hath never yet forsaken us. Wherefore, what is it that we want? Why is it that we hesitate? From Britain we can expect nothing but ruin. If she is once admitted to the government of America again, this Continent will not be worth living in. Jealousies will be always arising; insurrections will be constantly happening; and who will go forth to quell them? Who will venture his life to reduce his own countrymen to a foreign obedience? The difference between Pennsylvania and Connecticut, respecting some unlocated lands, shews the insignificance of a British government, and fully proves, that nothing but Continental authority can regulate Continental matters.

Another reason why the present time is preferable to all others, is, that the fewer our numbers are, the more land there is yet unoccupied, which instead of being lavished by the king on his worthless dependants, may be hereafter applied, not only to the discharge of the present debt, but to the constant support of government. No nation under heaven hath such an advantage as this.

The infant state of the Colonies, as it is called, so far from being against, is an argument in favor of independance. We are sufficiently numerous, and were we more so, we might be less united. It is a matter worthy of observation, that the more a country is peopled, the smaller their armies are. In military numbers, the ancients far exceeded the moderns: and the reason is evident, for trade being the consequence of population, men become too much absorbed thereby to attend to any thing else. Commerce diminishes the spirit, both of patriotism and military defence. And history sufficiently informs us, that the bravest atchievements were always accomplished in the non-age of a nation. With the increase of commerce, England hath lost its spirit. The city of London, notwithstanding its numbers, submits to continued insults with the patience of a coward. The more men have to lose, the less willing are they to venture. The rich are in general slaves to fear, and submit to courtly power with the trembling duplicity of a Spaniel.

Youth is the seed time of good habits, as well in nations as in individuals. It might be difficult, if not impossible, to form the Continent into one government half a century hence. The vast variety of interests, occasioned by an increase of trade and population, would create confusion. Colony would be against colony. Each being able might scorn each other's assistance: and while the proud and foolish gloried in their little distinctions, the wise would lament, that the union had not been formed before. Wherefore, the *present time* is the *true time* for establishing it. The intimacy which is contracted in infancy, and the friendship which is formed in misfortune, are, of all others, the most lasting and unalterable. Our present union is marked with both these characters: we are young, and we have been distressed; but our concord hath withstood our troubles, and fixes a memorable æra for posterity to glory in.

The present time, likewise, is that peculiar time, which never happens to a nation but once, *viz.* the time of forming itself into a government. Most nations have let slip the opportunity, and by that means have been compelled to receive laws from their conquerors, instead of making laws for themselves. First, they had a king, and then a form of government; whereas, the articles or charter of government, should be formed first, and men delegated to execute them afterward: but from the errors of other nations, let us learn wisdom, and lay hold of the present opportunity————*To begin government at the right end.*

When William the Conqueror subdued England, he gave them law at the point of the sword; and until we consent, that the seat of government, in America, be legally and authoritatively occupied, we shall be in danger of having it filled by some fortunate ruffian, who may treat us in the same manner, and then, where will be our freedom? where our property?

As to religion, I hold it to be the indispensible duty of all government, to protect all conscientious professors thereof, and I know of no other business which government hath to do therewith. Let a man throw aside that narrowness of soul, that selfishness of principle, which the niggards of all professions are so unwilling to part with, and he will be at once delivered of his fears on that head. Suspicion is the companion of mean souls, and the bane of all good society. For myself, I fully and conscientiously believe, that it is the will of the Almighty, that there should be diversity of religious opinions among us: It affords a larger field for our Christian kindness. Were we all of one way of thinking, our religious dispositions would want matter for probation; and on this liberal principle, I look on the various denominations among us, to be like children of the same family, differing only, in what is called, their Christian names.

In page thirty-one, I threw out a few thoughts on the propriety of a Continental Charter, (for I only presume to offer hints, not plans) and in this place, I take the liberty of re-mentioning the subject, by observing, that a charter is to be understood as a bond of solemn obligation, which the whole enters into, to support the right of every separate part, whether of religion, personal freedom, or property. A firm bargain and a right reckoning make long friends.

In a former page I likewise mentioned the necessity of a large and equal representation; and there is no political matter which more deserves our attention. A small number of electors, or a small number of representatives, are equally dangerous. But if the number of the representatives be not only small, but unequal, the danger is increased. As an instance of this, I mention the following; when the Associators petition[30] was before the House of Assembly of Pennsylvania; twenty-eight members only were present, all the Bucks county members, being eight, voted against it, and had seven of the Chester members done the same, this whole province had been governed by two counties only, and this danger it is always exposed to. The unwarrantable stretch likewise, which that house made in their last sitting, to gain an undue authority over the Delegates of that province, ought to warn the people at large, how they trust power out of their own hands. A set of instructions for the Delegates were put together, which in point of sense and business would have dishonored a schoolboy, and after being approved by a *few*, a *very few* without doors, were carried into the House, and there passed *in behalf of the whole colony;* whereas, did the whole colony know, with what ill-will that House hath entered on some necessary public measures, they would not hesitate a moment to think them unworthy of such a trust.

Immediate necessity makes many things convenient, which if continued would grow into oppressions. Expedience and right are different things. When the calamities of America required a consultation, there was no method so ready, or at that time so proper, as to appoint persons from the several Houses of Assembly for that purpose; and the wisdom with which they have proceeded hath preserved this continent from ruin. But as it is more than probable that we shall never be without a Congress, every well wisher to good order, must own, that the mode for choosing members of that body, deserves consideration. And I put it as a question to those, who make a study of mankind, whether *representation and election* is not too great a power for one and the same body of men to possess? When we are planning for posterity, we ought to remember, that virtue is not hereditary.

It is from our enemies that we often gain excellent maxims, and are frequently surprised into reason by their mistakes. Mr. Cornwall (one of the Lords of the Treasury) treated the petition of the New-York Assembly with contempt,[31] because *that* House, he said, consisted but of twenty-six members, which trifling number, he argued, could not with decency be put for the whole. We thank him for his involuntary honesty.*

To Conclude, however strange it may appear to some, or however unwilling they may be to think so, matters not, but many strong and striking reasons may be given, to shew, that nothing can settle our affairs so expeditiously as an open and determined declaration for independance. Some of which are,

First.—It is the custom of nations, when any two are at war, for some other powers, not engaged in the quarrel, to step in as mediators, and bring about the preliminaries of a peace: but while America calls herself the Subject of Great-Britain, no power, however well disposed she may be, can offer her mediation. Wherefore, in our present state we may quarrel on for ever.

Secondly.—It is unreasonable to suppose, that France or Spain will

---

*Those who would fully understand of what great consequence a large and equal representation is to a state, should read Burgh's political Disquisitions.[32]

give us any kind of assistance, if we mean only, to make use of that assistance for the purpose of repairing the breach, and strengthening the connection between Britain and America; because, those powers would be sufferers by the consequences.

Thirdly.—While we profess ourselves the subjects of Britain, we must, in the eye of foreign nations, be considered as rebels. The precedent is somewhat dangerous to *their peace,* for men to be in arms under the name of subjects; we, on the spot, can solve the paradox: but to unite resistance and subjection, requires an idea much too refined for common understanding.

Fourthly.—Were a manifesto to be published, and despatched to foreign courts, setting forth the miseries we have endured, and the peaceable methods we have ineffectually used for redress; declaring, at the same time, that not being able, any longer, to live happily or safely under the cruel disposition of the British court, we had been driven to the necessity of breaking off all connections with her; at the same time, assuring all such courts of our peaceable disposition towards them, and of our desire of entering into trade with them: Such a memorial would produce more good effects to this Continent, than if a ship were freighted with petitions to Britain.

Under our present denomination of British subjects, we can neither be received nor heard abroad: The custom of all courts is against us, and will be so, until, by an independance, we take rank with other nations.

These proceedings may at first appear strange and difficult; but, like all other steps which we have already passed over, will in a little time become familiar and agreeable; and, until an independance is declared, the Continent will feel itself like a man who continues putting off some unpleasant business from day to day, yet knows it must be done, hates to set about it, wishes it over, and is continually haunted with the thoughts of its necessity.

APPENDIX

Since the publication of the first edition of this pamphlet, or rather, on the same day on which it came out, the King's Speech[33] made its appearance in this city. Had the spirit of prophecy directed the birth of this production, it could not have brought it forth, at a more seasonable juncture, or a more necessary time. The bloody mindedness of the one, shew the necessity of pursuing the doctrine of the other. Men read by way of revenge. And the Speech, instead of terrifying, prepared a way for the manly principles of Independance.

Ceremony, and even, silence, from whatever motive they may arise, have a hurtful tendency, when they give the least degree of countenance to base and wicked performances; wherefore, if this maxim be admitted, it naturally follows, that the King's Speech, as being a piece of finished villany, deserved, and still deserves, a general execration both by the Congress and the people. Yet, as the domestic tranquillity of a nation, depends greatly, on the *chastity* of what may properly be called NATIONAL MANNERS, it is often better, to pass some things over in silent disdain, than to make use of such new methods of dislike, as might introduce the least innovation, on that guardian of our peace and safety. And, perhaps, it is chiefly owing to this prudent delicacy, that the King's Speech, hath not, before now, suffered a public execution. The Speech if it may be called one, is nothing better than a wilful audacious libel against the truth, the common good, and the existence of mankind; and is a formal and pompous method of offering up human sacrifices to the pride of tyrants. But this general massacre of mankind, is one of the privileges, and the certain consequence of Kings; for as nature knows them *not,* they know *not her,* and although they are beings of our *own* creating, they know not *us,* and are become the gods of their creators. The Speech hath one good quality, which is, that it is not calculated to deceive, neither can we, even if we would, be deceived by it. Brutality and tyranny appear on the face of it. It leaves us at no loss: And every line convinces, even in the moment of reading, that He, who hunts the woods for prey, the naked and untutored Indian, is less a Savage than the King of Britain.

Sir John Dalrymple,[34] the putative father of a whining jesuitical piece, fallaciously called, "*The Address of the people of* ENGLAND *to the inhabitants of* AMERICA," hath, perhaps, from a vain supposition, that the people *here* were to be frightened at the pomp and description of a king, given, (though very unwisely on his part) the real character of the present one: "But," says this writer, "if you are inclined to pay compliments to an administration, which we do not complain of," (meaning the Marquis of Rockingham's[35] at the repeal of the Stamp Act) "it is very unfair in you to withhold them from that prince, *by whose* NOD ALONE *they were permitted to do any thing.*" This is toryism with a witness! Here is idolatry even without a mask: And he who can calmly hear, and digest such doctrine, hath forfeited his claim to rationality—an apostate from the order of manhood; and ought to be considered—as one, who hath not only given up the proper dignity of man, but sunk himself beneath the rank of animals, and contemptibly crawl through the world like a worm.

However, it matters very little now, what the king of England either says or does; he hath wickedly broken through every moral and human obligation, trampled nature and conscience beneath his feet; and by a steady and constitutional spirit of insolence and cruelty, procured for himself an universal hatred. It is *now* the interest of America to provide for herself. She hath already a large and young family, whom it is more her duty to take care of, than to be granting away her property, to support a power who is become a reproach to the names of men and christians—YE—whose office it is to watch over the morals of a nation, of whatsoever sect or denomination ye are of, as well as ye, who, are more immediately the guardians of the public liberty, if ye wish to preserve your native country uncontaminated by European corruption, ye must in secret wish a separation—But leaving the moral part to private reflection, I shall chiefly confine my farther remarks to the following heads.

——

First. That it is the interest of America to be separated from Britain.

——

Secondly. Which is the easiest and most practicable plan, RECONCILIATION or INDEPENDANCE? with some occasional remarks.

——

In support of the first, I could, if I judged it proper, produce the opinion of some of the ablest and most experienced men on this continent; and whose sentiments, on that head, are not yet publicly known. It is in reality a self-evident position: For no nation in a state of foreign dependance, limited in its commerce, and cramped and fettered in its legislative powers, can ever arrive at any material eminence. America doth not yet know what opulence is; and although the progress which she hath made stands unparalleled in the history of other nations, it is but childhood, compared with what she would be capable of arriving at, had she, as she ought to have, the legislative powers in her own hands. England is, at this time, proudly covering what would do her no good, were she to accomplish it; and the Continent hesitating on a matter, which will be her final ruin if neglected. It is the commerce and not the conquest of America, by which England is to be benefited, and that would in a great measure continue, were the countries as independant of each other as France and Spain; because in many articles, neither can go to a better market. But it is the independance of this country on Britain or any other, which is now the main and only object worthy of contention, and which, like all other truths discovered by necessity, will appear clearer and stronger every day.

———

First. Because it will come to that one time or other.

———

Secondly. Because, the longer it is delayed the harder it will be to accomplish.

———

I have frequently amused myself both in public and private companies, with silently remarking, the specious errors of those who speak without reflecting. And among the many which I have heard, the following seems the most general, viz. that had this rupture happened forty or fifty years hence, instead of *now*, the Continent would have been more able to have shaken off the dependance. To which I reply, that our military ability, *at this time*, arises from the experience gained in the last war, and which in forty or fifty years time, would have been totally extinct. The Continent, would not, by that time, have had a General, or even a military officer left; and we, or those who may succeed us, would have been as ignorant of martial matters as the ancient Indians: And this single position, closely attended to, will unanswerably prove, that the present time is preferable to all others. The argument turns thus—at the conclusion of the last war, we had experience, but wanted numbers; and forty or fifty years hence, we should have numbers, without experience; wherefore, the proper point of time, must be some particular point between the two extremes, in which a sufficiency of the former remains, and a proper increase of the latter is obtained: And that point of time is the present time.

The reader will pardon this digression, as it does not properly come under the head I first set out with, and to which I again return by the following position, viz.

Should affairs be patched up with Britain, and she to remain the governing and sovereign power of America, (which, as matters are now circumstanced, is giving up the point intirely) we shall deprive ourselves of the very means of sinking the debt we have, or may contract. The value of the back lands which some of the provinces are clandestinely deprived of, by the unjust extension of the limits of Canada, valued only at five pounds sterling per hundred acres, amount to upwards of twenty-five millions, Pennsylvania currency; and the quit-rents at one penny sterling per acre, to two millions yearly.

It is by the sale of those lands that the debt may be sunk, without burthen to any, and the quit-rent reserved thereon, will always lessen, and in time, will wholly support the yearly expence of government. It matters not how long the debt is in paying, so that the lands when sold be applied to the discharge of it, and for the execution of which, the Congress for the time being, will be the continental trustees.

———

I proceed now to the second head, viz. Which is the easiest and most practicable plan, RECONCILIATION or INDEPENDENCE; with some occasional remarks.

———

He who takes nature for his guide is not easily beaten out of his argument, and on that ground, I answer *generally—That* INDEPENDANCE *being a* SINGLE SIMPLE LINE, *contained within ourselves; and reconciliation, a matter exceedingly perplexed and complicated, and in which, a treacherous capricious court is to interfere, gives the answer without a doubt.*

———

The present state of America is truly alarming to every man who is capable of reflexion. Without law, without government, without any other mode of power than what is founded on, and granted by courtesy. Held together by an unexampled concurrence of sentiment, which, is nevertheless subject to change, and which, every secret enemy is endeavouring to dissolve. Our present condition, is, Legislation without law; wisdom without a plan; a constitution without a name; and, what is strangely astonishing, perfect Independance contending for dependance. The instance is without a precedent; the case never existed before; and who can tell what may be the event? The property of no man is secure in the present unbraced system of things. The mind of the multitude is left at random, and seeing no fixed object before them, they pursue such as fancy or opinion starts. Nothing is criminal; there is no such thing as treason; wherefore, every one thinks himself at liberty to act as he pleases. The Tories dared not have assembled offensively, had they known that their lives, by that act, were forfeited to the laws of the state. A line of distinction should be drawn, between, English soldiers taken in battle, and inhabitants of America taken in arms. The first are prisoners, but the latter traitors. The one forfeits his liberty, the other his head.

Notwithstanding our wisdom, there is a visible feebleness in some of our proceedings which gives encouragement to dissentions. The Continental Belt is too losely buckled. And if something is not done in time, it will be too late to do any thing, and we shall fall into a state, in which, neither *Reconciliation* nor *Independance* will be practicable. The king and his worthless adherents are got at their old game of dividing the Continent, and there are not wanting among us, Printers, who will be busy in spreading specious falsehoods. The artful and hypocritical letter which appeared a few months ago in two of the New-York papers, and likewise in two others, is an evidence that there are men who want either judgment or honesty.

It is easy getting into holes and corners and talking of reconciliation: But do such men seriously consider, how difficult the task is, and how dangerous it may prove, should the Continent divide thereon. Do they take within their view, all the various orders of men whose situation and circumstances, as well as their own, are to be considered therein. Do they put themselves in the place of the sufferer whose *all* is *already* gone, and of the soldier, who hath quitted *all* for the defence of his country. If their ill judged moderation be suited to their own private situations *only*, regardless of others, the event will convince them, that "they are reckoning without their Host."

Put us, says some, on the footing we were on in sixty-three:[36] To which I answer, the request is not *now* in the power of Britain to comply with, neither will she propose it; but if it were, and even should be granted, I ask, as a reasonable question, By what means is such a corrupt and faithless court to be kept to its engagements? Another parliament, nay, even the present, may hereafter repeal the obligation, on the pretence, of its being violently obtained, or unwisely granted; and in that case, Where is our redress?—No going to law with nations; cannon are the barristers of Crowns; and the sword, not of justice, but of war, decides the suit. To be on the footing of sixty-three, it is not sufficient, that the laws only be put on the same state, but, that our circumstances, likewise, be put on the same state; Our burnt and destroyed towns[37] repaired or built up, our private losses made good, our public debts (contracted for defence) discharged; otherwise, we shall be millions worse than we were at that enviable period. Such a request, had it been complied with a year ago, would have won the heart and soul of the Continent—but now it is too late, "The Rubicon is passed."[38]

Besides, the taking up arms, merely to enforce the repeal of a pecuniary law, seems as unwarrantable by the divine law, and as repugnant to human feelings, as the taking up arms to enforce obedience thereto. The object, on either side, doth not justify the means; for the lives of men are too valuable to be cast away on such trifles. It is the violence which is done and threatened to our persons; the destruction of our property by an armed force; the invasion of our country by fire and sword, which conscientiously qualifies the use of arms: And the instant, in which such a mode of defence became necessary, all subjection to Britain ought to have ceased; and the independancy of America, should have been considered, as dating its æra from, and published by, *the first musket that was fired against her.* This line is a line of consistency; neither drawn by caprice, nor extended by ambition; but produced by a chain of events, of which the colonies were not the authors.

I shall conclude these remarks, with the following timely and well intended hints, We ought to reflect, that there are three different ways, by which an independancy may hereafter be effected; and that *one* of those *three,* will one day or other, be the fate of America, viz. By the legal voice of the people in Congress; by a military power; or by a mob: It may not always happen that our soldiers are citizens, and the multitude a body of reasonable men; virtue, as I have already remarked, is not hereditary, neither is it perpetual. Should an independancy be brought about by the first of those means, we have every opportunity and every encouragement before us, to form the noblest purest constitution on the face of the earth. We have it in our power to begin the world over again. A situation, similar to the present, hath not happened since the days of Noah until now. The birthday of a new world is at hand, and a race of men, perhaps as numerous as all Europe contains, are to receive their portion of freedom from the event of a few months. The Reflexion is awful—and in this point of view, How trifling, how ridiculous, do the little, paltry cavellings, of a few weak or interested men appear, when weighed against the business of a world.

Should we neglect the present favorable and inviting period, and an Independance be hereafter effected by any other means, we must charge the consequence to ourselves, or to those rather, whose narrow and prejudiced souls, are habitually opposing the measure, without either inquiring or reflecting. There are reasons to be given in support of Independance, which men should rather privately think of, than be publicly told of. We ought not now to be debating whether we shall be independant or not, but, anxious to accomplish it on a firm, secure, and honorable basis, and uneasy rather that it is not yet began upon. Every day convinces us of its necessity. Even the Tories (if such beings yet remain among us) should, of all men, be the most solicitous to promote it; for, as the appointment of committees at first, protected them from popular rage, so, a wise and well established form of government, will be the only certain means of continuing it securely to them. *Wherefore,* if they have not virtue enough to be WHIGS, they ought to have prudence enough to wish for Independance.

In short, Independance is the only BOND that can tye and keep us together. We shall then see our object, and our ears will be legally shut against the schemes of an intriguing, as well, as a cruel enemy. We shall then too, be on a proper footing, to treat with Britain; for there is reason to conclude, that the pride of that court, will be less hurt by treating with the American states for terms of peace, than with those, whom she denominates, "rebellious subjects," for terms of accommodation. It is our delaying it that encourages her to hope for conquest, and our backwardness tends only to prolong the war. As we have, without any good effect therefrom, withheld our trade to obtain a redress of our grievances, let us *now* try the alternative, by *independantly* redressing them ourselves, and then offering to open the trade. The mercantile and reasonable part in England, will be still with us; because, peace *with* trade, is preferable to war *without* it. And if this offer be not accepted, other courts may be applied to.

On these grounds I rest the matter. And as no offer hath yet been made to refute the doctrine contained in the former editions of this pamphlet, it is a negative proof, that either the doctrine cannot be re-

futed, or, that the party in favour of it are too numerous to be opposed.
WHEREFORE, instead of gazing at each other with suspicious or doubtful curiosity, let each of us, hold out to his neighbour the hearty hand
of friendship, and unite in drawing a line, which, like an act of obliv-
ion shall bury in forgetfulness every former dissention. Let the names
of Whig and Tory be extinct; and let none other be heard among us,
than those of *a good citizen, an open and resolute friend, and a virtuous sup-
porter of the* RIGHTS *of* MANKIND *and of the* FREE AND INDEPENDENT
STATES OF AMERICA.

TO THE REPRESENTATIVES OF THE RELIGIOUS SOCIETY OF
THE PEOPLE CALLED QUAKERS, OR TO SO MANY OF THEM
AS WERE CONCERNED IN PUBLISHING A LATE PIECE, ENTITLED
"THE ANCIENT TESTIMONY AND PRINCIPLES[39] OF
THE PEOPLE CALLED QUAKERS RENEWED,
WITH RESPECT TO THE KING AND GOVERNMENT,
AND TOUCHING THE COMMOTIONS NOW PREVAILING
IN THESE AND OTHER PARTS OF AMERICA ADDRESSED TO
THE PEOPLE IN GENERAL."

The Writer of this, is one of those few, who never dishonors religion
either by ridiculing, or cavilling at any denomination whatsoever. To
God, and not to man, are all men accountable on the score of religion.
Wherefore, this epistle is not so properly addressed to you as a reli-
gious, but as a political body, dabbling in matters, which the professed
Quietude of your Principles instruct you not to meddle with.

As you have, without a proper authority for so doing, put yourselves in the place of the whole body of the Quakers, so, the writer of
this, in order to be on an equal rank with yourselves, is under the necessity, of putting himself in the place of all those, who, approve the
very writings and principles, against which, your testimony is directed:
And he hath chosen this singular situation, in order, that you might
discover in him that presumption of character which you cannot see in
yourselves. For neither he nor you can have any claim or title to *Political Representation.*

When men have departed from the right way, it is no wonder that
they stumble and fall. And it is evident from the manner in which ye
have managed your testimony, that politics, (as a religious body of men)

is not your proper Walk; for however well adapted it might appear to you, it is, nevertheless, a jumble of good and bad put unwisely together, and the conclusion drawn therefrom, both unnatural and unjust.

The two first pages, (and the whole doth not make four) we give you credit for, and expect the same civility from you, because the love and desire of peace is not confined to Quakerism, it is the *natural,* as well the religious wish of all denominations of men. And on this ground, as men laboring to establish an Independant Constitution of our own, do we exceed all others in our hope, end, and aim. *Our plan is peace for ever.* We are tired of contention with Britain, and can see no real end to it but in a final separation. We act confidently, because for the sake of introducing an endless and uninterrupted peace, do we bear the evils and burthens of the present day. We are endeavoring, and will steadily continue to endeavor, to separate and dissolve a connexion which hath already filled our land with blood; and which, while the name of it remains, will be the fatal cause of future mischiefs to both countries.

We fight neither for revenge nor conquest; neither from pride nor passion; we are not insulting the world with our fleets and armies, nor ravaging the globe for plunder. Beneath the shade of our own vines are we attacked; in our own houses, and on our own lands, is the violence committed against us. We view our enemies in the character of Highwaymen and Housebreakers, and having no defence for ourselves in the civil law, are obliged to punish them by the military one, and apply the sword, in the very case, where you have before now, applied the halter——— Perhaps we feel for the ruined and insulted sufferers in all and every part of the continent, with a degree of tenderness which hath not yet made it's way into some of your bosoms. But be ye sure that ye mistake not the cause and ground of your Testimony. Call not coldness of soul, religion; nor put the *Bigot* in the place of the *Christian.*

O ye partial ministers of your own acknowledged principles. If the bearing arms be sinful, the first going to war must be more so, by all the difference between wilful attack and unavoidable defence. Wherefore, if ye really preach from conscience, and mean not to make a political hobby-horse of your religion, convince the world thereof, by proclaiming your doctrine to our enemies, *for they likwise bear* ARMS. Give us proof of your sincerity by publishing it at St. James's,[40] to the commanders in chief at Boston, to the Admirals and Captains who are piratically ravaging our coasts, and to all the murdering miscreants who are acting in authority under HIM whom ye profess to serve. Had ye the honest soul of * *Barclay*[41] ye would preach repentance to *your* king; Ye would tell the Royal Wretch his sins, and warn him of eternal ruin. Ye would not spend your partial invectives against the injured and the insulted only, but, like faithful ministers, would cry aloud and *spare none.* Say not that ye are persecuted, neither endeavour to make us the authors of that reproach, which, ye are bringing upon yourselves; for we testify unto all men, that we do not complain against you because ye are *Quakers,* but because ye pretend to *be* and are NOT Quakers.

Alas! it seems by the particular tendency of some part of your testimony, and other parts of your conduct, as if, all sin was reduced to, and comprehended in, *the act of bearing arms,* and that by the *people only.* Ye appear to us, to have mistaken party for conscience; because, the general tenor of your actions wants uniformity: And it is exceedingly difficult to us to give credit to many of your pretended scruples; because, we see them made by the same men, who, in the very instant that they are exclaiming against the mammon of this world, are nevertheless, hunting after it with a step as steady as Time, and an appetite as keen as Death.

The quotation which ye have made from Proverbs, in the third page of your testimony, that, "when a man's ways please the Lord, he maketh even his enemies to be at peace with him"; is very unwisely chosen on your part; because, it amounts to a proof, that the king's ways (whom ye are so desirous of supporting) do *not* please the Lord, otherwise, his reign would be in peace.

I now proceed to the latter part of your testimony, and that, for which all the foregoing seems only an introduction, viz.

"It hath ever been our judgment and principle, since we were called to profess the light of Christ Jesus, manifested in our consciences unto

---

* "Thou hast tasted of prosperity and adversity; thou knowest what it is to be banished thy native country, to be over-ruled as well as to rule, and set upon the throne; and being oppressed thou hast reason to know how *hateful* the *oppressor* is both to God and man: If after all these warnings and advertisements, thou dost not turn unto the Lord with all thy heart, but forget him who remembered thee in thy distress, and give up thyself to follow lust and vanity, surely great will be thy condemnation.—Against which snare, as well as the temptation of those who may or do feed thee, and prompt thee to evil, the most excellent and prevalent remedy will be, to apply thyself to that light of Christ which shineth in thy conscience, and which neither can, nor will flatter thee, nor suffer thee to be at ease in thy sins."

BARCLAY'S ADDRESS TO CHARLES II.

this day, that the sitting up and putting down kings and governments, is God's peculiar prerogative; for causes best known to himself: And that it is not our business to have any hand or contrivance therein; nor to be busy bodies above our station, much less to plot and contrive the ruin, or overturn of any of them, but to pray for the king, and safety of our nation, and good of all men: That we may live a peaceable and quiet life, in all godliness and honesty; *under the government which God is pleased to set over us.*"—If these are *really* your principles why do ye not abide by them? Why do ye not leave that, which ye call God's Work, to be managed by himself? These very principles instruct you to wait with patience and humility, for the event of all public measures, and to receive *that event* as the divine will towards you. *Wherefore,* what occasion is there for your *political testimony* if you fully believe what it contains? And the very publishing it proves, that either, ye do not believe what ye profess, or have not virtue enough to practise what ye believe.

The principles of Quakerism have a direct tendency to make a man the quiet and inoffensive subject of any, and every government *which is set over him.*[42] And if the setting up and putting down of kings and governments is God's peculiar prerogative, he most certainly will not be robbed thereof by us; wherefore, the principle itself leads you to approve of every thing, which ever happened, or may happen to kings as being his work. OLIVER CROMWELL[43] thanks you. CHARLES, then, died not by the hands of man; and should the present Proud Imitator of him, come to the same untimely end, the writers and publishers of the Testimony, are bound, by the doctrine it contains, to applaud the fact. Kings are not taken away by miracles, neither are changes in government brought about by any other means than such as are common and human; and such as we are now using. Even the dispersion of the Jews, though foretold by our Saviour, was effected by arms. Wherefore, as ye refuse to be the means of one side, ye ought not to be meddlers on the other; but to wait the issue in silence; and unless ye can produce divine authority, to prove, that the Almighty who hath created and placed this *new* world, at the greatest distance it could possibly stand, east and west, from every part of the old, doth, nevertheless, disapprove of its being independent of the corrupt and abandoned court of Britain, unless I say, ye can shew this, how can ye on the ground of your principles, justify the exciting and stirring up the people "firmly to unite in the *abhorrence* of all such *writings,* and *measures,* as evidence a desire and design to break off the *happy* connexion we have hitherto enjoyed, with the kingdom of Great-Britain, and our just and necessary subordination to the king, and those who are lawfully placed in authority under him." What a slap of the face is here! the men, who in the very paragraph before, have quietly and passively resigned up the ordering, altering, and disposal of kings and governments, into the hands of God, are now, recalling their principles, and putting in for a share of the business. Is it possible, that the conclusion, which is here justly quoted, can any ways follow from the doctrine laid down? The inconsistency is too glaring not to be seen; the absurdity too great not to be laughed at; and such as could only have been made by those, whose understandings were darkened by the narrow and crabby spirit of a dispairing political party; for ye are not to be considered as the whole body of the Quakers but only as a factional and fractional part thereof.

Here ends the examination of your testimony; (which I call upon no man to abhor, as ye have done, but only to read and judge of fairly;) to which I subjoin the following remark; "That the setting up and putting down of kings," most certainly mean, the making him a king, who is yet not so, and the making him no king who is already one. And pray what hath this to do in the present case? We neither mean to *set up* nor to *put down,* neither to *make* nor to *unmake,* but to have nothing to *do* with them. Wherefore, your testimony in whatever light it is viewed serves only to dishonor your judgement, and for many other reasons had better have been let alone than published.

———

First, Because it tends to the decrease and reproach of all religion whatever, and is of the utmost danger to society, to make it a party in political disputes.

———

Secondly, Because it exhibits a body of men, numbers of whom disavow the publishing political testimonies, as being concerned therein and approvers thereof.

———

Thirdly, Because it hath a tendency to undo that continental harmony and friendship which yourselves by your late liberal and charitable donations hath lent a hand to establish; and the preservation of which, is of the utmost consequence to us all.

———

And here without anger or resentment I bid you farewel. Sincerely wishing, that as men and christians, ye may always fully and uninterruptedly enjoy every civil and religious right; and be, in your turn, the means of securing it to others; but that the example which ye have unwisely set, of mingling religion with politics, *may be disavowed and reprobated by every inhabitant of* AMERICA.

FOUR LETTERS ON
INTERESTING SUBJECTS

1776

In his Four Letters, *Thomas Paine expands upon the ideas that he used in* Common Sense *to explain the logic of proposing American independence. Published anonymously sometime between May 22 and July 2, 1776, these essays were not identified as Paine's work until they were examined by A. Owen Aldridge, a distinguished American literature professor, in the late twentieth century. The* Letters, *like the early* American Crisis *papers Paine would write shortly, were published by the Philadelphia printing house of Steiner and Cist.*

Paine's Four Letters *were firmly grounded in the political storm that was raging in Philadelphia in the spring of 1776, and in these writings he added his voice to the cause of independence in his adopted town. Pennsylvania's elections on May 1 had given victory to the moderates who favored a reconciliation with Great Britain. On May 21, a mass meeting of four to seven thousand people was held on the State House (now Independence Hall) Square in Philadelphia. The meeting, responding to John Adams's May 15 call for each colony to establish provincial governments in the face of Britain's increasingly oppressive policies, took actions that were committed and active, if not quite within the confines of the law. The Pennsylvania Assembly elected May 1, they reasoned, had not been elected as a body to form a new government. Furthermore, the assembly's act the previous November, giving instructions to its Continental Congress delegates that they could not vote for any new form of government, alienated Pennsylvania from the other twelve colonies. The mass meeting overcame these problems by unanimously electing a one-hundred-member convention, chosen by the people, to carry out Congress's plan.*

Styner and Cist were correct when they noted at the front of the pamphlet "the rapid turn which Politics have taken within the course of a few days." Indeed, a citizen of Philadelphia might have seen the preceding weeks as a revolution. The Four Letters *were an integral part of this. In them, Paine showed his beliefs in the American cause, attacked Pennsylvania's conservative Proprietary Party, and then the very foundation upon which they based their beliefs: the character and policies of William Penn and his descendants. He showed his commitment to an America that would be independent as soon as possible, strengthened by its natural resources and supported by a written constitution.*

To the Public

The rapid turn which Politics have taken within the course of a few days, makes it almost impossible for the Press to keep pace therewith; which will account for some few remarks in the first and second of the following Letters, if they should not appear so necessary now as at the time of writing them.

LETTER I

Every man who acts beyond the line of private life, must expect to pass through two severe examinations. First, as to his motives, secondly, as to his conduct: On the former of these depends his character for honesty; on the latter for wisdom. The question is, how are we to know a man's motives? I answer, by tracing his conduct back on himself, as you would a stream to the fountain-head, and comparing the measures he pursues with his own private interest and dependencies; and the conclusion will be, that if no visible connexion appears between them, we are obliged, on the grounds of justice and generosity, to believe that such a man acts from reason and principle; for if this criterion be taken away, there is no other general one to know men by. On the other hand, if on examining from a man's conduct back to the man himself, we find a place of an hundred or a thousand a year at the bottom, or some advantage equivalent thereto, and find likewise that all his measures have been continually and invariably directed to support the party in *every thing* which supports him in his place or office, we may, without hesitation, set that man down for an interested time-serving tool.

We used to feel a mighty indignity at hearing a king's custom-house officer, of forty or fifty pounds a year, bawling out in support of every measure of his employers; and the cause of this dislike in us was, because his motives had the appearance of selfishness; yet we have every reason to believe that the same servile principle produced the late Remonstrance, and drew together the whole tribe of Crown and Proprietary dependants to give it countenance; who, by fermenting the prejudices of some, and working on the weakness of others, endeavoured to render themselves formidable by a party. Why is it, that every governor, and almost every officer under them, throughout the Continent, have uniformly trodden in the same steps? but because that ONE slavish mercenary principle has governed all. Scarcely a man amongst them have had either honesty or fortitude enough, to ask his conscience or his judgment a question. Did men reason with themselves ever so little, they would soon conclude, that the King and his Ministers could not be for *ever right*, nor the opposition, either in England or America, for *ever wrong*. Wisdom cannot be all on one side, nor ignorance all on the other; yet this levee of dependents have never dared to doubt any thing, but obeyed as implicitly as if their employers had been divine, and travelled on through thick and thin, without once enquiring into the cause, or reflecting on the consequence. The case was, that their places were at stake, and *that all commanding thought* superseded every other.

Reason and conscience seem unnecessary endowments to men in such stations; for as they use them not, they need them not, and their chiefest excellence consists in a kind of magnetical obedience, which, having no choice of its own, is governed implicitly by the influence of some other. However degrading this servile character may seem, it is nevertheless a just description of almost every man who held an office under George the Third; and the misfortune to these "*middle provinces*" has been, that the circle of duplicity was considerably enlarged therein by the addition of the Proprietary interest to that of the Crown. Did those persons see themselves in the same light which others view them in, their confidence would fail to support them in the measures they have been pursuing. The indecency of meddling and making in political matters is the same in them, as in the lowest custom-house officer under the Crown; neither does it answer their purpose; for their motives being known, their opinion passes for nothing, and their credit sinks by the very means they take to prop it up.

To the impertinence of office there have been added in this province an affectation of rank: The Proprietary party,[1] who headed the opposers of independence, set out under the assumed distinction of "men of consequence;" although it happens very unfortunately for them, that in the line of extraction they are much beneath the generality of the other inhabitants. No reflection ought to be made on any man on account of birth, provided that his manners rises decently with his circumstances, and that he affects not to forget the level he came from; when he does, he ought to be led back and shewn the mortifying picture of originality. Riches in a new country are unavoidable to the descendants of the early settlers; because the lands at that time were purchased for a trifle, and rendered valuable afterwards by the addition and industry of new-comers: A capital of ten pounds well laid out in land a century ago, would, without either care or genius either in the heir or the owner, been by this time an estate; and perhaps it is owing to this accidental manner of becoming rich, that wealth does not obtain the same degree of influence here, which it does in old countries. Rank, at present, in America is derived more from qualification than property; a sound moral character, amiable manners and firmness in principle constitute the first class, and will continue to do so till the origin of families be forgotten, and the proud follies of the old world over-run the simplicity of the new.

But to return. There is a more principal consequence for such men to contemplate than bare disappointment and disgrace. A contest for government is not to be considered as an election. The whole affair is now taking a most serious turn. The transition from Toryism to treason is nearly effected, and the rude custom of Tarring and Feathering will soon give way to the severer punishment of the gibbet. Disaffection and treachery have only received strength and encouragement from former lenity; and, until an example be made of some leading ones, the evil will continue increasing. It may perhaps be asked, what sort of people are we now to call Tories? I answer, every one who contends or argues for the supremacy of the king of England over the colonies. We have at this time but two general denominations of persons, *Independents* and *Tories,* or, if you please, *Traitors;* for to endeavour now either by words or ways to unite America to the crown and government of Britain, is the same kind of crime as it would be for a citizen of London to propose uniting England to the crown and government of France. This is plain doctrine, but it may perhaps save some man or other from the gallows; and, however it be relished by many, it is nevertheless a duty due to society to shew such men their danger fully, and warn them of the consequences. If, after that, they fall, their blood be upon their own head.

But the circumstance which most affects a generous mind is, that those men generally draw into their party a number of unwary, unsuspicious persons, by false and fraudulent pretences. There are men at this time who are base enough to give out that Britain wants to be reconciled—that we may make matters up if we will—and that it is our own fault if we do not—and, after painting a horrid picture of war, charge the whole guilt thereof upon the Continent. It was partly by artifices of this kind that the promoters of the Remonstrance procured signers thereto: Therefore, for the sake of such deceived persons, I'll state the case truly, and leave it to their reflection. Have not every mode for reconciliation been tried?—Have a stone been left unturned that could possibly effect it?—Have not petition after petition been sent and rejected?—Have not the petition from the Assembly of New-York met with the same fate with those of the Congress?—Have not every petition of the city of London and other parts of England been indignantly disregarded, and the petitioners, in some cases, accused of aiding a rebellion?—Have not every conciliatory plan, proposed by our friends in either house of parliament, failed even without a chance?—Is there now one untried method left to proceed upon, or a single hope left to stand upon?—Have not the British court amused us with Commissioners, while at the same time she was privately negociating for foreign troops?—Have she not now cut off every possibility of an accommodation by first declaring us rebels, and then declaring that rebels must be subdued before they can be treated with? Is this the case, or is it not? You that sculk into holes and corners, and exclaim against independency, can you disprove these things, or even bring the truth of them into suspicion? If you can not, the case will be, that those whom ye deceive will soon turn your accusers.

If a general review be taken of the conduct of Britain, it will confirm the suspicion which many discerning men, both on this and the other side the water, had at first, which was, that the British court wished from the beginning of this dispute to come to an open rupture with the Continent, that she might have a colourable pretence to possess herself of the whole. The long and scandalous list of placemen and pensioners, and the general profligacy and prodigality of the present reign, exceed the annual supplies. England is drained by taxes, and Ireland impoverished to almost the last farthing, yet the farce of state must be kept up, every thing must give way to the wants and vices of a court. America was the only remaining spot to which their oppression and extortion had not fully reached; and they considered her as a fallow field, from which a large income might be drawn, if politically broken up; but the experiment of the stamp-act had taught them to know that they must not hope to effect it by taxation. It is generally believed that Mr. Grenville[2] had nothing more in view in getting the stamp-act passed than the raising a revenue in America quietly; and it is fully believed by many, that the present king and ministry had *no revenue* in view in passing the tea-act; their object was a quarrel, by which they expected to accomplish the whole at once, and taxation was only the bone to quarrel about. To see America in arms is probably the very thing they wished for—the unpardonable sin which they wanted her to commit; because it furnished them with a pretence for declaring us rebels; and persons conquered under that character forfeit their all, be it where it will, or what it will, to the crown. And as Britain had no apprehension of the military strength of the Continent, nor any doubt of easily subduing it, she would, from motives of political avarice, prefer conquest to any mode of accommodation whatsoever; and it is on this ground only that the continued obstinacy of her conduct can be accounted for.

Some, perhaps, will object to the harshness of this supposition, and endeavour to disprove it by referring to Lord North's[3] conciliatory plan of the 20th of February, 1775, wherein the Colonies are left to tax themselves: To which I reply, that that scheme, instead of weakening, corroborates the suspicion; for, there is strong reason to believe, that the British court never wished to have even that plan, bad as it was, adopted by the Colonies; and this is presumptively proved by her beginning on hostilities between the time of passing that resolve and the time of the different assemblies meeting to deliberate thereon. Had no private orders been given to General Gage,[4] he undoubtedly would have avoided any new aggravation in the interim. He was acquainted with the resolve of the 20th of February upwards of three weeks before his famous expedition to Lexington and Concord, and knew likewise that no assembly had at that time met on the business. Truly has it been said that the tender mercies of the wicked are cruel; and when all the circumstances attending this resolve are compared, they amount to a strong presumption that it was only hung out to amuse the English while an effectual military method was taken to aggravate the Colonies to reject it, till, by driving them to hostilities, she might crush them with arms in their hands, and make them glad to compound for their lives with the surrender of their property. That "*nothing but a good battle would do*" was very common language two years ago in many companies in London; and what has happened since shews that such a scheme was in real contemplation.

A few weak or wicked men among ourselves, for the sake of keeping up a division, may talk of reconciliation; but Britain has no such thought; the amazing expence she has put herself to is a sufficient proof against it: Her aim is to get or lose the whole, and repay the millions she has expended, either by laying on us a heavy yearly tribute, if she can, or by immediately seizing our property. We have now no middle-line; and none but an idiot or a villain would endeavour to spread such notions. That it is the design of Britain to set up military governments throughout the provinces, if ever they come into her hands again, is doubted by no man of sense and reflection; and likewise, that we have no other mercy to expect from her but a repetition of all those savage and hellish oppressions and cruelties which she so unrelentingly inflicted on the wretched inhabitants of the East-Indies. Thank GOD! we have had a long warning given us to prepare; and, when every disadvantage which we had to encounter, from the want both of materials and experience, be considered, together with the opposition from the ignorant and disaffected among us, it is nearly a miracle that we are so well prepared.

The king and his ministers in all their speeches and harangues have constantly held out that the Americans were aiming at independence. Pity but we could have taken the hint sooner! for all our present distresses, arising from a scarcity of goods, are owing to our not thinking of independence *soon enough*. Our non-importation agreement[5] ought to have ceased immediately on the breaking-out of hostilities, and instead thereof we ought to have doubled or tribled our imports; and this would have been the case, had it not been for the absurd and destructive doctrine of reconciliation: because, the moment we had adopted the plan of separation we should have seen the necessity of laying in an additional stock. In short, reconciliation is a doctrine which has driven us to the edge of ruin, and the man that hereafter mentions it as a plan, ought to be considered and treated as a traitor to his country.

LETTER II

The interest of the Provinces, like that of individuals, is two-fold, public and private; for in the same rank which an individual stands in to the public, do the provinces stand in to the Continent; and he who in the present affairs looks no farther than the province he lives in, is moved thereto by the same spirit which inclines a selfish man to look no farther than himself; and in the same manner in which private interest undermines a community, does a narrow provincial spirit sap the Continental welfare: An open generous hearted man, and an open generous hearted province, are characters on the same line. A number of misers trading constantly with one another, would grow poor by their covetousness, and the same circumstance would happen with the Colonies were they to adopt a miserly provincial spirit. The happiness of individuals is secured to them by the community, and the happiness of the separate Colonies can only be secured by the Continent; and as the former yields up a part for that purpose, so must the latter. In the future regulations of trade there will undoubtedly happen instances in which some one or more provinces, like some one or more individuals, may wish it were otherwise; but as the same restrictions may happen to all in their turn, the reasonableness of submitting to them will appear to all.

The more any one province may flourish, the better it will be for the rest, and it matters not where riches begin at, because the commerce carried on between the Colonies will spread it through all; and that province which receives it first, either from Europe or the West-Indies, is only in the state of the Spaniards, who first dig it. There is but very little probability that jealousy between the Colonies on account of trade can ever happen, because most of their principal articles of commerce differ from each other, and will continue to do so while the difference of soil and situation remain; and the communication being by this natural necessity always kept open, it will happen, that no one can grow rich without communicating a share of that riches to the rest, and in the like manner, no province can grow poor without communicating a part of its poverty to others; and on these grounds it is as much our interest, as it is our duty, to promote the happiness of other provinces as of our own. Were Spain, Portugal, and other nations, with whom

Britain trades, to grow poor, Britain would grow poor in the same proportion; and the argument is much stronger respecting the Colonies, because they have a common national debt between them, for the payment of which they are reciprocally securities. Countries at war are obliquely benefited by each other's poverty, because inability is equal to a defeat, but the contrary is true in commerce. In short, the number of commercial reasons, which might be produced to shew the advantages flowing from a perfect harmony and union of the Colonies, sufficiently proves likewise that nothing but poverty and destruction can attend their separation.

Besides, as none of the Colonies separately are able to repel the force of Great-Britain, and as it is impossible that she can make an attack on all at once, or were she to do so, her strength would be so divided as to be comparatively less than that of any single province; therefore our preservation, as a people, depends upon our Union. Were Britain to attack the Continent in three places at once, each attack might be repulsed with a proportion of strength equal to four provinces; if in four places, with a force equal to three; if in six, with the force of two, exclusive of the thirteenth: And the knowledge of being thus supported and assisted by each other, is a comfortable and encouraging reflection to men under arms.

But the condition of our affairs *now* is such, that the union *must* be supported; and any Colony that should revolt therefrom, would instantly become a seat of war. The whole *must* go together, and it would be treason in any one province to act separately from the rest. Were Pennsylvania, Maryland, New-York, or the Jersies, to attempt such a thing, they would instantly be invaded by the adjoining ones, and perhaps the far greater part of their own inhabitants would assist in subduing the revolters. What safety would there be for this city, if the Jersey shore were possessed by the enemy? or what safety would the Jersies be in, were the Pennsylvania shore occupied in the same manner? and so on for the rest. Neither can the neutrality of any province be admitted, because it would enable Britain to bring a larger detachment against the resisting ones. A great part of our strength lies in the variety of objects which a coast so extensive as ours produces to an enemy; while she is meditating a stroke in one quarter, her attention, by some new circumstance, is called away to another. The part she has to act is likewise infinitely greater than ours: Her object is conquest, ours only to keep possession. She is conquered in not conquering us, whether we defeat her or not; and would be obliged to quit the Continent on the same principle that she quitted Boston, could we embarrass her in the same manner. While her force is small she may sculk about the coast, and pick up a living, but when her whole expedition arrives, the matter will be short with her; she must either conquer or depart; and if we can but prevent the first, the latter must follow. In short, we may conquer without a battle, but she cannot.

I shall conclude this letter with remarking, that the Tories have been exceedingly fond of impressing us with the necessity of what they call a perfect union, and that we cannot hope to succeed unless we are all in one mind. For my part I am quite of a different opinion, and think that a disunion is now the thing necessary: Every province either has or must undergo a purgation; it is the lot of all. Whigs and Tories cannot unite; they *must* separate; and the sooner the separation takes place the better. Those who are Tories now, mean never to be otherwise; therefore it is needless to wait for them. The Proprietary party have the honour of standing out to the last; they have distinguished themselves as much by their folly as their obstinacy, and on our part we have this consolation, that a union with them would only have weakened us, and produced the same kind of peaceable destruction in the political constitution which opium does in the natural one.

LETTER III

The Charter, called, the Royal Charter for this province,[6] was granted by Charles the Second, king of England, and dated at Westminster, the 4th day of March, 1681.

Interest and Time have an amazing influence over the understanding of mankind, and reconcile them to almost every species of absurdity and injustice. We have, with little or no hesitation, accustomed ourselves to look on these Crown grants as if the givers of them had really a right so to do; yet what was this right of theirs founded on? I answer, on the most villainous injustice. Had the kings of England first entered into treaty with the Indians for any part of their lands, and purchased them at ever so small a consideration, they would then have had a fair right either to have granted or disposed of them: But the case was otherwise, and the claims of the Crown was founded only on the poor pretence of sailing by, and looking at them; or, what is rather worse, because some distressed adventurous navigator was invited on shore, and civilly treated by the gaping gazing natives. This putting foot upon land was called "*taking possession of it in the king's name;*" and is that which gives him, forsooth, a right to give away the whole country. Suppose the Indian chiefs had taken it in their heads to have disposed of England in the same manner, we certainly should have laughed at their folly; but had they been able to have established their claim, we should have moved heaven and earth to have chastised their imposition: Yet the right of the one was equally as good as the other.

Any individual has a natural privilege to settle in any part of the world that suits him, and this custom all nations agree in; an Indian may settle in England, or elsewhere, purchase and occupy lands, and an European may settle in America for the same purposes, without injustice in either case: but for the kings of one country to assume a right to give away the lands in another, which they never were in possession of, either by treaty or purchase, is no better than qualified robbery, and downright arbitrary power. No man arguing from the reasonableness of things, could ever view a king's charter granting away lands which were at that time in the possession of the natives, in any other light, than as an obligation, which the Crown bound itself under, not to disturb the adventurers in whatever settlements they might make, or in whatever possessions they might afterwards acquire in America. And *William Penn,* by entering into treaty with the Indians[7] for the sale of the lands contained within the Charter from Charles the Second, seemed by that procedure to question Charles's right to grant such a Charter, and that his own title under that Charter only was not sufficiently good; and if the groundwork be defective, it of course renders the whole so. In any case, the granting Charters with such extensive privileges to individuals is incompatible with the spirit of freedom, and would in time extinguish it; but in this case it interfered with property, by obliging the emigrants to purchase lands of *William Penn,* for his particular emolument, and at just what price he pleased to set thereon; when they might have purchased the same of the natives at three or four thousand times less price. At the time that the Proprietaries bought of the Indians at the high rate, as it was called, of *Twopence Half-penny per Hundred acres,* they sold them again for *Fifteen pounds per Hundred acres, and one Half-penny sterling per acre quit-rent.* Perhaps no country in Europe can furnish greater instances of imposition and extortion than is to be found in the conduct of the Proprietaries of Pennsylvania.

The above Charter is contained in twenty-three sections. A striking absurdity appears in the first of them; which is, that *William Penn*, one of the first and most principal of the people called Quakers, and who held even the bearing of arms to be sinful, should, nevertheless, accept from Charles the Second the grant of the province of *Pennsylvania*, as a reward, for a *"signal battle and victory fought and obtained by his father, under James, duke of York, against the Dutch fleet, commanded by the Heer van Opdam, in the year 1665."** To *William Penn*, therefore, this province was the price of blood. If it was, as some say, for wages due to his father as an Admiral, he is the more guilty under that excuse; because, in that case, he took the pay of a soldier, though in any case he gave, contrary to his principles, an oblique approbation of war, and exhibited a striking instance of a convenient conscience.[8]

The first, second and third sections treat wholly of the soil, and speak of *William Penn* as proprietor *only*, no mention being made in either of them respecting the government.

By the fourth section Charles the Second hath endeavoured to grant and bestow on *William Penn* and his *Heirs* a power which no man or monarch on earth ever had or can have a right to give, viz. that of appointing him and his heirs the perpetual and absolute governors of Pennsylvania. Where there are no people, there can be no government; it is the people that constitute the government; and to give away a government is giving away the people, in the same manner that giving the proprietaryship was giving the soil. What right could Charles the Second, a deceased tyrant of the last century, have to appoint a governor for the present generation, or declare that the heirs of *William Penn* should be the Lords and Masters of persons to be born a thousand years hence? Are the inhabitants of the earth to be conveyed or transferred away, by virtue of a scrap of paper, from generation to generation, like so many head of cattle, or so many acres of land? Is such a thought, or such an act, consistent with human rights? Yet *William Penn*, regardless of every sacred privilege of freedom, carried the principle of tyranny higher than any of the Stuart family ever did; for by his

---

* First section in the Charter.

Will he directed the government of Pennsylvania to be SOLD. However some may endeavour to refine or explain away the sense of words I know not, but this I know, that there is no difference between selling a government and selling the people, because it is obliging them, like horses, to take for their master and rider any one who has money enough to come up to the sellers price.

> "I *William Penn*, Esq; so called, &c. give and dispose of my estate in manner following:——The GOVERNMENT of *my* province of Pennsylvania, and territories thereunto belonging, and ALL POWERS relating thereto, I give and devise to the most honourable the Earl of Oxford, and Earl Mortimer, and to William, Earl Pawlet, so called, and their heirs, upon trust, to dispose thereof to the Queen, *or to any other person,* to the best advantage and profit they can."
>
> WILLIAM PENN'S LAST WILL.

Neither in this part, nor in any other part of the will, is there any exception respecting the purchaser. The only condition is, the "best advantage and profit." He might be of any denomination of religion, or of none; a man of reputation, or not; a gentleman, or a gambler; if he could but raise the money, that was all. In short, the will of William Penn is as great a violation of the rights of nature as ever appeared upon a Christian record.——When governments are put up for sale, farewell liberty: It is time, and high time, that the Being of man should be extinct, when such articles appear at public market. By what pretence the government of this province hath remained in the Proprietary family since doth not appear; whether they inherit under the Charter, or by purchase under the will: However, neither is good; the first being a nullity, and the second an infamous traffic.

The Charter of Charles the Second says, "William Penn and his heirs" generally, by which it should seem that if any of them have any right, all of them have the same: A joint heirship, male and female. Had they been a prolific family, we might have had four or five hundred governors by this time, all of them claiming under the charter; quarrelling, and perhaps fighting for superiority with each other; and CATO, like the vicar of Bray,[9] the unprincipled chaplain of every conqueror; the purchases made by the inhabitants from *one* proprietor and governor disputed by another, or invalidated by a successor, till no body knew from whom to purchase. In fine, the evils and confusion occasioned by the obscurity of succession in the Proprietary family, would have been so great in a little time, and is even now so embarrassing, that is the present dissolution and suppression of all governments under the Crown of England had not fortunately happened, something must have been done in this province to have regulated the concerns thereof, and secured the purchasers in their possessions; otherwise we might have had heirs and lords coming from every part of Europe, "whose fathers were the Lord knows who."

William Penn, having obtained the Royal Charter, as it is called, acted very humbly under it for some little time; his first system of government is modestly entitled, "The frame of government of the province of Pennsylvania, in America, together with certain laws AGREED upon in England by the governor and divers freemen of the aforesaid province; to be farther explained and confirmed *there* by the first Provincial Council, if *they* see *meet*." By this the governor was to have three votes in passing or rejecting any bill, but not a negative upon the whole; but Mr. *Penn,* in less than one year, found means to get that agreement abolished, and in the forming of what he calls a Charter, managed matters so artfully, as to obtain a negative, in lieu of three votes; for which he was severely reprimanded by a future Assembly in 1704, in which they tell him, "That by a subtile contrivance and artifice of thine, laid deeper than the capacities of some could fathom, or the circumstances of many admit them time to consider of, a way was found out (by thee) to lay that aside, and introduce another Charter." "We see no just cause thou had to insist upon a negative upon bills to be passed into laws in General Assemblies." It ought to be remembered, that, according to Charles the Second's Charter, *William Penn* was only empowered to make laws with the *Consent of Freemen.* But this was not sufficiently lordly; and he soon took on himself, in imitation of his benefactor Charles, to issue out *his* Charter likewise, in the proud and arbitrary stile of "*I do* GRANT *and* DECLARE," &c. His piece, entitled, "*The Charter of privileges,*[10] GRANTED *by* WILLIAM PENN, *Esq; to the inhabitants of Pennsylvania, and territories,*" is an insult on their understanding; it ought at least to have been entitled, "A Charter of privileges, AGREED upon and CONFIRMED between William Penn and the inhabitants of Pennsylvania." Whenever a person undertakes to grant a thing, it implies that the thing which he grants was once his own.

William Penn, in this sense, might grant his lands, but that he should assume to himself the Popish power of granting liberty of conscience, and undertake to define, by a single act of his own, called a Charter, what degree of personal and political privilege we shall enjoy as freemen, is truly ridiculous. Liberty and liberty of conscience both would have a poor foundation indeed, were they to be received as privileges granted to us by William Penn. Every man who understands the true value of them will disdain to say he receives them in such a narrow line. We hold them immediately from GOD; and though it is our reciprocal duty to guarantee them to each other, we cannot be the givers of them. All Charters, which are the acts of a single man, are a species of tyranny; because they substitute the will of ONE as a law for ALL. They ought to have no Being in a free country; and no country can be free that has them. William Penn, in his Charter, called the Charter of privileges, has very arrogantly undertaken to lay down what shall be the law of this land. If this be not a species of arbitrary power, I know not what is. The people had certainly as good a right to have made a Charter for him as he for them: And it matters not what the Charter contains; the thing is, that he had no authority for that purpose, any more than he had to have granted a passport to heaven. All constitutions should be contained in some written Charter; but *that* Charter should be the act of *all* and not of *one man*. Magna Charta was not a grant from the Crown, but only agreed or acceded to by the Crown, being first drawn up and framed by the people.

Charters, as has been already observed, when granted by individuals, are not only a species of tyranny, but of the worse kind of tyranny; because the granters of them undertake, by an act of their own, to fix what the constitution of a country shall be; which is a higher authority than the giving out temporary laws. Perhaps there was not an inhabitant of this province who would have suffered William Penn to have made a law of his own mere accord, or would have looked upon such an act of his as a law: Yet, that they should suffer him to form a Charter of his own mere accord, describing the perpetual mode of government for this province, taking to himself, and giving to them, just what proportions he pleased, was very extraordinary! But he allowed them to sit on their own adjournments.—Mighty condescension, truly! The case was, he had no right either to tell them they should, or they should not, the whole of his authority being confined to the making of "laws with the consent of the freemen;" and all beyond that was arrogance and arbitrary power.

But, having assumed the prerogative of granting a Charter, he soon after assumed the right of explaining it in such manner as best suited his purpose: First, by claiming to himself the authority of proroguing and dissolving the assembly at pleasure, and summoning them by writs; and secondly, that he should have a negative on the laws passed in this province, whether he acted as governor or not, "saving always," says he in his instructions to deputy-governor Evans, "to me and my heirs, our *final assent* to all such bills as thou shalt pass." But in both these he miscarried.

The contentions which have arisen between the governors of this province and the people, since the time of its first settlements, are various and numerous, and can only be attributed to that astonishing absurdity of having the proprietaryship and governorship invested in one person. The composition is as impolitic and unnatural as it would be to leave a man to determine his own wager, or sit as judge in his own cause. The interest of the proprietor and the people, being like that of buyer and seller, it was impossible but that they would sometimes disagree; and in that case, the proprietor, being likewise governor, with the power of appointing judges, disposing of all offices, and having a negative upon all laws, was quite an over-match for the people; and of this the assembly in deputy-governor Morris's[11] administration seemed fully sensible. "If we are thus," say they, "to be driven from bill to bill, without one solid reason afforded us, and can raise no money for the relief and security of our country, until we shall fortunately hit on the *only* bill the governor is allowed to pass, or till we consent to make such as the governor or proprietaries direct us to make, we see little use of assemblies in this particular; and we think we might as well leave it to the governor or proprietaries to make *for us* what laws they please, and save ourselves and the province the expence and trouble. All debates and reasonings are vain, where proprietary instructions, just or unjust, right or wrong, must inviolably be observed. We have only to find *out*, if we *can*, what they are, and then *submit* and *obey*."

The Charter of privileges was accompanied with another, called "*The Charter for the* CITY *of* PHILADELPHIA," from which the Corporation derives all their authority. In the preamble William Penn says, "I have, by virtue of the king's letters patent, under the great seal of England, erected the said town into a borough, and do, by these presents, erect the said town and borough into a CITY." What William Penn meant by erecting the town and borough into a CITY, I am wholly at a loss to know, as that name particularly signifies an *Episcopal Town,* or place where the bishop's *See* is held.—*See*—*Seety*—or *City.* All towns in England are thus distinguished, and never otherwise, except Westminster, which was once a See—as, See or City of Canterbury—See or City of York—See or City of London, of Bath and Wells—of Bristol—of Salisbury, &c. &c. &c. and no place is called a City which has not a bishop's See: Wherefore William Penn's Charter, establishing a Corporation for the See or City of Philadelphia, is a sort of nullity in itself.

As to Corporations themselves, they are without exception so many badges of kingly tyranny, and tend, like every other species of useless pomp, to the oppression and impoverishment of the place, without one single advantage arising from them. They keep up a perpetual spirit of distinction and faction, engross emoluments and advantages to themselves, which ought to be employed to better purposes, and generally get into quarrels and lawsuits with the other part of the inhabitants. They diminish the freedom of every place where they exist. The most flourishing towns in England, as, Birmingham, Sheffield, Manchester, have no Corporations. A sufficient number of justices and a jury annually chosen, which shall regularly account with their successors for the monies which they may receive or pay in a year, are found to answer every *good* purpose much better.

But of all Corporations that of Philadelphia is the most obnoxious, its power resembling that of an hermaphrodite,[12] or is at least a kind of aristocratical Corporation made hereditary by adoption.

LETTER IV

Among the many publications which have appeared on the subject of political Constitutions, none, that I have seen, have properly defined what is meant by *a Constitution,* that word having been bandied about without any determinate sense being affixed thereto. A Constitution, and a form of government, are frequently confounded together, and spoken of as synonimous things; whereas they are not only different, but are established for different purposes: All countries have some form of government, but few, or perhaps none, have truly a Constitution. The form of government in England is by a king, lords and commons; but if you ask an Englishman what he means when he speaks of the English Constitution, he is unable to give you any answer. The truth is, the English have no fixed Constitution. The prerogative of the crown, it is true, is under several restrictions; but the legislative power, which includes king, lords and commons, is under none; and whatever acts *they* pass, are laws, be they ever so oppressive or arbitrary. England is likewise defective in Constitution in three other material points, viz. The crown, by virtue of a patent from itself, can increase the number of the lords (one of the legislative branches) at his pleasure. Queen Ann[13] created six in one day, for the purpose of making a majority for carrying a bill then passing, who were afterwards distinguished by the name of the six occasional lords. Lord Bathurst,[14] the father of the present chancellor, is the only surviving one. The crown can likewise, by a patent, incorporate any town or village, small or great, and empower it to send members to the house of commons, and fix what the precise number of the electors shall be. And an act of the legislative power, that is, an act of king, lords, and commons, can again diminish the house of commons to what number they please, by disfranchising any county, city or town.

It is easy to perceive that individuals by agreeing to erect forms of government, (for the better security of themselves) must give up some part of their liberty for that purpose; and it is the particular business of a Constitution to mark out *how much* they shall give up. In this sense it is easy to see that the English have no Constitution, because they have given up every thing; their legislative power being unlimited without either condition or controul, except in the single instance of trial by Juries. No country can be called *free* which is governed by an absolute power; and it matters not whether it be an absolute royal power or an absolute legislative power, as the consequences will be the same to the people. That England is governed by the latter, no man can deny, there being, as is said before, no Constitution in that country which says to the legislative powers, "Thus far shalt thou go, and no farther." There is nothing to prevent them passing a law which shall exempt themselves from the payment of taxes, or which shall give the house of commons power to sit for life, or to fill up the vacancies by appointing others, like the Corporation of Philadelphia. In short, an act of parliament, to use a court phrase, can do any thing but make a man a woman.

A Constitution, when completed, resolves the two following questions: First, What shall the form of government be? And secondly, what shall be its power? And the last of these two is far more material than the first. The Constitution ought likewise to make provision in those cases where it does not empower the legislature to act.

The forms of government are numerous, and perhaps the simplest is the best. The notion of checking by having different houses, has but little weight with it, when inquired into, and in all cases it tends to embarrass and prolong business; besides, what kind of checking is it that one house is to receive from another? or which is the house that is most to be trusted to? They may fall out about forms and precedence, and check one another's honour and tempers, and thereby produce petulances and ill-will, which a more simple form of government would have prevented. That some kind of convenience might now and then arise from having two houses, is granted, and the same may be said of twenty houses; but the question is, whether such a mode would not produce more hurt than good. The more houses the more parties; and perhaps the ill consequence to this country would be, that the landed interest would get into one house, and the commercial interest into the other; and by that means a perpetual and dangerous opposition would be kept up, and no business be got through: Whereas, were there a large, equal and annual representation in one house *only*, the different parties, by being thus blended together, would hear each others arguments, which advantage they cannot have if they sit in different houses. To say, there ought to be two houses, because there are two sorts of interest, is the very reason why there ought to be but one, and *that one* to consist of every sort. The lords and commons in England formerly made but one house; and it is evident, that by separating men you lessen the quantity of knowledge, and increase the difficulties of business. However, let the form of government be what it may, in this, or other provinces, so long as it answers the purpose of the people, and they approve it, they will be happy under it. That which suits one part of the Continent may not in every thing suit another; and when each is pleased, however variously, the matter is ended. No man is a true republican, or worthy of the name, that will not give up his single voice to that of the public: his private opinion he may retain; it is obedience only that is his duty.

The chief convenience arising from two houses is, that the second may sometimes amend small imperfections which would otherwise pass; yet, there is nearly as much chance of their making alterations for the worse as the better; and the supposition that a single house may become arbitrary, can with more reason be said of two; because their strength is greater. Besides, when all the supposed advantages arising from two houses are put together, they do not appear to balance the disadvantage. A division in one house will not retard business, but serves rather to illustrate; but a difference between two houses may produce serious consequences. In queen Ann's reign a quarrel arose between the upper and lower house, which was carried to such a pitch that the nation was under very terrifying apprehensions, and the house of commons was dissolved to prevent worse mischief. A like instance was nearly happening about six years ago, when the members of each house very affrontingly turned one another by force out of doors: The two best bills in the last sessions in England were entirely lost by having two houses; the bill for encreasing liberty of conscience, by taking off the necessity of subscription to the thirty-nine articles, Athanasian creed, &c. after passing the lower house by a very great majority, was thrown out by the upper one; and at the time that the nation was starving with the high price of corn, the bill for regulating the importation and exportation of grain, after passing the lower house, was lost by a *difference* between the two, and when returned from the upper one was thrown on the floor by the commons, and indignantly trampled under foot.—Perhaps most of the Colonies will have two houses, and it will probably be of benefit to have some little difference in the forms of government, as those which do not like one, may reside in another, and by trying different experiments, the best form will the sooner be found out, as the preference at present rests on conjecture.

Government is generally distinguished into three parts, Executive, Legislative and Judicial; but this is more a distinction of words than things. Every king or governor in giving his assent to laws acts legislatively, and not executively: The house of lords in England is both a legislative and judicial body. In short, the distinction is perplexing, and however we may refine and define, there is no more than two powers in any government, viz. the power to make laws, and the power to execute them; for the judicial power is only a branch of the executive, the CHIEF of every country being the first magistrate.

A CONSTITUTION should lay down some permanent ratio, by which the representation should afterwards encrease or decrease with the number of inhabitants; for the right of representation, which is a natural one, ought not to depend upon the will and pleasure of future legislatures. And for the same reason perfect liberty of conscience; security of person against unjust imprisonments, similar to what is called the Habeas Corpus act; the mode of trial in all law and criminal cases; in short, all the great rights which man never mean, nor ever ought, to lose, should be *guaranteed*, not *granted*, by the Constitution; for at the forming a Constitution we ought to have in mind, that whatever is left to be secured by law only, may be altered by another law. That Juries ought to be judges of law, as well as fact, should be clearly described; for though in some instances Juries may err, it is generally from tenderness, and on the right side. A man cannot be *guilty* of a *good* action, yet if the fact only is to be proved (which is Lord Mansfield's[15] doctrine) and the Jury not empowered to determine in their own minds, whether the fact proved to be done is a crime or not, a man may hereafter be found guilty of going to church or meeting.

There is one circumstance respecting trial by Juries which seems to deserve attention; which is, whether a Jury of Twelve persons, which cannot bring in a verdict unless they are all of one mind, or appear so; or, whether a Jury of not less than Twenty-five, a majority of which shall make a verdict, is the safest to be trusted to? The objections against an Jury of Twelve are, that the necessity of being unanimous prevents the freedom of speech, and causes men sometimes to conceal their own opinions, and follow that of others; that it is a kind of terrifying men into a verdict, and that a strong hearty obstinate man who can bear starving twenty-four or forty-eight hours, will distress the rest into a compliance; that there is no difference, in effect, between hunger and the point of a bayonet, and that under such circumstances a Jury is not, nor can be free. In favour of the latter it is said, that the least majority is thirteen; that the dread of the consequences of disagreeing being removed, men will speak freer, and that justice will thereby have a fairer chance.

It is the part of a Constitution to fix the manner in which the officers of government shall be chosen, and determine the principal outlines of their power, their time of duration, manner of commissioning them, &c. The line, so far as respects their election, seems easy, which is, by the representatives of the people; provincial officers can be chosen no other way, because the whole province cannot be convened, any more than the whole of the Associators could be convened for choosing generals. Civil officers for towns and countries may easily be chosen by election. The mode of choosing delegates for Congress deserves consideration, as they are not officers but legislators. Positive provincial instructions have a tendency to disunion, and, if admitted, will one day or other rend the Continent of America. A continental Constitution, when fixed, will be the best boundaries of Congressional power, and in matters for the general good, they ought to be as free as assemblies. The notion, which some have, of excluding the military from the legislature is unwise, because it has a tendency to make them form a distinct party of their own. Annual elections, strengthened by some kind of periodical exclusion, seem the best guard against the encroachments of power; suppose the exclusion was triennial, that is, that no person should be returned a member of assembly for more than three succeeding years, nor be capable of being returned again till he had been absent three years. Such a mode would greatly encrease the circle of knowledge, make men cautious how they acted, and prevent the disagreeableness of giving offence, by removing some, to make room for others of equal, or perhaps superior, merit. Something of the same kind may be practiced respecting Presidents or Governors, not to be eligible after a certain number of returns; and as no person, after filling that rank, can, consistent with character, descend to any other office or employment; and as it may not always happen that the most wealthy are the most capable, some decent provision therefore should be made for them in their retirement, because it is a retirement from the world. Whoever reflects on this, will see many good advantages arising from it.

Modest and decent honorary titles, so as they be neither hereditary, nor convey legislative authority, are of use in a state; they are, when properly conferred, the badges of merit. The love of the public is the chief reward which a generous man seeks; and, surely! if *that* be an honour, the mode of conferring it must be so likewise.

Next to the forming a good Constitution, is the means of preserving it. If once the legislative power breaks in upon it, the effect will be the same as if a kingly power did it. The Constitution, in either case, will receive its death wound, and "the outward and visible sign," or mere form of government only will remain. "I wish," says Lord Camden,[16] "that the maxim of Machiavel was followed, that of examining a Constitution, at certain periods, according to its first principles; this would correct abuses, and supply defects." The means here pointed out for preserving a Constitution are easy, and some article in the Constitution may provide, that at the expiration of every seven or any other number of years a *Provincial Jury* shall be elected, to enquire if any inroads have been made in the Constitution, and to have power to remove them; but not to make alterations, unless a clear majority of all the inhabitants shall so direct.

Farther observations were intended to have been offered in these letters, but the sudden turn of military affairs hath prevented them; I shall therefore conclude with remarking, that perfection in government, like perfection in all other earthly things, is not to be hoped for. A single house, or a duplication of them, will alike have their evils; and the defect is incurable, being founded in the nature of man, and the instability of things.

THE AMERICAN CRISES

Paine's title for the pamphlet The American Crisis, Number 1, *published on December 19, 1776, aptly described the feelings of many in the first days of the American war for independence. The exhilarating days following the Continental Congress's approval of Thomas Jefferson's Declaration of Independence on July 4 had been followed by months of defeats. The American army, under General George Washington, had recently fled across the Delaware River, reeling from several defeats in New York and New Jersey. Troops under General William Howe had captured New York City on September 15.*

Paine had joined the Pennsylvania Associators, a militia group, shortly after the approval of the Declaration, and began serving as secretary to General Daniel Roberdeau, then became aide-de-camp to General Nathaniel Greene at Fort Lee, New Jersey. When the British army crossed the Hudson on November 20, Paine was one of the soldiers who joined Washington in the retreat across New Jersey.

Paine left the army a short time later to return to Philadelphia to write. His first American Crisis *was a rallying cry to the American people and their disheartened army. Its impact was profound. General Washington had the essay read to his troops on the banks of the Delaware River as they prepared to cross to attack Trenton on December 26. James Cheetham, eventually one of Paine's bitter enemies, described the essay's impact in saying "the number was read in the camp, to every corporal's guard, and in the army and out of it had more than the intended effect."*

The tone, and times, of the final Crisis *were much different. Published on April 19, 1783, in the* Pennsylvania Packet, *the pamphlet's number celebrates the thirteen states of the union just as its publication date commemorates the eighth anniversary of the Battle of Lexington and Concord. By that date, the American army had been victorious at Yorktown, and the United*

States Congress had declared a cessation of war on April 11, 1783. On September 23, the Treaty of Paris would formally end the war.

"It was the cause of America that made me an author," Paine wrote in The Last Crisis. *In the essay, he first uses the word* Revolution *to describe what he and his adopted country had gone through in the preceding eight years. At the end of that revolution, he appears to show obvious pride in the way the country was created and the benefits that will shape its future.*

THE AMERICAN CRISIS
NUMBER I
DECEMBER 19, 1776

These are the times that try men's souls: The summer soldier and the sunshine patriot will, in this crisis, shrink from the service of his country; but he that stands it NOW, deserves the love and thanks of man and woman. Tyranny, like hell, is not easily conquered; yet we have this consolation with us, that the harder the conflict, the more glorious the triumph. What we obtain too cheap, we esteem too lightly:—'Tis dearness only that gives every thing its value. Heaven knows how to set a proper price upon its goods; and it would be strange indeed, if so celestial an article as FREEDOM should not be highly rated. Britain, with an army to enforce her tyranny, has declared,[1] that she has a right (*not only to* TAX) but "*to* BIND *us in* ALL CASES WHATSOEVER," and if being *bound in that manner* is not slavery, then is there not such a thing as slavery upon earth. Even the expression is impious, for so unlimited a power can belong only to GOD.

Whether the Independence of the Continent was declared too soon, or delayed too long, I will not now enter into as an argument; my own simple opinion is, that had it been eight months earlier, it would have been much better. We did not make a proper use of last winter, neither could we, while we were in a dependent state. However, the fault, if it were one, was all our own; we have none to blame but ourselves*. But no great deal is lost yet; all that Howe has been doing for this month past is rather a ravage than a conquest, which the spirit of the Jersies a year ago would have quickly repulsed, and which time and a little resolution will soon recover.

---

* "The present winter" (meaning the last) "is worth an age, if rightly employed, but if lost, or neglected, the whole Continent will partake of the evil; and there is no punishment that man does not deserve, but he who, or what, or where he will, that may be the means of sacrificing a season so precious and useful."   COMMON SENSE.

I have as little superstition in me as any man living, but my secret opinion has ever been, and still is, that GOD almighty will not give up a people to military destruction, or leave them unsupportedly to perish, who had so earnestly and so repeatedly sought to avoid the calamities of war, by every decent method which wisdom could invent. Neither have I so much of the infidel in me, as to suppose, that HE has relinquished the government of the world, and given us up to the care of devils; and as I do not, I cannot see on what grounds the king of Britain can look up to heaven for help against us. A common murderer, a highwayman, or a housebreaker, has as good a pretence as he.

'Tis surprising to see how rapidly a panic will sometimes run through a country. All nations and ages have been subject to them: Britain has trembled like an ague at the report of a French fleet of flat bottomed boats; and in the fourteenth century the whole English army, after ravaging the kingdom of France, was driven back like men petrified with fear; and this brave exploit was performed by a few broken forces collected and headed by a woman, Joan of Arc. Would, that Heaven might inspire some Jersey maid to spirit up her countrymen, and save her fair fellow-sufferers from ravage and ravishment! Yet panics, in some cases, have their uses; they produce as much good as hurt. Their duration is always short; the mind soon grows thro' them, and acquires a firmer habit than before. But their peculiar advantage is, that they are the touchstones of sincerity and hypocrisy, and bring things and men to light, which might otherwise have lain for ever undiscovered. In fact, they have the same effect on secret traitors, which an imaginary apparition would upon a private murderer. They sift out the hidden thoughts of man, and hold them up in public to the world. Many a disguised Tory has lately shewn his head, that shall penitentially solemnize with curses the day on which Howe arrived upon the Delaware.

As I was with the troops at fort Lee, and marched with them to the edge of Pennsylvania, I am well acquainted with many circumstances, which those, who lived at a distance, know but little or nothing of. Our situation there was exceedingly cramped, the place being on a narrow neck of land between the North river and the Hackensack. Our force was inconsiderable, being not one fourth so great as Howe could bring against us. We had no army at hand to have relieved the garrison, had we shut ourselves up and stood on the defence. Our ammunition, light artillery, and the best part of our stores, had been removed upon the apprehension that Howe would endeavour to penetrate the Jersies, in which case fort Lee could be of no use to us; for it must occur to every thinking man, whether in the army or not, that these kind of field forts are only for temporary purposes, and last in use no longer than the enemy directs his force against the particular object, which such forts are raised to defend. Such was our situation and condition at fort Lee on the morning of the 20th of November, when an officer arrived with information, that the enemy with 200 boats had landed about seven or eight miles above: Major General Green,[2] who commanded the garrison, immediately ordered them under arms, and sent express to his Excellency General Washington at the town of Hackensack, distant by the way of the ferry six miles. Our first object was to secure the bridge over the Hackensack, which laid up the river between the enemy and us, about six miles from us and three from them. General Washington arrived in about three quarters of an hour, and marched at the head of the troops towards the bridge, which place I expected we should have a brush for; however, they did not chuse to dispute it with us, and the greatest part of our troops went over the bridge, the rest over the ferry, except some which passed at a mill on a small creek, between the bridge and the ferry, and made their way through some marshy grounds up to the town of Hackensack, and there passed the river. We brought off as much baggage as the waggons could contain, the rest was lost. The simple object was to bring off the garrison, and to march them on till they could be strengthened by the Jersey or Pennsylvania militia, so as to be enabled to make a stand. We staid four days at Newark, collected in our out-posts with some of the Jersey militia, and marched out twice to meet the enemy on information of their being advancing, though our numbers were greatly inferiour to theirs. Howe, in my little opinion, committed a great error in generalship, in not throwing a body of forces off from Staaten Island through Amboy, by which means he might have seized all our stores at Brunswick, and intercepted our march into Pennsylvania. But, if we believe the power of hell to be limited, we must likewise believe that their agents are under some providential controul.

I shall not now attempt to give all the particulars of our retreat to the Delaware; suffice it for the present to say, that both officers and men, though greatly harassed and fatigued, frequently without rest, covering, or provision, the inevitable consequences of a long retreat, bore it with a manly and a martial spirit. All their wishes were one, which was, that the country would turn out and help them to drive the enemy back. Voltaire has remarked, that king William never appeared to full advantage but in difficulties and in action; the same remark may be made on General Washington, for the character fits him. There is a natural firmness in some minds which cannot be unlocked by triffles, but which, when unlocked, discovers a cabinet of fortitude; and I reckon it among those kind of public blessings, which we do not immediately see, that GOD hath blest him with uninterrupted health, and given him a mind that can even flourish upon care.

I shall conclude this paper with some miscellaneous remarks on the state of our affairs; and shall begin with asking the following question, Why is it that the enemy hath left the New-England provinces, and made these middle ones the seat of war? The answer is easy: New-England is not infested with Tories, and we are.[3] I have been tender in raising the cry against these men, and used numberless arguments to shew them their danger, but it will not do to sacrifice a world to either their folly or their baseness. The period is now arrived, in which either they or we must change our sentiments, or one or both must fall. And what is a Tory? Good GOD! what is he? I should not be afraid to go with an hundred Whigs against a thousand Tories, were they to attempt to get into arms. Every Tory is a coward, for a servile, slavish, self-interested fear is the foundation of Toryism; and a man under such influence, though he may be cruel, never can be brave.

But before the line of irrecoverable seperation be drawn between us, let us reason the matter together: Your conduct is an invitation to the enemy, yet not one in a thousand of you has heart enough to join him. Howe is as much deceived by you as the American cause is injured by you. He expects you will all take up arms, and flock to his standard with muskets on your shoulders. Your opinions are of no use to him, unless you support him personally, for 'tis soldiers, and not Tories, that he wants.

I once felt all that kind of anger, which a man ought to feel, against the mean principles that are held by the Tories: A noted one, who kept a tavern at Amboy, was standing at his door, with as pretty a child in his hand, about eight or nine years old, as most I ever saw, and after speaking his mind as freely as he thought was prudent, finished with this unfatherly expression, " *Well! Give me peace in my day.*" Not a man lives on the Continent but fully believes that a seperation must some time or other finally take place, and a generous parent would have said, "*If there must be trouble, let it be in my day, that my child may have peace;*" and this single reflection, well applied, is sufficient to awaken every man to duty. Not a place upon earth might be so happy as America. Her situation is remote from all the wrangling world, and she has nothing to do but to trade with them. A man may easily distinguish in himself between temper and principle, and I am as confident, as I am that GOD governs the world, that America will never be happy till she gets clear of foreign dominion. Wars, without ceasing, will break out till that period arrives, and the Continent must in the end be conqueror; for, though the flame of liberty may sometimes cease to shine, the coal never can expire.

America did not, nor does not, want force; but she wanted a proper application of that force. Wisdom is not the purchase of a day, and it is no wonder that we should err at first sitting off. From an excess of tenderness, we were unwilling to raise an army, and trusted our cause to the temporary defence of a well meaning militia. A summer's experience has now taught us better; yet with those troops, while they were collected, we were able to set bounds to the progress of the enemy, and, thank GOD! they are again assembling. I always considered a militia as the best troops in the world for a sudden exertion, but they will not do for a long campaign. Howe, it is probable, will make an attempt on this city;[4] should he fail on this side the Delaware, he is ruined; if he succeeds, our cause is not ruined. He stakes all on his side against a part of ours; admitting he succeeds, the consequence will be, that armies from both ends of the Continent will march to assist their suffering friends in the middle States; for he cannot go every where, it is impossible. I consider Howe as the greatest enemy the Tories have; he is bringing a war into their country, which, had it not been for him and partly for themselves, they had been clear of. Should he now be expelled, I wish, with all the devotion of a Christian, that the names of Whig and Tory may never more be mentioned; but should the Tories give him encouragement to come, or assistance if he come, I as sincerely wish that our next year's arms may expell them from the Continent, and the Congress appropriate their possessions to the relief of those who have suffered in well doing. A single successful battle next year will settle the whole. America could carry on a two years war by the confiscation of the property of disaffected persons, and be made happy by their expulsion. Say not that this is revenge, call it rather the soft resentment of a suffering people, who, having no object in view but the GOOD of ALL, have staked their OWN ALL upon a seemingly doubtful event. Yet it is folly to argue against determined hardness; eloquence may strike the ear, and the language of sorrow draw forth the tear of compassion, but nothing can reach the heart that is steeled with prejudice.

Quitting this class of men, I turn with the warm ardour of a friend to those who have nobly stood, and are yet determined to stand the matter out; I call not upon a few, but upon all; not on THIS State or THAT State, but on EVERY State; up and help us; lay your shoulders to the wheel; better have too much force than too little, when so great an object is at stake. Let it be told to the future world, that in the depth of winter, when nothing but hope and virtue could survive, that the city and the country, alarmed at one common danger, came forth to meet and to repulse it. Say not, that thousands are gone, turn out your tens of thousands; throw not the burthen of the day upon Providence, but "*shew your faith by your works,*" that GOD may bless you. It matters not where you live, or what rank of life you hold,[5] the evil or the blessing will reach you all. The far and the near, the home counties and the back, the rich and the poor, shall suffer or rejoice alike. The heart that feels not now, is dead: The blood of his children shall curse his cowardice, who shrinks back at a time when a little might have saved the whole, and made *them* happy. I love the man that can smile in trouble, that can gather strength from distress, and grow brave by reflection. 'Tis the business of little minds to shrink, but he whose heart is firm, and whose conscience approves his conduct, will pursue his principles unto death. My own line of reasoning is to myself as strait and clear as a ray of light. Not all the treasures of the world, so far as I believe, could have induced me to support an offensive war, for I think it murder; but if a thief break into my house, burn and destroy my property, and kill or threaten to kill me, or those that are in it, and to "*bind me in all cases whatsoever,*" to his absolute will, am I to suffer it? What signifies it to me, whether he who does it, is a king or a common man; my countryman or not my countryman? whether it is done by an individual villain, or an army of them? If we reason to the root of things we shall find no difference; neither can any just cause be assigned why we should punish in the one case, and pardon in the other. Let them call me rebel, and wel-come, I feel no concern from it; but I should suffer the misery of devils, were I to make a whore of my soul by swearing allegiance to one, whose character is that of a sottish, stupid, stubborn, worthless, brutish man. I conceive likewise a horrid idea in receiving mercy from a being, who at the last day shall be shrieking to the rocks and mountains to cover him, and fleeing with terror from the orphan, the widow and the slain of America.

There are cases which cannot be overdone by language, and this is one. There are persons too who see not the full extent of the evil that threatens them; they solace themselves with hopes that the enemy, if they succeed, will be merciful. It is the madness of folly to expect mercy from those who have refused to do justice; and even mercy, where conquest is the object, is only a trick of war. The cunning of the fox is as murderous as the violence of the wolfe; and we ought to guard equally against both. Howe's first object is partly by threats and partly by promises, to terrify or seduce the people to deliver up their arms, and receive mercy. The ministry recommended the same plan to Gage, and this is what the Tories call making their peace; "*a peace which passeth all understanding*" *indeed!* A peace which would be the immediate fore-runner of a worse ruin than any we have yet thought of. Ye men of Pennsylvania, do reason upon those things! Were the back counties to give up their arms, they would fall an easy prey to the Indians, who are all armed. This perhaps is what some Tories would not be sorry for. Were the home counties to deliver up their arms, they would be ex-posed to the resentment of the back counties, who would then have it in their power to chastise their defection at pleasure. And were any one State to give up its arms, THAT State must be garrisoned by all Howe's army of Britons and Hessians to preserve it from the anger of the rest. Mutual fear is a principal link in the chain of mutual love, and woe be to that State that breaks the compact. Howe is mercifully invit-ing you to barbarous destruction, and men must be either rogues or fools that will not see it. I dwell not upon the vapours of imagination; I bring reason to your ears; and in language, as plain as A, B, C, hold up truth to your eyes.

I thank GOD that I fear not. I see no real cause for fear. I know our situation well, and can see the way out of it. While our army was col-lected, Howe dared not risk a battle, and it is no credit to him that he decamped from the White Plains, and waited a mean opportunity to ravage the defenceless Jersies; but it is great credit to us, that, with an handful of men, we sustained an orderly retreat for near an hundred miles, brought off our ammunition, all our field-pieces, the greatest part of our stores, and had four rivers to pass. None can say that our retreat was precipitate, for we were near three weeks in performing it, that the country might have time to come in. Twice we marched back to meet the enemy and remained out till dark. The sign of fear was not seen in our camp, and had not some of the cowardly and disaffected inhabitants spread false alarms thro' the country, the Jersies had never been ravaged. Once more we are again collected and collecting; our new army at both ends of the Continent is recruiting fast, and we shall be able to open the next campaign with sixty thousand men, well armed and cloathed. This is our situation, and who will may know it. By perseverance and fortitude we have the prospect of a glorious issue; by cowardice and submission, the sad choice of a variety of evils—a ravaged country—a depopulated city—habitations without safety, and slavery without hope—our homes turned into barracks and baudyhouses for Hessians, and a future race to provide for whose fathers we shall doubt of. Look on this picture, and weep over it!—and if there yet remains one thoughtless wretch who believes it not, let him suffer it unlamented.

THE LAST CRISIS
NUMBER XIII
APRIL 19, 1783

"The times that tried mens souls,"* are over—and the greatest and compleatest revolution the world ever knew is gloriously and happily accomplished.

But to pass from the extremes of danger to safety—from the tumult of war, to the tranquility of peace, though sweet in contemplation, requires a gradual composure of the senses to receive it. Even calmness has the power of stunning when it opens too instantly upon us. The long and raging hurricane that should cease in a moment, would leave us in a state rather of wonder than enjoyment: and some moments of recollection must pass before we could be capable of tasting the full felicity of repose. There are but few instances, in which the mind is fitted for sudden transitions: it takes in its pleasure by reflection and comparison, and those must have time to act, before the relish of new scenes is compleat.

In the present case—the mighty magnitude of the object—the various uncertainties of fate it has undergone—the numerous and complicated dangers we have suffered or escaped—the eminence we now stand on, and the vast prospect before us, must all conspire to impress us with contemplation.

To see it in our power to make a world happy—to teach mankind the art of being so—to exhibit on the theatre of the universe a character hitherto unknown—and to have, as it were, a new creation entrusted to our hands, and hence that command reflection, and can neither be too highly estimated, nor too gratefully received.

In this pause then of recollection—while the storm is ceasing, and the long agitated mind vibrating to a rest, let us look back on the

*"These are the times that try mens souls." Crisis No. 1. Published December 19, 1776.

scenes we have passed, and learn from experience what is yet to be done.

Never, I say, had a country so many openings to happiness as this. Her sitting out into life, like the rising of a fair morning, was unclouded and promising. Her cause was good. Her principles just and liberal. Her temper serene and firm. Her conduct regulated by the nicest steps of order, and every thing about her wore the mark of honor.

It is not every country (perhaps there is not another in the world) that can boast so fair an origin. Even the first settlement of America corresponds with the character of the revolution. Rome, once the proud mistress of the universe, was originally a band of ruffians. Plunder and rapine made her rich, and her oppression of millions made her great. But America needs never be ashamed to tell her birth, nor relate the stages by which she rose to empire.

The remembrance, then, of what is past, if it operates rightly, must inspire her with the most laudable of all ambition, that of adding to the fair fame she began with. The world has seen her great in adversity. Struggling, without a thought of yielding, beneath accumulated difficulties. Bravely, nay proudly, encountering distress, and rising in resolution as the storm encreased. All this is justly due to her, for her fortitude has merited the character.—Let, then, the world see that she can bear prosperity; and that her honest virtue in time of peace, is equal to the bravest virtue in time of war.

She is now descending to the scenes of quiet and domestic life. Not beneath the cypress shade of disappointment, but to enjoy in her own land, and under her own vine, the sweets of her labours, and the reward of her toil.—In this situation, may she never forget, that a fair national reputation is of as much importance as independence. That it possesses a charm which wins upon the world, and makes even enemies civil. That it gives a dignity which is often superior to power, and commands a reverence where pomp and splendor fail.

It would be a circumstance ever to be lamented and never to be forgotten, were a single blot, from any cause whatsoever, suffered to fall on a revolution, which to the end of time must be an honor to the age that accomplished it: and which has contributed more to enlighten the world, and diffuse a spirit of freedom and liberality among mankind, than any human event (if this may be called one) that ever preceded it.

It is not among the least of the calamities of a long continued war, that it unhinges the mind from those nice sensations which at other times appear so amiable. The continual spectacle of woe blunts the finer feelings, and the necessity of bearing with the sight renders it familiar. In like manner, are many of the moral obligations of society weakened, till the custom of acting by necessity, becomes an apology where it is truly a crime. Yet let but a nation conceive rightly of its character, and it will be chastely just in protecting it. None ever began with a fairer than America, and none can be under a greater obligation to preserve it.

The debt which America has contracted, compared with the cause she has gained, and the advantages to flow from it, ought scarcely to be mentioned. She has it in her choice to do, and to live, as happily, as she pleases. The world is in her hands. She has now no foreign power to monopolize her commerce, perplex her legislation, or controul her prosperity. The struggle is over, which must one day have happened, and, perhaps, never could have happened at a better time.* And instead

---

* That the revolution began at the exact period of time best fitted to the purpose, is sufficiently proved by the event.—But the great hinge on which the whole machine turned is the UNION OF THE STATES: and this union was naturally produced by the inability of any one state to support itself against a foreign enemy without the assistance of the rest.

Had the states severally been less able than they were when the war began, their united strength would not have been equal to the undertaking, and they must, in all human probability, have failed—And on the other hand, had they severally been more able, they might not have seen, or, what is more, might not have felt, the necessity of uniting; and either by attempting to stand alone, or in small confederacies, would have been separately conquered.

Now, as we cannot see a time (and many years must pass away before it can arrive) when the strength of any one state, or of several united, can be equal to the whole of the present united states, and as we have seen the extreme difficulty of collectively prosecuting the war to a successful issue, and preserving our national importance in the world, therefore, from the experience we have had, and the knowledge we have gained, we must, unless we make a waste of wisdom, be strongly impressed with the advantage, as well as the necessity, of strengthening that happy union which has been our salvation, and without which we should have been a ruined people.

While I was writing this note, I cast my eye on the pamphlet COMMON SENSE, from which I shall make an extract, as it applies exactly to the case. It is as follows.

'I have never met with a man, either in England or America, who hath not confessed his opinion that a separation between the countries would take place one time or other: And there is no instance in which we have shewn less judgment, than in endeavouring to describe, what we call, the ripeness or fitness of the continent for independence.

'As all men allow the measure, and differ only in their opinion of the time, let us, in order to remove mistakes, take a general survey of things, and endeavour, if possible, to find out the

of a domineering master, she has gained an Ally,[6] whose examplary greatness, and universal liberality, have extorted a confession even from her enemies.

With the blessings of peace, independence, and an universal commerce, the states, individually and collectively, will have leisure and opportunity to regulate and establish their domestic concerns, and to put it beyond the power of calumny to throw the least reflection on their honor. Character is much easier kept than recovered, and that man, if any such there be, who, from any sinister views, or littleness of soul, lends unseen his hand to injure it, contrives a wound it will never be in his power to heal.

As we have established an inheritance for posterity, let that inheritance descend with every mark of an honorable conveyance. The little it will cost, compared with the worth of the states, the greatness of the object, and the value of national character, will be a profitable exchange.

But that which must more forcibly strike a thoughtful penetrating mind, and which includes and renders easy all inferior concerns, is the UNION OF THE STATES. On this, our great national character depends. It is this which must give us importance abroad and security at home. It is through this only that we are, or can be nationally known in the world. It is the flag of the united states which renders our ships and commerce safe on the seas, or in a foreign port. Our Mediterranean passes must be obtained under the same stile. All our treaties, whether of alliance, peace, or commerce, are formed under the sovereignty of the united states, and Europe knows us by no other name or title.

The division of the empire into states is for our own convenience, but abroad this distinction ceases. The affairs of each state are local. They can go no farther than to itself. And were the whole worth of even the richest of them expended in revenue, it would not be sufficient to support sovereignty against a foreign attack. In short, we have

---

VERY TIME. But we need not go far, the enquiry ceases at once, for, THE TIME HATH FOUND US. The general concurrence, the glorious union of all things prove the fact.

'It is not in numbers, but in a union, that our great strength lies. The continent is just arrived at that pitch of strength, in which no single colony is able to support itself, and the whole, when united, can accomplish the matter; and either more or less than this, might be fatal in its effects.'

PAMPHLET COMMON SENSE.

no other national sovereignty than as united states. It would even be fatal for us if we had—too expensive to be maintained, and impossible to be supported. Individuals or individual states may call themselves what they please; but the world, and especially the world of enemies, is not to be held in awe by the whistling of a name. Sovereignty must have power to protect all the parts that compose and constitute it: and as UNITED STATES we are equal to the importance of the title, but otherwise we are not. Our union well and wisely regulated and cemented, is the cheapest way of being great—the easiest way of being powerful, and the happiest invention in government which the circumstances of America can admit of.—Because it collects from each state, that, which, by being inadequate, can be of no use to it, and forms an aggregate that serves for all.

The states of Holland are an unfortunate instance of the effects of individual sovereignty.[7] Their disjointed condition exposes them to numerous intrigues, losses, calamities, and enemies; and the almost impossibility of bringing their measures to a decision, and that decision into execution, is to them, and would be to us, a source of endless misfortune.

It is with confederate states as with individuals in society; something must be yielded up to make the whole secure. In this view of things we gain by what we give, and draw an annual interest greater than the capital.—I ever feel myself hurt when I hear the union, that great palladium of our liberty and safety, the least irreverently spoken of. It is the most sacred thing in the constitution of America, and that which every man should be the most proud and tender of. Our citizenship in the united states is our national character. Our citizenship in any particular state is only our local distinction. By the latter we are known at home, by the former to the world. Our great title is, AMERICANS; our inferior one varies with the place.

So far as my endeavours could go, they have all been directed to conciliate the affections, unite the interests, and draw and keep the mind of the country together; and the better to assist in this foundation work of the revolution, I have avoided all places of profit or office, either in the state I live in, or in the united states; kept myself at a distance from all parties and party connections, and even disregarded all private and inferior concerns: and when we take into view the great work we have gone through, and feel, as we ought to feel, the just importance of it, we shall then see, that the little wranglings and indecent contentions of personal party, are as dishonorable to our characters, as they are injurious to our repose.

It was the cause of America that made me an author. The force with which it struck my mind, and the dangerous condition the country appeared to me in, by courting an impossible and unnatural reconciliation with those who were determined to reduce her, instead of striking out into the only line that could cement and save her, A DECLARATION OF INDEPENDENCE, made it impossible for me, feeling as I did, to be silent: and if, in the course of more than seven years, I have rendered her any service, I have likewise added something to the reputation of literature, by freely and disinterestedly employing it in the great cause of mankind, and shewing there may be genius without prostitution.

Independence always appeared to me practicable and probable; provided the sentiment of the country could be formed and held to the object: and there is no instance in the world, where a people so extended, and wedded to former habits of thinking, and under such a variety of circumstances, were so instantly and effectually pervaded, by a turn in politics, as in the case of independence, and who supported their opinion, undiminished, through such a succession of good and ill fortune, till they crowned it with success.

But as the scenes of war are closed, and every man preparing for home and happier times, I therefore take my leave of the subject. I have most sincerely followed it from beginning to end, and through all its turns and windings: and whatever country I may hereafter be in, I shall always feel an honest pride at the part I have taken and acted, and a gratitude to Nature and Providence for putting it in my power to be of some use to mankind.

COMMON SENSE.
Philadelphia, April 19, 1783.

LETTER TO THE
ABBÉ RAYNAL

When Thomas Paine wrote his Letter to the Abbé Raynal *in 1782, he was emerging as a writer from issues that were colonial or local in nature, to those addressing a wider world of ideas.*

Paine had a great deal in common with Guillaume Raynal, the Parisian former priest who had become one of the leading intellectuals of pre-Revolutionary France. Both men believed in religious liberty; both were Europeans who believed that the enlightened future of humanity rested in America. But Paine saw the Abbé's Revolution de l'Amerique, *published in translation in 1781 as a supplement to his famous* Histoire philosophique et politique des . . . deux Indes, *as misrepresenting the history of the causes of the American Revolution. Raynal emphasized the colonists' anger over taxation (an idea he likely drew from John Dickinson's* Letters from an American Farmer, *then in vogue in France). Paine countered in the essay that follows that the Americans were always guided by the highest principles, and had been brutally oppressed by the British.*

Paine saw the intellectual debate in his Raynal pamphlet as his entrée into the republic of letters, the international community of thinkers in the late-eighteenth-century Atlantic world. This Letter *was intended for a European audience. He had traveled to France in January 1781, stayed there until August, and gained an understanding both of the Franco-American alliance as well as the impact of writing on popular support for the American cause.*

By now, Paine was a paid writer. Early that year, George Washington, Robert Morris, and Robert R. Livingston had prepared a plan which paid Paine $800 annually to write essays in support of the American economic *cause. In May, Chevalier Anne Cesar de La Luzerne, France's minister to the United States, "remitted to Mr. Paine 50 guineas, and ... exhorted him to exercise his pen on objects of the same kind," fearing that Raynal's portrayal of the superficiality of America's grievances would bring the alliance or himself under attack. Paine crafted this argument, first in* The Crisis No. 11 *in May 1782 and then in the Raynal letter, published in August.*

INTRODUCTION

A London translation of an original work in France, by the Abbé Raynal,[1] which treats of the Revolution of North America, having been reprinted in Philadelphia and other parts of the continent, and as the distance at which the Abbé is placed from the American theater of war and politics, has occasioned him to mistake several facts, or misconceive the causes or principles by which they were produced, the following tract, therefore, is published with a view to rectify them, and prevent even accidental errors from intermixing with history, under the sanction of time and silence.

The editor of the London edition has entitled it, "The Revolution of America, by the ABBÉ RAYNAL," and the American printers have followed the example. But I have understood, and I believe my information just, that the piece, which is more properly reflections on the Revolution, was unfairly purloined from the printer whom the Abbé employed, or from the manuscript copy, and is only part of a larger work then in the press, or preparing for it. The person who procured it, appears to have been an Englishman, and though, in an advertisement prefixed to the London edition, he has endeavored to gloss over the embezzlement with professions of patriotism, and to soften it with high encomiums on the author, yet the action in any view in which it can be placed, is illiberal and unpardonable.

In the course of his travels (says he), the translator happily succeeded in obtaining a copy of this exquisite little piece which has not made its appearance from any press. He publishes a French edition, in favor of those who feel its eloquent reasoning more forcibly in its native language, at the same time with the following translation of it: in which he has been desirous, perhaps in vain, that all the warmth, the grace, the strength, the dignity of the original, should not be lost. And he flatters himself, that the indulgence of the illustrious historian will not be wanting to a man, who, of his own motion, has taken the liberty to give this composition to the public, only from a strong persuasion, that its momentous argument will be useful in a critical conjuncture, to that country which he loves with an ardor that can be exceeded only by the nobler flame, which burns in the bosom of the philanthropic author, for the freedom and happiness of all the countries upon earth.

This plausibility of setting off a dishonorable action, may pass for patriotism and sound principles with those who do not enter into its demerits, and whose interest is not injured nor their happiness affected thereby. But it is more than probable, notwithstanding the declarations it contains, that the copy was obtained for the sake of profiting by the sale of a new and popular work, and that the professions are but a garb to the fraud.

It may with propriety be marked, that in all countries where litera-ture is protected, and it never can flourish where it is not, the works of an author are his legal property; and to treat letters in any other light than this, is to banish them from the country, or strangle them in the birth.

The embezzlement from the Abbé Raynal, was, it is true, commit-ted by one country upon another, and therefore shows no defect in the laws of either. But it is nevertheless a breach of civil manners and lit-erary justice: neither can it be any apology, that because the countries are at war, literature shall be entitled to depradation.*

But the forestalling the Abbé's publication by London editions, both in French and English, and thereby not only defrauding him and throwing an expensive publication on his hands by anticipating the sale, are only the smaller injuries which such conduct may occasion. A man's opinions, whether written or in thought, are his own, until he pleases to publish them himself; and it is adding cruelty to injustice, to make him the author of what future reflection, or better information, might occasion him to suppress or amend. There are declarations and

---

* The state of literature in America must one day become a subject of legislative consid-eration. Hitherto, it has been a disinterested volunteer in the service of the Revolution, and no man thought of profits: but when peace shall give time and opportunity for study, the country will deprive itself of the honor and service of letters and the improvement of sci-ence, unless sufficient laws are made to prevent depredations on literary property. It is well worth remarking, that Russia, who but a few years ago was scarcely known in Europe, owes a large share of her present greatness to the close attention she has paid, and the wise en-couragement she has given, to every branch of science and learning: and we have almost the same instance in France, in the reign of Louis XIV.

sentiments in the Abbé's piece which, for my own part, I did not expect to find, and such as himself, on a revisal, might have seen occasion to change; but the anticipated piracy effectually prevented his having the opportunity, and precipitated him into difficulties, which, had it not been for such ungenerous fraud, might not have happened.

This mode of making an author appear before his time, will appear still more ungenerous, when we consider how very few men there are in any country, who can at once, and without the aid of reflection and revisal, combine warm passions with a cool temper, and the full expansion of the imagination with the natural and necessary gravity of judgment, so as to be rightly balanced within themselves, and to make a reader feel, fancy, and understand justly at the same time. To call three powers of the mind into action at once, in a manner that neither shall interrupt, and that each shall aid and invigorate the other, is a talent very rarely possessed.

It often happens that the weight of an argument is lost by the wit of setting it off; or the judgment disordered by an intemperate irritation of the passions: yet a certain degree of animation must be felt by the writer, and raised in the reader, in order to interest the attention; and a sufficient scope given to the imagination, to enable it to create in the mind a sight of the persons, characters and circumstances of the subject: for without these, the judgment will feel little or no excitement to office, and its determinations will be cold, sluggish, and imperfect.

But if either or both of the two former are raised too high, or heated too much, the judgment will be jostled from its seat, and the whole matter, however important in itself, will diminish into a pantomime of the mind, in which we create images that promote no other purpose than amusement.

The Abbé's writings bear evident marks of that extension and rapidness of thinking and quickness of sensation, which of all others require revisal, and the more particularly so, when applied to the living characters of nations or individuals in a state of war. The least misinformation or misconception leads to some wrong conclusion, and an error believed, becomes the progenitor of others. And, as the Abbé has suffered some inconveniences in France, by mistaking certain circumstances of the war, and the characters of the parties therein, it becomes some apology for him that those errors were precipitated into the world by the avarice of an ungenerous enemy.

LETTER TO THE ABBÉ RAYNAL

To an author of such distinguished reputation as the Abbé Raynal, it might very well become me to apologize for the present undertaking; but, as *to be right* is the first wish of philosophy, and the first principle of history, he will, I presume, accept from me a declaration of my motives, which are those of doing justice, in preference to any complimental apology I might otherwise make. The Abbé, in the course of his work, has, in some instances, extolled without a reason, and wounded without a cause. He has given fame where it was not deserved, and withheld it where it was justly due; and appears to be so frequently in and out of temper with his subjects and parties, that few or none of them are decisively and uniformly marked.

It is yet too soon to write the history of the Revolution, and whoever attempts it precipitately, will unavoidably mistake characters and circumstances, and involve himself in error and difficulty. Things, like men, are seldom understood rightly at first sight. But the Abbé is wrong even in the foundation of his work; that is, he has misconceived and mis-stated the causes which produced the rupture between England and her then colonies, and which led on, step by step, unstudied and uncontrived on the part of America, to a revolution, which has engaged the attention, and affected the interest of Europe.

To prove this, I shall bring forward a passage, which, though placed towards the latter part of the Abbé's work, is more intimately connected with the beginning; and in which, speaking of the original cause of the dispute, he declares himself in the following manner:

None (says he), of those energetic causes, which have produced so many revolutions upon the globe, existed in North America. Neither religion nor laws had there been outraged. The blood of martyrs or patriots had not there streamed from scaffolds. Morals had not there been insulted. Manners, customs, habits, no object dear to nations, had there been the sport of ridicule. Arbitrary power had not there torn any inhabitant from the arms of his family and friends, to drag him to a dreary dungeon. Public order had not been there inverted. The principles of administration had not been changed there; and the maxims of government had there always remained the same. The whole question was reduced to the knowing whether the mother country had, or had not, a right to lay, directly or indirectly, a slight tax upon the colonies.

On this extraordinary passage, it may not be improper, in general terms, to remark, that none can feel like those who suffer; and that for a man to be a competent judge of the provocatives, or as the Abbé styles them, the energetic causes of the Revolution, he must have resided at the time in America.

The Abbé, in saying that the several particulars he has enumerated, did not exist in America, and neglecting to point out the particular period, in which he means they did not exist, reduces thereby his declaration to a nullity, by taking away all meaning from the passage.

They did not exist in 1763, and they all existed before 1776; consequently as there was a time when they did *not*, and another, when they *did* exist, the *time when* constitutes the essence of the fact, and not to give it is to withhold the only evidence which proves the declaration right or wrong, and on which it must stand or fall. But the declaration as it now appears, unaccompanied by time, has an effect in holding out to the world, that there was no real cause for the Revolution, because it denies the existence of all those causes, which are supposed to be justifiable, and which the Abbé styles energetic.

I confess myself exceedingly at a loss to find out the time to which the Abbé alludes; because, in another part of the work, in speaking of the Stamp Act, which was passed in 1764, he styles it "an *usurpation* of the Americans' *most precious and sacred rights.*" Consequently he here admits the most energetic of all causes, that is, *an usurpation of their most precious and sacred rights,* to have existed in America twelve years before the Declaration of Independence, and ten years before the breaking out of hostilities. The time, therefore, in which the paragraph is true, must be antecedent to the Stamp Act, but as at that time there was no revolution, nor any idea of one, it consequently applies without a meaning; and as it cannot, on the Abbé's own principle, be applied to any time *after* the Stamp Act, it is therefore a wandering, solitary paragraph, connected with nothing and at variance with everything.

The Stamp Act, it is true, was repealed in two years after it was passed, but it was immediately followed by one of infinitely more mischievous magnitude; I mean the Declaratory Act, which asserted the right, as it was styled, of the British Parliament, *"to bind America in all cases whatsoever."*

If then the Stamp Act was an usurpation of the Americans' most precious and sacred rights, the Declaratory Act[2] left them no rights at all; and contained the full grown seeds of the most despotic government ever exercised in the world. It placed America not only in the lowest, but in the basest state of vassalage; because it demanded an unconditional submission in everything, or as the act expressed it, *in all cases whatsoever:* and what renders this act the more offensive, is, that it appears to have been passed as an act of mercy; truly then may it be said, that *the tender mercies of the wicked are cruel.*

All the original charters from the Crown of England, under the faith of which the adventurers from the Old World settled in the new, were by this act displaced from their foundations; because, contrary to the nature of them, which was that of a compact, they were now made subject to repeal or alteration at the mere will of one party only. The whole condition of America was thus put into the hands of the Parliament or Ministry, without leaving to her the least right in any case whatsoever.

There is no despotism to which this iniquitous law did not extend; and though it might have been convenient in the execution of it, to have consulted manners and habits, the principle of the act made all tyranny legal. It stopped nowhere. It went to everything. It took in with it the whole life of a man, or if I may so express it, an eternity of circumstances. It is the nature of law to require obedience, but this demanded servitude; and the condition of an American, under the operation of it, was not that of a subject, but a vassal. Tyranny has often been established *without* law and sometimes *against* it, but the history of mankind does not produce another instance, in which it has been established *by* law. It is an audacious outrage upon civil government, and cannot be too much exposed, in order to be sufficiently detested.

Neither could it be said after this, that the legislature of that country any longer made laws for this, but that it gave out commands; for wherein differed an act of Parliament constructed on this principle, and operating in this manner, over an unrepresented people, from the orders of a military establishment?

The Parliament of England, with respect to America, was not septennial but *perpetual.* It appeared to the latter a body always in being. Its election or expiration were to her the same as if its members succeeded by inheritance, or went out by death, or lived forever, or were appointed to it as a matter of office. Therefore, for the people of England to have any just conception of the mind of America, respecting this extraordinary act, they must suppose all election and expiration in that country to cease forever, and the present Parliament, its heirs, etc., to be perpetual; in this case, I ask, what would the most clamorous of them think, were an act to be passed, declaring the right of *such a Parliament* to bind *them* in all cases whatsoever? For this word *whatsoever* would go as effectually to their *Magna Charta, Bill of Rights, trial by juries, etc.,* as it went to the charters and forms of government in America.

I am persuaded, that the gentleman to whom I address these remarks, will not, after the passing of this act, say, "that the *principles* of administration had not been *changed* in America, and that the maxims of government had there been *always the same.*" For here is, in principle, a total overthrow of the whole; and not a subversion only, but an annihilation of the foundation of liberty and absolute domination established in its stead.

The Abbé likewise states the case exceedingly wrong and injuriously, when he says, that "*the whole* question was reduced to the knowing whether the mother country had, or had not, a right to lay, directly or indirectly, a *slight* tax upon the colonies." This was *not the whole* of the question; neither was the *quantity* of the tax the object either to the Ministry or to the Americans. It was the principle, of which the tax made but a part, and the quantity still less, that formed the ground on which America resisted.

The tax on tea,[3] which is the tax here alluded to, was neither more nor less than an experiment to establish the practice of a declaratory law upon; modeled into the more fashionable phrase *of the universal supremacy of Parliament.* For until this time the declaratory law had lain dormant, and the framers of it had contented themselves with barely declaring an opinion.

Therefore the *whole* question with America, in the opening of the dispute, was, shall we be bound in all cases whatsoever by the British Parliament, or shall we not? For submission to the tea or tax act implied an acknowledgment of the Declaratory Act, or, in other words, of the universal supremacy of Parliament, which as they never intended to do, it was necessary they should oppose it, in its first stage of execution.

It is probable the Abbé has been led into this mistake by perusing detached pieces in some of the American newspapers; for, in a case where all were interested, everyone had a right to give his opinion; and there were many, who, with the best intentions, did not choose the best, nor indeed the true ground, to defend their cause upon. They felt themselves right by a general impulse, without being able to separate, analyze, and arrange the parts.

I am somewhat unwilling to examine too minutely into the whole of this extraordinary passage of the Abbé, lest I should appear to treat it with severity; otherwise I could show that not a single declaration is justly founded: for instance, the reviving an obsolete act of the reign of Henry VIII[4] and fitting it to the Americans, by authority of which they were to be seized and brought from America to England, and there imprisoned and tried for any supposed offenses, was, in the worst sense of the words, *to tear them, by the arbitrary power of Parliament, from the arms of their families and friends, and drag them not only to dreary but distant dungeons.* Yet this act was contrived some years before the breaking out of hostilities. And again, though the blood of martyrs and patriots had not streamed on the scaffolds, it streamed in the streets, in the massacre of the inhabitants of Boston,[5] by the British soldiery in the year 1770.

Had the Abbé said that the causes which produced the Revolution in America were originally *different* from those which produced revolutions in other parts of the globe, he had been right. Here the value and quality of liberty, the nature of government, and the dignity of man, were known and understood, and the attachment of the Americans to these principles produced the Revolution, as a natural and almost unavoidable consequence. They had no particular family to set up or pull down. Nothing of personality was incorporated with their cause. They started even-handed with each other, and went no faster into the several stages of it, than they were driven by the unrelenting and imperious conduct of Britain. Nay, in the last act, the Declaration of Independence, they had nearly been too late; for had it not been declared at the exact time it was, I see no period in their affairs since, in which it could have been declared with the same effect, and probably not at all.

But the object being formed before the reverse of fortune took place, that is, before the operations of the gloomy campaign of 1776, their honor, their interest, their everything, called loudly on them to maintain it; and that glow of thought and energy of heart, which even a distant prospect of independence inspires, gave confidence to their hopes, and resolution to their conduct, which a state of dependence could never have reached. They looked forward to happier days and scenes of rest, and qualified the hardships of the campaign by contemplating the establishment of their new-born system.

If, on the other hand, we take a review of what part Britain has acted, we shall find everything which ought to make a nation blush—the most vulgar abuse, accompanied by that species of haughtiness which distinguishes the hero of a mob from the character of a gentleman. It was equally as much from her manners as from her injustice that she lost the colonies. By the latter she provoked their principles, by the former she wore out their temper: and it ought to be held out as an example to the world, to show how necessary it is to conduct the business of government with civility. In short, other revolutions may have originated in caprice, or generated in ambition; but here, the most unoffending humility was tortured into rage, and the infancy of existence made to weep.

A union so extensive, continued and determined, suffering with patience and never in despair, could not have been produced by common causes. It must be something capable of reaching the whole soul of man and arming it with perpetual energy. It is in vain to look for precedents among the revolutions of former ages, to find out, by comparison, the causes of this.

The spring, the progress, the object, the consequences, nay, the men, their habits of thinking, and all the circumstances of the country, are different. Those of other nations are, in general, little more than the history of their quarrels. They are marked by no important character in the annals of events; mixed in the mass of general matters, they occupy but a common page; and while the chief of the successful partisans stepped into power, the plundered multitude sat down and sorrowed. Few, very few of them are accompanied with reformation, either in government or manners; many of them with the most consummate profligacy. Triumph on the one side and misery on the other were the only events. Pains, punishments, torture, and death were made the business of mankind, until compassion, the fairest associate of the heart, was driven from its place, and the eye, accustomed to continual cruelty, could behold it without offense.

But as the principles of the present Revolution differed from those which preceded it, so likewise did the conduct of America both in government and war. Neither the foul finger of disgrace nor the bloody hand of vengeance has hitherto put a blot upon her fame. Her victories have received lustre from a greatness of lenity; and her laws have been permitted to slumber, where they might justly be awakened to punish. War, so much the trade of the world, has here been only the business of necessity; and when the necessity shall cease, her very enemies must confess, that as she drew the sword in her just defense, she used it without cruelty, and sheathed it without revenge.

As it is not my design to extend these remarks to a history, I shall now take my leave of this passage of the Abbé, with an observation, which, until something unfolds itself to convince me otherwise, I cannot avoid believing to be true;—which is, that it was the fixed determination of the British Cabinet to quarrel with America at all events.

They (the members who composed the Cabinet) had no doubt of success, if they could once bring it to the issue of a battle, and they expected from a conquest, what they could neither propose with decency, nor hope for by negotiation. The charters and constitutions of the colonies were become to them matters of offense, and their rapid progress in property and population were disgustingly beheld as the growing and natural means of independence. They saw no way to retain them long but by reducing them in time. A conquest would at once have made them both lords and landlords; and put them in the possession both of the revenue and the rental. The whole trouble of government would have ceased in a victory, and a final end put to remonstrance and debate.

The experience of the Stamp Act had taught them how to quarrel with the advantages of cover and convenience, and they had nothing to do but to renew the scene, and put contention into motion. They hoped for a rebellion, and they made one. They expected a declaration of independence, and they were not disappointed. But after this, they looked for victory, and they obtained a defeat.

If this be taken as the generating cause of the contest, then is every part of the conduct of the British Ministry consistent from the commencement of the dispute, until the signing the Treaty of Paris, after which, conquest becoming doubtful, they retreated to negotiation, and were again defeated.

. . . .

Though I am not surprised to see the Abbé mistaken in matters of history, acted at such a distance from his sphere of immediate observation, yet I am more than surprised to find him wrong (or at least what appears so to me) in the well enlightened field of philosophical reflection. Here the materials are his own; created by himself, and the error, therefore, is an act of the mind.

Hitherto my remarks have been confined to circumstance; the order in which they arose, and the events they produced. In these, my information being better than the Abbé's, my task was easy. How I may succeed in controverting matters of sentiment and opinion, with one whom years, experience, and long established reputation have placed in a superior line, I am less confident in; but as they fall within the scope of my observations it would be improper to pass them over.

From this part of the Abbé's work to the latter end, I find several expressions, which appear to me to start, with cynical complexion, from the path of liberal thinking, or at least they are so involved as to lose many of the beauties which distinguish other parts of the performance.

The Abbé having brought his work to the period when the Treaty of Alliance between France and the United States[6] commenced, proceeds to make some remarks thereon.

In short (says he), philosophy, whose first sentiment is the desire to see all governments just and all people happy, in casting her eyes upon this alliance of a monarchy, with a people who are defending their liberty, *is curious to know its motive. She sees at once too clearly, that the happiness of mankind has no part in it.*

Whatever train of thinking or of temper the Abbé might be in, when he penned this expression, matters not. They will neither qualify the sentiment, nor add to its defect. If right, it needs no apology; if wrong, it merits no excuse. It is sent into the world as an opinion of philosophy, and may be examined without regard to the author.

It seems to be a defect, connected with ingenuity, that it often employs itself more in matters of curiosity, than usefulness. Man must be the privy councillor of fate, or something is not right. He must know the springs, the whys and wherefores of everything, or he sits down unsatisfied. Whether this be a crime, or only a caprice of humanity, I am not inquiring into. I shall take the passage as I find it, and place my objections against it.

It is not so properly the *motives* which *produced* the alliance, as the *consequences* which are to be *produced from it*, that mark out the field of philosophical reflection. In the one we only penetrate into the barren cave of secrecy, where little can be known, and everything may be misconceived; in the other, the mind is presented with a wide extended prospect of vegetative good, and sees a thousand blessings budding into existence.

But the expression, even within the compass of the Abbé's meaning, sets out with an error, because it is made to declare that which no man has authority to declare. Who can say that the happiness of mankind made *no part of the motives* which produced the alliance? To be able to declare this, a man must be possessed of the mind of all the parties concerned, and know that their motives were something else.

In proportion as the independence of America became contemplated and understood, the local advantages of it to the immediate actors, and the numerous benefits it promised mankind, appeared to be every day increasing; and we saw not a temporary good for the present race only, but a continued good to all posterity; these motives, therefore, added to those which preceded them, became the motives on the part of America, which led her to propose and agree to the Treaty of Alliance, as the best effectual method of extending and securing happiness; and therefore, with respect to us, the Abbé is wrong.

France, on the other hand, was situated very differently. She was not acted upon by necessity to seek a friend, and therefore her motive in becoming one, has the strongest evidence of being good, and that which is so, must have some happiness for its object. With regard to herself, she saw a train of conveniences worthy her attention. By lessening the power of an enemy, whom at the same time she sought neither to destroy nor distress, she gained an advantage without doing an evil, and created to herself a new friend by associating with a country in misfortune.

The springs of thought that lead to actions of this kind, however political they may be, are nevertheless naturally beneficent; for in all causes, good or bad, it is necessary there should be a fitness in the mind, to enable it to act in character with the object: therefore, as a bad cause cannot be prosecuted with a good motive, so neither can a good cause be long supported by a bad one: and as no man acts without a motive, therefore in the present instance, as they cannot be bad, they must be admitted to be good. But the Abbé sets out upon such an extended scale, that he overlooks the degrees by which it is measured, and rejects the beginning of good, because the end comes not out at once.

It is true that bad motives may in some degree be brought to support a good cause or prosecute a good object; but it never continues long, which is not the case with France; for either the object will reform the mind, or the mind corrupt the object, or else not being able, either way, to get into unison, they will separate in disgust: and this natural, though unperceived progress of association or contention between the mind and the object, is the secret cause of fidelity or defection. Every object a man pursues, is, for the time, a kind of mistress to his mind: if both are good or bad, the union is natural; but if they are in reverse, and neither can seduce nor yet reform the other, the opposition grows into dislike, and a separation follows.

When the cause of America first made its appearance on the stage of the universe, there were many, who, in the style of adventurers and fortune-hunters, were dangling in its train, and making their court to it with every profession of honor and attachment. They were loud in its praise and ostentatious in its service. Every place echoed with their ardor or their anger, and they seemed like men in love. But, alas! they were fortune-hunters. Their expectations were excited, but their minds were unimpressed; and finding it not to their purpose, nor themselves reformed by its influence, they ceased their suit, and in some instances deserted and betrayed it.

There were others, who at first beheld America with indifference, and unacquainted with her character were cautious of her company. They treated her as one who, under the fair name of liberty, might conceal the hideous figure of anarchy, or the gloomy monster of tyranny. They knew not what she was. If fair, she was fair indeed. But still she was suspected and though born among us appeared to be a stranger.

Accident with some, and curiosity with others, brought on a distant acquaintance. They ventured to look at her. They felt an inclination to speak to her. One intimacy led to another, till the suspicion wore away, and a change of sentiment gradually stole upon the mind; and having no self-interest to serve, no passion of dishonor to gratify, they became enamored of her innocence, and, unaltered by misfortune or uninfluenced by success, shared with fidelity in the varieties of her fate.

This declaration of the Abbé's respecting motives, has led me unintentionally into a train of metaphysical reasoning; but there was no other avenue by which it could properly be approached. To place presumption against presumption, assertion against assertion, is a mode of opposition that has no effect; and therefore the more eligible method was to show that the declaration does not correspond with the natural progress of the mind, and the influence it has upon our conduct. I shall now quit this part and proceed to what I have before stated, namely, that it is not so properly the motives which produced the alliance, as the consequences to be procured from it, that mark out the field of philosophical reflection.

It is an observation I have already made in some former publications, that the circle of civilization is yet incomplete. Mutual wants have formed the individuals of each country into a kind of national society, and here the progress of civilization has stopped. For it is easy to see, that nations with regard to each other (notwithstanding the ideal civil law, which every one explains as it suits him) are like individuals in a state of nature. They are regulated by no fixed principle, governed by no compulsive law, and each does independently what it pleases or what it can.

Were it possible we could have known the world when in a state of barbarism, we might have concluded that it never could be brought into the order we now see it. The untamed mind was then as hard, if not harder, to work upon in its individual state, than the national mind is in its present one. Yet we have seen the accomplishment of one, why then should we doubt that of the other?

There is a greater fitness in mankind to extend and complete the civilization of nations with each other at this day, than there was to begin it with the unconnected individuals at first; in the same manner that it is somewhat easier to put together the materials of a machine after they are formed, than it was to form them from original matter. The present condition of the world, differing so exceedingly from what it formerly was, has given a new cast to the mind of man, more than what he appears to be sensible of. The wants of the individual, which first produced the idea of society, are now augmented into the wants of the nation, and he is obliged to seek from another country what before he sought from the next person.

Letters, the tongue of the world, have in some measure brought all mankind acquainted, and by an extension of their uses are every day promoting some new friendship. Through them distant nations became capable of conversation, and losing by degrees the awkwardness of strangers, and the moroseness of suspicion, they learn to know and understand each other. Science, the partisan of no country, but the beneficent patroness of all, has liberally opened a temple where all may meet. Her influence on the mind, like the sun on the chilled earth, has long been preparing it for higher cultivation and further improvement. The philosopher of one country sees not an enemy in the philosopher of another: he takes his seat in the temple of science, and asks not who sits beside him.

This was not the condition of the barbarian world. Then the wants of men were few and the objects within his reach. While he could acquire these, he lived in a state of individual independence; the consequence of which was, there were as many nations as persons, each contending with the other, to secure something which he had, or to obtain something which he had not. The world had then no business to follow, no studies to exercise the mind. Their time was divided between sloth and fatigue. Hunting and war were their chief occupations; sleep and food their principal enjoyments.

Now it is otherwise. A change in the mode of life has made it necessary to be busy; and man finds a thousand things to do now which before he did not. Instead of placing his ideas of greatness in the rude achievements of the savage, he studies arts, sciences, agriculture and commerce, the refinements of the gentleman, the principles of society, and the knowledge of the philosopher.

There are many things which in themselves are neither morally good nor bad, but they are productive of consequences, which are strongly marked with one or other of these characters. Thus commerce, though in itself a moral nullity, has had a considerable influence in tempering the human mind. It was the want of objects in the ancient world, which occasioned in them such a rude and perpetual turn for war. Their time hung on their hands without the means of employment. The indolence they lived in afforded leisure for mischief, and being all idle at once, and equal in their circumstances, they were easily provoked or induced to action.

But the introduction of commerce furnished the world with objects, which, in their extent, reach every man, and give him something to think about and something to do; by these his attention is mechanically drawn from the pursuits which a state of indolence and an unemployed mind occasioned, and he trades with the same countries, which in former ages, tempted by their productions, and too indolent to purchase them, he would have gone to war with.

Thus, as I have already observed, the condition of the world being materially changed by the influence of science and commerce, it is put into a fitness not only to admit of, but to desire, an extension of civilization. The principal and almost only remaining enemy, it now has to encounter, is *prejudice*; for it is evidently the interest of mankind to agree and make the best of life. The world has undergone its divisions of empire, the several boundaries of which are known and settled. The idea of conquering countries, like the Greeks and Romans, does not now exist; and experience has exploded the notion of going to war for the sake of profit. In short, the objects for war are exceedingly diminished, and there is now left scarcely anything to quarrel about, but what arises from that demon of society, prejudice, and the consequent sullenness and untractableness of the temper.

There is something exceedingly curious in the constitution and operation of prejudice. It has the singular ability of accommodating itself to all the possible varieties of the human mind. Some passions and vices are but thinly scattered among mankind, and find only here and there a fitness of reception. But prejudice, like the spider, makes every place its home. It has neither taste nor choice of situation, and all that it requires is room. Everywhere, except in fire or water, a spider will live.

So, let the mind be as naked as the walls of an empty and forsaken tenement, gloomy as a dungeon, or ornamented with the richest abilities of thinking, let it be hot, cold, dark or light, lonely or inhabited, still prejudice, if undisturbed, will fill it with cobwebs, and live, like the spider, where there seems nothing to live on. If the one prepares her food by poisoning it to her palate and her use, the other does the same;

and as several of our passions are strongly characterized by the animal world, prejudice may be denominated the spider of the mind.

Perhaps no two events ever united so intimately and forcibly to combat and expel prejudice, as the Revolution of America and the alliance with France. Their effects are felt, and their influence already extends as well to the Old World as the New. Our style and manner of thinking have undergone a revolution more extraordinary than the political revolution of the country. We see with other eyes; we hear with other ears; and think with other thoughts, than those we formerly used. We can look back on our own prejudices, as if they had been the prejudices of other people.

We now see and know they were prejudices and nothing else; and, relieved from their shackles, enjoy a freedom of mind, we felt not before. It was not all the argument, however powerful, nor the reasoning, however eloquent, that could have produced this change, so necessary to the extension of the mind, and the cordiality of the world, without the two circumstances of the Revolution and the alliance.

Had America dropped quietly from Britain, no material change in sentiment had taken place. The same notions, prejudices, and conceits would have governed in both countries, as governed them before, and, still the slaves of error and education, they would have traveled on in the beaten track of vulgar and habitual thinking. But brought about by the means it has been, both with regard to ourselves, to France and England, every corner of the mind is swept of its cobwebs, poison and dust, and made fit for the reception of generous happiness.

Perhaps there never was an alliance on a broader basis, than that between America and France, and the progress of it is worth attending to. The countries had been enemies, not properly of themselves, but through the medium of England.[7] They originally had no quarrel with each other, nor any cause for one, but what arose from the interest of England, and her arming America against France. At the same time, the Americans at a distance from, and unacquainted with, the world, and tutored in all the prejudices which governed those who governed them, conceived it their duty to act as they were taught. In doing this, they expended their substance to make conquests, not for themselves, but for their masters, who in return treated them as slaves.

A long succession of insolent severity, and the separation finally occasioned by the commencement of hostilities at Lexington, on the nineteenth of April, 1775, naturally produced a new disposition of thinking. As the mind closed itself toward England, it opened itself toward the world, and our prejudices like our oppressions, underwent, though less observed, a mental examination; until we found the former as inconsistent with reason and benevolence, as the latter were repugnant to our civil and political rights.

. . . .

But the subsequent conduct of the British Cabinet has shown that this was not their plan of politics, and consequently their motives must be sought for in another line.

The truth is, that the British had formed a very humble opinion of the Dutch nation. They looked on them as a people who would submit to anything; that they might insult them as they liked, plunder them as they pleased, and still the Dutch dared not to be provoked.

If this be taken as the opinion of the British Cabinet, the measure is easily accounted for; because it goes on the supposition, that when, by a declaration of hostilities, they had robbed the Dutch of some millions sterling (and to rob them was popular), they could make peace with them again whenever they pleased, and on almost any terms the British Ministry should propose. And no sooner was the plundering committed, than the accommodation was set on foot and failed.

When once the mind loses the sense of its own dignity, it loses, likewise, the ability of judging of it in another. And the American war has thrown Britain into such a variety of absurd situations, that, arguing from herself, she sees not in what conduct national dignity consists in other countries. From Holland she expected duplicity and submission, and this mistake arose from her having acted, in a number of instances during the present war, the same character herself.

To be allied to, or connected with, Britain seems to be an unsafe and impolitic situation. Holland and America are instances of the reality of this remark. Make those countries the allies of France or Spain, and Britain will court them with civility and treat them with respect; make them her own allies, and she will insult and plunder them. In the first case, she feels some apprehensions at offending them because they have support at hand; in the latter, those apprehensions do not exist. Such, however, has hitherto been her conduct.

Another measure which has taken place since the publication of the Abbé's work, and likewise since the time of my beginning this letter, is the change in the British Ministry.[8] What line the new Cabinet will pursue respecting America is, at this time, unknown; neither is it very material, unless they are seriously disposed to a general and honorable peace.

Repeated experience has shown, not only the impracticability of conquering America, but the still higher impossibility of conquering her mind, or recalling her back to her former condition of thinking. Since the commencement of the war, which is now approaching to eight years, thousands and tens of thousands have advanced, and are daily advancing into the first state of manhood, who know nothing of Britain but as a barbarous enemy, and to whom the independence of America appears as much the natural and established government of the country, as that of England does to an Englishman.

And, on the other hand, thousands of the aged, who had British ideas, have dropped, and are daily dropping, from the stage of business and life. The natural progress of generation and decay operates every hour to the disadvantage of Britain. Time and death, hard enemies to contend with, fight constantly against her interest; and the bills of mortality,[9] in every part of America, are the thermometers of her decline. The children in the streets are from their cradle bred to consider her as their only foe. They hear of her cruelties; of their fathers, uncles, and kindred killed; they see the remains of burned and destroyed houses, and the common tradition of the school they go to, tells them, *those things were done by the British.*

These are circumstances which the mere English state politician, who considers man only in a state of manhood, does not attend to. He gets entangled with parties coeval or equal with himself at home, and thinks not how fast the rising generation in America is growing beyond knowledge of them, or they of him. In a few years all personal remembrances will be lost, and who is king or minister in England, will be little known and scarcely inquired after.

The new British Administration is composed of persons who have ever been against the war, and who have constantly reprobated all the violent measures of the former one. They considered the American war as destructive to themselves, and opposed it on that ground. But what are these things to America? She has nothing to do with English parties. The ins and the outs are nothing to her. It is the whole country she is at war with, or must be at peace with.

Were every minister in England a Chatham,[10] it would now weigh little or nothing in the scale of American politics. Death has preserved to the memory of this statesman, *that fame,* which he, by living, would have lost. His plans and opinions, toward the latter part of his life, would have been attended with as many evil consequences, and as much reprobated here as those of Lord North; and considering him a wise man, they abound with inconsistencies amounting to absurdities.

It has apparently been the fault of many in the late minority to suppose that America would agree to certain terms with them, were they in place, which she would not even listen to, from the then Administration. This idea can answer no other purpose than to prolong the war; and Britain may, at the expense of many more millions, learn the fatality of such mistakes. If the new Ministry wisely avoid this hopeless policy, they will prove themselves better pilots and wiser men than they are conceived to be; for it is every day expected to see their bark strike upon some hidden rock and go to pieces.

But there is a line in which they may be great. A more brilliant opening needs not to present itself; and it is such an one as true magnanimity would improve, and humanity rejoice in.

A total reformation is wanted in England. She wants an expanded mind—a heart which embraces the universe. Instead of shutting herself up in an island, and quarreling with the world, she would derive more lasting happiness, and acquire more real riches, by generously mixing with it, and bravely saying, I am the enemy of none. It is not now a time for little contrivances or artful politics. The European world is too experienced to be imposed upon, and America too wise to be duped. It must be something new and masterly that can succeed. The idea of seducing America from her independence, or corrupting her from her alliance, is a thought too little for a great mind, and impossible for any honest one, to attempt. Whenever politics are applied to debauch mankind from their integrity, and dissolve the virtue of human nature, they become detestable; and to be a statesman on this plan, is to be a commissioned villain. He who aims at it, leaves a vacancy in his character, which may be filled up with the worst of epithets.

If the disposition of England should be such, as not to agree to a general and honorable peace, and the war must, at all events, continue longer, I cannot help wishing that the alliances which America has or may enter into, may become the only objects of the war. She wants an opportunity of showing to the world that she holds her honor as dear and sacred as her independence, and that she will in no situation forsake those whom no negotiations could induce to forsake her. Peace, to every reflecting mind, is a desirable object; but *that peace* which is accompanied with a ruined character, becomes a crime to the seducer, and a curse upon the seduced.

But where is the impossibility or even the great difficulty of England's forming a friendship with France and Spain, and making it a national virtue to renounce forever those prejudiced inveteracies it has been her custom to cherish; and which, while they serve to sink her with an increasing enormity of debt, by involving her in fruitless wars, become likewise the bane of her repose, and the destruction of her manners? We had once the fetters that she has now, but experience has shown us the mistake, and thinking justly, has set us right.

The true idea of a great nation, is that which extends and promotes the principles of universal society; whose mind rises above the atmosphere of local thoughts, and considers mankind, of whatever nation or profession they may be, as the work of one Creator. The rage for conquest has had its fashion, and its day. Why may not the amiable virtues have the same? The Alexander and Cæsars of antiquity have left behind them their monuments of destruction, and are remembered with hatred; while those more exalted characters, who first taught society and science, are blessed with the gratitude of every age and country. Of more use was *one* philosopher, though a heathen, to the world, than all the heathen conquerors that ever existed.

Should the present Revolution be distinguished by opening a new system of extended civilization, it will receive from heaven the highest evidence of approbation; and as this is a subject to which the Abbé's powers are so eminently suited, I recommend it to his attention with the affection of a friend, and the ardor of a universal citizen.[11]

POSTSCRIPT

Since closing the foregoing letter, some intimations respecting a general peace have made their way to America. On what authority or foundation they stand, or how near or remote such an event may be, are circumstances I am not inquiring into. But as the subject must sooner or later become a matter of serious attention, it may not be improper, even at this early period, candidly to investigate some points that are connected with it, or lead toward it.

The independence of America is at this moment as firmly established as that of any other country in a state of war. It is not length of time, but power that gives stability. Nations at war know nothing of each other on the score of antiquity. It is their present and immediate strength, together with their connections, that must support them. To which we may add, that a right which originated to-day, is as much a right, as if it had the sanction of a thousand years; and therefore the independence and present governments of America are in no more danger of being subverted, because they are modern, than that of England is secure, because it is ancient.

The politics of Britain, so far as respects America, were originally conceived in idiotism, and acted in madness. There is not a step which bears the smallest trace of rationality. In her management of the war, she has labored to be wretched, and studied to be hated; and in all her former propositions for accommodation, she has discovered a total ignorance of mankind, and of those natural and unalterable sensations by which they are so generally governed. How she may conduct herself in the present or future business of negotiating a peace, is yet to be proved.

He is a weak politician who does not understand human nature, and penetrate into the effect which measures of government will have upon the mind. All the miscarriages of Britain have arisen from this defect. The former Ministry acted as if they supposed mankind to be *without a mind*; and the present Ministry, as if America was *without a memory*. The one must have supposed we were incapable of feeling; and the other that we could not remember injuries.

There is likewise another line in which politicians mistake, which is, that of not rightly calculating, or rather of misjudging, the consequences which any given circumstance will produce. Nothing is more frequent, as well in common as in political life, than to hear people complain, that such or such means produced an event directly contrary to their intentions. But the fault lies in their not judging rightly what the event would be; for the means produced only its proper and natural consequences.

It is very probably that, in a treaty of peace, Britain will contend for some post or other in North America, perhaps Canada or Halifax, or both: and I infer this from the known deficiency of her politics, which have ever yet made use of means whose natural event was against both her interest and her expectation. But the question with her ought to be, whether it is worth her while to hold them, and what will be the consequences.

Respecting Canada, one or other of the two following will take place, *viz.*: If Canada should become populous, it will revolt; and if it does not become so, it will not be worth the expense of holding. And the same may be said of Halifax, and the country round it. But Canada *never will* be populous; neither is there any occasion for contrivances on one side or the other, for nature alone will do the whole.

Britain may put herself to great expenses in sending settlers to Canada; but the descendants of those settlers will be Americans, as other descendants have been before them. They will look round and see the neighboring states sovereign and free, respected abroad and trading at large with the world; and the natural love of liberty, the advantages of commerce, the blessings of independence, and of a happier climate, and a richer soil, will draw them southward; and the effect will be, that Britain will sustain the expense, and America reap the advantage.

One would think that the experience which Britain has had of America, would entirely sicken her of all thoughts of continental colonization, and any part she might retain will only become to her a field of jealousy and thorns, of debate and contention, forever struggling for privileges, and meditating revolt. She may form new settlements, but they will be for us; they will become part of the United States of America; and that against all her contrivances to prevent it, or without any endeavors of ours to promote it. In the first place she cannot draw from them a revenue, until they are able to pay one, and when they are so they will be above subjection. Men soon become attached to the soil they live upon, and incorporated with the prosperity of the place: and it signifies but little what opinions they come over with, for time, interest, and new connections will render them obsolete, and the next generation know nothing of them.

Were Britain truly wise, she would lay hold of the present opportunity to disentangle herself from all continental embarrassments in North America, and that not only to avoid future broils and troubles, but to save expenses. To speak explicitly on the matter, I would not, were I an European power, have Canada, under the conditions that Britain must retain it, could it be given to me. It is one of those kind of dominions that is, and ever will be, a constant charge upon any foreign holder.

As to Halifax, it will become useless to England after the present war, and the loss of the United States. A harbor, when the dominion is gone, for the purpose of which only it was wanted, can be attended only with expense. There are, I doubt not, thousands of people in England, who suppose, that these places are a profit to the nation, whereas they are directly the contrary, and instead of producing any revenue, a considerable part of the revenue of England is annually drawn off, to support the expense of holding them.

Gibraltar is another instance of national ill-policy. A post which in time of peace is not wanted, and in time of war is of no use, must at all times be useless. Instead of affording protection to a navy, it requires the aid of one to maintain it. To suppose that Gibraltar commands the Mediterranean, or the pass into it, or the trade of it, is to suppose a detected falsehood; because though Britain holds the post she has lost the other three, and every benefit she expected from it. And to say that all this happens because it is besieged by land and water, is to say nothing, for this will always be the case in time of war, while France and Spain keep up superior fleets, and Britain holds the place. So that, though, as an impenetrable, inaccessible rock, it may be held by the one, it is always in the power of the other to render it useless and excessively chargeable.

I should suppose that one of the principal objects of Spain in besieging it, is to show to Britain, that though she may not take it, she can command it, that is she can shut it up, and prevent its being used as a harbor, though not as a garrison. But the short way to reduce Gibraltar is to attack the British fleet; for Gibraltar is as dependent on a fleet for support, as a bird is on its wings for food, and when wounded there it starves.

There is another circumstance which the people of England have not only not attended to, but seem to be utterly ignorant of, and that is, the difference between permanent power and accidental power, considered in a national sense.

By permanent power, I mean, a natural, inherent, and perpetual ability in a nation, which though always in being, may not be always in action, or not advantageously directed; and by accidental power, I mean, a fortunate or accidental disposition or exercise of national strength, in whole or in part.

There undoubtedly was a time when any one European nation, with only eight or ten ships of war, equal to the present ships of the line, could have carried terror to all others, who had not begun to build a navy, however great their natural ability might be for that purpose: but this can be considered only as accidental, and not as a standard to compare permanent power by, and could last no longer than until those powers built as many or more ships than the former. After this a larger fleet was necessary, in order to be superior; and a still larger would again supersede it. And thus mankind have gone on building fleet upon fleet, as occasion or situation dictated. And this reduces it to an original question, which is: Which power can build and man the largest number of ships? The natural answer to which is, that power which has the largest revenue and the greatest number of inhabitants, provided its situation of coast affords sufficient conveniences.

France being a nation on the continent of Europe, and Britain an island in its neighborhood, each of them derived different ideas from their different situations. The inhabitants of Britain could carry on no foreign trade, nor stir from the spot they dwelt upon, without the assistance of shipping; but this was not the case with France. The idea therefore of a navy did not arise to France from the same original and immediate necessity which produced it to England. But the question is, that when both of them turn their attention, and employ their revenues the same way, which can be superior?

The annual revenue of France is nearly double that of England, and her number of inhabitants more than twice as many. Each of them has the same length of coast on the Channel, besides which, France has several hundred miles extent on the Bay of Biscay, and an opening on the Mediterranean: and every day proves that practice and exercise make sailors, as well as soldiers, in one country as well as another.

If, then, Britain can maintain a hundred ships of the line, France can as well support a hundred and fifty, because her revenue and her population are as equal to the one, as those of England are to the other. And the only reason why she has not done it is because she has not till very lately attended to it. But when she sees, as she now does, that a navy is the first engine of power, she can easily accomplish it.

England, very falsely, and ruinously for herself, infers that because she had the advantage of France, while France had the smaller navy, that for that reason it is always to be so. Whereas it may be clearly seen that the strength of France has never yet been tried on a navy, and that she is able to be as superior to England in the extent of a navy, as she is in the extent of her revenues and her population. And England may lament the day, when, by her insolence and injustice, she provoked in France a maritime disposition.

It is in the power of the combined fleets to conquer every island in the West Indies, and reduce all the British Navy in those places. For were France and Spain to send their whole naval force in Europe to those islands it would not be in the power of Britain to follow them with an equal force. She would still be twenty or thirty ships inferior, were she to send every vessel she had, and in the meantime all the foreign trade to England would lay exposed to the Dutch.

It is a maxim which, I am persuaded, will ever hold good, and more especially in naval operations, that a great power ought never to move in detachments, if it can possibly be avoided; but to go with its whole force to some important object, the reduction of which shall have a decisive effect upon the war. Had the whole of the French and Spanish fleets in Europe come last spring to the West Indies, every island had been their own, Rodney[12] their prisoner, and his fleet their prize. From the United States the combined fleets can be supplied with provisions, without the necessity of drawing them from Europe, which is not the case with England.

Accident has thrown some advantages in the way of England, which, from the inferiority of her navy, she had not a right to expect. For though she had been obliged to fly before the combined fleets, yet Rodney has twice had the fortune to fall in with detached squadrons, to which he was superior in numbers: the first off Cape St. Vincent, where he had nearly two to one, and the other in the West Indies, where he had a majority of six ships. Victories of this kind almost produce themselves. They are won without honor, and suffered without disgrace: and are ascribable to the chance of meeting, not to the superiority of fighting. For the same admiral, under whom they were obtained, was unable, in three former engagements, to make the least impression on a fleet consisting of an equal number of ships with his own, and compounded for the events by declining the actions.*

To conclude: if it may be said that Britain has numerous enemies, it likewise proves that she has given numerous offenses. Insolence is sure to provoke hatred, whether in a nation or an individual. That want of manners in the British Court may be seen even in its birthdays' and New Year's odes, which are calculated to infatuate the vulgar, and disgust the man of refinement; and her former overbearing rudeness, and insufferable injustice on the seas, have made every commercial nation her foe. Her fleets were employed as engines of prey, and acted on the surface of the deep the character which the shark does beneath it. On the other hand, the combined powers are taking a popular part, and will render their reputation immortal, by establishing the perfect freedom of the ocean, to which all countries have a right, and are interested in accomplishing. The sea is the world's highway; and he who arrogates a prerogative over it transgresses the right, and justly brings on himself the chastisement of nations.

Perhaps it might be of some service to the future tranquillity of mankind if an article were introduced into the next general peace that no one nation should, in time of peace, exceed a certain number of ships of war. Something of this kind seems necessary; for according to the present fashion, half of the world will get upon the water, and there appears to be no end to the extent to which navies may be carried. Another reason is that navies add nothing to the manners or morals of a people. The sequestered life which attends the service, prevents the opportunities of society, and is too apt to occasion a coarseness of ideas and of language, and that more in ships of war than in the commercial employ; because in the latter they mix more with the world, and are nearer related to it. I mention this remark as a general one: and not applied to any one country more than to another.

* See the accounts, either English or French, of three actions, in the West Indies, between Count de Guichen and Admiral Rodney, in 1780.

Britain has now had the trial of above seven years, with an expense of nearly an hundred million pounds sterling; and every month in which she delays to conclude a peace costs her another million sterling, over and above her ordinary expenses of government, which are a million more; so that her total *monthly* expense is two million pounds sterling, which is equal to the whole *yearly* expenses of America, all charges included. Judge then who is best able to continue it.

She has likewise many atonements to make to an injured world, as well in one quarter as in another. And instead of pursuing that temper of arrogance, which serves only to sink her in the esteem, and entail on her the dislike of all nations, she would do well to reform her manners, retrench her expenses, live peaceably with her neighbors, and think of war no more.

Philadelphia, August 21, 1782.

RIGHTS OF MAN

PART THE SECOND

COMBINING PRINCIPLE AND PRACTICE

1792

With the completion of the war for independence, Thomas Paine returned to France in April 1787, and in August returned to his native country, England. For the next several years, Paine traveled back and forth across the English Channel. During this period, Paine showed himself to be a true man of the Enlightenment, engaging not just in debate over politics and government, but in a host of other intellectual pursuits, including the method of constructing an iron bridge—a topic that would interest him for years to come.

Paine was in France in July 1789 when the Bastille, the symbol of the oppressive feudal system, was attacked by the Paris mob. Now seeing himself increasingly as a "citizen of the world," Paine threw his support behind the French Revolution. He published essays on it, met with his old friend the Marquis de Lafayette, and corresponded with British Parliamentarian Edmund Burke on the topic. While Paine and Burke had held many similar ideas on earlier American issues, they differed greatly on the meaning of the situation in France. Burke's Reflections on the Revolution in France *was published in Britain on November 1, 1790, and the following February the first part of Paine's* Rights of Man *was published. The ideas in the pamphlet were so controversial that Joseph Johnson, Paine's printer, withdrew the pamphlet shortly after it was released, and it would not be widely available for another month, when publisher J. Jordan released it. Paine insisted that the essay be brought out in cheap editions, for which he received no royalties, so it would have the widest possible audience.*

By the time Rights of Man, Part Two *was released on February 16,*

1792, Paine's world had changed. He had become a leading voice for individual rights, and his circle included women's rights advocate Mary Wollstonecraft and poet Joel Barlow. Paine had also become a lightning rod for conservative forces in England, who feared his anti-royal, anti-aristocratic republican ideas as well as his views on Great Britain's economy. Prime Minister William Pitt's government had subsidized the publication of a critical biography of Paine the year before. On May 21, Paine received a summons to appear in court on charges of seditious libel for the ideas expressed in Rights of Man. As Paine awaited trial in London, the French monarchy fell and the National Assembly conferred honorary French citizenship on him. On September 6, 1792, Paine was elected to the French National Convention. A week later, Paine arrived at Calais. On September 21, he voted to formally abolish the monarchy and proclaim the French Republic, and a month later was selected to help craft the first written French constitution. As Paine helped create the new French government, widespread anger against him grew in Britain. Crowds burned him in effigy, and government-supported anti-Paine tracts were published. On December 18, 1792, a British court convicted Paine in absentia for seditious libel.

To M. De La Fayette

After an acquaintance of nearly fifteen years, in difficult situations in America, and various consultations in Europe, I feel a pleasure in presenting to you this small treatise, in gratitude for your services to my beloved America, and as a testimony of my esteem for the virtues, public and private, which I know you to possess.

The only point upon which I could ever discover that we differed, was not as to principles of government, but as to time. For my own part, I think it equally as injurious to good principles to permit them to linger, as to push them on too fast. That which you suppose accomplishable in fourteen or fifteen years, I may believe practicable in a much shorter period. Mankind, as it appears to me, are always ripe enough to understand their true interest, provided it be presented clearly to their understanding, and that in a manner not to create suspicion by any thing like self-design, nor offend by assuming too much. Where we would wish to reform we must not reproach.

When the American revolution was established, I felt a disposition to sit serenely down and enjoy the calm. It did not appear to me that any object could afterwards arise great enough to make me quit tranquillity, and feel as I had felt before. But when principle, and not place, is the energetic cause of action, a man, I find, is every where the same.

I am now once more in the public world; and as I have not a right to contemplate on so many years of remaining life as you have, I am resolved to labour as fast as I can; and as I am anxious for your aid and your company, I wish you to hasten your principles, and overtake me.

If you make a campaign the ensuing spring, which it is most probable there will be no occasion for, I will come and join you. Should the campaign commence, I hope it will terminate in the extinction of German despotism, and in establishing the freedom of all Germany. When France shall be surrounded with revolutions, she will be in peace and safety, and her taxes, as well as those of Germany, will consequently become less.

> Your sincere,
> Affectionate Friend,
> THOMAS PAINE.
> *London, Feb.* 9, 1792.

PREFACE

When I began the chapter entitled the *"Conclusion"* in the former part of the RIGHTS OF MAN, published last year, it was my intention to have extended it to a greater length; but in casting the whole matter in my mind which I wished to add, I found that I must either make the work too bulky, or contract my plan too much. I therefore brought it to a close as soon as the subject would admit, and reserved what I had further to say to another opportunity.

Several other reasons contributed to produce this determination. I wished to know the manner in which a work, written in a style of thinking and expression different to what had been customary in England, would be received before I proceeded farther. A great field was opening to the view of mankind by means of the French Revolution. Mr. Burke's outrageous opposition thereto brought the controversy into England. He attacked principles which he knew (from information) I would contest with him, because they are principles I believe to be good, and which I have contributed to establish, and conceive myself bound to defend. Had he not urged the controversy, I had most probably been a silent man.

Another reason for deferring the remainder of the work was, that Mr. Burke promised in his first publication to renew the subject at another opportunity, and to make a comparison of what he called the English and French Constitutions. I therefore held myself in reserve for him. He has published two works since, without doing this; which he certainly would not have omitted, had the comparison been in his favour.

In his last work, *"His appeal from the new to the old Whigs,"* he has quoted about ten pages from the *Rights of Man,* and having given himself the trouble of doing this, says, "he shall not attempt in the smallest degree to refute them," meaning the principles therein contained. I am enough acquainted with Mr. Burke to know, that he would if he could. But instead of contesting them, he immediately after consoles himself with saying, that "he has done his part."—He has not done his part. He has not performed his promise of a comparison of constitutions. He started the controversy, he gave the challenge, and has fled from it; and he is now a *case in point* with his own opinion, that, "*the age of chivalry is gone!*"

The title, as well as the substance of his last work, his "*Appeal*," is his condemnation. Principles must stand on their own merits, and if they are good they certainly will. To put them under the shelter of other men's authority, as Mr. Burke has done, serves to bring them into suspicion. Mr. Burke is not very fond of dividing his honours, but in this case he is artfully dividing the disgrace.

But who are those to whom Mr. Burke has made his appeal? A set of childish thinkers and half-way politicians born in the last century; men who went no farther with any principle than as it suited their purpose as a party; the nation was always left out of the question; and this has been the character of every party from that day to this. The nation sees nothing in such works, or such politics worthy its attention. A little matter will move a party, but it must be something great that moves a nation.

Though I see nothing in Mr. Burke's Appeal worth taking much notice of, there is, however, one expression upon which I shall offer a few remarks.—After quoting largely from the *Rights of Man,* and declining to contest the principles contained in that work, he says, "This will most probably be done (*if such writings shall be thought to deserve any other refutation than that of criminal justice*) by others, who may think with Mr. Burke and with the same zeal."

In the first place, it has not yet been done by any body. Not less, I believe, than eight or ten pamphlets intended as answers to the former part of the "Rights of Man" have been published by different persons, and not one of them, to my knowledge, has extended to a second edition, nor are even the titles of them so much as generally remembered. As I am averse to unnecessarily multiplying publications, I have answered none of them. And as I believe that a man may write himself out of reputation when nobody else can do it, I am careful to avoid that rock.

But as I would decline unnecessary publications on the one hand, so would I avoid every thing that might appear like sullen pride on the other. If Mr. Burke, or any person on his side the question, will produce an answer to the "Rights of Man," that shall extend to an half, or even to a fourth part of the number of copies to which the Rights of Man extended, I will reply to his work. But until this be done, I shall so far take the sense of the public for my guide (and the world knows I am not a flatterer) that what they do not think worth while to read, is not worth mine to answer. I suppose the number of copies to which the first part of the *Rights of Man* extended, taking England, Scotland, and Ireland, is not less than between forty and fifty thousand.

I now come to remark on the remaining part of the quotation I have made from Mr. Burke.

"If," says he, "such writings shall be thought to deserve any other refutation than that of *criminal* justice."

Pardoning the pun, it must be *criminal* justice indeed that should condemn a work as a substitute for not being able to refute it. The greatest condemnation that could be passed upon it would be a refutation. But in proceeding by the method Mr. Burke alludes to, the condemnation would, in the final event, pass upon the criminality of the process and not upon the work, and in this case, I had rather be the author, than be either the judge, or the jury, that should condemn it.

But to come at once to the point. I have differed from some professional gentlemen on the subject of prosecutions, and I since find they are falling into my opinion, which I will here state as fully, but as concisely as I can.

I will first put a case with respect to any law, and then compare it with a government, or with what in England is, or has been, called a constitution.

It would be an act of despotism, or what in England is called arbitrary power, to make a law to prohibit investigating the principles, good or bad, on which such a law, or any other is founded.

If a law be bad, it is one thing to oppose the practice of it, but it is quite a different thing to expose its errors, to reason on its defects, and to shew cause why it should be repealed, or why another ought to be substituted in its place. I have always held it an opinion (making it also my practice) that it is better to obey a bad law, making use at the same time of every argument to shew its errors and procure its repeal, than forcibly to violate it; because the precedent of breaking a bad law might weaken the force, and lead to a discretionary violation, of those which are good.

The case is the same with respect to principles and forms of government, or to what are called constitutions and the parts of which they are composed.

It is for the good of nations, and not for the emolument or aggrandizement of particular individuals, that government ought to be established, and that mankind are at the expence of supporting it. The defects of every government and constitution, both as to principle and form must, on a parity of reasoning, be as open to discussion as the defects of a law, and it is a duty which every man owes to society to point them out. When those defects, and the means of remedying them are generally seen by a nation, that nation will reform its government or its constitution in the one case, as the government repealed or reformed the law in the other. The operation of government is restricted to the making and the administering of laws; but it is to a nation that the right of forming or reforming, generating or regenerating constitutions and governments belong; and consequently those subjects, as subjects of investigation, are always before a country *as a matter of right,* and cannot, without invading the general rights of that country, be made subjects for prosecution. On this ground I will meet Mr. Burke whenever he please. It is better that the whole argument should come out, than to seek to stifle it. It was himself that opened the controversy, and he ought not to desert it.

I do not believe that monarchy and aristocracy will continue seven years longer in any of the enlightened countries in Europe. If better reasons can be shewn for them than against them, they will stand; if the contrary, they will not. Mankind are not now to be told they shall not think, or they shall not read; and publications that go no further than to investigate principles of government, to invite men to reason and to reflect, and to shew the errors and excellences of different systems, have a right to appear. If they do not excite attention, they are not worth the trouble of a prosecution; and if they do, the prosecution will amount to nothing, since it cannot amount to a prohibition of reading.

This would be a sentence on the public, instead of the author, and would also be the most effectual mode of making or hastening revolutions.

On all cases that apply universally to a nation, with respect to systems of government, a jury of *twelve* men is not competent to decide. When there are no witnesses to be examined, no facts to be proved, and where the whole matter is before the whole public, and the merits or demerits of it resting on their opinion; and where there is nothing to be known in a court, but what every body knows out of it, every twelve men is equally as good a jury as the other, and would most probably reverse each other's verdict; or from the variety of their opinions, not be able to form one. It is one case, whether a nation approve a work, or a plan; but it is quite another case, whether it will commit to any such jury the power of determining whether that nation have a right to, or shall reform its government, or not. I mention those cases, that Mr. Burke may see I have not written on Government without reflecting on what is Law, as well as on what are Rights.—The only effectual jury in such cases would be, a convention of the whole nation fairly elected; for in all such cases the whole nation is the vicinage. If Mr. Burke will propose such a jury, I will wave all privileges of being the citizen of another country, and, defending its principles, abide the issue, provided he will do the same; for my opinion is, that his work and his principles would be condemned instead of mine.

As to the prejudices which men have from education and habit, in favour of any particular form or system of government, those prejudices have yet to stand the test of reason and reflection. In fact, such prejudices are nothing. No man is prejudiced in favour of a thing, knowing it to be wrong. He is attached to it on the belief of its being right; and when he see it is not so, the prejudice will be gone. We have but a defective idea of what prejudice is. It might be said, that until men think for themselves the whole is prejudice, and *not opinion;* for that only is opinion which is the result of reason and reflection. I offer this remark, that Mr. Burke may not confide too much in what has been the customary prejudices of the country.

I do not believe that the people of England have ever been fairly and candidly dealt by. They have been imposed upon by parties, and by men assuming the character of leaders. It is time that the nation should rise above those trifles. It is time to dismiss that inattention which has so long been the encouraging cause of stretching taxation to excess. It is time to dismiss all those songs and toasts which are calculated to enslave, and operate to suffocate reflection. On all such subjects men have but to think, and they will neither act wrong nor be misled. To say that any people are not fit for freedom, is to make poverty their choice, and to say they had rather be loaded with taxes than not. If such a case could be proved, it would equally prove, that those who govern are not fit to govern them, for they are a part of the same national mass.

But admitting governments to be changed all over Europe; it certainly may be done without convulsion or revenge. It is not worth making changes or revolutions, unless it be for some great national benefit; and when this shall appear to a nation, the danger will be, as in America and France, to those who oppose; and with this reflection I close my Preface.

THOMAS PAINE.
London, Feb. 9, 1792.

INTRODUCTION

What Archimedes[1] said of the mechanical powers, may be applied to Reason and Liberty: "*Had we,*" said he, "*a place to stand upon, we might raise the world.*"

The revolution of America presented in politics what was only theory in mechanics. So deeply rooted were all the governments of the old world, and so effectually had the tyranny and the antiquity of habit established itself over the mind, that no beginning could be made in Asia, Africa, or Europe, to reform the political condition of man. Freedom had been hunted round the globe; reason was considered as rebellion; and the slavery of fear had made men afraid to think.

But such is the irresistible nature of truth, that all it asks, and all it wants, is the liberty of appearing. The sun needs no inscription to distinguish him from darkness; and no sooner did the American governments display themselves to the world, than despotism felt a shock, and man began to contemplate redress.

The independence of America, considered merely as a separation from England, would have been a matter but of little importance, had it not been accompanied by a revolution in the principles and practice of governments. She made a stand, not for herself only, but for the world, and looked beyond the advantages herself could receive. Even the Hessian, though hired to fight against her, may live to bless his defeat; and England, condemning the viciousness of its government, rejoice in its miscarriage.

As America was the only spot in the political world, where the principles of universal reformation could begin, so also was it the best in the natural world. An assemblage of circumstances conspired not only to give birth, but to add gigantic maturity to its principles. The scene which that country presents to the eye of a spectator, has something in it which generates and encourages great ideas. Nature appears to him in magnitude. The mighty objects he beholds, act upon his mind by enlarging it, and he partakes of the greatness he contemplates.—Its first settlers were emigrants from different European nations, and of diversified professions of religion, retiring from the governmental persecutions of the old world, and meeting in the new, not as enemies, but as brothers. The wants which necessarily accompany the cultivation of a wilderness produced among them a state of society, which countries, long harassed by the quarrels and intrigues of governments, had neglected to cherish. In such a situation man becomes what he ought. He sees his species, not with the inhuman idea of a natural enemy, but as kindred; and the example shews to the artificial world, that man must go back to Nature for information.

From the rapid progress which America makes in every species of improvement, it is rational to conclude, that if the governments of Asia, Africa, and Europe, had begun on a principle similar to that of America, or had not been very early corrupted therefrom, that those countries must by this time have been in a far superior condition to what they are. Age after age has passed away, for no other purpose than to behold their wretchedness.—Could we suppose a spectator who knew nothing of the world, and who was put into it merely to make his observations, he would take a great part of the old world to be new, just struggling with the difficulties and hardships of an instant settlement. He could not suppose that the hordes of miserable poor, with which old countries abound, could be any other than those who had not yet had time to provide for themselves. Little would he think they were the consequence of what in such countries is called government.

If, from the more wretched parts of the old world, we look at those which are in an advanced stage of improvement, we still find the greedy hand of government thrusting itself into every corner and crevice of industry, and grasping the spoil of the multitude. Invention is continually exercised, to furnish new pretences for revenue and taxation. It watches prosperity as its prey, and permits none to escape without a tribute.

As revolutions have begun, (and as the probability is always greater against a thing beginning, than of proceeding after it has begun), it is natural to expect that other revolutions will follow. The amazing and still increasing expences with which old governments are conducted, the numerous wars they engage in or provoke, the embarrassments they throw in the way of universal civilization and commerce, and the oppression and usurpation they act at home, have wearied out the patience, and exhausted the property of the world. In such a situation, and with the examples already existing, revolutions are to be looked for. They are become subjects of universal conversation, and may be considered as the *Order of the day*.

If systems of government can be introduced, less expensive, and more productive of general happiness, than those which have existed, all attempts to oppose their progress will in the end be fruitless. Reason, like time, will make its own way, and prejudice will fall in a combat with interest. If universal peace, civilization, and commerce, are ever to be the happy lot of man, it cannot be accomplished but by a revolution in the system of governments. All the monarchical governments are military. War is their trade, plunder and revenue their objects. While such governments continue, peace has not the absolute security of a day. What is the history of all monarchical governments, but a disgustful picture of human wretchedness, and the accidental respite of a few years repose? Wearied with war, and tired with human butchery, they sat down to rest and called it peace. This certainly is not the condition that Heaven intended for man; and if *this be monarchy*, well might monarchy be reckoned among the sins of the Jews.

The revolutions which formerly took place in the world, had nothing in them that interested the bulk of mankind. They extended only to a change of persons and measures but not of principles, and rose or fell among the common transactions of the moment. What we now behold, may not improperly be called a *"counter revolution."* Conquest and tyranny, at some early period, dispossessed man of his rights, and he is now recovering them. And as the tide of all human affairs has its ebb and flow in directions contrary to each other, so also is it in this. Government founded on a *moral theory, on a system of universal peace, on the indefensible hereditary Rights of Man,* is now revolving from west to east, by a stronger impulse than the government of the sword revolved from east to west. It interests not particular individuals, but nations, in its progress, and promises a new æra to the human race.

The danger to which the success of revolutions is most exposed, is that of attempting them before the principles on which they proceed, and the advantages to result from them, are sufficiently seen and understood. Almost every thing appertaining to the circumstances of a nation, has been absorbed and confounded under the general and mysterious word *government.* Though it avoids taking to its account the errors it commits, and the mischiefs it occasions, it fails not to arrogate to itself whatever has the appearance of prosperity. It robs industry of its honours, by pedanticly making itself the cause of its effects; and purloins from the general character of man, the merits that appertain to him as a social being.

It may therefore be of use, in this day of revolutions, to discriminate between those things which are the effect of government, and those which are not. This will best be done by taking a review of society and civilization, and the consequences resulting therefrom, as things distinct from what are called governments. By beginning with this investigation, we shall be able to assign effects to their proper cause, and analize the mass of common errors.

CHAPTER I:

OF SOCIETY AND CIVILIZATION

Great part of that order which reigns among mankind is not the effect of government. It has its origin in the principles of society and the natural constitution of man. It existed prior to government, and would exist if the formality of government was abolished. The mutual dependance and reciprocal interest which man has upon man, and all the parts of a civilized community upon each other, create that great chain of connection which holds it together. The landholder, the farmer, the manufacturer, the merchant, the tradesman, and every occupation, prospers by the aid which each receives from the other, and from the whole. Common interest regulates their concerns, and forms their law; and the laws which common usage ordains, have a greater influence than the laws of government. In fine, society performs for itself almost every thing which is ascribed to government.

To understand the nature and quantity of government proper for man, it is necessary to attend to his character. As Nature created him for social life, she fitted him for the station she intended. In all cases she made his natural wants greater than his individual powers. No one man is capable, without the aid of society, of supplying his own wants; and those wants, acting upon every individual, impel the whole of them into society, as naturally as gravitation acts to a center.

But she has gone further. She has not only forced man into society, by a diversity of wants, which the reciprocal aid of each other can supply, but she has implanted in him a system of social affections, which, though not necessary to his existence, are essential to his happiness. There is no period in life when this love for society ceases to act. It begins and ends with our being.

If we examine, with attention, into the composition and constitution of man, the diversity of his wants, and the diversity of talents in different men for reciprocally accommodating the wants of each other, his propensity to society, and consequently to preserve the advantages resulting from it, we shall easily discover, that a great part of what is called government is mere imposition.

Government is no farther necessary than to supply the few cases to which society and civilization are not conveniently competent; and instances are not wanting to shew, that every thing which government can usefully add thereto, has been performed by the common consent of society, without government.

For upwards of two years from the commencement of the American war, and to a longer period in several of the American States, there were no established forms of government. The old governments had been abolished, and the country was too much occupied in defence, to employ its attention to establishing new governments; yet during this interval, order and harmony were preserved as inviolate as in any country in Europe. There is a natural aptness in man, and more so in society, because it embraces a greater variety of abilities and resource, to accommodate itself to whatever situation it is in. The instant formal government is abolished, society begins to act. A general association takes place, and common interest produces common security.

So far is it from being true, as has been pretended, that the abolition of any formal government is the dissolution of society, that it acts by a contrary impulse, and brings the latter the closer together. All that part of its organization which it had committed to its government, devolves again upon itself, and acts through its medium. When men, as well from natural instinct, as from reciprocal benefits, have habituated themselves to social and civilized life, there is always enough of its principles in practice to carry them through to make any changes they may find necessary or convenient to make in their government. In short, man is so naturally a creature of society, that it is almost impossible to put him out of it.

Formal government makes but a small part of civilized life; and when even the best that human wisdom can devise is established, it is a thing more in name and idea, than in fact. It is to the great and fundamental principles of society and civilization—to the common usage universally consented to, and mutually and reciprocally maintained—to the unceasing circulation of interest, which, passing through its million channels, invigorates the whole mass of civilized man—it is to these things, infinitely more than to any thing which even the best instituted government can perform, that the safety and prosperity of the individual and of the whole depends.

The more perfect civilization is, the less occasion has it for government, because the more does it regulate its own affairs, and govern itself; but so contrary is the practice of old governments to the reason of the case, that the expences of them increase in the proportion they ought to diminish. It is but few general laws that civilized life requires, and those of such common usefulness, that whether they are enforced by the forms of government or not, the effect will be nearly the same. If we consider what the principles are that first condense men into society, and what the motives that regulate their mutual intercourse afterwards, we shall find, by the time we arrive at what is called government, that nearly the whole of the business is performed by the natural operation of the parts upon each other.

Man, with respect to all those matters, is more a creature of consistency than he is aware, or that governments would wish him to believe. All the great laws of society are laws of nature. Those of trade and commerce, whether with respect to the intercourse of individuals, or of nations, are laws of mutual and reciprocal interest. They are followed and obeyed, because it is the interest of the parties so to do, and not on account of any formal laws their governments may impose or interpose.

But how often is the natural propensity to society disturbed or destroyed by the operations of government! When the latter, instead of being ingrafted on the principles of the former, assumes to exist for itself, and acts by partialities of favour and oppression, it becomes the cause of the mischiefs it ought to prevent.

If we look back to the riots and tumults, which at various times have happened in England, we shall find, that they did not proceed from the want of a government, but that government was itself the generating cause; instead of consolidating society it divided it; it deprived it of its natural cohesion, and engendered discontents and disorders, which otherwise would not have existed. In those associations which men promiscuously form for the purpose of trade, or of any concern, in which government is totally out of the question, and in which they act merely on the principles of society, we see how naturally the various parties unite; and this shews, by comparison, that governments, so far from being always the cause or means of order, are often the destruction of it. The riots of 1780[2] had no other source than the remains of those prejudices, which the government itself had encouraged. But with respect to England there are also other causes.

Excess and inequality of taxation, however disguised in the means, never fail to appear in their effects. As a great mass of the community are thrown thereby into poverty and discontent, they are constantly on the brink of commotion; and, deprived, as they unfortunately are, of the means of information, are easily heated to outrage. Whatever the apparent cause of any riots may be, the real one is always want of happiness. It shews that something is wrong in the system of government, that injures the felicity by which society is to be preserved.

But as fact is superior to reasoning, the instance of America presents itself to confirm these observations.—If there is a country in the world, where concord, according to common calculation, would be least expected, it is America. Made up, as it is, of people from different nations*, accustomed to different forms and habits of government, speaking different languages, and more different in their modes of worship, it would appear that the union of such a people was impracticable; but by the simple operation of constructing government on the principles of society and the rights of man, every difficulty retires, and all the parts are brought into cordial unison. There, the poor are not oppressed, the rich are not privileged. Industry is not mortified by the splendid extravagance of a court rioting at its expence. Their taxes are few, because their government is just: and as there is nothing to render them wretched, there is nothing to engender riots and tumults.

A metaphysical man, like Mr. Burke, would have tortured his invention to discover how such a people could be governed. He would have supposed that some must be managed by fraud, others by force, and all by some contrivance; that genius must be hired to impose upon ignorance, and shew and parade to fascinate the vulgar. Lost in the abundance of his researches, he would have resolved and re-resolved, and finally overlooked the plain and easy road that lay directly before him.

One of the great advantages of the American revolution has been, that it led to a discovery of the principles, and laid open the imposition of governments. All the revolutions till then had been worked within the atmosphere of a court, and never on the great floor of a nation. The parties were always of the class of courtiers; and whatever was their rage for reformation, they carefully preserved the fraud of the profession.

In all cases they took care to represent government as a thing made up of mysteries, which only themselves understood; and they hid from the understanding of the nation, the only thing that was beneficial to

---

* That part of America which is generally called New-England, including New-Hampshire, Massachusetts, Rhode-Island, and Connecticut, is peopled chiefly by English descendants. In the state of New-York, about half are Dutch, the rest English, Scotch, and Irish. In New-Jersey, a mixture of English and Dutch, with some Scotch and Irish. In Pennsylvania, about one third are English, another Germans, and the remainder Scotch and Irish, with some Swedes. The States to the southward have a greater proportion of English than the middle States, but in all of them there is a mixture; and besides those enumerated, there are a considerable number of French, and some few of all the European nations lying on the coast. The most numerous religious denomination are the Presbyterians; but no one sect is established above another, and all men are equally citizens.

know, namely, *That government is nothing more than a national association acting on the principles of society.*

———

Having thus endeavoured to shew, that the social and civilized state of man is capable of performing within itself, almost every thing necessary to its protection and government, it will be proper, on the other hand, to take a review of the present old governments, and examine whether their principles and practice are correspondent thereto.

CHAPTER II:
OF THE ORIGIN OF THE PRESENT OLD GOVERNMENTS

It is impossible that such governments as have hitherto existed in the world, could have commenced by any other means than a total violation of every principle sacred and moral. The obscurity in which the origin of all the present old governments is buried, implies the iniquity and disgrace with which they began. The origin of the present government of America and France will ever be remembered, because it is honourable to record it; but with respect to the rest, even Flattery has consigned them to the tomb of time, without an inscription.

It could have been no difficult thing in the early and solitary ages of the world, while the chief employment of men was that of attending flocks and herds, for a banditti of ruffians to overrun a country, and lay it under contributions. Their power being thus established, the chief of the band contrived to lose the name of Robber in that of Monarch; and hence the origin of Monarchy and Kings.

The origin of the government of England, so far as relates to what is called its line of monarchy, being one of the latest, is perhaps the best recorded. The hatred which the Norman invasion and tyranny begat, must have been deeply rooted in the nation, to have outlived the contrivance to obliterate it. Though not a courtier will talk of the cur-feu bell, not a village in England has forgotten it.

Those bands of robbers having parcelled out the world and divided it into dominions, began, as is naturally the case, to quarrel with each other. What at first was obtained by violence, was considered by others as lawful to be taken, and a second plunderer succeeded the first. They alternately invaded the dominions which each had assigned to himself, and the brutality with which they treated each other explains the original character of monarchy. It was ruffian torturing ruffian. The conqueror considered the conquered, not as his prisoner, but his property. He led him in triumph rattling in chains, and doomed him, at pleasure, to slavery or death. As time obliterated the history of their beginning, their successors assumed new appearances, to cut off the entail of their disgrace, but their principles and objects remained the same. What at first was plunder, assumed the softer name of revenue; and the power originally usurped, they affected to inherit.

From such beginning of governments, what could be expected, but a continual system of war and extortion? It has established itself into a trade. The vice is not peculiar to one more than to another, but is the common principle of all. There does not exist within such governments, a stamina whereon to ingraft reformation; and the shortest and most effectual remedy is to begin anew.

What scenes of horror, what perfection of iniquity, present themselves in contemplating the character, and reviewing the history of such governments! If we would delineate human nature with a baseness of heart, and hypocrisy of countenance, that reflection would shudder at and humanity disown, it is kings, courts, and cabinets, that must sit for the portrait. Man, naturally as he is, with all his faults about him, is not up to the character.

Can we possibly suppose that if governments had originated in a right principle, and had not an interest in pursuing a wrong one, that the world could have been in the wretched and quarrelsome condition we have seen it? What inducement has the farmer, while following the plough, to lay aside his peaceful pursuits, and go to war with the farmer of another country? or what inducement has the manufacturer? What is dominion to them, or to any class of men in a nation? Does it add an acre to any man's estate, or raise its value? Are not conquest and defeat each of the same price, and taxes the never-failing consequence?—Though this reasoning may be good to a nation, it is not so to a government. War is the Pharo table of governments, and nations the dupes of the game.

If there is any thing to wonder at in this miserable scene of governments, more than might be expected, it is the progress which the peaceful arts of agriculture, manufacture and commerce have made, beneath such a long accumulating load of discouragement and oppression. It serves to shew, that instinct in animals does not act with stronger impulse, than the principles of society and civilization operate in man. Under all discouragements, he pursues his object, and yields to nothing but impossibilities.

CHAPTER III:
OF THE OLD AND NEW SYSTEMS
OF GOVERNMENT

Nothing can appear more contradictory than the principles on which the old governments began, and the condition to which society, civilization, and commerce, are capable of carrying mankind. Government on the old system, is an assumption of power, for the aggrandisement of itself; on the new, a delegation of power, for the common benefit of society. The former supports itself by keeping up a system of war; the latter promotes a system of peace, as the true means of enriching a nation. The one encourages national prejudices; the other promotes universal society, as the means of universal commerce. The one measures its prosperity, by the quantity of revenue it extorts; the other proves its excellence, by the small quantity of taxes it requires.

Mr. Burke has talked of old and new whigs. If he can amuse himself with childish names and distinctions, I shall not interrupt his pleasure. It is not to him, but to the Abbé Sieyes,[3] that I address this chapter. I am already engaged to the latter gentleman, to discuss the subject of monarchial government; and as it naturally occurs in comparing the old and new systems, I make this the opportunity of presenting to him my observations. I shall occasionally take Mr. Burke in my way.

Though it might be proved that the system of government now called the NEW, is the most ancient in principle of all that have existed, being founded on the original inherent Rights of Man: yet, as tyranny and the sword have suspended the exercise of those rights for many centuries past, it serves better the purpose of distinction to call it the *new*, than to claim the right of calling it the old.

The first general distinction between those two systems, is, that the one now called the old is *hereditary*, either in whole or in part; and the new is entirely *representative*. It rejects all hereditary government:

First, As being an imposition on mankind.

Secondly, As inadequate to the purposes for which government is necessary.

With respect to the first of these heads—It cannot be proved by what right hereditary government could begin: neither does there exist within the compass of mortal power, a right to establish it. Man has no authority over posterity in matters of personal right; and therefore, no man, or body of men, had, or can have, a right to set up hereditary government. Were even ourselves to come again into existence, instead of being succeeded by posterity, we have not now the right of taking from ourselves the rights which would then be ours. On what ground, then, do we pretend to take them from others?

All hereditary government is in its nature tyranny. An heritable crown, or an heritable throne, or by what other fanciful name such things may be called, have no other significant explanation than that mankind are heritable property. To inherit a government, is to inherit the people, as if they were flocks and herds.

With respect to the second head, that of being inadequate to the purposes for which government is necessary, we have only to consider what government essentially is, and compare it with the circumstances to which hereditary succession is subject.

Government ought to be a thing always in full maturity. It ought to be so constructed as to be superior to all the accidents to which individual man is subject; and therefore, hereditary succession, by being *subject to them all*, is the most irregular and imperfect of all the systems of government.

We have heard the *Rights of Man* called a *levelling* system; but the only system to which the word *levelling* is truly applicable, is the hereditary monarchical system. It is a system of *mental levelling*. It indiscriminately admits every species of character to the same authority. Vice and virtue, ignorance and wisdom, in short, every quality, good or bad, is put on the same level. Kings succeed each other, not as rationals, but as animals. It signifies not what their mental or moral characters are. Can we then be surprised at the abject state of the human mind in monarchical countries, when the government itself is formed on such an abject levelling system?—It has no fixed character. To-day it is one thing; to-morrow it is something else. It changes with the temper of every succeeding individual, and is subject to all the varieties of each. It is government through the medium of passions and accidents. It appears under all the various characters of childhood, decrepitude, dotage, a thing at nurse, in leading-strings, or in crutches. It reverses the wholesome order of nature. It occasionally puts children over men, and the conceits of non-age over wisdom and experience. In short, we cannot conceive a more ridiculous figure of government, than hereditary succession, in all its cases, presents.

Could it be made a decree in nature, or an edict registered in heaven, and man could know it, that virtue and wisdom should invariably appertain to hereditary succession, the objections to it would be removed; but when we see that nature acts as if she disowned and sported with the hereditary system; that the mental characters of successors, in all countries, are below the average of human understanding; that one is a tyrant, another an ideot, a third insane, and some all three together, it is impossible to attach confidence to it, when reason in man has power to act.

It is not to the Abbé Sieyes that I need apply this reasoning; he has already saved me that trouble, by giving his own opinion upon the case. "If it be asked," says he, "what is my opinion with respect to hereditary right, I answer, without hesitation, That, in good theory, and hereditary transmission of any power or office, can never accord with the laws of a true representation. Hereditaryship is, in this sense, as much an attaint upon principle, as an outrage upon society. But let us," continues he, "refer to the history of all elective monarchies and principalities: Is there one in which the elective mode is not worse than the hereditary succession?"

As to debating on which is the worst of the two, is admitting both to be bad; and herein we are agreed. The preference which the Abbé has given is a condemnation of the thing that he prefers. Such a mode of reasoning on such a subject is inadmissible, because it finally amounts to an accusation upon Providence, as if she had left to man no other choice with respect to government than between two evils, the best of which he admits to be "*an attaint upon principle, and an outrage upon society.*"

Passing over, for the present, all the evils and mischiefs which monarchy has occasioned in the world, nothing can more effectually

prove its uselessness in a state of *civil government,* than making it hereditary. Would we make any office hereditary that required wisdom and
abilities to fill it? and where wisdom and abilities are not necessary,
such an office, whatever it may be, is superfluous or insignificant.

Hereditary succession is a burlesque upon monarchy. It puts it in
the most ridiculous light, by presenting it as an office which any child
or ideot may fill. It requires some talents to be a common mechanic;
but, to be a king, requires only the animal figure of man—a sort of
breathing automaton. This sort of superstition may last a few years
more, but it cannot long resist the awakened reason and interest of
man.

As to Mr. Burke, he is a stickler for monarchy, not altogether as a
pensioner, if he is one, which I believe, but as a political man. He has
taken up a contemptible opinion of mankind, who, in their turn, are
taking up the same of him. He considers them as a herd of beings that
must be governed by fraud, effigy and shew; and an idol would be as
good a figure of monarchy with him, as a man. I will, however, do him
the justice to say, that, with respect to America, he has been very com-
plimentary. He always contended, at least in my hearing, that the people of America were more enlightened than those of England, or of
any country in Europe; and that therefore the imposition of shew was
not necessary in their governments.

Though the comparison between hereditary and elective monarchy, which the Abbé has made, is unnecessary to the case, because the
representative system rejects both; yet, were I to make the comparison,
I should decide contrary to what he has done.

The civil wars which have originated from contested hereditary
claims, are more numerous, and have been more dreadful, and of
longer continuance, than those which have been occasioned by election. All the civil wars in France arose from the hereditary system; they
were either produced by hereditary claims, or by the imperfection of
the hereditary form, which admits of regencies, or monarchy at nurse.
With respect to England, its history is full of the same misfortunes.
The contests for succession between the Houses of York and Lancaster, lasted a whole century; and others of a similar nature, have renewed themselves since that period. Those of 1715 and 1745,[4] were of
the same kind. The succession war for the crown of Spain,[5] embroiled
almost half Europe. The disturbances in Holland are generated from

the hereditaryship of the Stadtholder. A government calling itself free, with an hereditary office, is like a thorn in the flesh, that produces a fermentation which endeavours to discharge it.

But I might go further, and place also foreign wars, of whatever kind, to the same cause. It is by adding the evil of hereditary succession to that of monarchy, that a permanent family-interest is created, whose constant objects are dominion and revenue. Poland, though an elective monarchy, has had fewer wars than those which are hereditary; and it is the only government that has made a voluntary essay, though but a small one, to reform the condition of the country.

Having thus glanced at a few of the defects of the old, or hereditary systems of government, let us compare it with the new, or representative system.

The representative system takes society and civilization for its basis; nature, reason, and experience, for its guide.

Experience, in all ages, and in all countries, has demonstrated, that it is impossible to controul Nature in her distribution of mental powers. She gives them as she pleases. Whatever is the rule by which she, apparently to us, scatters them among mankind, that rule remains a secret to man. It would be as ridiculous to attempt to fix the hereditaryship of human beauty, as of wisdom. Whatever wisdom constituently is, it is like a seedless plant; it may be reared when it appears, but it cannot be voluntarily produced. There is always a sufficiency somewhere in the general mass of society for all purposes; but with respect to the parts of society, it is continually changing its place. It rises in one to-day, in another to-morrow, and has most probably visited in rotation every family of the earth, and again withdrawn.

As this is the order of nature, the order of government must necessarily follow it, or government will, as we see it does, degenerate into ignorance. The hereditary system, therefore, is as repugnant to human wisdom, as to human rights; and is as absurd, as it is unjust.

As the republic of letters[6] brings forward the best literary productions, by giving to genius a fair and universal chance; so the representative system of government is calculated to produce the wisest laws, by collecting wisdom from where it can be found. I smile to myself when I contemplate the ridiculous insignificance into which literature and all the sciences would sink, were they made hereditary; and I carry the same idea into governments. An hereditary governor is as inconsistent as an hereditary author. I know not whether Homer or Euclid had sons: but I will venture an opinion, that if they had, and had left their works unfinished, those sons could not have completed them.

Do we need a stronger evidence of the absurdity of hereditary government, than is seen in the descendants of those men, in any line of life, who once were famous? Is there scarcely an instance in which there is not a total reverse of the character? It appears as if the tide of mental faculties flowed as far as it could in certain channels, and then forsook its course, and arose in others. How irrational then is the hereditary system which establishes channels of power, in company with which wisdom refuses to flow! By continuing this absurdity, man is perpetually in contradiction with himself; he accepts, for a king, or a chief magistrate, or a legislator, a person whom he would not elect for a constable.

It appears to general observation, that revolutions create genius and talents; but those events do no more than bring them forward. There is existing in man, a mass of sense lying in a dormant state, and which, unless something excites it to action, will descend with him, in that condition, to the grave. As it is to the advantage of society that the whole of its faculties should be employed, the construction of government ought to be such as to bring forward, by a quiet and regular operation, all that extent of capacity which never fails to appear in revolutions.

This cannot take place in the insipid state of hereditary government, not only because it prevents, but because it operates to benumb. When the mind of a nation is bowed down by any political superstition in its government, such as hereditary succession is, it loses a considerable portion of its powers on all other subjects and objects. Hereditary succession requires the same obedience to ignorance, as to wisdom; and when once the mind can bring itself to pay this indiscriminate reverence, it descends below the stature of mental manhood. It is fit to be great only in little things. It acts a treachery upon itself, and suffocates the sensations that urge to detection.

Though the ancient governments present to us a miserable picture of the condition of man, there is one which above all others exempts itself from the general description. I mean the democracy of the Athenians. We see more to admire, and less to condemn, in that great, extraordinary people, than in any thing which history affords.

Mr. Burke is so little acquainted with constituent principles of government, that he confounds democracy and representation together. Representation was a thing unknown in the ancient democracies. In those the mass of the people met and enacted laws (grammatically speaking) in the first person. Simple democracy was no other than the common-hall of the ancients. It signifies the *form*, as well as the public principle of the government. As these democracies increased in population, and the territory extended, the simple democratical form became unwieldy and impracticable; and as the system of representation was not known, the consequence was they either degenerated convulsively into monarchies, or became absorbed into such as then existed. Had the system of representation been then understood, as it now is, there is no reason to believe that those forms of government, now called monarchical or aristocratical, would ever have taken place. It was the want of some method to consolidate the parts of society, after it became too populous, and too extensive for the simple democratical form, and also the lax and solitary condition of shepherds and herdsmen in other parts of the world, that afforded opportunities to those unnatural modes of government to begin.

As it is necessary to clear away the rubbish of errors, into which the subject of government has been thrown, I shall proceed to remark on some others.

It has always been the political craft of courtiers and court-governments, to abuse something which they called republicanism; but what republicanism was, or is, they never attempt to explain. Let us examine a little into this case.

The only forms of government are, the democratical, the aristocratical, the monarchical, and what is now called the representative.

What is called a *republic*, is not any *particular form* of government. It is wholly characteristical of the purport, matter, or object for which government ought to be instituted, and on which it is to be employed, RES-PUBLICA, the public affairs, or the public good; or, literally translated, the *public thing*. It is a word of a good original, referring to what ought to be the character and business of government; and in this sense it is naturally opposed to the word *monarchy*, which has a base original signification. It means arbitrary power in an individual person; in the exercise of which, *himself*, and not the *res-publica*, is the object.

Every government that does not act on the principle of a *Republic*, or in other words, that does not make the *res-publica* its whole and sole object, is not a good government. Republican government is no other than government established and conducted for the interest of the public, as well individually as collectively. It is not necessarily connected with any particular form, but it most naturally associates with the representative form, as being best calculated to secure the end for which a nation is at the expence of supporting it.

Various forms of government have affected to style themselves a republic. Poland calls itself a republic, which is an hereditary aristocracy, with what is called an elective monarchy. Holland calls itself a republic, which is chiefly aristocratical, with an hereditary stadtholdership. But the government of America, which is wholly on the system of representation, is the only real republic in character and in practice, that now exists. Its government has no other object than the public business of the nation, and therefore it is properly a republic; and the Americans have taken care of THIS, and no other, shall always be the object of their government, by their rejecting every thing hereditary, and establishing government on the system of representation only.

Those who have said that a republic is not a *form* of government calculated for countries of great extent, mistook, in the first place, the *business* of a government, for a *form* of government; for the *res-publica* equally appertains to every extent of territory and population. And, in the second place, if they meant any thing with respect to *form,* it was the simple democratical form, such as was the mode of government in the ancient democracies, in which there was no representation. The case, therefore, is not, that a republic cannot be extensive, but that it cannot be extensive on the simple democratical form; and the question naturally presents itself, *What is the best form of government for conducting the* RES-PUBLICA, *or the* PUBLIC BUSINESS *of a nation, after it becomes too extensive and populous for the simple democratical form?*

It cannot be monarchy, because monarchy is subject to an objection of the same amount to which the simple democratical form was subject.

It is possible that an individual may lay down a system of principles, on which government shall be constitutionally established to any extent of territory. This is no more than an operation of the mind, acting by its own powers. But the practice upon those principles, as applying to the various and numerous circumstances of a nation, its agriculture, manufacture, trade, commerce, &c. &c. requires a knowledge of a different kind, and which can be had only from the various parts of society. It is an assemblage of practical knowledge, which no one individual can possess; and therefore the monarchical form is as much limited, in useful practice, from the incompetency of knowledge, as was the democratical form, from the multiplicity of population. The one degenerates, by extension, into confusion; the other, into ignorance and incapacity, of which all the great monarchies are an evidence. The monarchical form, therefore, could not be a substitute for the democratical, because it has equal inconveniences.

Much less could it when made hereditary. This is the most effectual of all forms to preclude knowledge. Neither could the high democratical mind have voluntarily yielded itself to be governed by children and idiots, and all the motley insignificance of character, which attends such a mere animal-system, the disgrace and the reproach of reason and of man.

As to the aristocratical form, it has the same vices and defects with the monarchical, except that the chance of abilities is better from the proportion of numbers, but there is still no security for the right use and application of them*.

Referring, then, to the original simple democracy, it affords the true data from which government on a large scale can begin. It is incapable of extension, not from its principle, but from the inconvenience of its form; and monarchy and aristocracy, from their incapacity. Retaining, then, democracy as the ground, and rejecting the corrupt systems of monarchy and aristocracy, the representative system naturally presents itself; remedying at once the defects of the simple democracy as to form, and the incapacity of the other two with respect to knowledge.

Simple democracy was society governing itself without the aid of secondary means. By ingrafting representation upon democracy, we arrive at a system of government capable of embracing and confederating all the various interests and every extent of territory and population; and that also with advantages as much superior to hereditary government, as the republic of letters is to hereditary literature.

It is on this system that the American government is founded. It is

---

* For a character of aristocracy, the reader is referred to *Rights of Man*, Part I. Page 70.

representation ingrafted upon democracy. It has fixed the form by a scale parallel in all cases to the extent of the principle. What Athens was in miniature, America will be in magnitude. The one was the wonder of the ancient world; the other is becoming the admiration and model of the present. It is the easiest of all the forms of government to be understood, and the most eligible in practice; and excludes at once the ignorance and insecurity of the hereditary mode, and the inconvenience of the simple democracy.

It is impossible to conceive a system of government capable of acting over such an extent of territory, and such a circle of interests, as is immediately produced by the operation of representation. France, great and populous as it is, is but a spot in the capaciousness of the system. It adapts itself to all possible cases. It is preferable to simple democracy even in small territories. Athens, by representation, would have outrivalled her own democracy.

That which is called government, or rather that which we ought to conceive government to be, is no more than some common center, in which all the parts of society unite. This cannot be accomplished by any method so conducive to the various interests of the community, as by the representative system. It concentrates the knowledge necessary to the interest of the parts, and of the whole. It places government in a state of constant maturity. It is, as has been already observed, never young, never old. It is subject neither to nonage, nor dotage. It is never in the cradle, nor on crutches. It admits not of a separation between knowledge and power, and is superior, as government always ought to be, to all the accidents of individual man, and is therefore superior to what is called monarchy.

A nation is not a body, the figure of which is to be represented by the human body; but is like a body contained within a circle, having a common center, in which every radius meets; and that center is formed by representation. To connect representation with what is called monarchy, is eccentric government. Representation is of itself the delegated monarchy of a nation, and cannot debase itself by dividing it with another.

Mr. Burke has two or three times, in his parliamentary speeches, and in his publications, made use of a jingle of words that convey no ideas. Speaking of government, he says, "It is better to have monarchy for its basis, and republicanism for its corrective, than republicanism for its basis, and monarchy for its corrective."—If he means that it is better to correct folly with wisdom, than wisdom with folly, I will no otherwise contend with him, than that it would be much better to reject the folly entirely.

But what is this thing which Mr. Burke calls monarchy? Will he explain it? All men can understand what representation is; and that it must necessarily include a variety of knowledge and talents. But, what security is there for the same qualities on the part of monarchy? or, when this monarchy is a child, where then is the wisdom? What does it know about government? Who then is the monarch, or where is the monarchy? If it is to be performed by regency, it proves it to be a farce. A regency is a mock species of republic, and the whole of monarchy deserves no better description. It is a thing as various as imagination can paint. It has none of the stable character that government ought to possess. Every succession is a revolution, and every regency a counter-revolution. The whole of it is a scene of perpetual court cabal and intrigue, of which Mr. Burke is himself an instance. To render monarchy consistent with government, the next in succession should not be born a child, but a man at once, and that man a Solomon. It is ridiculous that nations are to wait, and government be interrupted, till boys grow to be men.

Whether I have too little sense to see, or too much to be imposed upon; whether I have too much or too little pride, or of any thing else, I leave out of the question; but certain it is, that what is called monarchy, always appears to me a silly, contemptible thing. I compare it to something kept behind a curtain, about which there is a great deal of bustle and fuss, and a wonderful air of seeming solemnity; but when, by any accident, the curtain happens to be open, and the company see what it is, they burst into laughter.

In the representative system of government, nothing of this can happen. Like the nation itself, it possesses a perpetual stamina, as well of body as of mind, and presents itself on the open theatre of the world in a fair and manly manner. Whatever are its excellences or its defects, they are visible to all. It exists not by fraud and mystery; it deals not in cant and sophistry; but inspires a language, that, passing from heart to heart, is felt and understood.

We must shut our eyes against reason, we must basely degrade our understanding, not to see the folly of what is called monarchy. Nature is orderly in all her works; but this is a mode of government that counteracts nature. It turns the progress of the human faculties upside down. It subjects age to be governed by children, and wisdom by folly.

On the contrary, the representative system is always parallel with the order and immutable laws of nature, and meets the reason of man in every part. For example:

In the American federal government, more power is delegated to the President of the United States, than to any other individual member of congress. He cannot, therefore, be elected to this office under the age of thirty-five years. By this time the judgment of man becomes matured, and he has lived long enough to be acquainted with men and things, and the country with him.—But on the monarchical plan, (exclusive of the numerous chances there are against every man born into the world, of drawing a prize in the lottery of human faculties), the next in succession, whatever he may be, is put at the head of a nation, and of a government, at the age of eighteen years. Does this appear like an act of wisdom? Is it consistent with the proper dignity and the manly character of a nation? Where is the propriety of calling such a lad the father of the people?—In all other cases, a person is a minor until the age of twenty-one years. Before this period, he is not trusted with the management of an acre of land, or with the heritable property of a flock of sheep, or an herd of swine; but, wonderful to tell! he may, at the age of eighteen years, be trusted with a nation.

That monarchy is all a bubble, a mere court artifice to procure money, is evident, (at least to me), in every character in which it can be viewed. It would be impossible, on the rational system of representative government, to make out a bill of expences to such an enormous amount as this deception admits. Government is not of itself a very chargeable institution. The whole expence of the federal government of America, founded, as I have already said, on the system of representation, and extending over a country nearly ten times as large as England, is but six hundred thousand dollars, or one hundred and thirty-five thousand pounds sterling.

I presume, that no man in his sober senses, will compare the character of any of the kings of Europe with that of General Washington. Yet, in France, and also in England, the expence of the civil list[7] only, for the support of one man, is eight times greater than the whole expence of the federal government in America. To assign a reason for this, appears almost impossible. The generality of people in America, especially the poor, are more able to pay taxes, than the generality of people either in France or England.

But the case is, that the representative system diffuses such a body of knowledge throughout a nation, on the subject of government, as to explode ignorance and preclude imposition. The craft of courts cannot be acted on that ground. There is no place for mystery; no where for it to begin. Those who are not in the representation, know as much of the nature of business as those who are. An affectation of mysterious importance would there be scouted. Nations can have no secrets; and the secrets of courts, like those of individuals, are always their defects.

In the representative system, the reason for every thing must publicly appear. Every man is a proprietor in government, and considers it a necessary part of his business to understand. It concerns his interest, because it affects his property. He examines the cost, and compares it with the advantages; and above all, he does not adopt the slavish custom of following what in other governments are called LEADERS.

It can only be by blinding the understanding of man, and making him believe that government is some wonderful mysterious thing, that excessive revenues are obtained. Monarchy is well calculated to ensure this end. It is the popery of government; a thing kept up to amuse the ignorant, and quiet them into taxes.

The government of a free country, properly speaking, is not in the persons, but in the laws. The enacting of those requires no great expence; and when they are administered, the whole of civil government is performed—the rest is all court contrivance.

CHAPTER IV:
OF CONSTITUTIONS

That men mean distinct and separate things when they speak of constitutions and of governments, is evident; or, why are those terms distinctly and separately used? A constitution is not the act of a government, but of a people constituting a government; and government without a constitution, is power without a right.

All power exercised over a nation, must have some beginning. It must be either delegated, or assumed. There are no other sources. All delegated power is trust, and all assumed power is usurpation. Time does not alter the nature and quality of either.

In viewing this subject, the case and circumstances of America present themselves as in the beginning of a world; and our enquiry into the origin of government is shortened, by referring to the facts that have arisen in our own day. We have no occasion to roam for information into the obscure field of antiquity, nor hazard ourselves upon conjecture. We are brought at once to the point of seeing government begin, as if we had lived in the beginning of time. The real volume, not of history, but of facts, is directly before us, unmutilated by contrivance, or the errors of tradition.

I will here concisely state the commencement of the American constitutions; by which the difference between constitutions and governments will sufficiently appear.

It may not be improper to remind the reader, that the United States of America consist of thirteen separate states, each of which established a government for itself, after the declaration of independence, done the fourth of July 1776. Each state acted independently of the rest, in forming its government; but the same general principle pervades the whole. When the several state governments were formed, they proceeded to form the federal government, that acts over the whole in all matters which concern the interest of the whole, or which relate to the intercourse of the several states with each other, or with foreign nations. I will begin with giving an instance from one of the state governments, (that of Pennsylvania), and then proceed to the federal government.

The state of Pennsylvania, though nearly of the same extent of territory as England, was then divided into only twelve counties. Each of those counties had elected a committee at the commencement of the dispute with the English government; and as the city of Philadelphia, which also had its committee, was the most central for intelligence, it became the center of communication to the several county committees. When it became necessary to proceed to the formation of a government, the committee of Philadelphia proposed a conference of all the county committees, to be held in that city, and which met the latter end of July 1776.

Though these committees had been elected by the people, they were not elected expressly for the purpose, nor invested with the authority, of forming a constitution; and as they could not, consistently with the American idea of rights, assume such a power, they could only confer upon the matter, and put it into a train of operation. The conferrees, therefore, did no more than state the case, and recommend to the several counties to elect six representatives for each county, to meet in convention at Philadelphia, with powers to form a constitution,[8] and propose it for public consideration.

This convention, of which Benjamin Franklin was president, having met and deliberated, and agreed upon a constitution, they next ordered it to be published, not as a thing established, but for the consideration of the whole people, their approbation or rejection, and then adjourned to a stated time. When the time of adjournment was expired, the convention re-assembled; and as the general opinion of the people in approbation of it was then known, the constitution was signed, sealed, and proclaimed on the *authority of the people* and the original instrument deposited as a public record. The convention then appointed a day for the general election of the representatives who were to compose the government, and the time it should commence; and having done this, they dissolved, and returned to their several homes and occupations.

In this constitution were laid down, first, a declaration of rights. Then followed the form which the government should have, and the powers it should possess—the authority of the courts of judicature, and of juries—the manner in which elections should be conducted, and the proportion of representatives to the number of electors—the time which each succeeding assembly should continue, which was one year—the mode of levying, and of accounting for the expenditure, of public money—of appointing public officers, &c. &c. &c.

No article of this constitution could be altered or infringed at the discretion of the government that was to ensue. It was to that government a law. But as it would have been unwise to preclude the benefit of experience, and in order also to prevent the accumulation of errors, if any should be found, and to preserve an unison of government with the circumstances of the state at all times, the constitution provided, that, at the expiration of every seven years, a convention should be elected, for the express purpose of revising the constitution, and making alterations, additions, or abolitions therein, if any such should be found necessary.

Here we see a regular process—a government issuing out of a constitution, formed by the people in their original character; and that constitution serving, not only as an authority, but as a law of controul to the government. It was the political bible of the state. Scarcely a family was without it. Every member of the government had a copy; and nothing was more common, when any debate arose on the principle of a bill, or on the extent of any species of authority, than for the members to take the printed constitution out of their pocket, and read the chapter with which such matter in debate was connected.

Having thus given an instance from one of the states, I will shew the proceedings by which the federal constitution of the United States arose and was formed.

Congress, at its two first meetings, in September 1774, and May 1775, was nothing more than a deputation from the legislatures of the several provinces, afterwards states; and had no other authority than what arose from common consent, and the necessity of its acting as a public body. In every thing which related to the internal affairs of America, congress went no further than to issue recommendations to the several provincial assemblies, who at discretion adopted them or not. Nothing on the part of congress was compulsive; yet, in this situation, it was more faithfully and affectionately obeyed, than was any government in Europe. This instance, like that of the national assembly in France, sufficiently shews, that the strength of government does not consist in any thing *within* itself, but in the attachment of a nation, and the interest which the people feel in supporting it. When this is lost, government is but a child in power; and though, like the old government of France, it may harrass individuals for a while, it but facilitates its own fall.

After the declaration of independence, it became consistent with the principle on which representative government is founded, that the authority of congress should be defined and established. Whether that authority should be more or less than congress then discretionarily exercised, was not the question. It was merely the rectitude of the measure.

For this purpose, the act, called the act of confederation,[9] (which was a sort of imperfect federal constitution), was proposed, and, after long deliberation, was concluded in the year 1781. It was not the act of congress, because it is repugnant to the principles of representative government that a body should give power to itself. Congress first informed the several states, of the powers which it conceived were necessary to be invested in the union, to enable it to perform the duties and services required from it; and the states severally agreed with each other, and concentrated in congress those powers.

It may not be improper to observe, that in both those instances, (the one of Pennsylvania, and the other of the United States), there is no such thing as the idea of a compact between the people on one side, and the government on the other. The compact was that of the people with each other, to produce and constitute a government. To suppose that any government can be a party in a compact with the whole people, is to suppose it to have existence before it can have a right to exist. The only instance in which a compact can take place between the people and those who exercise the government, is, that the people shall pay them, while they chuse to employ them.

Government is not a trade which any man or body of men has a right to set up and exercise for his own emolument, but is altogether a trust, in right of those by whom the trust is delegated, and by whom it is always resumeable. It has of itself no rights; they are altogether duties.

Having thus given two instances of the original formation of a constitution, I will shew the manner in which both have been changed since their first establishment.

The powers vested in the governments of the several states, by the state constitutions, were found, upon experience, to be too great; and those vested in the federal government, by the act of confederation, too little. The defect was not in the principle, but in the distribution of power.

Numerous publications, in pamphlets and in the newspapers, appeared, on the propriety and necessity of new modelling the federal government. After some time of public discussion, carried on through the channel of the press, and in conversations, the state of Virginia, experiencing some inconvenience with respect to commerce, proposed holding a continental conference; in consequence of which, a deputation from five or six of the state assemblies met at Anapolis[10] in Maryland, in 1786. This meeting, not conceiving itself sufficiently authorised to go into the business of a reform, did no more than state their general opinions of the propriety of the measure, and recommend that a convention of all the states should be held the year following.

This convention met at Philadelphia in May 1787, of which General Washington was elected president. He was not at that time connected with any of the state governments, or with congress. He delivered up his commission when the war ended,[11] and since then had lived a private citizen.

The convention went deeply into all the subjects; and having, after a variety of debate and investigation, agreed among themselves upon the several parts of a federal constitution, the next question was, the manner of giving it authority and practice.

For this purpose, they did not, like a cabal of courtiers, send for a Dutch Stadtholder, or a German Elector;[12] but they referred the whole matter to the sense and interest of the country.

They first directed, that the proposed constitution should be published. Secondly, that each state should elect a convention, expressly for the purpose of taking it into consideration, and of ratifying or rejecting it; and that as soon as the approbation and ratification of any nine states should be given, that those states should proceed to the election of their proportion of members to the new federal government; and that the operation of it should then begin, and the former federal government cease.

The several states proceeded accordingly to elect their conventions. Some of those conventions ratified the constitution by very large majorities, and two or three unanimously. In others there were much debate and division of opinion. In the Massachusetts convention, which met at Boston, the majority was not above nineteen or twenty, in about three hundred members; but such is the nature of representative government, that it quietly decides all matters by majority. After the debate in the Massachusetts convention was closed, and the vote taken, the objecting members rose, and declared, "*That though they had argued and voted against it, because certain parts appeared to them in a different light to what they appeared to other members; yet, as the vote had decided in favour of the constitution as proposed, they should give it the same practical support as if they had voted for it.*"

As soon as nine states had concurred, (and the rest followed in the order their conventions were elected), the old fabric of the federal government was taken down, and the new one erected, of which General Washington is president.—In this place I cannot help remarking, that the character and services of this gentleman are sufficient to put all those men called kings to shame. While they are receiving from the sweat and labours of mankind, a prodigality of pay, to which neither their abilities nor their services can entitle them, he is rendering every service in his power, and refusing every pecuniary reward. He accepted no pay as commander in chief; he accepts none as president of the United States.

After the new federal constitution was established, the state of Pennsylvania, conceiving that some parts of its own constitution required to be altered, elected a convention for that purpose. The proposed alterations were published, and the people concurring therein, they were established.

In forming those constitutions, or in altering them, little or no inconvenience took place. The ordinary course of things was not interrupted, and the advantages have been much. It is always the interest of a far greater number of people in a nation to have things right, than to let them remain wrong; and when public matters are open to debate, and the public judgment free, it will not decide wrong, unless it decides too hastily.

In the two instances of changing the constitutions, the governments then in being were not actors either way. Government has no right to make itself a party in any debate respecting the principles or modes of forming, or of changing, constitutions. It is not for the benefit of those who exercise the powers of government, that constitutions, and the governments issuing from them, are established. In all those matters, the right of judging and acting are in those who pay, and not in those who receive.

A constitution is the property of a nation, and not of those who exercise the government. All the constitutions of America are declared to be established on the authority of the people. In France, the word nation is used instead of the people; but in both cases, a constitution is a thing antecedent to the government, and always distinct therefrom.

In England, it is not difficult to perceive that every thing has a constitution, except the nation. Every society and association that is established, first agreed upon a number of original articles, digested into form, which are its constitution. It then appointed its officers, whose powers and authorities are described in that constitution, and the government of that society then commenced. Those officers, by whatever name they are called, have no authority to add to, alter, or abridge the original articles. It is only to the constituting power that this right belongs.

From the want of understanding the difference between a constitution and a government, Dr. Johnson,[13] and all writers of his description, have always bewildered themselves. They could not but perceive, that there must necessarily be a *controuling* power existing somewhere, and they placed this power in the discretion of the persons exercising the government, instead of placing it in a constitution formed by the nation. When it is in a constitution, it has the nation for its support, and the natural and the political controuling powers are together. The laws which are enacted by governments, controul men only as individuals, but the nation, through its constitution, controuls the whole government, and has a natural ability so to do. The final controuling power, therefore, and the original constituting power, are one and the same power.

Dr. Johnson could not have advanced such a position in any country where there was a constitution; and he is himself an evidence, that no such thing as a constitution exists in England.—But it may be put as a question, not improper to be investigated, That if a constitution does not exist, how came the idea of its existence so generally established?

In order to decide this question, it is necessary to consider a constitution in both its cases:—First, as creating a government and giving it powers. Secondly, as regulating and restraining the powers so given.

If we begin with William of Normandy, we find that the government of England was originally a tyranny, founded on an invasion and conquest of the country. This being admitted, it will then appear, that the exertion of the nation, at different periods, to abate that tyranny, and render it less intolerable, has been credited for a constitution.

Magna Charta,[14] as it was called, (it is now like an almanack of the same date), was no more than compelling the government to renounce a part of its assumptions. It did not create and give powers to government in the manner a constitution does; but was, as far as it went, of the nature of a re-conquest, and not of a constitution; for could the nation have totally expelled the usurpation, as France has done its despotism, it would then have had a constitution to form.

The history of the Edwards and the Henries, and up to the commencement of the Stuarts, exhibits as many instances of tyranny as could be acted within the limits to which the nation had restricted it. The Stuarts endeavoured to pass those limits, and their fate is well known.[15] In all those instances we see nothing of a constitution, but only of restrictions on assumed power.

After this, another William, descended from the same stock, and claiming from the same origin, gained possession; and of the two evils, *James* and *William*, the nation preferred what it thought the least; since, from circumstances, it must take one. The act, called the Bill of Rights, comes here into view. What is it, but a bargain, which the parts of the government made with each other to divide powers, profits, and privileges? You shall have so much, and I will have the rest; and with respect to the nation, it said, for *your share*, YOU *shall have the right of petitioning*. This being the case, the bill of rights is more properly a bill of wrongs, and of insult. As to what is called the convention parliament,[16] it was a thing that made itself, and then made the authority by which it acted. A few persons got together, and called themselves by that name. Several of them had never been elected, and none of them for the purpose.

From the time of William, a species of government arose, issuing out of this coalition bill of rights; and more so, since the corruption introduced at the Hanover succession by the agency of Walpole; that can be described by no other name than a despotic legislation. Though the parts may embarrass each other, the whole has no bounds; and the only right it acknowledges out of itself, is the right of petitioning. Where then is the constitution either that gives or that restrains power?

It is not because a part of the government is elective, that makes it less a despotism, if the persons so elected, possess afterwards, as a parliament, unlimited powers. Election, in this case, becomes separated from representation, and the candidates are candidates for despotism.

I cannot believe that any nation, reasoning on its own rights, would have thought of calling those things *a constitution*, if the cry of constitution had not been set up by the government. It has got into circulation like the words *bore* and *quoz*, by being chalked up in the speeches of parliament, as those words were on window shutters and door posts;

but whatever the constitution may be in other respects, it has undoubtedly been *the most productive machine of taxation that was ever invented*. The taxes in France, under the new constitution, are not quite thirteen shillings per head*, and the taxes in England, under what is called its present constitution, are forty-eight shillings and sixpence per head, men, women, and children, amounting to nearly seventeen millions sterling, besides the expence of collection, which is upwards of a million more.

In a country like England, where the whole of the civil government is executed by the people of every town and county, by means of parish officers, magistrates, quarterly sessions, juries, and assize; without any trouble to what is called the government, or any other expence to the revenue than the salary of the judges, it is astonishing how such a mass of taxes can be employed. Not even the internal defence of the country is paid out of the revenue. On all occasions, whether real or contrived, recourse is continually had to new loans and new taxes. No wonder, then, that a machine of government so advantageous to the advocates of a court, should be so triumphantly extolled! No wonder, that St. James's or St. Stephen's should echo with the continual cry of constitution! No wonder, that the French revolution should be reprobated, and the *res-publica* treated with reproach! The *red book* of England, like the red book of France,[17] will explain the reason†.

———

I will now, by way of relaxation, turn a thought or two to Mr. Burke. I ask his pardon for neglecting him so long.

"America," says he, (in his speech on the Canada constitution bill[18]) "never dreamed of such absurd doctrine as the *Rights of Man*."

Mr. Burke is such a bold presumer, and advances his assertions and

———

*The whole amount of the assessed taxes of France, for the present year, is three hundred millions of livres, which is twelve millions and a half sterling; and the incidental taxes are estimated at three millions, making in the whole fifteen millions and a half; which, among twenty-four millions of people, is not quite thirteen shillings per head. France has lessened her taxes since the revolution, nearly nine millions sterling annually. Before the revolution, the city of Paris paid a duty of upwards of thirty per cent. on all articles brought into the city. This tax was collected at the city gates. It was taken off on the first of last May, and the gates taken down.

† What was called the *livre rouge*, or the red book, in France, was not exactly similar to the court calendar in England; but it sufficiently shewed how a great part of the taxes was lavished.

his premises with such a deficiency of judgment, that, without troubling ourselves about principles of philosophy or politics, the mere logical conclusions they produce, are ridiculous. For instance,

If governments, as Mr. Burke asserts, are not founded on the Rights of MAN, and are founded on *any rights* at all, they consequently must be founded on the rights of *something* that is *not man*. What then is that something?

Generally speaking, we know of no other creatures that inhabit the earth than man and beast; and in all cases, where only two things offer themselves, and one must be admitted, a negation proved on any one, amounts to an affirmative on the other; and therefore, Mr. Burke, by proving against the Rights of *Man*, proves in behalf of the *beast*; and consequently, proves that government is a beast: and as difficult things sometimes explain each other, we now see the origin of keeping wild beasts in the Tower; for they certainly can be of no other use than to shew the origin of the government. They are in the place of a constitution. O John Bull,[19] what honours thou hast lost by not being a wild beast. Thou mightest, on Mr. Burke's system, have been in the Tower for life.

If Mr. Burke's arguments have not weight enough to keep one serious, the fault is less mine than his; and as I am willing to make an apology to the reader for the liberty I have taken, I hope Mr. Burke will also make his for giving the cause.

Having thus paid Mr. Burke the compliment of remembering him, I return to the subject.

———

From the want of a constitution in England to restrain and regulate the wild impulse of power, many of the laws are irrational and tyrannical, and the administration of them vague and problematical.

The attention of the government of England, (for I rather chuse to call it by this name, than the English government) appears, since its political connection with Germany, to have been so completely engrossed and absorbed by foreign affairs, and the means of raising taxes, that it seems to exist for no other purposes. Domestic concerns are neglected; and, with respect to regular law, there is scarcely such a thing.

Almost every case now must be determined by some precedent, be that precedent good or bad, or whether it properly applies or not; and the practice is become so general, as to suggest a suspicion, that it proceeds from a deeper policy than at first sight appears.

Since the revolution of America, and more so since that of France, this preaching up the doctrine of precedents, drawn from times and circumstances antecedent to those events, has been the studied practice of the English government. The generality of those precedents are founded on principles and opinions, the reverse of what they ought; and the greater distance of time they are drawn from, the more they are to be suspected. But by associating those precedents with a superstitious reverence for ancient things, as monks shew relics and call them holy, the generality of mankind are deceived into the design. Governments now act as if they were afraid to awaken a single reflection in man. They are softly leading him to the sepulchre of precedents, to deaden his faculties and call his attention from the scene of revolutions. They feel that he is arriving at knowledge faster than they wish, and their policy of precedents is the barometer of their fears. This political popery, like the ecclesiastical popery of old, has had its day, and is hastening to its exit. The ragged relic and the antiquated precedent, the monk and the monarch, will moulder together.

Government by precedent, without any regard to the principle of the precedent, is one of the vilest systems that can be set up. In numerous instances, the precedent ought to operate as a warning, and not as an example, and requires to be shunned instead of imitated; but instead of this, precedents are taken in the lump, and put at once for constitution and for law.

Either the doctrine of precedents is policy to keep man in a state of ignorance, or it is a practical confession that wisdom degenerates in governments as governments increase in age, and can only hobble along by the stilts and crutches of precedents. How is it that the same persons who would proudly be thought wiser than their predecessors, appear at the same time only as the ghosts of departed wisdom? How strangely is antiquity treated! To answer some purposes it is spoken of as the times of darkness and ignorance, and to answer others, it is put for the light of the world.

If the doctrine of precedents, is to be followed, the expences of government need not continue the same. Why pay men extravagantly, who have but little to do? If every thing that can happen is already in precedent, legislation is at an end, and precedent, like a dictionary, determines every case. Either, therefore, government has arrived at its dotage, and requires to be renovated, or all the occasions for exercising its wisdom have occured.

We now see all over Europe, and particularly in England, the curious phænomenon of a nation looking one way, and a government the other—the one forward and the other backward. If governments are to go on by precedent, while nations go on by improvement, they must at last come to a final separation; and the sooner, and the more civilly, they determine this point, the better*.

———

Having thus spoken of constitutions generally, as things distinct from actual governments, let us proceed to consider the parts of which a constitution is composed.

Opinions differ more on this subject, than with respect to the whole. That a nation ought to have a constitution, as a rule for the conduct of its government, is a simple question in which all men, not directly courtiers, will agree. It is only on the component parts that questions and opinions multiply.

But this difficulty, like every other, will diminish when put into a train of being rightly understood.

The first thing is, that a nation has a right to establish a constitution.

Whether it exercises this right in the most judicious manner at first, is quite another case. It exercises it agreeably to the judgment it possesses; and by continuing to do so, all errors will at last be exploded.

When this right is established in a nation, there is no fear that it will be employed to its own injury. A nation can have no interest in being wrong.

Though all the constitutions of America are on one general principle, yet no two of them are exactly alike in their component parts, or in the distribution of the powers which they give to the actual governments. Some are more, and others less complex.

* In England, the improvements in agriculture, useful arts, manufactures, and commerce, have been made in opposition to the genius of its government, which is that of following precedents. It is from the enterprize and industry of the individuals, and their numerous associations, in which, tritely speaking, government is neither pillow nor bolster, that these improvements had proceeded. No man thought about the government, or who was *in,* or who was *out,* when he was planning or executing those things; and all he had to hope, with respect to government, was, *that it would let him alone.* Three or four very silly ministerial news-papers are continually offending against the spirit of national improvement, by ascribing it to a minister. They may with as much truth ascribe this book to a minister.

In forming a constitution, it is first necessary to consider what are the ends for which government is necessary? Secondly, what are the best means, and the least expensive, for accomplishing those ends?

Government is nothing more than a national association; and the object of this association is the good of all, as well individually as collectively. Every man wishes to pursue his occupation, and to enjoy the fruits of his labours, and the produce of his property in peace and safety, and with the least possible expence. When these things are accomplished, all the objects for which government ought to be established are answered.

It has been customary to consider government under three distinct general heads. The legislative, the executive, and the judicial.

But if we permit our judgment to act unincumbered by the habit of multiplied terms, we can perceive no more than two divisions of power, of which civil government is composed, namely, that of legislating or enacting laws, and that of executing or administering them. Every thing, therefore, appertaining to civil government, classes itself under one or other of these two divisions.

So far as regards the execution of the laws, that which is called the judicial power, is strictly and properly the executive power of every country. It is that power to which every individual has appeal, and which causes the laws to be executed; neither have we any other clear idea with respect to the official execution of the laws. In England, and also in America and France, this power begins with the magistrate, and proceeds up through all the courts of judicature.

I leave to courtiers to explain what is meant by calling monarchy the executive power. It is merely a name in which acts of government are done; and any other, or none at all, would answer the same purpose. Laws have neither more nor less authority on this account. It must be from the justness of their principles, and the interest which a nation feels therein, that they derive support; if they require any other than this, it is a sign that something in the system of government is imperfect. Laws difficult to be executed cannot be generally good.

With respect to the organization of the *legislative power*, different modes have been adopted in different countries. In America it is generally composed of two houses. In France it consists but of one, but in both countries it is wholly by representation.

The case is, that mankind (from the long tyranny of assumed

power) have had so few opportunities of making the necessary trials on modes and principles of government, in order to discover the best, *that government is but now beginning to be known,* and experience is yet wanting to determine many particulars.

The objections against two houses are, first, that there is an inconsistency in any part of a whole legislature, coming to a final determination by vote on any matter, whilst *that matter,* with respect to *that whole,* is yet only in a train of deliberation, and consequently open to new illustrations.

Secondly, That by taking the vote on each, as a separate body, it always admits of the possibility, and is often the case in practice, that the minority governs the majority, and that, in some instances, to a degree of great inconsistency.

Thirdly, That two houses arbitrarily checking or controuling each other is inconsistent; because it cannot be proved, on the principles of just representation, that either should be wiser or better than the other. They may check in the wrong as well as in the right,—and therefore, to give the power where we cannot give the wisdom to use it, nor be assured of its being rightly used, renders the hazard at least equal to the precaution*.

The objection against a single house is, that it is always in a condi-

---

* With respect to the two houses, of which the English Parliament is composed, they appear to be effectually influenced into one, and, as a legislature, to have no temper of its own. The minister, whoever he at any time may be, touches it as with an opium wand, and it sleeps obedience.

But if we look at the distinct abilities of the two houses, the difference will appear so great, as to shew the inconsistency of placing power where there can be no certainty of the judgment to use it. Wretched as the state of representation is in England, it is manhood compared with what is called the house of Lords; and so little is this nick-named house regarded, that the people scarcely inquire at any time what it is doing. It appears also to be most under influence, and the furthest removed from the general interest of the nation. In the debate on engaging in the Russian and Turkish war, the majority in the house of peers in favour of it was upwards of ninety, when in the other house, which is more than double its numbers, the majority was sixty-three.

The proceedings on Mr. Fox's bill, respecting the rights of juries, merits also to be noticed. The persons called the peers were not the objects of that bill. They are already in possession of more privileges than that bill gave to others. They are their own jury, and if any of that house were prosecuted for a libel, he would not suffer, even upon conviction, for the first offence. Such inequality in laws ought not to exist in any country. The French constitution says, That *the law is the same to every individual, whether to protect or to punish. All are equal in its sight.*

tion of committing itself too soon.—But it should at the same time be remembered, that when there is a constitution which defines the power, and establishes the principles within which a legislature shall act, there is already a more effectual check provided, and more powerfully operating, than any other check can be. For example,

Were a bill to be brought into any of the American legislatures, similar to that which was passed into an act by the English parliament, at the commencement of George the First, to extend the duration of the assemblies to a longer period than they now sit, the check is in the constitution, which in effect says, *Thus far shalt thou go and no further.*

But in order to remove the objection against a single house, (that of acting with too quick an impulse,) and at the same time to avoid the inconsistencies, in some cases absurdities, arising from two houses, the following method has been proposed as an improvement upon both.

First, To have but one representation.

Secondly, To divide that representation, by lot, into two or three parts.

Thirdly, That every proposed bill, shall be first debated in those parts by succession, that they may become the hearers of each other, but without taking any vote. After which the whole representation to assemble for a general debate and determination by vote.

To this proposed improvement has been added another, for the purpose of keeping the representation in a state of constant renovation; which is, that one-third of the representation of each county, shall go out at the expiration of one year, and the number be replaced by new elections.—Another third at the expiration of the second year replaced in like manner, and every third year to be a general election*.

But in whatever manner the separate parts of a constitution may be arranged, there is *one* general principle that distinguishes freedom from slavery, which is, that all *hereditary government over a people is to them a species of slavery, and representative government is freedom.*

Considering government in the only light in which it should be considered, that of a NATIONAL ASSOCIATION; it ought to be so constructed as not to be disordered by any accident happening among the

---

* As to the state of representation in England, it is too absurd to be reasoned upon. Almost all the represented parts are decreasing in population, and the unrepresented parts are increasing. A general convention of the nation is necessary to take the whole state of its government into consideration.

parts; and, therefore, no extraordinary power, capable of producing such an effect, should be lodged in the hands of any individual. The death, sickness, absence, or defection, of any one individual in a government, ought to be a matter of no more consequence, with respect to the nation, than if the same circumstance had taken place in a member of the English Parliament, or the French National Assembly.

Scarcely any thing presents a more degrading character of national greatness, than its being thrown into confusion by any thing happening to, or acted by, an individual; and the ridiculousness of the scene is often increased by the natural insignificance of the person by whom it is occasioned. Were a government so constructed, that it could not go on unless a goose or a gander were present in the senate, the difficulties would be just as great and as real on the flight or sickness of the goose, or the gander, as if it were called a King. We laugh at individuals for the silly difficulties they make to themselves, without perceiving, that the greatest of all ridiculous things are acted in governments*.

All the constitutions of America are on a plan that excludes the childish embarrassments which occur in monarchical countries. No suspension of government can there take place for a moment, from any circumstance whatever. The system of representation provides for every thing, and is the only system in which nations and governments can always appear in their proper character.

As extraordinary power, ought not to be lodged in the hands of any individual, so ought there to be no appropriations of public money to any person, beyond what his services in a state may be worth. It signifies not whether a man be called a president, a king, an emperor, a

---

* It is related, that in the canton of Berne, in Swisserland, it had been customary, from time immemorial, to keep a bear at the public expence, and the people had been taught to believe, that if they had not a bear they should all be undone. It happened some years ago, that the bear, then in being, was taken sick and died too suddenly to have his place immediately supplied with another. During this interregnum the people discovered, that the corn grew, and the vintage flourished, and the sun and moon continued to rise and set, and every thing went on the same as before, and, taking courage from these circumstances, they resolved not to keep any more bears; for, said they, "a bear is a very voracious, expensive animal, and we were obliged to pull out his claws, lest he should hurt the citizens."

The story of the bear of Berne was related in some of the French news-papers, at the time of the flight of Louis XVI. and the application of it to monarchy could not be mistaken in France; but it seems, that the aristocracy of Berne applied it to themselves, and have since prohibited the reading of French news-papers.

senator, or by any other name, which propriety or folly may devise, or arrogance assume, it is only a certain service he can perform in the state; and the service of any such individual in the rotine of office, whether such office be called monarchical, presidential, senatorial, or by any other name or title, can never exceed the value of ten thousand pounds a year. All the great services that are done in the world are performed by volunteer characters, who accept nothing for them; but the rotine of office is always regulated to such a general standard of abilities as to be within the compass of numbers in every country to perform, and therefore cannot merit very extraordinary recompence. *Government,* says Swift, *is a plain thing, and fitted to the capacity of many heads.*

It is inhuman to talk of a million sterling a year, paid out of the public taxes of any country, for the support of any individual, whilst thousands who are forced to contribute thereto, are pining with want, and struggling with misery. Government does not consist in a contrast between prisons and palaces, between poverty and pomp; it is not instituted to rob the needy of his mite, and increase the wretchedness of the wretched.—But of this part of the subject I shall speak hereafter, and confine myself at present to political observations.

When extraordinary power and extraordinary pay are allotted to any individual in a government, he becomes the center, round which every kind of corruption generates and forms. Give to any man a million a year, and add thereto the power of creating and disposing of places, at the expence of a country, and the liberties of that country are no longer secure. What is called the splendor of a throne is no other than the corruption of the state. It is made up of a band of parasites, living in luxurious indolence, out of the public taxes.

When once such a vicious system is established it becomes the guard and protection of all inferior abuses. The man who is in the receipt of a million a year is the last person to promote a spirit of reform, lest, in the event, it should reach to himself. It is always his interest to defend inferior abuses, as so many out-works to protect the citadel; and in this species of political fortification, all the parts have such a common dependence that it is never to be expected they will attack each other*.

---

* It is scarcely possible to touch on any subject, that will not suggest an allusion to some corruption in governments. The simile of "*fortifications,*" unfortunately involves with it a circumstance, which is directly in point with the matter above alluded to.

Monarchy would not have continued so many ages in the world, had it not been for the abuses it protects. It is the master-fraud, which shelters all others. By admitting a participation of the spoil, it makes itself friends; and when it ceases to do this, it will cease to be the idol of courtiers.

As the principle on which constitutions are now formed rejects all hereditary pretentions to government, it also rejects all that catalogue of assumptions known by the name of prerogatives.

If there is any government where prerogatives might with apparent safety be entrusted to any individual, it is in the fœderal government of America. The President of the United States of America is elected only for four years. He is not only responsible in the general sense of the word, but a particular mode is laid down in the constitution for trying him. He cannot be elected under thirty-five years of age; and he must be a native of the country.

In a comparison of these cases with the government of England, the difference when applied to the latter amounts to an absurdity. In England the person who exercises prerogative is often a foreigner; always half a foreigner, and always married to a foreigner. He is never in full natural or political connection with the country, is not responsible for any thing, and becomes of age at eighteen years; yet such a person is permitted to form foreign alliances, without even the knowledge of the nation, and to make war and peace without its consent.

But this is not all. Though such a person cannot dispose of the government, in the manner of a testator, he dictates the marriage con-

---

Among the numerous instances of abuse which have been acted or protected by governments, ancient or modern, there is not a greater than that of quartering a man and his heirs upon the public, to be maintained at its expence.

Humanity dictates a provision for the poor; but by what right, moral or political, does any government assume to say, that the person called the Duke of Richmond, shall be maintained by the public? Yet, if common report is true, not a beggar in London can purchase his wretched pittance of coal, without paying towards the civil list of the Duke of Richmond. Were the whole produce of this imposition but a shilling a year, the iniquitous principle would be still the same; but when it amounts, as it is said to do, to not less than twenty thousand pounds *per ann.* the enormity is too serious to be permitted to remain—This is one of the effects of monarchy and aristocracy.

In stating this case, I am led by no personal dislike. Though I think it mean in any man to live upon the public, the vice originates in the government; and so general is it become, that whether the parties are in the ministry or in the opposition, it makes no difference: they are sure of the guarantee of each other.

nections, which, in effect, accomplishes a great part of the same end. He cannot directly bequeath half the government to Prussia, but he can form a marriage partnership that will produce almost the same thing. Under such circumstances, it is happy for England that she is not situated on the continent, or she might, like Holland, fall under the dictatorship of Prussia. Holland, by marriage, is as effectually governed by Prussia, as if the old tyranny of bequeathing the government had been the means.

The presidency in America, (or, as it is sometimes called, the executive,) is the only office from which a foreigner is excluded,[20] and in England it is the only one to which he is admitted. A foreigner cannot be a member of parliament, but he may be what is called a King. If there is any reason for excluding foreigners, it ought to be from those offices where mischief can most be acted, and where, by uniting every bias of interest and attachment, the trust is best secured.

But as nations proceed in the great business of forming constitutions, they will examine with more precision into the nature and business of that department which is called the executive. What the legislative and judicial departments are, every one can see; but with respect to what, in Europe, is called the executive, as distinct from those two, it is either a political superfluity or a chaos of unknown things.

Some kind of official department, to which reports shall be made from the different parts of a nation, or from abroad, to be laid before the national representatives, is all that is necessary; but there is no consistency in calling this the executive; neither can it be considered in any other light than as inferior to the legislative. The sovereign authority in any country is the power of making laws, and every thing else is an official department.

Next to the arrangement of the principles and the organization of the several parts of a constitution, is the provision to be made for the support of the persons to whom the nation shall confide the administration of the constitutional powers.

A nation can have no right to the time and services of any person at his own expence, whom it may chuse to employ or entrust in any department whatever; neither can any reason be given for making provision for the support of any one part of a government and not for the other.

But, admitting that the honour of being entrusted with any part of a government is to be considered a sufficient reward, it ought to be so to every person alike. If the members of the legislature of any country are to serve at their own expence, that which is called the executive, whether monarchical, or by any other name, ought to serve in like manner. It is inconsistent to pay the one, and accept the service of the other gratis.

In America, every department in the government is decently provided for; but no one is extravagantly paid. Every member of Congress and of the assemblies, is allowed a sufficiency for his expences. Whereas in England, a most prodigal provision is made for the support of one part of the government, and none for the other, the consequence of which is, that the one is furnished with the means of corruption, and the other is put into the condition of being corrupted. Less than a fourth part of such expence, applied as it is in America, would remedy a great part of the corruption.

Another reform in the American constitutions, is the exploding all oaths of personality. The oath of allegiance in America is to the nation only. The putting any individual as a figure for a nation is improper. The happiness of a nation is the superior object, and therefore the intention of an oath of allegiance ought not to be obscured by being figuratively taken, to, or in the name of, any person. The oath, called the civic oath, in France, viz. the "*nation, the law, and the king,*" is improper. If taken at all, it ought to be as in America, to the nation only. The law may or may not be good; but, in this place, it can have no other meaning, than as being conducive to the happiness of the nation, and therefore is included in it. The remainder of the oath is improper, on the ground, that all personal oaths ought to be abolished. They are the remains of tyranny on one part, and slavery on the other; and the name of the CREATOR ought not to be introduced to witness the degradation of his creation; or if taken, as is already mentioned, as figurative of the nation, it is in this place redundant. But whatever apology may be made for oaths at the first establishment of a government, they ought not to be permitted afterwards. If a government requires the support of oaths, it is a sign that it is not worth supporting, and ought not to be supported. Make government what it ought to be, and it will support itself.

To conclude this part of the subject:—One of the greatest improvements that has been made for the perpetual security and progress of constitutional liberty, is the provision which the new constitutions make for occasionally revising, altering, and amending them.

The principle upon which Mr. Burke formed his political creed, that "*of binding and controlling posterity to the end of time, and of renouncing and abdicating the rights of all posterity for ever,*" is now become too detestable to be made a subject of debate; and, therefore, I pass it over with no other notice than exposing it.

Government is but now beginning to be known. Hitherto it has been the mere exercise of power, which forbad all effectual enquiry into rights, and grounded itself wholly on possession. While the enemy of liberty was its judge, the progress of its principles must have been small indeed.

The constitutions of America, and also that of France, have either affixed a period for their revision, or laid down the mode by which improvements shall be made. It is perhaps impossible to establish any thing that combines principles with opinions and practice, which the progress of circumstances, through a length of years, will not in some measure derange, or render inconsistent; and, therefore, to prevent inconveniences accumulating, till they discourage reformations or provoke revolutions, it is best to provide the means of regulating them as they occur. The Rights of Man are the rights of all generations of men, and cannot be monopolized by any. That which is worth following, will be followed for the sake of its worth; and it is in this that its security lies, and not in any conditions with which it may be encumbered. When a man leaves property to his heirs, he does not connect it with an obligation that they shall accept it. Why then should we do otherwise with respect to constitutions?

The best constitution that could now be devised, consistent with the condition of the present moment, may be far short of that excellence which a few years may afford. There is a morning of reason rising upon man on the subject of government, that has not appeared before. As the barbarism of the present old governments expires, the moral condition of nations with respect to each other will be changed. Man will not be brought up with the savage idea of considering his species as his enemy, because the accident of birth gave the individuals existence in countries distinguished by different names; and as constitutions have always some relation to external as well as to domestic circumstances, the means of benefiting by every change, foreign or domestic, should be a part of every constitution.

We already see an alteration in the national disposition of England and France towards each other, which, when we look back to only a few years, is itself a revolution. Who could have foreseen, or who would have believed, that a French National Assembly would ever have been a popular toast in England, or that a friendly alliance of the two nations should become the wish of either. It shews, that man, were he not corrupted by governments; is naturally the friend of man, and that human nature is not of itself vicious. That spirit of jealousy and ferocity, which the governments of the two countries inspired, and which they rendered subservient to the purpose of taxation, is now yielding to the dictates of reason, interest, and humanity. The trade of courts is beginning to be understood, and the affectation of mystery, with all the artificial sorcery by which they imposed upon mankind, is on the decline. It has received its death-wound; and though it may linger, it will expire.

Government ought to be as much open to improvement as any thing which appertains to man, instead of which it has been monopolized from age to age, by the most ignorant and vicious of the human race. Need we any other proof of their wretched management, than the excess of debts and taxes with which every nation groans, and the quarrels into which they have precipitated the world?

Just emerging from such a barbarous condition, it is too soon to determine to what extent of improvement government may yet be carried. For what we can foresee, all Europe may form but one great republic, and man be free of the whole.

CHAPTER V:
WAYS AND MEANS OF IMPROVING THE CONDITION OF EUROPE, INTERSPERSED WITH MISCELLANEOUS OBSERVATIONS.

In contemplating a subject that embraces with equatorial magnitude the whole region of humanity, it is impossible to confine the pursuit in one single direction. It takes ground on every character and condition that appertains to man, and blends the individual, the nation, and the world.

From a small spark, kindled in America, a flame has arisen, not to be extinguished. Without consuming, like the *Ultima Ratio Regum,* it winds its progress from nation to nation, and conquers by a silent operation. Man finds himself changed, he scarcely perceives how. He acquires a knowledge of his rights by attending justly to his interest, and discovers in the event that the strength and powers of despotism consist wholly in the fear of resisting it, and that, in order *"to be free, it is sufficient that he wills it."*

Having in all the preceding parts of this work endeavoured to establish a system of principles as a basis, on which governments ought to be erected; I shall proceed in this, to the ways and means of rendering them into practice. But in order to introduce this part of the subject with more propriety, and stronger effect, some preliminary observations, deducible from, or connected with, those principles, are necessary.

Whatever the form or constitution of government may be, it ought to have no other object than the *general* happiness. When, instead of this, it operates to create and encrease wretchedness in any of the parts of society, it is on a wrong system, and reformation is necessary.

Customary language has classed the condition of man under the two descriptions of civilized and uncivilized life. To the one it has ascribed felicity and affluence; to the other hardship and want. But, however, our imagination may be impressed by painting and comparison, it is nevertheless true, that a great portion of mankind, in what are called civilized countries, are in a state of poverty and wretchedness, far below the condition of an Indian. I speak not of one country, but of all. It is so in England, it is so all over Europe. Let us enquire into the cause.

It lies not in any natural defect in the principles of civilization, but in preventing those principles having an universal operation; the consequence of which is, a perpetual system of war and expence, that drains the country, and defeats the general felicity of which civilization is capable.

All the European governments (France now excepted) are constructed not on the principle of universal civilization, but on the reverse of it. So far as those governments relate to each other, they are in the same condition as we conceive of savage uncivilized life; they put themselves beyond the law as well of GOD as of man, and are, with respect to principle and reciprocal conduct, like so many individuals in a state of nature.

The inhabitants of every country, under the civilization of laws, easily civilize together, but governments being yet in an uncivilized state, and almost continually at war, they pervert the abundance which civilized life produces to carry on the uncivilized part to a greater extent. By thus engrafting the barbarism of government upon the internal civilization of a country, it draws from the latter, and more especially from the poor, a great portion of those earnings, which should be applied to their own subsistence and comfort.—Apart from all reflections of morality and philosophy, it is a melancholy fact, that more than one-fourth of the labour of mankind is annually consumed by this barbarous system.

What has served to continue this evil, is the pecuniary advantage, which all the governments of Europe have found in keeping up this state of uncivilization. It affords to them pretences for power, and revenue, for which there would be neither occasion nor apology, if the circle of civilization were rendered compleat. Civil government alone, or the government of laws, is not productive of pretences for many taxes; it operates at home, directly under the eye of the country, and precludes the possibility of much imposition. But when the scene is laid in the uncivilized contention of governments, the field of pretences is enlarged, and the country, being no longer a judge, is open to every imposition, which governments please to act.

Not a thirtieth, scarcely a fortieth, part of the taxes which are raised in England are either occasioned by, or applied to, the purposes of civil government. It is not difficult to see, that the whole which the actual government does in this respect, is to enact laws, and that the country administers and executes them, at its own expence, by means of magistrates, juries, sessions, and assize, over and above the taxes which it pays.

In this view of the case, we have two distinct characters of government; the one the civil government, or the government of laws, which operates at home, the other the court or cabinet government, which operates abroad, on the rude plan of uncivilized life; the one attended with little charge, the other with boundless extravagance; and so distinct are the two, that if the latter were to sink, as it were by a sudden opening of the earth, and totally disappear, the former would not be deranged. It would still proceed, because it is the common interest of the nation that it should, and all the means are in practice.

Revolutions, then, have for their object, a change in the moral condition of governments, and with this change the burthen of public taxes will lessen, and civilization will be left to the enjoyment of that abundance, of which it is now deprived.

In contemplating the whole of this subject, I extend my views into the department of commerce. In all my publications, where the matter would admit, I have been an advocate for commerce, because I am a friend to its effects. It is a pacific system, operating to cordialize mankind, by rendering nations, as well as individuals, useful to each other. As to mere theoretical reformation, I have never preached it up. The most effectual process is that of improving the condition of man by means of his interest; and it is on this ground that I take my stand.

If commerce were permitted to act to the universal extent it is capable, it would extirpate the system of war, and produce a revolution in the uncivilized state of governments. The invention of commerce has arisen since those governments began, and is the greatest approach towards universal civilization, that has yet been made by any means not immediately flowing from moral principles.

Whatever has a tendency to promote the civil intercourse of nations, by an exchange of benefits, is a subject as worthy of philosophy as of politics. Commerce is no other than the traffic of two individuals, multiplied on a scale of numbers; and by the same rule that nature intended the intercourse of two, she intended that of all. For this purpose she has distributed the materials of manufactures and commerce, in various and distant parts of a nation and of the world; and as they cannot be procured by war so cheaply or so commodiously as by commerce, she has rendered the latter the means of extirpating the former.

As the two are nearly the opposites of each other, consequently, the uncivilized state of European governments is injurious to commerce. Every kind of destruction or embarrassment serves to lessen the quantity, and it matters but little in what part of the commercial world the reduction begins. Like blood, it cannot be taken from any of the parts, without being taken from the whole mass in circulation, and all partake of the loss. When the ability in any nation to buy is destroyed, it equally involves the seller. Could the government of England destroy the commerce of all other nations, she would most effectually ruin her own.

It is possible that a nation may be the carrier for the world, but she cannot be the merchant. She cannot be the seller and the buyer of her own merchandize. The ability to buy must reside out of herself; and, therefore, the prosperity of any commercial nation is regulated by the prosperity of the rest. If they are poor she cannot be rich, and her condition, be it what it may, is an index of the height of the commercial tide in other nations.

That the principles of commerce, and its universal operation may be understood, without understanding the practice, is a position that reason will not deny; and it is on this ground only that I argue the subject. It is one thing in the counting-house, in the world it is another. With respect to its operation it must necessarily be contemplated as a reciprocal thing; that only one half its powers resides within the nation, and that the whole is as effectually destroyed by destroying the half that resides without, as if the destruction had been committed on that which is within; for neither can act without the other.

When in the last, as well as in former wars, the commerce of England sunk, it was because the general quantity was lessened every where; and it now rises, because commerce is in a rising state in every nation. If England, at this day, imports and exports more than at any former period, the nations with which she trades must necessarily do the same; her imports are their exports, and *vice versa*.

There can be no such thing as a nation flourishing alone in commerce; she can only participate; and the destruction of it in any part must necessarily affect all. When, therefore, governments are at war, the attack is made upon the common stock of commerce, and the consequence is the same as if each had attacked his own.

The present increase of commerce is not to be attributed to ministers, or to any political contrivances, but to its own natural operations in consequence of peace. The regular markets had been destroyed, the channels of trade broken up, the high road of the seas infested with robbers of every nation, and the attention of the world called to other objects. Those interruptions have ceased, and peace has restored the deranged condition of things to their proper order*.

It is worth remarking, that every nation reckons the balance of

---

* In America, the increase of commerce is greater in proportion than in England. It is, at this time, at least one half more than at any period prior to the revolution. The greatest number of vessels cleared out of the port of Philadelphia, before the commencement of the war, was between eight and nine hundred. In the year 1788, the number was upwards of twelve hundred. As the state of Pennsylvania is estimated as an eighth part of the United States in population, the whole number of vessels must now be nearly ten thousand.

trade in its own favour; and therefore something must be irregular in the common ideas upon this subject.

The fact, however, is true, according to what is called a balance; and it is from this cause that commerce is universally supported. Every nation feels the advantage, or it would abandon the practice: but the deception lies in the mode of making up the accounts, and in attributing what are called profits to a wrong cause.

Mr. Pitt has sometimes amused himself, by shewing what he called a balance of trade from the custom-house books. This mode of calculation, not only affords no rule that is true, but one that is false.

In the first place, Every cargo that departs from the custom-house, appears on the books as an export; and, according to the custom-house balance, the losses at sea, and by foreign failures, are all reckoned on the side of profit, because they appear as exports.

Secondly, Because the importation by the smuggling trade does not appear on the custom-house books, to arrange against the exports.

No balance, therefore, as applying to superior advantages, can be drawn from those documents; and if we examine the natural operation of commerce, the idea is fallacious; and if true, would soon be injurious. The great support of commerce consists in the balance being a level of benefits among all nations.

Two merchants of different nations trading together, will both become rich, and each makes the balance in his own favour; consequently, they do not get rich out of each other; and it is the same with respect to the nations in which they reside. The case must be, that each nation must get rich out of its own means, and increases that riches by something which it procures from another in exchange.

If a merchant in England sends an article of English manufacture abroad, which costs him a shilling at home, and imports something which sells for two, he makes a balance of one shilling in his own favour; but this is not gained out of the foreign nation or the foreign merchant, for he also does the same by the article he receives, and neither has a balance of advantage upon the other. The original value of the two articles in their proper countries were but two shillings; but by changing their places, they acquire a new idea of value, equal to double what they had at first, and that increased value is equally divided.

There is no otherwise a balance on foreign than on domestic commerce. The merchants of London and Newcastle trade on the same principles, as if they resided in different nations, and make their balances in the same manner: yet London does not get rich out of Newcastle, any more than Newcastle out of London: but coals, the merchandize of Newcastle, have an additional value at London, and London merchandize has the same at Newcastle.

Though the principle of all commerce is the same, the domestic, in a national view, is the part of the most beneficial; because the whole of the advantages, on both sides, rests within the nation; whereas, in foreign commerce, it is only a participation of one half.

The most unprofitable of all commerce is that connected with foreign dominion. To a few individuals it may be beneficial, merely because it is commerce; but to the nation it is a loss. The expence of maintaining dominion more than absorbs the profits of any trade. It does not increase the general quantity in the world, but operates to lessen it; and as a greater mass would be afloat by relinquishing dominion, the participation without the expence would be more valuable than a greater quantity with it.

But it is impossible to engross commerce by dominion; and therefore it is still more fallacious. It cannot exist in confined channels, and necessarily breaks out by regular or irregular means, that defeat the attempt; and to succeed would be still worse. France, since the revolution, has been more than indifferent as to foreign possessions; and other nations will become the same, when they investigate the subject with respect to commerce.

To the expence of dominion is to be added that of navies, and when the amount of the two are subtracted from the profits of commerce, it will appear, that what is called the balance of trade, even admitting it to exist, is not enjoyed by the nation, but absorbed by the government.

The idea of having navies for the protection of commerce is delusive. It is putting the means of destruction for the means of protection. Commerce needs no other protection than the reciprocal interest which every nation feels in supporting it—it is common stock—it exists by a balance of advantages to all; and the only interruption it meets, is from the present uncivilized state of governments, and which it is its common interest to reform*.

---

* When I saw Mr. Pitt's mode of estimating the balance of trade, in one of his parliamentary speeches, he appeared to me to know nothing of the nature and interest of commerce; and no man has more wantonly tortured it than himself. During a period of peace, it

Quitting this subject, I now proceed to other matters—As it is necessary to include England in the prospect of a general reformation, it is proper to enquire into the defects of its government. It is only by each nation reforming its own, that the whole can be improved, and the full benefit of reformation enjoyed. Only partial advantages can flow from partial reforms.

France and England are the only two countries in Europe where a reformation in government could have successfully begun. The one secure by the ocean, and the other by the immensity of its internal strength, could defy the malignancy of foreign despotism. But it is with revolutions as with commerce, the advantages increase by their becoming general, and double to either what each would receive alone.

As a new system is now opening to the view of the world, the European courts are plotting to counteract it. Alliances, contrary to all former systems,[21] are agitating, and a common interest of courts is forming against the common interest of man. This combination draws a line that runs throughout Europe, and presents a cause so entirely new, as to exclude all calculations from former circumstances. While despotism warred with despotism, man had no interest in the contest; but in a cause that unites the soldier with the citizen, and nation with nation, the despotism of courts, though it feels the danger, and meditates revenge, is afraid to strike.

No question has arisen within the records of history that pressed with the importance of the present. It is not whether this or that party shall be in or out, or whig or tory, or high or low shall prevail; but whether man shall inherit his rights, and universal civilization take place? Whether the fruits of his labours shall be enjoyed by himself, or consumed by the profligacy of governments? Whether robbery shall be banished from courts, and wretchedness from countries?

When, in countries that are called civilized, we see age going to the workhouse and youth to the gallows, something must be wrong in the system of government. It would seem, by the exterior appearance of such countries, that all was happiness; but there lies hidden from the eye of common observation, a mass of wretchedness that has scarcely any other chance, than to expire in poverty or infamy. Its entrance into

has been havocked with the calamities of war. Three times has it been thrown into stagnation, and the vessels unmaned by impressing, within less than four years of peace.

life is marked with the presage of its fate; and until this is remedied, it is in vain to punish.

Civil government does not consist in executions; but in making that provision for the instruction of youth, and the support of age, as to exclude, as much as possible, profligacy from the one, and despair from the other. Instead of this, the resources of a country are lavished upon kings, upon courts, upon hirelings, imposters, and prostitutes; and even the poor themselves, with all their wants upon them, are compelled to support the fraud that oppresses them.

Why is it, that scarcely any are executed but the poor? The fact is a proof, among other things, of a wretchedness in their condition. Bred up without morals, and cast upon the world without a prospect, they are the exposed sacrifice of vice and legal barbarity. The millions that are superfluously wasted upon governments, are more than sufficient to reform those evils, and to benefit the condition of every man in a nation, not included within the purlieus of a court. This I hope to make appear in the progress of this work.

It is the nature of compassion to associate with misfortune. In taking up this subject is seek no recompence—I fear no consequence. Fortified with that proud integrity, that disdains to triumph or to yield, I will advocate the Rights of Man.

It is to my advantage that I have served an apprenticeship to life. I know the value of moral instruction, and I have seen the danger of the contrary.

At an early period, little more than sixteen years of age, raw and adventurous, and heated with the false heroism of a master* who had served in a man of war, I began the carver of my own fortune, and entered on board the Terrible, Privateer, Capt. Death. From this adventure I was happily prevented by the affectionate and moral remonstrance of a good father, who, from his own habits of life, being of the Quaker profession, must begin to look upon me as lost. But the impression, much as it effected at the time, began to wear away, and I entered afterwards in the King of Prussia Privateer, Capt. Mendez, and went with her to sea. Yet, from such a beginning, and with all the inconvenience of early life against me, I am proud to say, that with a perseverance undismayed by difficulties, a disinterestedness that com-

---

* Rev. William Knowles, master of the grammar school of Thetford, in Norfolk.

pelled respect, I have not only contributed to raise a new empire in the world, founded on a new system of government, but I have arrived at an eminence in political literature, the most difficult of all lines to succeed and excel in, which aristocracy, with all its aids, has not been able to reach or to rival.

Knowing my own heart, and feeling myself, as I now do, superior to all the skirmish of party, the inveteracy of interested or mistaken opponents, I answer not to falsehood or abuse, but proceed to the defects of the English government*.

* Politics and self-interest have been so uniformly connected, that the world, from being so often deceived, has a right to be suspicious of public characters: but with regard to myself, I am perfectly easy on this head. I did not, at my first setting out in public life, nearly seventeen years ago, turn my thoughts to subjects of government from motives of interest; and my conduct from that moment to this, proves the fact. I saw an opportunity, in which I thought I could do some good, and I followed exactly what my heart dictated. I neither read books, nor studied other people's opinions. I thought for myself. The case was this:

During the suspension of the old governments in America, both prior to, and at the breaking out of hostilities, I was struck with the order and decorum with which every thing was conducted; and impressed with the idea, that a little more than what society naturally performed, was all the government that was necessary; and that monarchy and aristocracy were frauds and impositions upon mankind. On these principles I published the pamphlet *Common Sense.* The success it met with was beyond any thing since the invention of printing. I gave the copy right up to every state in the union, and the demand ran to not less than one hundred thousand copies. I continued the subject in the same manner, under the title of the *Crisis,* till the complete establishment of the revolution.

After the declaration of independence, Congress unanimously, and unknown to me, appointed me secretary in the foreign department. This was agreeable to me, because it gave me the opportunity of seeing into the abilities of foreign courts, and their manner of doing business. But a misunderstanding arising between congress and me, respecting one of their commissioners, then in Europe, Mr. Silas Deane, I resigned the office, and declined, at the same time, the pecuniary offers made me by the ministers of France and Spain, M. Gerard and Don Juan Mirralles.

I had by this time so completely gained the ear and confidence of America, and my own independence was become so visible as to give me a range in political writing, beyond, perhaps, what any man ever possessed in any country; and what is more extraordinary, I held it undiminished to the end of the war, and enjoy it in the same manner to the present moment. As my object was not myself, I set out with the determination, and happily with the disposition, of not being moved by praise or censure, friendship or calumny, nor of being drawn from my purpose by any personal altercation; and the man who cannot do this, is not fit for a public character.

When the war ended, I went from Philadelphia to Borden-Town, on the east bank of the Delaware, where I have a small place. Congress was at this time at Prince-Town, fifteen miles distant; and General Washington had taken his headquarters at Rocky-Hill, within the neighbourhood of Congress, for the purpose of resigning up his commission, (the object for which he accepted it being accomplished,) and of retiring to private life. While he was on this business, he wrote me the letter which I here subjoin.

Rocky-Hill, Sept. 10, 1783

I have learned since I have been at this place, that you are at Borden-Town. Whether for the sake of retirement or œconomy, I know not. Be it for either, for both, or whatever it may, if you will come to this place, and partake with me, I shall be exceedingly happy to see you at it.

Your presence may remind Congress of your past services to this country; and if it is in my power to impress them, command my best exertions with freedom, as they will be rendered chearfully by one, who entertains a lively sense of the importance of your works, and who, with much pleasure, subscribes himself,

YOUR SINCERE FRIEND,
G. WASHINGTON

During the war, in the latter end of the year 1780, I formed to myself a design of coming over to England; and communicated it to General Greene, who was then in Philadelphia, on his route to the southward, General Washington being then at too great a distance to communicate with immediately. I was strongly impressed with the idea, that if I could get over to England, without being known, and only remain in safety till I could get out a publication, that I could open the eyes of the country with respect to the madness and stupidity of its government. I saw that the parties in parliament had pitted themselves as far as they could go, and could make no new impressions on each other. General Greene entered fully into my views; but the affair of Arnold and André happening just after, he changed his mind, and, under strong apprehensions for my safety, wrote very pressingly to me from Anapolis, in Maryland, to give up the design, which, with some reluctance, I did. Soon after this I accompanied Col. Lawrens, son of Mr. Lawrens, who was then in the Tower, to France, on business from Congress. We landed at L'Orient; and while I remained there, he being gone forward, a circumstance occurred, that renewed my former design. An English packet from Falmouth to New-York, with the government dispatches on board, was brought into L'Orient. That a packet should be taken, is no extraordinary thing; but that the dispatches should be taken with it, will scarcely be credited, as they are always slung at the cabin window, in a bag loaded with cannon-ball, and ready to be sunk at a moment. The fact, however, is as I have stated it, for the dispatches came into my hands, and I read them. The capture, as I was informed, succeeded by the following stratagem:—The captain of the Madame privateer, who spoke English, on coming up with the packet, passed himself for the captain of an English frigate, and invited the captain of the packet on board, which, when done, he sent some of his own hands back, and secured the mail. But be the circumstance of the capture what it may, I speak with certainty as to the government dispatches. They were sent up to Paris, to Count Vergennes, and when Col. Lawrens and myself returned to America, we took the originals to Congress.

By these dispatches I saw into the stupidity of the English cabinet, far more than I otherwise could have done, and I renewed my former design. But Col. Lawrens was so unwilling to return alone; more especially, as among other matters, we had a charge of upwards of two hundred thousand pounds sterling in money, that I gave into his wishes, and finally gave up my plan. But I am now certain, that if I could have executed it, that it would not have been altogether unsuccessful.

I begin with charters and corporations.

It is a perversion of terms to say, that a charter gives rights. It operates by a contrary effect, that of taking rights away. Rights are inherently in all the inhabitants; but charters, by annulling those rights in the majority, leave the right by exclusion in the hands of a few. If charters were constructed so as to express in direct terms, *"that every inhabitant, who is not a member of a corporation, shall not exercise the right of voting,"* such charters would, in the face, be charters, not of rights, but of exclusion. The effect is the same under the form they now stand; and the only persons on whom they operate, are the persons whom they exclude. Those whose rights are guaranteed, by not being taken away, exercise no other rights, than as members of the community they are entitled to without a charter; and, therefore, all charters have no other than an indirect negative operation. They do not give rights to A, but they make a difference in favour of A by taking away the right of B, and consequently are instruments of injustice.

But charters and corporations have a more extensive evil effect, than what relates merely to elections. They are sources of endless contentions in the places where they exist; and they lessen the common rights of national society. A native of England, under the operation of these charters and corporations, cannot be said to be an Englishman in the full sense of the word. He is not free of the nation, in the same manner that a Frenchman is free of France, and an American of America. His rights are circumscribed to the town, and, in some cases, to the parish of his birth; and all other parts, though in his native land, are to him as a foreign country. To acquire a residence in these, he must undergo a local naturalization by purchase, or he is forbidden or expelled the place. This species of feudality is kept up to aggrandize the corporations at the ruin of towns; and the effect is visible.

The generality of corporation towns are in a state of solitary decay, and prevented from further ruin, only by some circumstance in their situation, such as a navigable river, or a plentiful surrounding country. As population is one of the chief sources of wealth, (for without it land itself has no value,) every thing which operates to prevent it must lessen the value of property; and as corporations have not only this tendency, but directly this effect, they cannot but be injurious. If any policy were to be followed, instead of that of general freedom, to every person to settle where he chose, (as in France or America,) it would be more consistent to give encouragement to new comers, than to prelude their admission by exacting premiums from them*.

The persons most immediately interested in the abolition of corporations, are the inhabitants of the towns where corporations are established. The instances of Manchester, Birmingham, and Sheffield, shew, by contrast, the injury which those Gothic institutions are to property and commerce. A few examples may be found, such as that of London, whose natural and commercial advantage, owing to its situation on the Thames, is capable of bearing up against the political evils of a corporation; but in almost all other cases the fatality is too visible to be doubted or denied.

Though the whole nation is not so directly affected by the depression of property in corporation towns as the inhabitants themselves, it partakes of the consequence. By lessening the value of property, the quantity of national commerce is curtailed. Every man is a customer in proportion to his ability; and as all parts of a nation trade with each other, whatever affects any of the parts, must necessarily communicate to the whole.

As one of the houses of the English parliament is, in a great measure, made up of elections from these corporations; and as it is unnatural that a pure stream should flow from a foul fountain, its vices are but a continuation of the vices of its origin. A man of moral honour and good political principles, cannot submit to the mean drudgery and disgraceful arts, by which such elections are carried. To be a successful candidate, he must be destitute of the qualities that constitute a just legislator: and being, thus disciplined to corruption by the mode of entering into parliament, it is not to be expected that the representative should be better than the man.

Mr. Burke, in speaking of the English representation, has advanced

---

* It is difficult to account for the origin of charter and corporation towns, unless we suppose them to have arisen out of, or been connected with, some species of garrison service. The times in which they began justify this idea. The generality of those towns have been garrisons; and the corporations were charged with the care of the gates of the towns, when no military garrison was present. Their refusing or granting admission to strangers, which has produced the custom of giving, selling, and buying freedom, has more of the nature of garrison authority than civil government. Soldiers are free of all corporations throughout the nation, by the same propriety that every soldier is free of every garrison, and no other persons are. He can follow any employment, with the permission of his officers, in any corporation town throughout the nation.

as bold a challenge as ever was given in the days of chivalry. "Our representation," says he, "has been found *perfectly adequate to all the purposes* for which a representation of the people can be desired or devised. I defy," continues he, "the enemies of our constitution to shew the contrary."——This declaration from a man, who has been in constant opposition to all the measures of parliament the whole of his political life, a year or two excepted, is most extraordinary; and, comparing him with himself, admits of no other alternative, than that he acted against his judgment as a member, or has declared contrary to it as an author.

But it is not in the representation only that the defects lie, and therefore I proceed in the next place to the aristocracy.

What is called the House of Peers,[22] is constituted on a ground very similar to that, against which there is a law in other cases. It amounts to a combination of persons in one common interest. No reason can be given, why an house of legislation should be composed entirely of men whose occupation consists in letting landed property, than why it should be composed of those who hire, or of brewers, or bakers, or any other separate class of men.

Mr. Burke calls this house, "*the great ground and pillar of security to the landed interest.*" Let us examine this idea.

What pillar of security does the landed interest require more than any other interest in the state, or what right has it to a distinct and separate representation from the general interest of a nation? The only use to be made of this power, (and which it has always made,) is to ward off taxes from itself, and throw the burthen upon such articles of consumption by which itself would be least affected.

That this has been the consequence, (and will always be the consequence of constructing governments on combinations,) is evident with respect to England, from the history of its taxes.

Notwithstanding taxes have encreased and multiplied upon every article of common consumption, the land-tax, which more particularly affects this "pillar," has diminished. In 1788, the amount of the land-tax was 1,950,000£. which is half a million less than it produced almost an hundred years ago*, notwithstanding the rentals are in many instances doubled since that period.

Before the coming of the Hanoverians, the taxes were divided in

* See Sir John Sinclair's *History of the Revenue.* The land-tax in 1646 was £2,473,499.

nearly equal proportions between the land and articles of consumption, the land bearing rather the largest share: but since that æra, nearly thirteen millions annually of new taxes have been thrown upon consumption. The consequence of which has been a constant encrease in the number and wretchedness of the poor, and in the amount of the poor-rates. Yet here again the burthen does not fall in equal proportions on the aristocracy with the rest of the community. Their residences, whether in town or country, are not mixed with the habitations of the poor. They live apart from distress, and the expence of relieving it. It is in manufacturing towns and labouring villages that those burthens press the heaviest; in many of which it is one class of poor supporting another.

Several of the most heavy and productive taxes are so contrived, as to give an exemption to this pillar, thus standing in its own defence. The tax upon beer brewed for sale does not affect the aristocracy, who brew their own beer free of this duty. It falls only on those who have not conveniency or ability to brew, and who must purchase it in small quantities. But what will mankind think of the justice of taxation, when they know, that this tax alone, from which the aristocracy are from circumstances exempt, is nearly equal to the whole of the land-tax, being in the year 1788, and it is not less now, 1,666,152£. and with its proportion of the taxes on malt and hops, it exceeds it.—That a single article, thus partially consumed, and that chiefly by the working part, should be subject to a tax, equal to that on the whole rental of a nation, is, perhaps, a fact not to be paralleled in the histories of revenues.

This is one of the consequences resulting from an house of legislation, composed on the ground of a combination of common interest; for whatever their separate politics as to parties may be, in this they are united. Whether a combination acts to raise the price of any article for sale, or the rate of wages; or whether it acts to throw taxes from itself upon another class of the community, the principle and the effect are the same; and if the one be illegal, it will be difficult to shew that the other ought to exist.

It is to no use to say, that taxes are first proposed in the house of commons; for as the other house has always a negative, it can always defend itself; and it would be ridiculous to suppose that its acquiescence in the measures to be proposed were not understood before hand. Besides which, it has obtained so much influence by borough-traffic, and so many of its relations and connections are distributed on both sides of the commons, as to give it, besides an absolute negative in one house, a preponderancy in the other, in all matters of common concern.

It is difficult to discover what is meant by the *landed interest,* if it does not mean a combination of aristocratical land-holders, opposing their own pecuniary interest to that of the farmer, and every branch of trade, commerce, and manufacture. In all other respects it is the only interest that needs no partial protection. It enjoys the general protection of the world. Every individual, high or low, is interested in the fruits of the earth; men, women, and children, of all ages and degrees, will turn out to assist the farmer, rather than a harvest should not be got in; and they will not act thus by any other property. It is the only one for which the common prayer of mankind is put up, and the only one that can never fail from the want of means. It is the interest, not of the policy, but of the existence of man, and when it ceases he must cease to be.

No other interest in a nation stands on the same united support. Commerce, manufactures, arts, sciences, and every thing else, compared with this, are supported but in parts. Their prosperity or their decay has not the same universal influence. When the vallies laugh and sing, it is not the farmer only, but all creation that rejoices. It is a prosperity that excludes all envy; and this cannot be said of any thing else.

Why then does Mr. Burke talk of his house of peers, as the pillar of the landed interest? Were that pillar to sink into the earth, the same landed property would continue, and the same ploughing, sowing, and reaping would go on. The aristocracy are not the farmers who work the land, and raise the produce, but are the mere consumers of the rent; and when compared with the active world, are the drones, a seraglio of males, who neither collect the honey nor form the hive, but exist only for lazy enjoyment.

Mr. Burke, in his first essay, called aristocracy, "*the Corinthian capital of polished society.*" Towards compleating the figure, he has now added the *pillar;* but still the base is wanting; and whenever a nation chuses to act a Samson, not blind, but bold, down go the temple of Dagon, the Lords and the Philistines.

If a house of legislation is to be composed of men of one class, for the purpose of protecting a distinct interest, all the other interests should have the same. The inequality, as well as the burthen of taxation, arises from admitting it in one case, and not in all. Had there been an house of farmers, there had been no game laws; or an house of merchants and manufacturers, the taxes had neither been so unequal nor so excessive. It is from the power of taxation being in the hands of those who can throw so great a part of it from their own shoulders, that it has raged without a check.

Men of small or moderate estates, are more injured by the taxes being thrown on articles of consumption, than they are eased by warding it from landed property, for the following reasons:

First, They consume more of the productive taxable articles, in proportion to their property, than those of large estates.

Secondly, Their residence is chiefly in towns, and their property in houses; and the encrease of the poor-rates, occasioned by taxes on consumption, is in much greater proportion than the land-tax has been favoured. In Birmingham, the poor-rates are not less than seven shillings in the pound. From this, as is already observed, the aristocracy are in a great measure exempt.

These are but a part of the mischiefs flowing from the wretched scheme of an house of peers.

As a combination, it can always throw a considerable portion of taxes from itself; and as an hereditary house, accountable to nobody, it resembles a rotten borough,[23] whose consent is to be courted by interest. There are but few of its members, who are not in some mode or other participaters, or disposers of the public money. One turns a candle-holder, or a lord in waiting; another a lord of the bed-chamber, a groom of the stole, or any insignificant nominal office, to which a salary is annexed, paid out of the public taxes, and which avoids the direct appearance of corruption. Such situations are derogatory to the character of man; and where they can be submitted to, honour cannot reside.

To all these are to be added the numerous dependants, the long list of younger branches and distant relations, who are to be provided for at the public expence: in short, were an estimation to be made of the charge of aristocracy to a nation, it will be found nearly equal to that of supporting the poor. The Duke of Richmond alone (and there are cases similar to his) takes away as much for himself as would maintain two thousand poor and aged persons. Is it, then, any wonder, that under such a system of government, taxes and rates have multiplied to their present extent?

In stating these matters, I speak an open and disinterested language, dictated by no passion but that of humanity. To me, who have not only refused offers, because I thought them improper, but have declined rewards I might with reputation have accepted, it is no wonder that meanness and imposition appear disgustful. Independence is my happiness, and I view things as they are, without regard to place or person; my country is the world, and my religion is to do good.

Mr. Burke, in speaking of the aristocratical law of primogeniture, says, "it is the standing law of our landed inheritance; and which, without question, has a tendency, and I think," continues he, "a happy tendency, to preserve a character of weight and consequence."

Mr. Burke may call this law what he pleases, but humanity and impartial reflection will denounce it a law of brutal injustice. Were we not accustomed to the daily practice, and did we only hear of it as the law of some distant part of the world, we should conclude that the legislators of such countries had not yet arrived at a state of civilization.

As to its preserving a character of *weight and consequence,* the case appears to me directly the reverse. It is an attaint upon character; a sort of privateering on family property. It may have weight among dependent tenants, but it gives none on a scale of national, and, much less of universal character. Speaking for myself, my parents were not able to give me a shilling, beyond what they gave me in education; and to do this they distressed themselves: yet, I possess more of what is called consequence, in the world, than any one in Mr. Burke's catalogue of aristocrats.

Having thus glanced at some of the defects of the two houses of parliament, I proceed to what is called the crown upon which I shall be very concise.

It signifies a nominal office of a million sterling a year, the business of which consists in receiving the money. Whether the person be wise or foolish, sane or insane, a native or a foreigner, matters not. Every ministry acts upon the same idea that Mr. Burke writes, namely, that the people must be hood-winked, and held in superstitious ignorance by some bugbear or other; and what is called the crown answers this purpose, and therefore it answers all the purposes to be expected from it. This is more than can be said of the other two branches.

The hazard to which this office is exposed in all countries, is not from any thing that can happen to the man, but from what may happen to the nation—the danger of its coming to its senses.

It has been customary to call the crown the executive power, and the custom is continued, though the reason has ceased.

It was called the *executive,* because the person whom it signified used, formerly, to fit in the character of a judge, in administering or executing the laws. The tribunals were then a part of the court. The power, therefore, which is now called the judicial, is what was called the executive; and, consequently, one or other of the terms is redundant, and one of the offices useless. When we speak of the crown now, it means nothing; it signifies neither a judge nor a general: besides which it is the laws that govern, and not the man. The old terms are kept up, to give an appearance of consequence to empty forms; and the only effect they have is that of increasing expences.

Before I proceed to the means of rendering governments more conducive to the general happiness of mankind, than they are at present, it will not be improper to take a review of the progress of taxation in England.

It is a general idea, that when taxes are once laid on, they are never taken off. However true this may have been of late, it was not always so. Either, therefore, the people of former times were more watchful over government than those of the present, or government was administered with less extravagance.

It is now seven hundred years since the Norman conquest, and the establishment of what is called the crown. Taking this portion of time in seven separate periods of one hundred years each, the amount of the annual taxes, at each period, will be as follows:—

Annual amount of taxes levied by William the Conqueror, beginning in the year 1066,	£. 400,000
Annual amount of taxes at one hundred years from the conquest, (1166)	200,000
Annual amount of taxes at two hundred years from the conquest, (1266)	150,000
Annual amount of taxes at three hundred years from the conquest, (1366)	130,000
Annual amount of taxes at four hundred years from the conquest, (1466)	100,000

These statements, and those which follow, are taken from Sir John Sinclair's History of the Revenue;[24] by which it appears that taxes continued decreasing for four hundred years, at the expiration of which time they were reduced three-fourths, viz. from four hundred thousand pounds to one hundred thousand. The people of England of the present day, have a traditionary and historical idea of the bravery of their ancestors; but whatever their virtues or their vices might have been, they certainly were a people who would not be imposed upon, and who kept government in awe as to taxation, if not as to principle. Though they were not able to expel the monarchical usurpation, they restricted it to a republican œconomy of taxes.

Let us now review the remaining three hundred years.

Annual amount of taxes at five hundred years from the conquest, (1566) — —	£. 500,000
Annual amount of taxes at six hundred years from the conquest, (1666) — —	1,800,000
Annual amount of taxes at the present time, (1791) — —	17,000,000

The difference between the first four hundred years and the last three, is so astonishing, as to warrant an opinion, that the national character of the English has changed. It would have been impossible to have dragooned the former English, into the excess of taxation that now exists; and when it is considered that the pay of the army, the navy, and of all the revenue-officers, is the same now as it was above a hundred years ago, when the taxes were not above a tenth part of what they are at present, it appears impossible to account for the enormous increase and expenditure, on any other ground, than extravagance, corruption, and intrigue*.

* Several of the court newspapers have of late made frequent mention of Wat Tyler. That his memory should be traduced by court sycophants, and all those who live on the spoil of a public, is not to be wondered at. He was, however, the means of checking the rage and injustice of taxation in his time, and the nation owed much to his valour. The history is concisely this:—In the time of Richard the second, a poll-tax was levied, of one shilling per head, upon every person in the nation, of whatever estate or condition, on poor as well as rich, above the age of fifteen years. If any favour was shewn in the law, it was to the rich rather than to the poor; as no person could be charged more than twenty shillings for himself, family, and servants, though ever so numerous; while all other families, under the number of twenty, were charged per head. Poll-taxes had always been odious; but this being also oppressive and unjust, it excited, as it naturally must, universal detestation among the poor and middle classes. The person known by the name of Wat Tyler, whose proper name was Walter, and a tyler by trade, lived in Deptford. The gatherer of the poll-tax, on coming to his house, demanded tax for one of his daughters, whom Tyler declared was under the age of fif-

With the revolution of 1688, and more so since the Hanover succession, came the destructive system of continental intrigues, and the rage for foreign wars and foreign dominion; systems of such secure mystery that the expences admit of no accounts; a single line stands for millions. To what excess taxation might have extended, had not the French revolution contributed to break up the system, and put an end to pretences, is impossible to say. Viewed, as that revolution ought to be, as the fortunate means of lessening the load of taxes of both countries, it is of as much importance to England as to France; and, if properly improved to all the advantages of which it is capable, and to which it leads, deserve as much celebration in one country as the other.

In pursuing this subject, I shall begin with the matter that first presents itself, that of lessening the burthen of taxes; and shall then add such matters and propositions, respecting the three countries of England, France, and America, as the present prospect of things appears to justify: I mean, an alliance of the three, for the purposes that will be mentioned in their proper place.

What has happened may happen again. By the statement before shewn of the progress of taxation, it is seen, that taxes have been lessened to a fourth part of what they had formerly been. Though the present circumstances do not admit of the same reduction, yet it ad-

---

teen. The tax-gatherer insisted on satisfying himself, and began an indecent examination of the girl, which enraging the father, he struck him with a hammer, that brought him to the ground, and was the cause of his death.

This circumstance served to bring the discontents to an issue. The inhabitants of the neighbourhood espoused the cause of Tyler, who, in a few days was joined, according to some histories, by upwards of fifty thousand men, and chosen their chief. With this force he marched to London, to demand an abolition of the tax, and a redress of other grievances. The court, finding itself in a forlorn condition, and unable to make resistance, agreed, with Richard at its head, to hold a conference with Tyler in Smithfield, making many fair professions, courtier like, of its dispositions to redress the oppressions. While Richard and Tyler were in conversation on these matters, each being on horseback, Walworth, then mayor of London, and one of the creatures of the court, watched an opportunity, and like a cowardly assassin, stabbed Tyler with a dagger; and two or three others falling upon him, he was instantly sacrificed.

Tyler appears to have been an intrepid disinterested man, with respect to himself. All his proposals made to Richard, were on a more just and public ground, than those which had been made to John by the Barons; and notwithstanding the sycophancy of historians, and men like Mr. Burke, who seek to gloss over a base action of the court by traducing Tyler, his fame will outlive their falsehood. If the Barons merited a monument to be erected in Runnymede, Tyler merits one in Smithfield.

mits of such a beginning, as may accomplish that end in less time, than in the former case.

The amount of taxes for the year, ending at Michaelmas 1788, was as follows:

Land-tax,	- -	£ 1,950,000
Customs,	- -	3,789,274
Excise, (including old and new malt,)		6,751,727
Stamps,	- -	1,278,214
Miscellaneous taxes and incidents,		1,803,755
		£ 15,572,970

Since the year 1788, upwards of one million, new taxes, have been laid on, besides the produce from the lotteries; and as the taxes have in general been more productive since than before, the amount may be taken, in round numbers, at

£ 17,000,000

N. B. The expence of collection and the drawbacks, which together amount to nearly two millions, are paid out of the gross amount; and the above is the nett sum paid into the exchequer.

This sum of seventeen millions is applied to two different purposes; the one to pay the interest of the national debt, the other to the current expences of each year. About nine millions are appropriated to the former; and the remainder, being nearly eight millions to the latter. As to the million, said to be applied to the reduction of the debt, it is so much like paying with one hand and taking out with the other, as not to merit much notice.

It happened, fortunately for France, that she possessed national domains for paying off her debt, and thereby lessening her taxes: but as this is not the case in England, her reduction of taxes can only take place by reducing the current expences, which may now be done to the amount of four or five millions annually, as will hereafter appear. When this is accomplished, it will more than counterbalance the enormous charge of the American war; and the saving will be from the same source from whence the evil arose.

As to the national debt, however heavy the interest may be in taxes;

yet, as it serves to keep alive a capital, useful to commerce, it balances by its effects a considerable part of its own weight; and as the quantity of gold and silver in England is, by some means or other, short of its proper proportion*, (being not more than twenty millions, whereas it should be sixty,) it would, besides the injustice, be bad policy to extinguish a capital that serves to supply that defect. But with respect to the current expence, whatever is saved therefrom is gain. The excess may serve to keep corruption alive, but it has no re-action on credit and commerce, like the interest of the debt.

It is now very probable, that the English government (I do not mean the nation) is unfriendly to the French revolution. Whatever serves to expose the intrigue and lessen the influence of courts, by lessening taxation, will be unwelcome to those who feed upon the spoil. Whilst the clamour of French intrigue, arbitrary power, popery, and wooden shoes could be kept up, the nation was easily allured and alarmed into taxes. Those days are now past; deception, it is to be hoped, has reaped its last harvest, and better times are in prospect for both countries, and for the world.

Taking it for granted, that an alliance may be formed between England, France, and America, for the purposes hereafter to be mentioned, the national expences of France and England may consequently be lessened. The same fleets and armies will no longer be necessary to either, and the reduction can be made ship for ship on each side. But to accomplish these objects, the governments must necessarily be fitted to a common and correspondent principle. Confidence can never take place, while an hostile disposition remains in either, or where mystery and secrecy on one side, is opposed to candour and openness on the other.

These matters admitted, the national expences might be put back, *for the sake of a precedent*, to what they were at some period when France and England were not enemies. This, consequently, must be prior to the Hanover succession, and also to the revolution of 1688†. The first

---

* Foreign intrigue, foreign wars, and foreign dominions, will in a great measure account for the deficiency.

† I happened to be in England at the celebration of the centenary of the revolution of 1688. The characters of William and Mary have always appeared to me detestable; the one seeking to destroy his uncle, and the other her father, to get possession of power themselves;

instance that presents itself, antecedent to those dates, is in the very wasteful and profligate times of Charles the Second; at which time England and France acted as allies. If I have chosen a period of great extravagance, it will serve to shew modern extravagance in a still worse light; especially as the pay of the navy, the army, and the revenue officers has not encreased since that time.

The peace establishment was then as follows:—See Sir John Sinclair's History of the Revenue.

Navy,	-	-	300,000
Army,	-	-	212,000
Ordnance,	-	-	40,000
Civil List,	-	-	462,115
			£ 1,014,115

The parliament, however, settled the whole annual peace establishment at 1,200,000*. If we go back to the time of Elizabeth, the amount of all the taxes was but half a million, yet the nation sees nothing during that period, that reproaches it with want of consequence.

All circumstances then taken together, arising from the French revolution, from the approaching harmony and reciprocal interest of the two nations, the abolition of court intrigue on both sides, and the progress of knowledge in the science of government, the annual expenditure might be put back to one million and an half, viz.

---

yet, as the nation was disposed to think something of that event, I felt hurt at seeing it ascribe the whole reputation of it to a man who had undertaken it as a jobb, and who, besides what he otherwise got, charged six hundred thousand pounds for the expence of the little fleet that brought him from Holland. George the First acted the same close-fisted part as William had done, and bought the Duchy of Bremin with the money he got from England, two hundred and fifty thousand pounds over and above his pay as king; and having thus purchased it at the expence of England, added it to his Hanoverian dominions for his own private profit. In fact, every nation that does not govern itself, is governed as a jobb. England has been the prey of jobbs ever since the revolution.

* Charles, like his predecessors and successors, finding that war was the harvest of governments, engaged in a war with the Dutch, the expence of which encreased the annual expenditure to £1,800,000, as stated under the date of 1666; but the peace establishment was but £1,200,000.

Navy,	—	—	500,000
Army,	—	—	500,000
Expences of government,			500,000

£. 1,500,000

Even this sum is six times greater than the expences of government are in America, yet the civil internal government in England, (I mean that administered by means of quarter sessions, juries, and assize, and, which, in fact, is nearly the whole, and performed by the nation,) is less expence upon the revenue, than the same species and portion of government is in America.

It is time that nations should be rational, and not be governed like animals, for the pleasure of their riders. To read the history of kings, a man would be almost inclined to suppose that government consisted in stag-hunting, and that every nation paid a million a year to a huntsman. Man ought to have pride, or shame enough to blush at being thus imposed upon, and when he feel his proper character, he will. Upon all subjects of this nature, there is often passing in the mind, a train of ideas he has not yet accustomed himself to encourage and communicate. Restrained by something that puts on the character of prudence, he acts the hypocrite upon himself as well as to others. It is, however, curious to observe how soon this spell can be dissolved. A single expression, boldly conceived and uttered, will sometimes put a whole company into their proper feelings; and whole nations are acted upon in the same manner.

As to the offices of which any civil government may be composed, it matters but little by what names they are described. In the rotine of business, as before observed, whether a man be stiled a president, a king, an emperor, a senator, or any thing else, it is impossible that any service he can perform, can merit from a nation more than ten thousand pounds a year; and as no man should be paid beyond his services, so every man of a proper heart will not accept more. Public money ought to be touched with the most scrupulous consciousness of honour. It is not the produce of riches only, but of the hard earnings of labour and poverty. It is drawn even from the bitterness of want and misery. Not a beggar passes, or perishes in the streets whose mite is not in that mass.

Were it possible that the Congress of America, could be so lost to their duty, and to the interest of their constituents, as to offer General Washington, as president of America, a million a year, he would not, and he could not, accept it. His sense of honour is of another kind. It has cost England almost seventy millions sterling, to maintain a family imported from abroad, of very inferior capacity to thousands in the nation; and scarcely a year has passed that has not produced some new mercenary application. Even the physicians bills have been sent to the public to be paid. No wonder that jails are crowded, and taxes and poor-rates encreased. Under such systems, nothing is to be looked for but what has already happened; and, as to reformation, whenever it come, it must be from the nation, and not from the government.

To shew that the sum of five hundred thousand pounds is more than sufficient to defray all the expences of government, exclusive of navies and armies, the following estimate is added for any country, of the same extent as England.

In the first place, three hundred representatives, fairly elected, are sufficient for all the purposes to which legislation can apply, and preferable to a larger number. They may be divided into two or three houses, or meet in one, as in France, or in any manner a constitution shall direct.

As representation is always considered, in free countries, as the most honourable of all stations, the allowance made to it is merely to defray the expence which the representatives incur by that service, and not to it as an office.

If an allowance, at the rate of five hundred pounds *per ann.* be made to every representative, deducting for non-attendance, the expence, if the whole number attended for six months, each year, would be } £. 75,000

The official departments cannot reasonably exceed the following number, with the salaries annexed:

Three offices, at ten thousand pounds each			30,000
Ten ditto,	at £. 5000	each	50,000
Twenty ditto,	at £. 2000	each	40,000
Forty ditto,	at £. 1000	each	40,000
Two hundred ditto,	at £. 500	each	100,000
Three hundred ditto,	at £. 200	each	60,000

Five hundred ditto,	at £.	100	each	50,000
Seven hundred ditto,	at £.	75	each	52,500
				£. 497,500

If a nation chuse, it can deduct four *per cent.* from all offices, and make one of twenty thousand *per ann.*

All revenue officers are paid out of the monies they collect, and therefore, are not in this estimation.

The foregoing is not offered as an exact detail of offices, but to shew the number and rate of salaries which five hundred thousand pounds will support; and it will, on experience, be found impracticable to find business sufficient to justify even this expence. As to the manner in which office business is now performed, the Chiefs, in several offices, such as the post-office, and certain offices in the exchequer, &c. do little more than sign their names three or four times a year; and the whole duty is performed by under clerks.

Taking, therefore, one million and an half as a sufficient peace establishment for all the honest purposes of government, which is three hundred thousand pounds more than the peace establishment in the profligate and prodigal times of Charles the Second, (notwithstanding, as has been already observed, the pay and salaries of the army, navy, and revenue officers, continue the same as at that period,) there will remain a surplus of upwards of six millions out of the present current expences. The question then will be, how to dispose of this surplus.

Whoever has observed the manner in which trade and taxes twist themselves together, must be sensible to the impossibility of separating them suddenly.

First. Because the articles now on hand are already charged with the duty, and the reduction cannot take place on the present stock.

Secondly. Because, on all those articles on which the duty is charged in the gross, such as *per* barrel, hogshead, hundred weight, or tun, the abolition of the duty does not admit of being divided down so fully to relieve the consumer, who purchases by the pint, or the pound. The last duty laid on strong beer and ale, was three shillings *per* barrel, which, if taken off, would lessen the purchase only half a farthing *per* pint, and consequently, would not reach to practical relief.

This being the condition of a great part of the taxes, it will be necessary to look for such others as are free from this embarrassment, and where the relief will be direct and visible, and capable of immediate operation.

In the first place, then, the poor-rates are a direct tax which every house-keeper feels, and who knows also, to a farthing, the sum which he pays. The national amount of the whole of the poor rates is not positively known, but can be procured. Sir John Sinclair, in his History of the Revenue, has stated it at £. 2,100,587. A considerable part of which is expended in litigations, in which the poor, instead of being relieved, are tormented. The expence, however, is the same to the parish from whatever cause it arises.

In Birmingham, the amount of the poor-rates is fourteen thousand pounds a year. This, though a large sum, is moderate, compared with the population. Birmingham is said to contain seventy thousand souls, and on a proportion of seventy thousand to fourteen thousand pounds poor-rates, the national amount of poor-rates, taking the population of England at seven millions, would be but one million four hundred thousand pounds. It is, therefore, most probable, that the population of Birmingham is over-rated. Fourteen thousand pounds is the proportion upon fifty thousand souls, taking two millions of poor-rates as the national amount.

Be it, however, what it may, it is no other than the consequence of the excessive burthen of taxes, for, at the time when the taxes were very low, the poor were able to maintain themselves; and there were no poor-rates*. In the present state of things, a labouring man, with a wife and two or three children, does not pay less than between seven and eight pounds a year in taxes. He is not sensible of this, because it is disguised to him in the articles which he buys, and he thinks only of their dearness; but as the taxes take from him, at least, a fourth part of his yearly earnings, he is consequently disabled from providing for a family, especially, if himself, or any of them, are afflicted with sickness.

The first step, therefore, of practical relief, would be to abolish the poor-rates entirely, and in lieu thereof, to make a remission of taxes

---

* Poor-rates began about the time of Henry the Eighth, when the taxes began to encrease, and they have encreased as the taxes encreased ever since.

to the poor of double the amount of the present poor-rates, viz. four millions annually out of the surplus taxes. By this measure, the poor would be benefited two millions, and the house-keepers two millions. This alone would be equal to a reduction of one hundred and twenty millions of the national debt, and consequently equal to the whole expence of the American war.

It will then remain to be considered, which is the most effectual mode of distributing this remission of four millions.

It is easily seen, that the poor are generally composed of large families of children, and old people past their labour. If these two classes are provided for, the remedy will so far reach to the full extent of the case, that what remains will be incidental, and, in a great measure, fall within the compass of benefit clubs, which, though of humble invention, merit to be ranked among the best of modern institutions.

Admitting England to contain seven million of souls; if one-fifth thereof are of that class of poor which need support, the number will be one million four hundred thousand. Of this number, one hundred and forty thousand will be aged poor, as will be hereafter shewn, and for which a distinct provision will be proposed.

There will then remain one million two hundred and sixty thousand, which, at five souls to each family, amount to two hundred and fifty-two thousand families, rendered poor from the expence of children and the weight of taxes.

The number of children under fourteen years of age, in each of those families, will be found to be about five to every two families; some having two, and others three; some one, and others four, some none, and others five; but it rarely happens that more than five are under fourteen years of age, and after this age they are capable of service or of being apprenticed.

Allowing five children (under fourteen years) to every two families,

The number of children will be -   630,000
The number of parents were they
all living, would be   -   -   504,000

It is certain, that if the children are provided for, the parents are relieved of consequence, because it is from the expence of bringing up children that their poverty arises.

Having thus ascertained the greatest number that can be supposed to need support on account of young families, I proceed to the mode of relief or distribution, which is,

To pay as a remission of taxes to every poor family, out of the surplus taxes, and in room of poor-rates, four pounds a year for every child under fourteen years of age; enjoining the parents of such children to send them to school, to learn reading, writing, and common arithmetic; the ministers of every parish, of every denomination, to certify jointly to an office, for that purpose, that this duty is performed.

The amount of this expence will be,

> For six hundred and thirty thousand
> children, at four pounds *per ann.* each,   £. 2,520,000

By adopting this method, not only the poverty of the parents will be relieved, but ignorance will be banished from the rising generation, and the number of poor will hereafter become less, because their abilities, by the aid of education, will be greater. Many a youth, with good natural genius, who is apprenticed to a mechanical trade, such as a carpenter, joiner, millwright, shipwright, blacksmith, &c. is prevented getting forward the whole of his life, from the want of a little common education when a boy.

I now proceed to the case of the aged.

I divide age into two classes. First, the approach of age beginning at fifty. Secondly, old age commencing at sixty.

At fifty, though the mental faculties of man are in full vigour, and his judgment better than at any preceeding date, the bodily powers for laborious life are on the decline. He cannot bear the same quantity of fatigue as at an earlier period. He begins to earn less, and is less capable of enduring wind and weather; and in those more retired employments where much sight is required, he fails apace, and sees himself, like an old horse, beginning to be turned adrift.

At sixty his labour ought to be over, at least from direct necessity. It is painful to see old age working itself to death, in what are called civilized countries, for daily bread.

To form some judgment of the number of those above fifty years of age, I have several times counted the persons I met in the streets of London, men, women, and children, and have generally found that the average is about one in sixteen or seventeen. If it be said that aged persons do not come much in the streets, so neither do infants; and a great proportion of grown children are in schools, and in work shops as apprentices. Taking then sixteen for a divisor, the whole number of persons, in England, of fifty years and upwards of both sexes, rich and poor, will be four hundred and twenty thousand.

The persons to be provided for out of this gross number will be, husbandmen, common labourers, journeymen of every trade and their wives, sailors, and disbanded soldiers, worn out servants of both sexes, and poor widows.

There will be also a considerable number of middling tradesmen, who having lived decently in the former part of life, begin, as age approaches, to lose their business, and at last fall to decay.

Besides these, there will be constantly thrown off from the revolutions of that wheel, which no man can stop, nor regulate, a number from every class of life connected with commerce and adventure.

To provide for all those accidents, and whatever else may befal, I take the number of persons, who at one time or other of their lives, after fifty years of age, may feel it necessary or comfortable to be better supported, than they can support themselves, and that not as a matter of grace and favour, but of right, at one third of the whole number, which is one hundred and forty thousand, as stated in page 207, and for whom a distinct provision was proposed to be made. If there be more, society, notwithstanding the shew and pomposity of government, is in a deplorable condition in England.

Of this one hundred and forty thousand, I take one half, seventy thousand, to be of the age of fifty and under sixty, and the other half to be sixty years and upwards.—Having thus ascertained the probable proportion of the number of aged persons, I proceed to the mode of rendering their condition comfortable, which is,

To pay to every such person of the age of fifty years, and until he shall arrive at the age of sixty, the sum of six pounds *per ann.* out of the surplus taxes; and ten pounds *per ann.* during life after the age of sixty. The expence of which will be,

Seventy thousand persons at £.6 *per ann.*	420,000
Seventy thousand ditto at £.10 *per ann.*	700,000
	£. 1,120,000

This support, as already remarked, is not of the nature of a charity, but of a right. Every person in England, male and female, pays on an average in taxes, two pounds eight shillings and sixpence *per ann.* from the day of his (or her) birth; and, if the expence of collection be added, he pays two pounds eleven shillings and sixpence; consequently, at the end of fifty years he has paid one hundred and twenty-eight pounds fifteen shillings; and at sixty, one hundred and fifty-four pounds ten shillings. Converting, therefore, his (or her) individual tax into a tontine, the money he shall receive after fifty years, is but little more than the legal interest of the nett money he has paid; the rest is made up from those whose circumstances do not require them to draw such support, and the capital in both cases defrays the expences of government. It is on this ground that I have extended the probable claims to one third of the number of aged persons in the nation.—Is it then better that the lives of one hundred and forty thousand aged persons be rendered comfortable, or that a million a year of public money be expended on any one individual, and him often of the most worthless or insignificant character? Let reason and justice, let honour and humanity, let even hypocrisy, sycophancy and Mr. Burke, let George, let Louis, Leopold, Frederic, Catharine, Cornwallis, or Tippoo Saib, answer the question*.

---

* Reckoning the taxes by families, five to a family, each family pays on an average, 12*l.* 17*s.* 6*d. per ann.* to this sum are to be added the poor-rates. Though all pay taxes in the articles they consume, all do not pay poor-rates. About two millions are exempted, some as not being house-keepers, others as not being able, and the poor themselves who receive the relief. The average, therefore, of poor-rates on the remaining number, is forty shillings for every family of five persons, which makes the whole average amount of taxes and rates, 14*l.* 17*s.* 6*d.* For six persons, 17*l.* 17*s.* For seven persons, 20*l.* 16*s.* 6*d.*

The average of taxes in America, under the new or representative system of government, including the interest of the debt contracted in the war, and taking the population at four million of souls, which it now amounts to, and it is daily encreasing, is five shillings per head, men, women, and children. The difference, therefore, between the two governments, is as under,

	ENGLAND.			AMERICA.		
	l.	*s.*	*d.*	*l.*	*s.*	*d.*
For a family of five persons	14	17	6	1	5	0
For a family of six persons	17	17	0	1	10	0
For a family of seven persons	20	16	6	1	15	0

The sum thus remitted to the poor will be,

To two hundred and fifty-two thousand poor families, containing six hundred and thirty thousand children,	2,520,000
To one hundred and forty thousand aged persons,	1,120,000
- -	£ 3,640,000

There will then remain three hundred and sixty thousand pounds out of the four millions, part of which may be applied as follows:

After all the above cases are provided for, there will still be a number of families who, though not properly of the class of poor, yet find it difficult to give education to their children; and such children, under such a case, would be in a worse condition than if their parents were actually poor. A nation under a well regulated government, should permit none to remain uninstructed. It is monarchical and aristocratical government only that requires ignorance for its support.

Suppose then four hundred thousand children to be in this condition, which is a greater number than ought to be supposed, after the provisions already made, the method will be,

To allow for each of those children ten shillings a year for the expence of schooling, for six years each, which will give them six months schooling each year, and half a crown a year for paper and spelling books.

The expence of this will be annually* £250,000

There will then remain one hundred and ten thousand pounds.

Notwithstanding the great modes of relief which the best instituted

---

* Public schools do not answer the general purpose of the poor. They are chiefly in corporation towns, from which the country towns and villages are excluded; or if admitted, the distance occasions a great loss of time. Education, to be useful to the poor, should be on the spot; and the best method, I believe, to accomplish this, is to enable the parents to pay the expence themselves. There are always persons of both sexes to be found in every village, especially when growing into years, capable of such an undertaking. Twenty children, at ten shillings each, (and that not more than six months each year) would be as much as some livings amount to in the remote parts of England; and there are often distressed clergymen's widows to whom such an income would be acceptable. Whatever is given on this account to children answers two purposes, to them it is education, to those who educate them it is a livelihood.

and best principled government may devise, there will still be a number of smaller cases, which it is good policy as well as beneficence in a nation to consider.

Were twenty shillings to be given to every woman immediately on the birth of a child, who should make the demand, and none will make it whose circumstances do not require it, it might relieve a great deal of instant distress.

There are about two hundred thousand births yearly in England; and if claimed, by one fourth,

> The amount would be - 50,000
> And twenty shillings to every new-married
> couple who should claim in like manner.
> This would not exceed the sum of - £20,000

Also twenty thousand pounds to be appropriated to defray the funeral expences of persons, who, travelling for work, may die at a distance from their friends. By relieving parishes from this charge, the sick stranger will be better treated.

I shall finish this part of the subject with a plan adapted to the particular condition of a metropolis, such as London.

Cases are continually occurring in a metropolis different to those which occur in the country, and for which a different, or rather an additional mode of relief is necessary. In the country, even in large towns, people have a knowledge of each other, and distress never rises to that extreme height it sometimes does in a metropolis. There is no such thing in the country as persons, in the literal sense of the word, starved to death, or dying with cold from the want of a lodging. Yet such cases, and others equally as miserable, happen in London.

Many a youth comes up to London full of expectations, and with little or no money, and unless he gets immediate employment he is already half undone; and boys bred up in London without any means of a livelihood, and as it often happens of dissolute parents, are in a still worse condition; and servants long out of place are not much better off. In short, a world of little cases are continually arising, which busy or affluent life knows not of, to open the first door to distress. Hunger is not among the postponeable wants, and a day, even a few hours, in such a condition, is often the crisis of a life of ruin.

These circumstances, which are the general cause of the little thefts and pilferings that lead to greater, may be prevented. There yet remain twenty thousand pounds out of the four millions of surplus taxes, which, with another fund hereafter to be mentioned, amounting to about twenty thousand pounds more, cannot be better applied than to this purpose. The plan then will be,

First, To erect two or more buildings, or take some already erected, capable of containing at least six thousand persons, and to have in each of these places as many kinds of employment as can be contrived, so that every person who shall come may find something which he or she can do.

Secondly, To receive all who shall come, without enquiring who or what they are. The only condition to be, that for so much, or so many hours work, each person shall receive so many meals of wholesome food, and a warm lodging, at least as good as a barrack. That a certain portion of what each person's work shall be worth shall be reserved, and given to him, or her, on their going away; and that each person shall stay as long, or as short time, or come as often as he chuse, on these conditions.

If each person staid three months, it would assist by rotation twenty-four thousand persons annually, though the real number, at all times, would be but six thousand. By establishing an asylum of this kind, such persons to whom temporary distresses occur, would have an opportunity to recruit themselves, and be enabled to look out for better employment.

Allowing that their labour paid but one half the expence of supporting them, after reserving a portion of their earnings for themselves, the sum of forty thousand pounds additional would defray all other charges for even a greater number than six thousand.

The fund very properly convertible to this purpose, in addition to the twenty thousand pounds, remaining of the former fund, will be the produce of the tax upon coals, and so iniquitously and wantonly applied to the support of the Duke of Richmond. It is horrid that any man, more especially at the price coals now are, should live on the distresses of a community; and any government permitting such an abuse, deserves to be dismissed. This fund is said to be about twenty thousand pounds *per annum*.

I shall now conclude this plan with enumerating the several particulars, and then proceed to other matters.

The enumeration is as follows:

First, Abolition of two million poor-rates.

Secondly, Provision for two hundred and fifty-two thousand poor families.

Thirdly, Education for one million and thirty thousand children.

Fourthly, Comfortable provision for one hundred and forty thousand aged persons.

Fifthly, Donation of twenty shillings each for fifty thousand births.

Sixthly, Donation of twenty shillings each for twenty thousand marriages.

Seventhly, Allowance of twenty thousand pounds for the funeral expences of persons travelling for work, and dying at a distance from their friends.

Eighthly, Employment, at all times, for the casual poor in the cities of London and Westminster.

By the operation of this plan, the poor laws, those instruments of civil torture, will be superceded, and the wasteful expence of litigation prevented. The hearts of the humane will not be shocked by ragged and hungry children, and persons of seventy and eighty years of age begging for bread. The dying poor will not be dragged from place to place to breathe their last, as a reprisal of parish upon parish. Widows will have a maintenance for their children, and not be carted away, on the death of their husbands, like culprits and criminals; and children will no longer be considered as encreasing the distresses of their parents. The haunts of the wretched will be known, because it will be to their advantage, and the number of petty crimes, the offspring of distress and poverty, will be lessened. The poor, as well as the rich, will then be interested in the support of government, and the cause and apprehension of riots and tumults will cease.—Ye who sit in ease, and solace yourselves in plenty, and such there are in Turkey and Russia, as well as in England, and who say to yourselves, "Are we not well off," have ye thought of these things? When ye do, ye will cease to speak and feel for yourselves alone.

The plan is easy in practice. It does not embarrass trade by a sudden interruption in the order of taxes, but effects the relief by changing the application of them; and the money necessary for the purpose can be drawn from the excise collections, which are made eight times a year in every market town in England.

Having now arranged and concluded this subject, I proceed to the next.

Taking the present current expences at seven millions and an half, which is the least amount they are now at, there will remain (after the sum of one million and an half be taken for the new current expences, and four millions for the before-mentioned service) the sum of two millions; part of which to be applied as follows:

Though fleets and armies, by an alliance with France, will, in a great measure, become useless, yet the persons who have devoted themselves to those services, and have thereby unfitted themselves for other lines of life, are not to be sufferers by the means that make others happy. They are a different description of men to those who form or hang about a court.

A part of the army will remain at least for some years, and also of the navy, for which a provision is already made in the former part of this plan of one million, which is almost half a million more than the peace establishment of the army and navy in the prodigal times of Charles the Second.

Suppose then fifteen thousand soldiers to be disbanded, and to allow to each of those men three shillings a week during life, clear of all deductions, to be paid in the same manner as the Chelsea College pensioners[25] are paid, and for them to return to their trades and their friends; and also to add fifteen thousand sixpences per week to the pay of the soldiers who shall remain; the annual expence will be,

To the pay of fifteen thousand disbanded soldiers, at three shillings per week, -	£ 117,000
Additional pay to the remaining soldiers, -	19,500
Suppose that the pay to the officers of the disbanded corps be of the same amount as the sum allowed to the men, -	117,000
	253,500

To prevent bulky estimations, admit
the same sum to the disbanded navy
as to the army, and the same in-
crease of pay,   -   -   -   253,500
                                                                    ————
                                                  Total   507,000

Every year some part of this sum of half a million (I omit the odd
seven thousand pounds for the purpose of keeping the account unem-
barrassed) will fall in, and the whole of it in time, as it is on the ground
of life annuities, except the encreased pay of twenty-nine thousand
pounds. As it falls in, a part of the taxes may be taken off; for instance,
when thirty thousand pounds fall in the duty on hops may be wholly
taken off; and as other parts fall in, the duties on candles and soap may
be lessened, till at last they will totally cease.

There now remains at least one million and an half of surplus taxes.

The tax on houses and windows is one of those direct taxes, which,
like the poor-rates, is not confounded with trade; and, when taken off,
the relief will be instantly felt. This tax falls heavy on the middling
class of people.

The amount of this tax by the returns of 1788, was,

	l.	*s.*	*d.*
Houses and windows by the act of 1766,	385,459	11	7
Ditto ditto by the act of 1779,	130,739	14	5½
Total	516,199	6	0½

If this tax be struck off, there will then remain about one million of
surplus taxes, and as it is always proper to keep a sum in reserve, for incidental matters, it may be best not to extend reductions further, in the
first instance, but to consider what may be accomplished by other
modes of reform.

Among the taxes most heavily felt is the commutation tax. I shall,
therefore, offer a plan for its abolition, by substituting another in its
place, which will affect three objects at once:

First, That of removing the burthen to where it can best be borne.

Secondly, Restoring justice among families by a distribution of property.

Thirdly, Extirpating the overgrown influence arising from the unnatural law of primogeniture, and which is one of the principal sources of corruption at elections.

> The amount of the commutation
> tax by the returns of 1788,
> was,　　———　　　£ 771,657　　0　0

When taxes are proposed, the country is amused by the plausible language of taxing luxuries. One thing is called a luxury at one time, and something else at another; but the real luxury does not consist in the article, but in the means of procuring it, and this is always kept out of sight.

I know not why any plant or herb of the field should be a greater luxury in one country than another, but an overgrown estate in either is a luxury at all times, and as such is the proper object of taxation. It is, therefore, right to take those kind tax-making gentlemen up on their own word, and argue on the principle themselves have laid down, that of *taxing luxuries.* If they, or their champion Mr. Burke, who, I fear, is growing out of date like the man in armour, can prove that an estate of twenty, thirty, or forty thousand pounds a year is not a luxury, I will give up the argument.

Admitting that any annual sum, say for instance, one thousand pounds, is necessary or sufficient for the support of a family, consequently the second thousand is of the nature of a luxury, the third still more so, and by proceeding on, we shall at last arrive at a sum that may not improperly be called a prohibitable luxury. It would be impolitic to set bounds to property acquired by industry, and therefore it is right to place the prohibition beyond the probable acquisition to which industry can extend; but there ought to be a limit to property, or the accumulation of it, by bequest. It should pass in some other line. The richest in every nation have poor relations, and those often very near in consanguinity.

The following table of progressive taxation is constructed on the above principles, and as a substitute for the commutation tax. It will reach the point of prohibition by a regular operation, and thereby supercede the aristocratical law of primogeniture.

TABLE I

A tax on all estates of the clear yearly value of fifty pounds, after deducting the land tax, and up

		s.	d.	
To £ 500	—	0	3	per pound
From 500 to 1000	—	0	6	per pound
On the second thousand		0	9	per pound
On the third ditto	—	1	0	per pound
On the fourth ditto		1	6	per pound
On the fifth ditto	—	2	0	per pound
On the sixth ditto	—	3	0	per pound
On the seventh ditto		4	0	per pound
On the eighth ditto		5	0	per pound
On the ninth ditto	—	6	0	per pound
On the tenth ditto	—	7	0	per pound
On the eleventh ditto		8	0	per pound
On the twelfth ditto		9	0	per pound
On the thirteenth ditto		10	0	per pound
On the fourteenth ditto		11	0	per pound
On the fifteenth ditto		12	0	per pound
On the sixteenth ditto		13	0	per pound
On the seventeenth ditto		14	0	per pound
On the eighteenth ditto		15	0	per pound
On the nineteenth ditto		16	0	per pound
On the twentieth ditto		17	0	per pound
On the twenty-first ditto		18	0	per pound
On the twenty-second ditto		19	0	per pound
On the twenty-third ditto		20	0	per pound

The foregoing table shews the progression per pound on every progressive thousand. The following table shews the amount of the tax on every thousand separately, and in the last column, the total amount of all the separate sums collected.

TABLE II

An estate of £			d.		l.	s.	d.
	50	*per ann.* at	3	per pd. pays	0	12	6
	100		3		1	5	0
	200		3		2	10	0
	300		3		3	15	0
	400		3		5	0	0
	500		3		7	5	0

After 500*l.*—the tax of sixpence per pound takes place on the second 500*l.*—consequently an estate of 1000*l. per ann.* pays 21*l.*, 15*s.* and so on,

		l.		s.	d.		l.	s.	Total amount. l.	s.
For the	1st	500	at	0	3	per pound	7	5 }	21	15
	2d	500	at	0	6		14	10 }		
	2d	1000	at	0	9		37	10	59	5
	3d	1000	at	1	0		50	0	109	5
	4th	1000	at	1	6		75	0	184	5
	5th	1000	at	2	0		100	0	284	5
	6th	1000	at	3	0		150	0	434	5
	7th	1000	at	4	0		200	0	634	5
	8th	1000	at	5	0		250	0	880	5
	9th	1000	at	6	0		300	0	1180	5
	10th	1000	at	7	0		350	0	1530	5
	11th	1000	at	8	0		400	0	1930	5
	12th	1000	at	9	0		450	0	2380	5
	13th	1000	at	10	0		500	0	2880	5
	14th	1000	at	11	0		550	0	3430	5
	15th	1000	at	12	0		600	0	4030	5
	16th	1000	at	13	0		650	0	4680	5
	17th	1000	at	14	0		700	0	5380	5
	18th	1000	at	15	0		750	0	6130	5
	19th	1000	at	16	0		800	0	6930	5
	20th	1000	at	17	0		850	0	7780	5
	21st	1000	at	18	0		900	0	8680	5
	22d	1000	at	19	0		950	0	9630	5
	23d	1000	at	20	0		1000	0	10630	5

At the twenty-third thousand the tax becomes twenty shillings in the pound, and consequently every thousand beyond that sum can produce no profit but by dividing the estate. Yet formidable as this tax appears, it will not, I believe, produce so much as the commutation tax; should it produce more, it ought to be lowered to that amount upon estates under two or three thousand a year.

On small and middling estates it is lighter (as it is intended to be) than the commutation tax. It is not till after seven or eight thousand a year that it begins to be heavy. The object is not so much the produce of the tax, as the justice of the measure. The aristocracy has screened itself too much, and this serves to restore a part of the lost equilibrium.

As an instance of its screening itself, it is only necessary to look back at the first establishment of the excise laws, at what is called the Restoration, or the coming of Charles the Second. The aristocratical interest then in power, commuted the feudal services itself was under by laying a tax on beer brewed for *sale;* that is, they compounded with Charles for an exemption from those services for themselves and their heirs, by a tax to be paid by other people. The aristocracy do not purchase beer brewed for sale, but brew their own beer free of the duty, and if any commutation at that time were necessary, it ought to have been at the expence of those for whom the exemptions from those services were intended*; instead of which it was thrown on an entire different class of men.

But the chief object of this progressive tax (besides the justice of rendering taxes more equal than they are) is, as already stated, to extirpate the overgrown influence arising from the unnatural law of primogeniture, and which is one of the principal sources of corruption at elections.

It would be attended with no good consequences to enquire how such vast estates as thirty, forty, or fifty thousand a year could commence, and that at a time when commerce and manufactures were not in a state to admit of such acquisitions. Let it be sufficient to remedy

---

*The tax on beer brewed for sale, from which the aristocracy are exempt, is almost one million more than the present commutation tax, being by the returns of 1788, 1,666,152*l.* and consequently they ought to take on themselves the amount of the commutation tax, as they are already exempted from one which is almost one million greater.

the evil by putting them in a condition of descending again to the community, by the quiet means of apportioning them among all the heirs and heiresses of those families. This will be the more necessary, because hitherto the aristocracy have quartered their younger children and connections upon the public in useless posts, places, and offices, which when abolished will leave them destitute, unless the law of primogeniture be also abolished or superceded.

A progressive tax will, in a great measure, effect this object, and that as a matter of interest to the parties most immediately concerned, as will be seen by the following table; which shews the nett produce upon every estate, after subtracting the tax. By this it will appear, that after an estate exceeds thirteen or fourteen thousand a year, the remainder produces but little profit to the holder, and consequently will pass either to the younger children, or to other kindred.

TABLE III

Shewing the nett produce of every estate from one thousand to twenty-three thousand pounds a year.

No. of thousands per ann.	Total tax subtracted.	Nett produce.
	£.	£.
1000	21	979
2000	59	1941
3000	109	2891
4000	184	3816
5000	284	4716
6000	434	5566
7000	634	6366
8000	880	7120
9000	1180	7820
10,000	1530	8470
11,000	1930	9070
12,000	2380	9620
13,000	2880	10,120
14,000	3430	10,570
15,000	4030	10,970
16,000	4680	11,320
17,000	5380	11,620

No. of thousands per ann.	Total tax subtracted.	Nett produce.
	£.	£.
18,000	6130	11,870
19,000	6930	12,170
20,000	7780	12,220
21,000	8680	12,320
22,000	9630	12,370
23,000	10,630	12,370

N. B. The odd shillings are dropped in this table.

According to this table, an estate cannot produce more then 12,370*l.* clear of the land tax and the progressive tax, and therefore the dividing such estates will follow as a matter of family interest. An estate of 23,000*l.* a year, divided into five estates of four thousand each and one of three, will be charged only 1129*l.* which is but five *per cent.* but if held by one possessor will be charged 10,630*l.*

Although an enquiry into the origin of those estates be unnecessary, the continuation of them in their present state is another subject. It is a matter of national concern. As hereditary estates, the law has created the evil, and it ought also to provide the remedy. Primogeniture ought to be abolished, not only because it is unnatural and unjust, but because the country suffers by its operation. By cutting off (as before observed) the younger children from their proper portion of inheritance, the public is loaded with the expence of maintaining them; and the freedom of elections violated by the overbearing influence which this unjust monopoly of family property produces. Nor is this all. It occasions a waste of national property. A considerable part of the land of the country is rendered unproductive by the great extent of parks and chases[26] which this law serves to keep up, and this at a time when the annual production of grain is not equal to the national consumption*.—In short, the evils of the aristocratical system are so great and numerous, so inconsistent with every thing that is just, wise, natural, and beneficent, that when they are considered, there ought not to be a doubt that many, who are now classed under that description, will wish to see such a system abolished.

* See the reports on the corn trade.

What pleasure can they derive from contemplating the exposed condition, and almost certain beggary of their younger offspring? Every aristocratical family has an appendage of family beggars hanging round it, which in a few ages, or a few generations, are shook off, and console themselves with telling their tale in alms-houses, work-houses, and prisons. This is the natural consequence of aristocracy. The peer and the beggar are often of the same family. One extreme produces the other: to make one rich many must be made poor; neither can the system be supported by other means.

There are two classes of people to whom the laws of England are particularly hostile, and those the most helpless; younger children and the poor. Of the former I have just spoken; of the latter I shall mention one instance out of the many that might be produced, and with which I shall close this subject.

Several laws are in existence for regulating and limiting workmen's wages. Why not leave them as free to make their own bargains, as the lawmakers are to let their farms and houses? Personal labour is all the property they have. Why is that little, and the little freedom they enjoy to be infringed? But the injustice will appear stronger, if we consider the operation and effect of such laws. When wages are fixed by what is called a law, the legal wages remain stationary, while every thing else is in progression; and as those who make that law, still continue to lay on new taxes by other laws, they encrease the expence of living by one law, and take away the means by another.

But if those gentlemen law-makers and tax-makers thought it right to limit the poor pittance which personal labour can produce, and on which a whole family is to be supported, they certainly must feel themselves happily indulged in a limitation on their own part, of not less than twelve thousand a year, and that of property they never acquired, (nor probably any of their ancestors) and of which they have made so ill a use.

Having now finished this subject, I shall bring the several particulars into one view, and then proceed to other matters.

The first EIGHT ARTICLES are brought forward from page 214.

1. Abolition of two million poor-rates.
2. Provision for two hundred and fifty-two thousand poor families, at the rate of four pounds per head for each child under fourteen years of age; which, with the addition of two hundred and fifty thousand pounds, provides also education for one million and thirty thousand children.
3. Annuity of six pounds (per ann.) each for all poor persons, decayed tradesmen, or others (supposed seventy thousand) of the age of fifty years, and until sixty.
4. Annuity of ten pounds each for life for all poor persons, decayed tradesmen, and others (supposed seventy thousand) of the age of sixty years.
5. Donation of twenty shillings each for fifty thousand births.
6. Donation of twenty shillings each for twenty thousand marriages.
7. Allowance of twenty thousand pounds for the funeral expences of persons travelling for work, and dying at a distance from their friends.
8. Employment at all times for the casual poor in the cities of London and Westminster.

SECOND ENUMERATION

9. Abolition of the tax on houses and windows.
10. Allowance of three shillings per week for life to fifteen thousand disbanded soldiers, and a proportionable allowance to the officers of the disbanded corps.
11. Encrease of pay to the remaining soldiers of 19,500*l.* annually.
12. The same allowance to the disbanded navy, and the same encrease of pay, as to the army.
13. Abolition of the commutation tax.
14. Plan of a progressive tax, operating to extirpate the unjust and unnatural law of primogeniture, and the vicious influence of the aristocratical system*.

* When enquiries are made into the condition of the poor, various degrees of distress will most probably be found, to render a different arrangement preferable to that which is already proposed. Widows with families will be in greater want than where there are husbands living. There is also a difference in the expence of living in different countries; and more so in fuel.

There yet remains, as already stated, one million of surplus taxes. Some part of this will be required for circumstances that do not immediately present themselves, and such part as shall not be wanted, will admit a further reduction of taxes equal to that amount.

Among the claims that justice requires to be made, the condition of the inferior revenue officers will merit attention. It is a reproach to any government to waste such an immensity of revenue in sinecures and nominal and unnecessary places and offices, and not allow even a decent livelihood to those on whom the labour falls. The salary of the inferior officers of the revenue has stood at the petty pittance of less than fifty pounds a year for upwards of one hundred years. It ought to be seventy. About one hundred and twenty thousand pounds applied to this purpose, will put all those salaries in a decent condition.

This was proposed to be done almost twenty years ago, but the treasury-board then in being startled at it, as it might lead to similar expectations from the army and navy; and the event was, that the King, or somebody for him, applied to parliament to have his own salary raised an hundred thousand a year, which being done, every thing else was laid aside.

With respect to another class of men, the inferior clergy, I forbear to enlarge on their condition; but all partialities and prejudices for, or against, different modes and forms of religion aside, common justice will determine, whether there ought to be an income of twenty or thirty pounds a year to one man, and of ten thousand to another. I

	£.
Suppose then fifty thousand extraordinary cases, at the rate of 10*l.* per family per ann. ————	500,000
100,000 Families, at 8*l.* per family per ann. -	800,000
100,000 Families, at 7*l.* per family per ann. -	700,000
104,000 Families, at 5*l.* per family per ann. -	520,000
And instead of ten shillings per head for the education of other children, to allow fifty shillings per family for that purpose to fifty thousand families	250,000
	2,770,000
140,000 Aged persons as before,	1,120,000
	3,890,000

This arrangement amounts to the same sum as stated in page 211, including the 250,000*l.* for education; but it provides (including the aged people) for four hundred and four thousand families, which is almost one third of all the families in England.

speak on this subject with the more freedom, because I am known not to be a Presbyterian; and therefore the cant cry of court sycophants, about church and meeting, kept up to amuse and bewilder the nation, cannot be raised against me.

Ye simple men, on both sides the question, do ye not see through this courtly craft? If ye can be kept disputing and wrangling about church and meeting, ye just answer the purpose of every courtier, who lives the while on the spoil of the taxes, and laughs at your credulity. Every religion is good that teaches man to be good; and I know of none that instructs him to be bad.

All the before-mentioned calculations, suppose only sixteen millions and an half of taxes paid into the exchequer, after the expence of collection and drawbacks at the custom-house and excise-office are deducted; whereas the sum paid into the exchequer is very nearly, if not quite, seventeen millions. The taxes raised in Scotland and Ireland are expended in those countries, and therefore their savings will come out of their own taxes; but if any part be paid into the English exchequer, it might be remitted. This will not make one hundred thousand pounds a year difference.

There now remains only the national debt to be considered. In the year 1789, the interest, exclusive of the tontine, was 9,150,138l. How much the capital has been reduced since that time the minister best knows. But after paying the interest, abolishing the tax on houses and windows, the commutation tax, and the poor rates; and making all the provisions for the poor, for the education of children, the support of the aged, the disbanded part of the army and navy, and encreasing the pay of the remainder, there will be a surplus of one million.

The present scheme of paying off the national debt appears to me, speaking as an indifferent person, to be an ill-concerted, if not a fallacious job. The burthen of the national debt consists not in its being so many millions, or so many hundred millions, but in the quantity of taxes collected every year to pay the interest. If this quantity continue the same, the burthen of the national debt is the same to all intents and purposes, be the capital more or less. The only knowledge which the public can have of the reduction of the debt, must be through the reduction of taxes for paying the interest. The debt, therefore, is not reduced one farthing to the public by all the millions that have been paid; and it would require more money now to purchase up the capital, than when the scheme began.

Digressing for a moment at this point, to which I shall return again, I look back to the appointment of Mr. Pitt, as minister.

I was then in America. The war was over; and though resentment had ceased, memory was still alive.

When the news of the coalition arrived, though it was a matter of no concern to me as a citizen of America, I felt it as a man. It had something in it which shocked, by publicly sporting with decency, if not with principle. It was impudence in Lord North; it was want of firmness in Mr. Fox.[27]

Mr. Pitt was, at that time, what may be called a maiden character in politics. So far from being hackneyed, he appeared not to be initiated into the first mysteries of court intrigue. Every thing was in his favour. Resentment against the coalition served as friendship to him, and his ignorance of vice was credited for virtue. With the return of peace, commerce and prosperity would rise of itself; yet even this encrease was thrown to his account.

When he came to the helm the storm was over, and he had nothing to interrupt his course. It required even ingenuity to be wrong, and he succeeded. A little time shewed him the same sort of man as his predecessors had been. Instead of profiting by those errors which had accumulated a burthen of taxes unparalleled in the world, he sought, I might almost say, he advertised for enemies, and provoked means to encrease taxation. Aiming at something, he knew not what, he ransacked Europe and India for adventures, and abandoning the fair pretensions he began with, became the knight-errant of modern times.

It is unpleasant to see character throw itself away. It is more so to see one's-self deceived. Mr. Pitt had merited nothing, but he promised much. He gave symptoms of a mind superior to the meanness and corruption of courts. His apparent candour encouraged expectations; and the public confidence, stunned, wearied, and confounded by a chaos of parties, revived and attached itself to him. But mistaking, as he has done, the disgust of the nation against the coalition, for merit in himself, he has rushed into measures, which a man less supported would not have presumed to act.

All this seems to shew that change of ministers amounts to nothing.

One goes out, another comes in, and still the same measures, vices, and extravagance are pursued. It signifies not who is minister. The defect lies in the system. The foundation and the superstructure of the government is bad. Prop it as you please, it continually sinks into court government, and ever will.

I return, as I promised, to the subject of the national debt, that offspring of the Dutch-Anglo revolution, and its handmaid the Hanover succession.

But it is now too late to enquire how it began. Those to whom it is due have advanced the money; and whether it was well or ill spent, or pocketed, is not their crime. It is, however, easy to see, that as the nation proceeds in contemplating the nature and principles of government, and to understand taxes, and make comparisons between those of America, France, and England, it will be next to impossible to keep it in the same torpid state it has hitherto been. Some reform must, from the necessity of the case, soon begin. It is not whether these principles press with little or much force in the present moment. They are out. They are abroad in the world, and no force can stop them. Like a secret told, they are beyond recall; and he must be blind indeed that does not see that a change is already beginning.

Nine millions of dead taxes is a serious thing; and this not only for bad, but in a great measure for foreign government. By putting the power of making war into the hands of foreigners who came for what they could get, little else was to be expected than what has happened.

Reasons are already advanced in this work shewing that whatever the reforms in the taxes may be, they ought to be made in the current expences of government, and not in the part applied to the interest of the national debt. By remitting the taxes of the poor, *they* will be totally relieved, and all discontent on their part will be taken away; and by striking off such of the taxes as are already mentioned, the nation will more than recover the whole expence of the mad American war.

There will then remain only the national debt as a subject of discontent; and in order to remove, or rather to prevent this, it would be good policy in the stock-holders themselves to consider it as property, subject like all other property, to bear some portion of the taxes. It would give to it both popularity and security, and as a great part of its present inconvenience is balanced by the capital which it keeps alive, a measure of this kind would so far add to that balance as to silence objections.

This may be done by such gradual means as to accomplish all that is necessary with the greatest ease and convenience.

Instead of taxing the capital, the best method would be to tax the interest by some progressive ratio, and to lessen the public taxes in the same proportion as the interest diminished.

Suppose the interest was taxed one halfpenny in the pound the first year, a penny more the second, and to proceed by a certain ratio to be determined upon, always less than any other tax upon property. Such a tax would be subtracted from the interest at the time of payment, without any expence of collection.

One halfpenny in the pound would lessen the interest and consequently the taxes, twenty thousand pounds. The tax on waggons amounts to this sum, and this tax might be taken off the first year. The second year the tax on female servants, or some other of the like amount might also be taken off, and by proceeding in this manner, always applying the tax raised from the property of the debt towards its extinction, and not carry it to the current services, it would liberate itself.

The stockholders, notwithstanding this tax, would pay less taxes than they do now. What they would save by the extinction of the poor-rates, and the tax on houses and windows, and the commutation tax, would be considerably greater than what this tax, slow, but certain in its operation, amounts to.

It appears to me to be prudence to look out for measures that may apply under any circumstance that may approach. There is, at this moment, a crisis in the affairs of Europe that requires it. Preparation now is wisdom. If taxation be once let loose, it will be difficult to re-instate it; neither would the relief be so effectual, as to proceed by some certain and gradual reduction.

The fraud, hypocrisy, and imposition of governments, are now beginning to be too well understood to promise them any long career. The farce of monarchy and aristocracy, in all countries, is following that of chivalry, and Mr. Burke is dressing for the funeral. Let it then pass quietly to the tomb of all other follies, and the mourners be comforted.

The time is not very distant when England will laugh at itself for sending to Holland, Hanover, Zell, or Brunswick for men, at the expence of a million a year, who understood neither her laws, her language, nor her interest, and whose capacities would scarcely have fitted them for the office of a parish constable. If government could be trusted to such hands, it must be some easy and simple thing indeed, and materials fit for all the purposes may be found in every town and village in England.

When it shall be said in any country in the world, my poor are happy; neither ignorance nor distress is to be found among them; my jails are empty of prisoners, my streets of beggars; the aged are not in want, the taxes are not oppressive; the rational world is my friend, because I am the friend of its happiness: when these things can be said, then may that country boast its constitution and its government.

Within the space of a few years we have seen two Revolutions, those of America and France. In the former, the contest was long, and the conflict severe; in the latter, the nation acted with such a consolidated impulse, that having no foreign enemy to contend with, the revolution was complete in power the moment it appeared. From both those instances it is evident, that the greatest forces that can be brought into the field of revolutions, are reason and common interest. Where these can have the opportunity of acting, opposition dies with fear, or crumbles away by conviction. It is a great standing which they have now universally obtained; and we may hereafter hope to see revolutions, or changes in governments, produced with the same quiet operation by which any measure, determinable by reason and discussion, is accomplished.

When a nation changes its opinion and habits of thinking, it is no longer to be governed as before; but it would not only be wrong, but bad policy, to attempt by force what ought to be accomplished by reason. Rebellion consists in forcibly opposing the general will of a nation, whether by a party or by a government. There ought, therefore, to be in every nation a method of occasionally ascertaining the state of public opinion with respect to government. On this point the old government of France was superior to the present government of England, because, on extraordinary occasions, recourse could be had to what was then called the States General. But in England there are no such occasional bodies; and as to those who are now called Representatives, a great part of them are mere machines of the court, placemen, and dependants.

I presume, that though all the people of England pay taxes, not an hundredth part of them are electors, and the members of one of the houses of parliament represent nobody but themselves. There is, therefore, no power but the voluntary will of the people that has a right to act in any matter respecting a general reform; and by the same right that two persons can confer on such a subject, a thousand may. The object, in all such preliminary proceedings, is to find out what the general sense of a nation is, and to be governed by it. If it prefer a bad or defective government to a reform, or chuse to pay ten times more taxes than there is occasion for, it has a right so to do; and so long as the majority do not impose conditions on the minority, different to what they impose on themselves, though there may be much error, there is no injustice. Neither will the error continue long. Reason and discussion will soon bring things right, however wrong they may begin. By such a process no tumult is to be apprehended. The poor, in all countries, are naturally both peaceable and grateful in all reforms in which their interest and happiness is included. It is only by neglecting and rejecting them that they become tumultuous.

The objects that now press on the public attention are, the French revolution, and the prospect of a general revolution in governments. Of all nations in Europe, there is none so much interested in the French revolution as England. Enemies for ages, and that at a vast expence, and without any national object, the opportunity now presents itself of amicably closing the scene, and joining their efforts to reform the rest of Europe. By doing this, they will not only prevent the further effusion of blood, and encrease of taxes, but be in a condition of getting rid of a considerable part of their present burthens, as has been already stated. Long experience however has shewn, that reforms of this kind are not those which old governments wish to promote; and therefore it is to nations, and not to such governments, that these matters present themselves.

In the preceding part of this work, I have spoken of an alliance between England, France, and America, for purposes that were to be afterwards mentioned. Though I have no direct authority on the part of America, I have good reason to conclude, that she is disposed to enter into a consideration of such a measure, provided, that the governments with which she might ally, acted as national governments, and not as courts enveloped in intrigue and mystery. That France as a nation, and a national government, would prefer an alliance with England, is a matter of certainty. Nations, like individuals, who have long been enemies, without knowing each other, or knowing why, become the better friends when they discover the errors and impositions under which they had acted.

Admitting, therefore, the probability of such a connection, I will state some matters by which such an alliance, together with that of Holland, might render service, not only to the parties immediately concerned, but to all Europe.

It is, I think, certain, that if the fleets of England, France, and Holland were confederated, they could propose, with effect, a limitation to, and a general dismantling of all the navies in Europe, to a certain proportion to be agreed upon.

First, That no new ship of war shall be built by any power in Europe, themselves included.

Secondly, That all the navies now in existence shall be put back, suppose to one-tenth of their present force. This will save to France and England at least two million sterling annually to each, and their relative force be in the same proportion as it is now. If men will permit themselves to think, as rational beings ought to think, nothing can appear more ridiculous and absurd, exclusive of all moral reflections, than to be at the expence of building navies, filling them with men, and then hauling them into the ocean, to try which can sink each other fastest. Peace, which costs nothing, is attended with infinitely more advantage, than any victory with all its expence. But this, though it best answers the purpose of nations, does not that of court governments, whose habited policy is pretence for taxation, places, and offices.

It is, I think, also certain, that the above confederated powers, together with that of the United States of America, can propose with effect, to Spain, the independance of South America, and the opening those countries of immense extent and wealth to the general commerce of the world, as North America now is.

With how much more glory, and advantage to itself, does a nation act, when it exerts its powers to rescue the world from bondage, and to create itself friends, than when it employs those powers to encrease ruin, desolation, and misery. The horrid scene that is now acting by the

English government in the East-Indies, is fit only to be told of Goths and Vandals, who, destitute of principle, robbed and tortured the world they were incapable of enjoying.

The opening of South America would produce an immense field of commerce, and a ready money market for manufactures, which the eastern world does not. The East is already a country full of manufactures, the importation of which is not only an injury to the manufactures of England, but a drain upon its specie. The balance against England by this trade is regularly upwards of half a million annually sent out in the East-India ships in silver; and this is the reason, together with German intrigue, and German subsidies, there is so little silver in England.

But any war is harvest to such governments, however ruinous it may be to a nation. It serves to keep up deceitful expectations which prevent a people looking into the defects and abuses of government. It is the *lo here!* and the *lo there!* that amuses and cheats the multitude.

Never did so great an opportunity offer itself to England, and to all Europe, as is produced by the two Revolutions of America and France. By the former, freedom has a national champion in the Western world; and by the latter, in Europe. When another nation shall join France, despotism and bad government will scarcely dare to appear. To use a trite expression, the iron is becoming hot all over Europe. The insulted German and the enslaved Spaniard, the Russ and the Pole, are beginning to think. The present age will hereafter merit to be called the Age of reason, and the present generation will appear to the future as the Adam of a new world.

When all the governments of Europe shall be established on the representative system, nations will become acquainted, and the animosities and prejudices fomented by the intrigue and artifice of courts, will cease. The oppressed soldier will become a freeman; and the tortured sailor, no longer dragged along the streets like a felon, will pursue his mercantile voyage in safety. It would be better that nations should continue the pay of their soldiers during their lives, and give them their discharge and restore them to freedom and their friends, and cease recruiting, than retain such multitudes at the same expence, in a condition useless to society and themselves. As soldiers have hitherto been treated in most countries, they might be said to be without a friend. Shunned by the citizen on an apprehension of being enemies to liberty, and too often insulted by those who commanded them, their condition was a double oppression. But where genuine principles of liberty pervade a people, every thing is restored to order; and the soldier civily treated, returns the civility.

In contemplating revolutions, it is easy to perceive that they may arise from two distinct causes; the one, to avoid or get rid of some great calamity; the other, to obtain some great and positive good; and the two may be distinguished by the names of active and passive revolutions. In those which proceed from the former cause, the temper becomes incensed and sowered; and the redress, obtained by danger, is too often sullied by revenge. But in those which proceed from the latter, the heart, rather animated than agitated, enters serenely upon the subject. Reason and discussion, persuasion and conviction, become the weapons in the contest, and it is only when those are attempted to be suppressed that recource is had to violence. When men unite in agreeing that a *thing is good,* could it be obtained, such as relief from a burden of taxes and the extinction of corruption, the object is more than half accomplished. What they approve as the end, they will promote in the means.

Will any man say, in the present excess of taxation, falling so heavily on the poor, that a remission of five pounds annually of taxes to one hundred and four thousand poor families is not a *good thing?* Will he say, that a remission of seven pounds annually to one hundred thousand other poor families—of eight pounds annually to another hundred thousand poor families, and of ten pounds annually to fifty thousand poor and widowed families, are not *good things?* And to proceed a step farther in this climax, will he say, that to provide against the misfortunes to which all human life is subject, by securing six pounds annually for all poor, distressed, and reduced persons of the age of fifty and until sixty, and of ten pounds annually after sixty is not a *good thing?*

Will he say, that an abolition of two million of poor-rates to the house-keepers, and of the whole of the house and window-light tax and of the commutation tax is not a *good thing?* Or will he say, that to abolish corruption is a *bad thing?*

If, therefore, the good to be obtained be worthy of a passive, rational, and costless revolution, it would be bad policy to prefer waiting for a calamity that should force a violent one. I have no idea, considering the reforms which are now passing and spreading throughout Europe, that England will permit herself to be the last; and where the occasion and the opportunity quietly offer, it is better than to wait for a turbulent necessity. It may be considered as an honour to the animal faculties of man to obtain redress by courage and danger, but it is far greater honour to the rational faculties to accomplish the same object by reason, accommodation, and general consent*.

As reforms, or revolutions, call them which you please, extend themselves among nations, those nations will form connections and conventions, and when a few are thus confederated, the progress will be rapid, till despotism and corrupt government be totally expelled, at least out of two quarters of the world, Europe and America. The Algerine piracy may then be commanded to cease, for it is only by the malicious policy of old governments, against each other, that it exists.

Throughout this work, various and numerous as the subjects are, which I have taken up and investigated, there is only a single paragraph upon religion, viz. *"that every religion is good, that teaches man to be good."*

I have carefully avoided to enlarge upon the subject, because I am inclined to believe, that what is called the present ministry wish to see contentions about religion kept up, to prevent the nation turning its attention to subjects of government. It is, as if they were to say, *"Look that way, or any way, but this."*

But as religion is very improperly made a political machine, and the reality of it is thereby destroyed, I will conclude this work with stating in what light religion appears to me.

---

* I know it is the opinion of many of the most enlightened characters in France (there always will be those who see farther into events than others) not only among the general mass of citizens, but of many of the principal members of the former National Assembly, that the monarchical plan will not continue many years in that country. They have found out, that as wisdom cannot be made hereditary, power ought not; and that, for a man to merit a million stirling a year from a nation, he ought to have a mind capable of comprehending from an atom to a universe; which, if he had, he would be above receiving the pay. But they wished not to appear to lead the nation faster than its own reason and interest dictated. In all the conversations where I have been present upon this subject, the idea always was, that when such a time, from the general opinion of the nation, shall arrive, that the honourable and liberal method would be, to make a handsome present in fee simple to the person whoever he may be, that shall then be in the monarchical office, and for him to retire to the enjoyment of private life, possessing his share of general rights and privileges, and to be no more accountable to the public for his time and his conduct than any other citizen.

If we suppose a large family of children, who, on any particular day, or particular circumstance, made it a custom to present to their parent some token of their affection and gratitude, each of them would make a different offering, and most probably in a different manner. Some would pay their congratulations in themes of verse or prose, by some little devices, as their genius dictated, or according to what they thought would please; and, perhaps, the least of all, not able to do any of those things, would ramble into the garden, or the field, and gather what it thought the prettiest flower it could find, though, perhaps, it might be but a simple weed. The parent would be more gratified by such variety, than if the whole of them had acted on a concerted plan, and each had made exactly the same offering. This would have the cold appearance of contrivance, or the harsh one of controul. But of all unwelcome things, nothing could more afflict the parent than to know, that the whole of them had afterwards gotten together by the ears, boys and girls, fighting, scratching, reviling, and abusing each other about which was the best or the worst present.

Why may we not suppose, that the great Father of all is pleased with variety of devotion; and that the greatest offence we can act, is that by which we seek to torment and render each other miserable. For my own part, I am fully satisfied that what I am now doing, with an endeavour to conciliate mankind, to render their condition happy, to unite nations that have hitherto been enemies, and to extirpate the horrid practice of war, and break the chains of slavery and oppression, is acceptable in his sight, and being the best service I can perform, I act it chearfully.

I do not believe that any two men, on what are called doctrinal points, think alike who think at all. It is only those who have not thought that appear to agree. It is in this case as with what is called the British constitution. It has been taken for granted to be good, and encomiums have supplied the place of proof. But when the nation come to examine into its principles and the abuses it admits, it will be found to have more defects than I have pointed out in this work and the former.

As to what are called national religions, we may, with as much propriety, talk of national Gods. It is either political craft or the remains of the Pagan system, when every nation had its separate and particular deity. Among all the writers of the English church clergy, who have treated on the general subject of religion, the present Bishop of Landaff has not been excelled, and it is with much pleasure that I take the opportunity of expressing this token of respect.

I have now gone through the whole of the subject, at least, as far as it appears to me at present. It has been my intention for the five years I have been in Europe, to offer an address to the people of England on the subject of government, if the opportunity presented itself before I returned to America. Mr. Burke has thrown it in my way, and I thank him. On a certain occasion three years ago, I pressed him to propose a national convention to be fairly elected for the purpose of taking the state of the nation into consideration; but I found, that however strongly the parliamentary current was then setting against the party he acted with, their policy was to keep every thing within that field of corruption, and trust to accidents. Long experience had shewn that parliaments would follow any change of ministers, and on this they rested their hopes and their expectations.

Formerly, when divisions arose respecting governments, recourse was had to the sword, and a civil war ensued. That savage custom is exploded by the new system, and reference is had to national conventions. Discussion and the general will arbitrates the question, and to this, private opinion yields with a good grace, and order is preserved uninterrupted.

Some gentlemen have affected to call the principles upon which this work and the former part of *Rights of Man* are founded, "a new fangled doctrine." The question is not whether those principles are new or old, but whether they are right or wrong. Suppose the former, I will shew their effect by a figure easily understood.

It is now towards the middle of February. Were I to take a turn into the country, the trees would present a leafless winterly appearance. As people are apt to pluck twigs as they walk along, I perhaps might do the same, and by chance might observe, that a *single bud* on that twig had begun to swell. I should reason very unnaturally, or rather not reason at all, to suppose *this* was the *only* bud in England which had this appearance. Instead of deciding thus, I should instantly conclude, that the same appearance was beginning, or about to begin, every where; and though the vegetable sleep will continue longer on some trees and plants than on others, and though some of them may not *blossom* for two or three years, all will be in leaf in the summer, except those which are *rotten*. What pace the political summer may keep with the natural, no human foresight can determine. It is, however, not difficult to perceive that the spring is begun.—Thus wishing, as I sincerely do, freedom and happiness to all nations, I close the

SECOND PART.

Appendix

As the publication of this work has been delayed beyond the time intended, I think it not improper, all circumstances considered, to state the causes that have occasioned the delay.

The reader will probably observe, that some parts in the plan contained in this work for reducing the taxes, and certain parts in Mr. Pitt's speech at the opening of the present session, Tuesday, January 31, are so much alike, as to induce a belief, that either the Author had taken the hint from Mr. Pitt, or Mr. Pitt from the Author.—I will first point out the parts that are similar, and then state such circumstances as I am acquainted with, leaving the reader to make his own conclusion.

Considering it almost an unprecedented case, that taxes should be proposed to be taken off, it is equally as extraordinary that such a measure should occur to two persons at the same time; and still more so, (considering the vast variety and multiplicity of taxes) that they should hit on the same specific taxes. Mr. Pitt has mentioned, in his speech, the tax on *Carts* and *Waggons*—that on *Female Servants*—the lowering the tax on *Candles,* and the taking off the tax of three shillings on *Houses* having under seven windows.

Every one of those specific taxes are a part of the plan contained in this work, and proposed also to be taken off. Mr. Pitt's plan, it is true, goes no farther than to a reduction of three hundred and twenty thousand pounds; and the reduction proposed in this work to nearly six millions. I have made my calculations on only sixteen millions and an half of revenue, still asserting that it was "very nearly, if not quite, seventeen millions." Mr. Pitt states it at 16,690,000. I know enough of the matter to say, that he has not *over*stated it. Having thus given the particulars, which correspond in this work and his speech, I will state a chain of circumstances that may lead to some explanation.

The first hint for lessening the taxes, and that as a consequence flowing from the French revolution, is to be found in the ADDRESS and DECLARATION of the Gentlemen who met at the Thatched-House Tavern, August 20, 1791. Among many other particulars stated in that Address, is the following, put as an interrogation to the government opposers of the French Revolution. "*Are they sorry that the pretence for new oppressive taxes, and the occasion for continuing many old taxes will be at an end?*"

It is well known, that the persons who chiefly frequent the Thatched-House Tavern, are men of court connections, and so much did they take this Address and Declaration respecting the French revolution and the reduction of taxes in disgust, that the Landlord was under the necessity of informing the Gentlemen, who composed the meeting of the twentieth of August, and who proposed holding another meeting, that he could not receive them*.

What was only hinted at in the Address and Declaration, respecting taxes and principles of government, will be found reduced to a regular system in this work. But as Mr. Pitt's speech contains some of the same things respecting taxes, I now come to give the circumstances before alluded to.

The case is: This work was intended to be published just before the meeting of Parliament, and for that purpose a considerable part of the copy was put into the printer's hands in September, and all the remaining copy, as far as page 229, which contains the parts to which Mr.

---

* The gentleman who signed the address and declaration as chairman of the meeting, M. Horne Tooke, being generally supposed to be the person who drew it up, and having spoken much in commendation of it, has been jocularly accused of praising his own work. To free him from this embarrassment, and to save him the repeated trouble of mentioning the author, as he has not failed to do, I make no hesitation in saying, that as the opportunity of benefiting by the French Revolution easily occurred to me, I drew up the publication in question, and shewed it to him and some other gentlemen; who, fully approving it, held a meeting for the purpose of making it public, and subscribed to the amount of fifty guineas to defray the expence of advertising. I believe there are at this time, in England, a greater number of men acting on disinterested principles, and determined to look into the nature and practices of government themselves, and not blindly trust, as has hitherto been the case, either to government generally, or to parliaments, or to parliamentary opposition, than at any former period. Had this been done a century ago, corruption and taxation had not arrived to the height they are now at.

Pitt's speech is similar, was given to him full six weeks before the meeting of parliament, and he was informed of the time at which it was to appear. He had composed nearly the whole about a fortnight before the time of Parliament meeting, and had printed as far as page 199, and had given me a proof of the next sheet, up to page 209. It was then in sufficient forwardness to be out at the time proposed, as two other sheets were ready for striking off. I had before told him, that if he thought he should be straightened for time, I would get part of the work done at another press, which he desired me not to do. In this manner the work stood on the Tuesday fortnight preceding the meeting of Parliament, when all at once, without any previous intimation, though I had been with him the evening before, he sent me, by one of his workmen, all the remaining copy, from page 199, declining to go on with the work *on any consideration.*

To account for this extraordinary conduct I was totally at a loss, as he stopped at the part where the arguments on systems and principles of government closed, and where the plan for the reduction of taxes, the education of children, and the support of the poor and the aged begins; and still more especially, as he had, at the time of his beginning to print, and before he had seen the whole copy, offered a thousand pounds for the copy-right, together with the future copy-right of the former part of the Rights of Man. I told the person who brought me this offer that I should not accept it, and wished it not to be renewed, giving him as my reason, that though I believed the printer to be an honest man, I would never put it in the power of any printer or publisher to suppress or alter a work of mine, by making him master of the copy, or give to him the right of selling it to any minister, or to any other person, or to treat as a mere matter of traffic, that which I intended should operate as a principle.

His refusal to complete the work (which he could not purchase) obliged me to seek for another printer, and this of consequence would throw the publication back till after the meeting of Parliament, otherways it would have appeared that Mr. Pitt had only taken up a part of the plan which I had more fully stated.

Whether that gentleman, or any other, had seen the work, or any part of it, is more than I have authority to say. But the manner in which the work was returned, and the particular time at which this was done, and that after the offers he had made, are suspicious circumstances. I know what the opinion of booksellers and publishers is upon such a case, but as to my own opinion, I chuse to make no declaration. There are many ways by which proof sheets may be procured by other persons before a work publicly appear; to which I shall add a certain circumstance, which is,

A ministerial bookseller in Piccadilly who has been employed, as common report says, by a clerk of one of the boards closely connected with the ministry (the board of trade and plantation of which Hawksbury is president) to publish what he calls my Life (I wish his own life and that those of the cabinet were as good) used to have his books printed at the same printing-office that I employed; but when the former part of *Rights of Man* came out, he took his work away in dudgeon; and about a week or ten days before the printer returned my copy, he came to make him an offer of his work again, which was accepted. This would consequently give him admission into the printing-office where the sheets of this work were then lying; and as booksellers and printers are free with each other, he would have the opportunity of seeing what was going on.—Be the case however as it may, Mr. Pitt's plan, little and diminutive as it is, would have had a very awkward appearance, had this work appeared at the time the printer had engaged to finish it.

I have now stated the particulars which occasioned the delay, from the proposal to purchase, to the refusal to print. If all the Gentlemen are innocent, it is very unfortunate for them that such a variety of suspicious circumstances should, without any design, arrange themselves together.

Having now finished this part, I will conclude with stating another circumstance.

About a fortnight or three weeks before the meeting of Parliament, a small addition, amounting to about twelve shillings and six pence a year, was made to the pay of the soldiers, or rather, their pay was docked so much less. Some Gentlemen who knew, in part, that this work would contain a plan of reforms respecting the oppressed condition of soldiers, wished me to add a note to the work, signifying, that the part upon that subject had been in the printer's hands some weeks before that addition of pay was proposed. I declined doing this, lest it should be interpreted into an air of vanity, or an endeavour to excite suspicion (for which, perhaps, there might be no grounds) that some of the government gentlemen, had, by some means or other, made out what this work would contain: and had not the printing been interrupted so as to occasion a delay beyond the time fixed for publication, nothing contained in this appendix would have appeared.

THOMAS PAINE.

THE AGE OF REASON

PART ONE

BEING AN INVESTIGATION OF TRUE AND OF FABULOUS THEOLOGY

When The Age of Reason; Being an Investigation of True and of Fabulous Theology *was published in Paris in January 1794, Thomas Paine was in prison. He had been granted honorary French citizenship in 1792, and soon thereafter had taken up the seat to which he had been elected in the French National Convention. Paine had great hopes for France, a strong belief that the republican nation he had helped create in America would be re-created there. He believed in a written constitution for France, much like the ideas he had been expressing for years.*

But he did not want regicide. While Thomas Paine had supported the trial of King Louis XVI for treason, he did not support the sentence of death that had been given to the deposed monarch. Paine devised a proposal that would have imprisoned the king for a period, then exiled him to the United States. The plan was defeated, however, and Louis was executed January 21, 1793. On February 1, France declared war on Great Britain and the Netherlands; President Washington announced that the United States would remain neutral in this war between its old ally and its enemy. Paine was arrested on December 28, 1793, and placed in the Luxembourg Palace. He would remain there until November 4, 1794, when James Monroe helped secure his release. Paine's anger at George Washington for failing to help him during his imprisonment would last for years to come.

The essay that Paine wrote in the midst of these events proved to be the most controversial thing he did in a lifetime filled with controversy. Some contemporaries, and numerous later readers, branded Paine an infidel or atheist for what he said in The Age of Reason. Yet that was not what he believed. He saw the French headed toward atheism, pushed by centuries of the church's ignorance, superstition, and greed. From the vantage point of his own deistic beliefs, Paine saw the importance of human reason and the natural world in understanding the world God created.

The Age of Reason would become one of the intellectual monuments of the Enlightenment, changing both the way people viewed human nature and the way many people viewed Thomas Paine. "Before Paine it had been possible to be both a Christian and a deist," historian Eric Foner has written. Just as Paine's earlier writings had challenged the deference that kings, proprietors, or government officials could demand, The Age of Reason attacked the status quo of organized religion. Many would celebrate Paine's intellectual achievement in this pamphlet, his views on creation and the natural world, and his belief in humanity's ability to think. But others, including his old friends Samuel Adams and Benjamin Rush—the man who had suggested the title Common Sense for Paine's first published work—found the ideas expressed in The Age of Reason offensive, and refused to speak to him afterwards.

It has been my intention, for several years past, to publish my thoughts upon religion. I am well aware of the difficulties that attend the subject; and from that consideration, had reserved it to a more advanced period of life. I intended it to be the last offering I should make to my fellow-citizens of all nations; and that at a time when the purity of the motive that induced me to it, could not admit of a question, even by those who might disapprove the work.

The circumstance that has now taken place in France of the total abolition of the whole national order of priesthood,[1] and of every thing appertaining to compulsive systems of religion, and compulsive articles of faith, has not only precipitated my intention, but rendered a work of this kind exceedingly necessary; lest, in the general wreck of superstition, of false systems of government, and false theology, we lose sight of morality, of humanity, and of the theology that is true.

As several of my colleagues, and others of my fellow-citizens of France, have given me the example of making their voluntary and individual profession of faith, I also will make mine; and I do this with all that sincerity and frankness with which the mind of man communicates with itself.

I believe in one God, and no more; and I hope for happiness beyond this life.

I believe the equality of man, and I believe that religious duties consist in doing justice, loving mercy, and endeavouring to make our fellow-creatures happy.

But lest it should be supposed that I believe many other things in addition to these, I shall, in the progress of this work, declare the things I do not believe, and my reasons for not believing them.

I do not believe in the creed professed by the Jewish church, by the Roman church, by the Greek church, by the Turkish church, by the Protestant church, nor by any church that I know of. My own mind is my own church.

All national institutions of churches, whether Jewish, Christian, or

Turkish, appear to me no other than human inventions set up to ter-rify and enslave mankind, and monopolize power and profit.

I do not mean by this declaration to condemn those who believe otherwise. They have the same right to their belief as I have to mine. But it is necessary to the happiness of man, that he be mentally faith-ful to himself. Infidelity does not consist in believing, or in disbeliev-ing: it consists in professing to believe what he does not believe.

It is impossible to calculate the moral mischief, if I may so express it, that mental lying has produced in society. When a man has so far corrupted and prostituted the chastity of his mind, as to subscribe his professional belief to things he does not believe, he has prepared him-self for the commission of every other crime. He takes up the trade of a priest for the sake of gain, and in order to *qualify* himself for that trade, he begins with a perjury. Can we conceive any thing more de-structive to morality than this?

Soon after I had published the pamphlet, COMMON SENSE, in America, I saw the exceeding probability that a revolution in the Sys-tem of Government would be followed by a revolution in the System of Religion. The adulterous connection of church and state, wherever it had taken place, whether Jewish, Christian, or Turkish, had so effec-tually prohibited, by pains and penalties, every discussion upon estab-lished creeds, and upon first principles of religion, that until the system of government should be changed, those subjects could not be brought fairly and openly before the world: but that whenever this should be done, a revolution in the system of religion would follow. Human in-ventions and priest-craft would be detected: and man would return to the pure, unmixed, and unadulterated belief of one God, and no more.

Every national church or religion has established itself by pretend-ing some special mission from God communicated to certain indi-viduals. The Jews have their Moses; the Christians their Jesus Christ, their apostles and saints; and the Turks their Mahomet; as if the way to God was not open to every man alike.

Each of those churches show certain books which they call *revelation*, or the word of God. The Jews say, that their word of God was given by God to Moses face to face; the Christians say, that their word of God came by divine inspiration; and the Turks say, that their word of God (the Koran) was brought by an angel from Heaven. Each of those churches accuses the other of unbelief; and, for my own part, I disbelieve them all.

As it is necessary to affix right ideas to words, I will, before I proceed further into the subject, offer some observations on the word *revelation*. Revelation, when applied to religion, means something communicated *immediately* from God to man.

No one will deny or dispute the power of the Almighty to make such a communication if he pleases. But admitting, for the sake of a case, that something has been revealed to a certain person, and not revealed to any other person, it is revelation to that person only. When he tells it to a second person, a second to a third, a third to a fourth, and so on, it ceases to be a revelation to all those persons. It is revelation to the first person only, and *hearsay* to every other; and consequently, they are not obliged to believe it.

It is a contradiction in terms and ideas to call any thing a revelation that comes to us at second hand, either verbally or in writing. Revelation is necessarily limited to the first communication. After this, it is only an account of something which that person says was a revelation made to him; and though he may find himself obliged to believe it, it cannot be incumbent on me to believe it in the same manner, for it was not a revelation made to *me,* and I have only his word for it that it was made to *him.*

When Moses told the children of Israel that he received the two tables of the commandments from the hand of God, they were not obliged to believe him, because they had no other authority for it than his telling them so; and I have no other authority for it than some historian telling me so. The commandments carrying no internal evidence of divinity with them. They contain some good moral precepts, such as any man qualified to be a law-giver or a legislator could produce himself, without having recourse to supernatural intervention*.

When I am told that the Koran was written in Heaven, and brought to Mahomet by an angel, the account comes to near the same kind of hearsay evidence, and second hand authority, as the former. I did not see the angel myself, and therefore I have a right not to believe it.

When also I am told that a woman, called the Virgin Mary, said, or gave out, that she was with child without any cohabitation with a man, and that her betrothed husband, Joseph, said, that an angel told him so,

* This is, however, necessary to except the declaration, which says, that God *visits the sins of the fathers upon the children.* It is contrary to every principle of moral justice.

I have a right to believe them or not: such a circumstance required a much stronger evidence than their bare word for it: but we have not even this: for neither Joseph nor Mary wrote any such matter themselves. It is only reported by others that *they said so.* It is hearsay upon hearsay, and I do not chuse to rest my belief upon such evidence.

It is, however, not difficult to account for the credit that was given to the story of Jesus Christ being the Son of God. He was born when the Heathen mythology had still some fashion and repute in the world, and that mythology had prepared the people for the belief of such a story. Almost all the extraordinary men that lived under the Heathen mythology were reputed to be the sons of some of their gods. It was not a new thing at that time to believe a man to have been celestially begotten: the intercourse of gods with women was then a matter of familiar opinion. Their Jupiter, according to their accounts, had cohabited with hundreds; the story, therefore, had nothing in it either new, wonderful, or obscene; it was conformable to the opinions that then prevailed among the people called Gentiles, or mythologists, and it was those people only that believed it. The Jews who had kept strictly to the belief of one God, and no more, and who had always rejected the Heathen mythology, never credited the story.

It is curious to observe how the theory of what is called the Christian church, sprung out of the tail of the Heathen mythology. A direct incorporation took place in the first instance, by making the reputed founder to be celestially begotten. The trinity of gods that then followed was no other than a reduction of the formal plurality, which was about twenty or thirty thousand. The statue of Mary succeeded the statue of Diana of Ephesus.[2] The deification of heroes, changed into the cannonization of saints. The mythologists had gods for every thing; the Christian mythologists had saints for every thing. The church became as crouded with the one, as the pantheon had been with the other; and Rome was the place of both. The Christian theory is little else than the idolatry of the ancient mythologists, accommodated to the purposes of power and revenue; and it yet remains to reason and philosophy to abolish the amphibious fraud.

Nothing that is here said can apply, even with the most distant disrespect, to the *real* character of Jesus Christ. He was a virtuous and an amiable man. The morality that he preached and practised was of the most benevolent kind; and though similar systems of morality had been preached by Confucius, and by some of the Greek philosophers, many years before; by the Quakers since; and by many good men in all ages; it has not been exceeded by any.

Jesus Christ wrote no account of himself, of his birth, parentage, or any thing else. Not a line of what is called the New Testament is of his own writing. The history of him is altogether the work of other people; and as to the account given of his resurrection and ascension, it was the necessary counterpart to the story of his birth. His historians, having brought him into the world in a supernatural manner, were obliged to take him out again in the same manner, or the first part of the story must have fallen to the ground.

The wretched contrivance with which this latter part is told, exceeds every thing that went before it. The first part, that of the miraculous conception, was not a thing that admitted of publicity; and therefore the tellers of this part of the story had this advantage, that though they might not be credited, they could not be detected. They could not be expected to prove it, because it was not one of those things that admitted of proof, and it was impossible that the person of whom it was told could prove it himself.

But the resurrection of a dead person from the grave, and his ascension through the air, is a thing very different as to the evidence it admits of, to the invisible conception of a child in the womb. The resurrection and ascension, supposing them to have taken place, admitted of public and occular demonstration, like that of the ascension of a balloon, or the sun at noon day, to all Jerusalem at least. A thing which every body is required to believe, requires that the proof and evidence of it should be equal to all, and universal; and as the public visibility of this last related act was the only evidence that could give sanction to the former part, the whole of it falls to the ground, because that evidence never was given. Instead of this, a small number of persons, not more than eight or nine, are introduced as proxies for the whole world, to say, they *saw it*, and all the rest of the world are called upon to believe it. But it appears that Thomas did not believe the resurrection; and, as they say, would not believe, without having occular and manual demonstration himself. *So neither will I;* and the reason is equally as good for me and for every other person, as for Thomas.

It is in vain to attempt to palliate or disguise this matter. The story, so far as relates to the supernatural part, has every mark of fraud and imposition stamped upon the face of it. Who were the authors of it is as impossible for us now to know, as it is for us to be assured, that the books in which the account is related, were written by the persons whose names they bear. The best surviving evidence we now have respecting this affair is the Jews. They are regularly descended from the people who lived in the times this resurrection and ascension is said to have happened, and they say, *it is not true*. It has long appeared to me a strange inconsistency to cite the Jews as a proof of the truth of the story. It is just the same as if a man were to say, I will prove the truth of what I have told you, by producing the people who say it is false.

That such a person as Jesus Christ existed, and that he was crucified, which was the mode of execution at that day, are historical relations strictly within the limits of probability. He preached most excellent morality, and the equality of man; but he preached also against the corruptions and avarice of the Jewish priests, and this brought upon him the hatred and vengeance of the whole order of priest-hood. The accusation which those priests brought against him, was that of sedition and conspiracy against the Roman government, to which the Jews were then subject and tributary; and it is not improbable that the Roman government might have some secret apprehension of the effects of his doctrine as well as the Jewish priests; neither is it improbable that Jesus Christ had in contemplation the delivery of the Jewish nation from the bondage of the Romans. Between the two, however, this virtuous reformer and revolutionist lost his life.

It is upon this plain narrative of facts, together with another case I am going to mention, that the Christian mythologists, calling themselves the Christian church, have erected their fable, which for absurdity and extravagance is not exceeded by any thing that is to be found in the mythology of the ancients.

The ancient mythologists tell that the race of Giants made war against Jupiter, and that one of them threw an hundred rocks against him at one throw; that Jupiter defeated him with thunder, and confined him afterwards under Mount Etna; and that every time the Giant turns himself, Mount Etna belches fire. It is here easy to see that the circumstance of the mountain, that of its being a volcano, suggested the idea of the fable; and that the fable is made to fit and wind itself up with that circumstance.

The Christian mythologists tell that their Satan made war against the Almighty, who defeated him, and confined him afterwards, not under a mountain, but in a pit. It is here easy to see that the first fable suggested the idea of the second; for the fable of Jupiter and the Giants was told many hundred years before that of Satan.

Thus far the ancient and the Christian mythologists differ very little from each other. But the latter have contrived to carry the matter much farther. They have contrived to connect the fabulous part of the story of Jesus Christ, with the fable originating from Mount Etna: and in order to make all the parts of the story tye together, they have taken to their aid the traditions of the Jews; for the Christian mythology is made up partly from the ancient mythology, and partly from the Jewish traditions.

The Christian mythologists, after having confined Satan in a pit, were obliged to let him out again, to bring on the sequel of the fable. He is then introduced into the garden of Eden in the shape of a snake, or a serpent, and in that shape he enters into familiar conversation with Eve, who is no ways surprised to hear a snake talk; and the issue of this tête-à-tête is, that he persuades her to eat an apple, and the eating of that apple, damns all mankind.

After giving Satan this triumph over the whole creation, one would have supposed that the church mythologists would have been kind enough to send him back again to the pit; or, if they had not done this, that they would have put a mountain upon him, (for they say that their faith can remove a mountain) or have put him *under* a mountain, as the former mythologists had done, to prevent his getting again among the women, and doing more mischief. But instead of this, they leave him at large without even obliging him to give his parole. The secret of which is, that they could not do without him; and after being at the trouble of making him, they bribed him to stay. They promised him ALL the Jews, ALL the Turks by anticipation, nine-tenths of the world beside, and Mahomet into the bargain. After this, who can doubt the bountifulness of the Christian mythology?

Having thus made an insurrection and a battle in Heaven, in which none of the combatants could be either killed or wounded—put Satan into the pit—let him out again—given him a triumph over the whole creation—damned all mankind by the eating of an apple, these Christian mythologists bring the two ends of their fable together. They represent this virtuous and amiable man, Jesus Christ, to be at once both

God and man, and also the Son of God, celestially begotten on purpose to be sacrificed, because, they say, that Eve in her longing had eaten an apple.

Putting aside every thing that might excite laughter by its absurdity, or detestation by its prophaneness, and confinding ourselves merely to an examination of the parts, it is impossible to conceive a story more derogatory to the Almighty, more inconsistent with his wisdom, more contradictory to his power, than this story is.

In order to make for it a foundation to rise upon, the inventors were under the necessity of giving to the being, whom they call Satan, a power equally as great, if not greater, than they attribute to the Almighty. They have not only given him the power of liberating himself from the pit, after what they call his fall, but they have made that power increase afterwards to infinity. Before this fall, they represent him only as an angel of limited existence, as they represent the rest. After his fall, he becomes, by their account, omnipresent. He exists every where, and at the same time. He occupies the whole immensity of space.

Not content with this deification of Satan, they represent him as defeating by stratagem, in the shape of an animal of the creation, all the power and wisdom of the Almighty. They represent him as having compelled the Almighty to the *direct necessity* either of surrendering the whole of the creation to the government and sovereignty of this Satan, or of capitulating for its redemption by coming down upon earth, and exhibiting himself upon a cross in the shape of a man.

Had the inventors of this story told it the contrary way, that is, had they represented the Almighty as compelling Satan to exhibit *himself* on a cross in the shape of a snake, as a punishment for his new transgression, the story would have been less absurd, less contradictory. But instead of this, they make the transgressor triumph, and the Almighty fall.

That many good men have believed this strange fable, and lived very good lives under that belief (for credulity is not a crime) is what I have no doubt of. In the first place, they were educated to believe it, and they would have believed any thing else in the same manner. There are also many who have been so enthusiastically enraptured by what they conceived to be the infinite love of God to man, in making a sacrifice of himself, that the vehemence of the idea has forbidden and deterred them from examining into the absurdity and profaneness of the story.

The more unnatural any thing is, the more is it capable of becoming the object of dismal admiration.

But if objects for gratitude and admiration are our desire, do they not present themselves every hour to our eyes? Do we not see a fair creation prepared to receive us the instant we were born—a world furnished to our hands that cost us nothing? Is it we that light up the sun; that pour down the rain; and fill the earth with abundance? Whether we sleep or wake, the vast machinery of the universe still goes on. Are these things, and the blessings they indicate in future, nothing to us? Can our gross feelings be excited by no other subjects than tragedy and suicide? Or is the gloomy pride of man become so intolerable, that nothing can flatter it but a sacrifice of the Creator?

I know that this bold investigation will alarm many, but it would be paying too great a compliment to their credulity to forbear it upon that account. The times and the subject demand it to be done. The suspicion that the theory of what is called the Christian Church is fabulous, is becoming very extensive in all countries; and it will be a consolation to men staggering under that suspicion, and doubting what to believe and what to disbelieve, to see the subject freely investigated. I therefore pass on to an examination of the books called the Old and the New Testament.

These books, beginning with Genesis and ending with Revelations (which by the bye is a book of riddles that requires a revelation to explain it) are, we are told, the word of God. It is therefore proper for us to know who told us so, that we may know what credit to give to the report. The answer to this question is, that nobody can tell, except that we tell one another so. The case, however, historically appears to be as follows:

When the church mythologists established their system, they collected all the writings they could find, and managed them as they pleased. It is a matter altogether of uncertainty to us whether such of the writings as now appear, under the name of the Old and the new Testament, are in the same state in which those collectors say they found them; or whether they added, altered, abridged, or dressed them up.

Be this as it may, they decided by *vote* which of the books out of the collection they had made, should be the WORD OF GOD, and which should not. They rejected several; they voted others to be doubtful, such as the books called the Apocraphy;[3] and those books which had a majority of votes, were voted to be the word of God. Had they voted otherwise, all the people, since calling themselves Christians, had believed otherwise; for the belief of the one comes from the vote of the other. Who the people were that did all this, we know nothing of; they called themselves by the general name of the church; and this is all we know of the matter.

As we have no other external evidence or authority for believing those books to be the word of God, than what I have mentioned, which is no evidence or authority at all, I come, in the next place, to examine the internal evidence contained in the books themselves.

In the former part of this essay, I have spoken of revelation. I now proceed further with that subject, for the purpose of applying it to the books in question.

Revelation is a communication of something, which the person, to whom that thing is revealed, did not know before. For if I have done a thing, or seen it done, it needs no revelation to tell me I have done it, or seen it, nor to enable me to tell it, or to write it.

Revelation, therefore, cannot be applied to any thing done upon earth of which man is himself the actor or the witness; and consequently all the historical and anecdotal part of the Bible, which is almost the whole of it, is not within the meaning and compass of the word revelation, and therefore is not the word of God.

When Samson ran off with the gate-posts of Gaza, if he ever did so (and whether he did or not is nothing to us), or when he visited his Delilah, or caught his foxes, or did any thing else, what has revelation to do with these things? If they were facts, he could tell them himself; or his secretary, if he kept one, could write them, if they were worth either telling or writing; and if they were fictions, revelation could not make them true; and whether true or not, we are neither the better nor the wiser for knowing them.—When we contemplate the immensity of that Being, who directs and governs the incomprehensible WHOLE, of which the utmost ken of human sight can discover but a part, we ought to feel shame at calling such paltry stories the word of God.

As to the account of the creation, with which the book of Genesis opens, it has all the appearance of being a tradition which the Israelites had among them before they came into Egypt; and after their departure from that country, they put it at the head of their history, without telling, as it is most probable that they did not know, how they came by it. The manner in which the account opens, shews it to be traditionary. It begins abruptly. It is nobody that speaks. It is nobody that hears. It is addressed to nobody. It has neither first, second, nor third person. It has every criterion of being a tradition. It has no voucher. Moses does not take it upon himself by introducing it with the formality that he uses on other occasions, such as that of saying, *"The Lord spake unto Moses, saying."*

Why it has been called the Mosaic account of the creation, I am at a loss to conceive. Moses, I believe, was too good a judge of such subjects to put his name to that account. He had been educated among the Egyptians, who were a people as well skilled in science, and particularly in astronomy, as any people of their day; and the silence and caution that Moses observes, in not authenticating the account, is a good negative evidence that he neither told it, nor believed it.—The case is, that every nation of people has been world-makers, and the Israelites had as much right to set up the trade of world-making as any of the rest; and as Moses was not an Israelite, he might not chuse to contradict the tradition. The account, however, is harmless; and this is more than can be said for many other parts of the Bible.

Whenever we read the obscene stories, the voluptuous debaucheries, the cruel and torturous executions, the unrelenting vindictiveness, with which more than half the Bible is filled, it would be more consistent that we called it the word of a demon, than the word of God. It is a history of wickedness, that has served to corrupt and brutalize mankind; and, for my own part, I sincerely detest it, as I detest every thing that is cruel.

We scarcely meet with any thing, a few phrases excepted, but what deserves either our abhorrence, or our contempt, till we come to the miscellaneous parts of the Bible. In the anonymous publications, the Psalms and the book of Job, more particularly in the latter, we find a great deal of elevated sentiment reverentially expressed of the power and benignity of the Almighty; but they stand on no higher rank than many other compositions on similar subjects, as well before that time as since.

The Proverbs, which are said to be Solomon's, though most probably a collection (because they discover a knowledge of life, which his situation excluded him from knowing) are an instructive table of ethics. They are inferior in keenness to the Proverbs of the Spaniards, and not more wise and œconomical than those of the American Franklin.

All the remaining parts of the Bible, generally known by the name of the Prophets, are the works of the Jewish poets and itinerant preachers, who mixed poetry, anecdote, and devotion together; and those works still retain the air and stile of poetry, though in translation*.

There is not, throughout the whole book, called the Bible, any word that describes to us what we call a poet, nor any word that describes what we call poetry. The case is, that the word *prophet,* to which later times have affixed a new idea, was the Bible word for poet, and the word *prophesying* meant the art of making poetry. It also meant the art of playing poetry to a tune upon any instrument of music.

We read of prophesying with pipes, tabrets, and horns. Of prophesying with harps, with psalteries, with cymbals, and with every other instrument of music then in fashion. Were we now to speak of prophesying with a fiddle, or with a pipe and tabor, the expression would have no meaning, or would appear ridiculous, and to some people contemptuous, because we have changed the meaning of the word.

---

* As there are many readers who do not see that a composition is poetry unless it be in rhyme, it is for their information that I add this note.

Poetry consists principally in two things: Imagery and composition. The composition of poetry differs from that of prose in the manner of mixing long and short syllables together. Take a long syllable out of a line of poetry, and put a short one in the room of it, or put a long syllable where a short one should be, and that line will lose its poetical harmony. It will have an effect upon the line like that of misplacing a note in a song.

The imagery in those books, called the Prophets, appertains altogether to poetry. It is fictitious and often extravagant, and not admissible in any other kind of writing than poetry.

To shew that these writings are composed in poetical numbers, I will take ten syllables as they stand in the book, and make a line of the same number of syllables (heroic measure) that shall rhyme with the last word. It will then be seen, that the composition of those books is poetical measure. The instance I shall first produce is from Isaiah.

> *"Hear, O ye heavens, and give ear, O earth,"*
> 'Tis God himself that calls attention forth.

Another instance I shall quote is from the mournful Jeremiah, to which I shall add two other lines for the purpose of carrying out the figure, and shewing the intention of the poet.

> *O! that mine head were waters, and mine eyes*
> Were fountains, flowing like the liquid skies,
> Then would I give the mighty flood release,
> And weep a deluge for the human race.

The Age of Reason · 257

We are told of Saul being among the *prophets,* and also that he prophesied; but we are not told what *they prophesied,* nor what *he prophesied.* The case is, there was nothing to tell; for these prophets were a company of musicians and poets; and Saul joined in the concert; and this was called *prophesying.*

The account given of this affair in the book called Samuel, is, that Saul met a *company* of prophets; a whole company of them! coming down with a psaltery, a tabret, a pipe, and a harp, and that they prophesied, and that he prophesied with them. But it appears afterwards, that Saul prophesied badly, that is, he performed his part badly; for it is said, that "an *evil sprit from God** came upon Saul, and he prophesied."

Now were there no other passage in the book, called the Bible, than this, to demonstrate to us that we have lost the original meaning of the word *prophesy,* and substituted another meaning in its place, this alone would be sufficient; for it is impossible to use and apply the word *prophesy* in the place it is here used and applied, if we give to it the sense which later times have affixed to it. The manner in which it is here used strips it of all religious meaning, and shews that a man might then be a *prophet,* or might *prophesy,* as he may now be a poet, or a musician, without any regard to the morality or the immorality of his character. The word was originally a term of science, promiscuously applied to poetry and to music, and not restricted to any subject upon which poetry and music might be exercised.

Deborah and Barak are called prophets, not because they predicted any thing, but because they composed the poem or song that bears their name in celebration of an act already done: David is ranked among the prophets, for he was a musician; and was also reputed to be (though perhaps very erroneously) the author of the Psalms. But Abraham, Isaac, and Jacob, are not called prophets. It does not appear from any accounts we have that they could either sing, play music, or make poetry.

We are told of the greater and the lesser prophets. They might as well tell us of the greater and the lesser God; for there cannot be degrees in prophesying consistently with its modern sense. But there are

---

* As those men, who call themselves divines and commentators, are very fond of puzzling one another, I leave them to contest the meaning of the first part of the phrase, that of *an evil spirit of God.* I keep to my text, I keep to the meaning of the word prophesy.

degrees in poetry, and therefore the phrase is reconcilable to the case, when we understand by it the greater and the lesser poets.

It is altogether unnecessary, after this, to offer any observations upon what those men, stiled prophets, have written. The ax goes at once to the root, by shewing that the original meaning of the word has been mistaken, and consequently all the inferences that have been drawn from those books, the devotional respect that has been paid to them, and the laboured commentaries that have been written upon them, under that mistaken meaning, are not worth disputing about.—In many things, however, the writings of the Jewish poets deserve a better fate than that of being bound up, as they now are, with the trash that accompanies them, under the abused name of the word of God.

If we permit ourselves to conceive right ideas of things, we must necessarily affix the idea, not only of unchangeableness, but of the utter impossibility of any change taking place, by any means or accident whatever, in that which we would honour with the name of the word of God; and therefore the word of God cannot exist in any written or human language.

The continually progressive change to which the meaning of words is subject, the want of an universal language which renders translations necessary, the errors to which translations are again subject, the mistakes of copyists and printers, together with the possibility of wilful alteration, are of themselves evidences, that human language, whether in speech or in print, cannot be the vehicle of the word of God.—The word of God exists in something else.

Did the book, called the Bible, excel in purity of ideas and expression, all the books that are now extant in the world, I would not take it for my rule of faith, as being the word of God; because the possibility would nevertheless exist of my being imposed upon. But when I see throughout the greatest part of this book, scarcely any thing but a history of the grossest vices, and a collection of the most paltry and contemptible tales, I cannot dishonour my Creator by calling it by his name.

Thus much for the Bible. I now go on to the book called the New Testament. The *new* Testament! that is, the *new* Will, as if there could be two wills of the Creator.

Had it been the object or the intention of Jesus Christ to establish a new religion, he would undoubtedly have written the system himself, or *procured it to be written* in his life time. But there is no publication extant authenticated with his name. All the books called the New Testament were written after his death. He was a Jew by birth and by profession; and he was the son of God in like manner that every other person is:[4] for the Creator is the Father of All.

The first four books, called Matthew, Mark, Luke, and John, do not give a history of the life of Jesus Christ, but only detached anecdotes of him. It appears from these books, that the whole time of his being a preacher was not more than eighteen months; and it was only during this short time, that those men became acquainted with him. They make mention of him, at the age of twelve years, sitting, they say, among the Jewish doctors, asking and answering them questions. As this was several years before their accquaintance with him began, it is most probable they had this anecdote from his parents. From this time there is no account of him for about sixteen years. Where he lived, or how he employed himself during this interval, is not known. Most probably he was working at his father's trade, which was that of a carpenter. It does not appear that he had any school education, and the probability is that he could not write, for his parents were extremely poor, as appears from their not being able to pay for a bed when he was born.

It is somewhat curious that the three persons, whose names are the most universally recorded, were of very obscure parentage. Moses was a foundling, Jesus Christ was born in a stable, and Mahomet was a mule-driver. The first and the last of these men, were founders of different systems of religion; but Jesus Christ founded no new system. He called men to the practice of moral virtues, and the belief of one God. The great trait in his character is philanthropy.

The manner in which he was apprehended, shews that he was not much known at that time; and it shews also that the meetings he then held with his followers were in secret; and that he had given over, or suspended, preaching publicly. Judas could no otherways betray him than by giving information where he was, and pointing him out to the officers that went to arrest him; and the reason for employing and paying Judas to do this, could arise only from the causes already mentioned, that of his not being much known, and living concealed.

The idea of his concealment not only agrees very ill with his reputed divinity, but associates with it something of pusillanimity; and his being betrayed, or in other words, his being apprehended, on the information of one of his followers, shews that he did not intend to be apprehended, and consequently that he did not intend to be crucified.

The Christian mythologists tell us, that Christ died for the sins of the world, and that he came on *purpose to die*. Would it not then have been the same if he had died of a fever, or of the small-pox, of old age, or of any thing else?

The declaratory sentence which, they say, was passed upon Adam in case he eat of the apple; was not, that *thou shalt surely be crucified, but thou shalt surely die*. The sentence was death, and not the *manner of dying*. Crucifixion, therefore, or any other particular manner of dying, made no part of the sentence that Adam was to suffer, and consequently, even upon their own tactic, it could make no part of the sentence that Christ was to suffer in the room of Adam. A fever would have done as well as a cross, if there was any occasion for either.

This sentence of death which, they tell us, was thus passed upon Adam, must either have meant dying naturally, that is, ceasing to live, or, have meant what these mythologists call damnation: and consequently, the act of dying on the part of Jesus Christ, must, according to their system, apply as a prevention to one or other of these two *things* happening to Adam and to us.

That it does not prevent our dying is evident, because we all die; and if their accounts of longevity be true, men die faster since the crucifixion than before: and with respect to the second explanation, (including with it the *natural death* of Jesus Christ as a substitute for the *eternal death or damnation* of all mankind) it is impertinently representing the Creator as coming off, or revoking the sentence, by a pun or a quibble upon the word *death*. That manufacturer of quibbles, St. Paul, if he wrote the books that bear his name, has helped this quibble on, by making another quibble upon the word *Adam*. He makes there to be two Adams; the one who sins in fact, and suffers by proxy; the other who sins by proxy, and suffers in fact. A religion thus interlarded with quibble, subterfuge and pun, has a tendency to instruct its professors in the practice of these arts. They acquire the habit without being aware of the cause.

If Jesus Christ was the Being which those mythologists tell us he was, and that he came into this world to *suffer*, which is a word they sometimes use instead of *to die*, the only real suffering he could have endured would have been *to live*. His existence here was a state of exilement or transportation from Heaven, and the way back to his original country was to die.—In fine, every thing in this strange system is the reverse of what it pretends to be. It is the reverse of truth, and I become so tired with examining into its inconsistences and absurdities, that I hasten to the conclusion of it, in order to proceed to something better.

How much, or what parts of the books called the New Testament, were written by the persons whose names they bear, is what we can know nothing of, neither are we certain in what language they were originally written. The matters they now contain may be classed under two heads: anecdote, and epistolary correspondence.

The four books already mentioned, Matthew, Mark, Luke, and John, are altogether anecdotal. They relate events after they had taken place. They tell what Jesus Christ did and said, and what others did and said to him, and in several instances they relate the same event differently. Revelation is necessarily out of the question with respect to those books; not only because of the disagreement of the writers, but because revelation cannot be applied to the relating of facts by the persons who saw them done, nor to the relating or recording of any discourse or conversation by those who heard it. The book, called the Acts of the Apostels, an anonymous work, belongs also to the anecdotal part.

All the other parts of the New Testament, except the book of enigmas, called the Revelations, are a collection of letters under the name of Epistles; and the forgery of letters has been such a common practice in the world, that the probability is, at least, equal, whether they are genuine or forged. One thing, however, is much less equivocal, which is, that out of the matters contained in those books, together with the assistance of some old stories, the church has set up a system of religion very contradictory to the character of the person whose name it bears. It has set up a religion of pomp and of revenue in pretended imitation of a person whose life was humility and poverty.

The invention of a purgatory,[5] and of the releasing of souls therefrom, by prayers, bought of the church with money; the selling of pardons, dispensations, and indulgences, are revenue laws, without bearing that name, or carrying that appearance. But the case nevertheless is, that those things derive their origin from the proxysm of the crucifixion, and the theory deduced therefrom, which was, that one person could stand in the place of another, and could perform meritorious services for him. The probability therefore is, that the whole theory or doctrine of what is called the redemption (which is said to have been accomplished by the act of one person in the room of another) was originally fabricated on purpose to bring forward and build all those secondary and pecuniary redemptions upon; and that the passages in the books upon which the idea or theory of redemption is built, have been manufactured and fabricated for that purpose. Why are we to give this church credit, when she tells us that those books are genuine in every part, any more than we give her credit for every thing else she has told us; or for the miracles she says she has performed. That she *could* fabricate writings is certain, because she could write; and the composition of the writings in question, is of that kind, that any body might do it; and that she *did* fabricate them is not more inconsistent with probability, than that she should tell us, as she has done, that she could and did work miracles.

Since then no external evidence can, at this long distance of time, be produced to prove whether the church fabricated the doctrines called redemption or not (for such evidence, whether for or against, would be subject to the same suspicion of being fabricated) the case can only be referred to the internal evidence which the thing carries of itself; and this affords a very strong presumption of its being a fabrication. For the internal evidence is, that the theory or doctrine of redemption has for its basis, an idea of pecuniary justice, and not that of moral justice.

If I owe a person money, and cannot pay him, and he threatens to put me in prison, another person can take the debt upon himself, and pay it for me. But if I have committed a crime, every circumstance of the case is changed. Moral justice cannot take the innocent for the guilty, even if the innocent would offer itself. To suppose justice to do this, is to destroy the principle of its existence, which is the thing itself. It is then no longer justice. It is indiscriminate revenge.

This single reflection will shew that the doctrine of redemption is founded on a mere pecuniary idea corresponding to that of a debt which another person might pay; and as this pecuniary idea corresponds again with the system of second redemptions obtained through the means of money given to the church, for pardons, the probability is, that the same persons fabricated both the one and the other of those theories; and that, in truth, there is no such thing as redemption; that it is fabulous; and that man stands in the same relative condition with his Maker he ever did stand since man existed; and that it is his greatest consolation to think so.

Let him believe this, and he will live more consistently and morally than by any other system. It is by his being taught to contemplate himself as an out-law, as an out-cast, as a beggar, as a mumper, as one thrown, as it were, on a dunghill, at an immense distance from his Creator, and who must make his approaches by creeping and cringing to intermediate beings, that he conceives either a contemptuous disregard for every thing under the name of religion, or becomes indifferent, or turns, what he calls, devout. In the latter case, he consumes his life in grief, or the affectation of it. His prayers are reproaches. His humility is ingratitude. He calls himself a worm, and the fertile earth a dunghill; and all the blessings of life by the thankless name of vanities. He despises the choicest gift of God to man, the GIFT OF REASON; and having endeavoured to force upon himself the belief of a system against which reason revolts, he ungratefully calls it *human reason*, as if man could give reason to himself.

Yet with all this strange appearance of humility, and this contempt for human reason, he ventures into the boldest presumptions. He finds fault with every thing. His selfishness is never satisfied: his ingratitude is never at an end. He takes on himself to direct the Almighty what to do, even in the government of the universe. He prays dictatorily. When it is sun-shine, he prays for rain, and when it is rain, he prays for sunshine. He follows the same idea in every thing that he prays for; for what is the amount of all his prayers, but an attempt to make the Almighty change his mind, and act otherwise than he does. It is as if he were to say—thou knowest not so well as I.

But some perhaps will say, are we to have no word of God—No revelation? I answer yes. There is a word of God; there is a revelation.

THE WORD OF GOD IS THE CREATION WE BEHOLD: And it is in *this word*, which no human invention can counterfeit or alter, that God speaketh universally to man.

Human language is local and changeable, and is therefore incapable of being used as the means of unchangeable and universal information. The idea that God sent Jesus Christ to publish, as they say, the glad tidings to all nations, from one end of the earth unto the other, is consistent only with the ignorance of those who know nothing of the extent of the world, and who believed, as those world-saviours believed, and continued to believe, for several centuries (and that in contradiction to the discoveries of philosophers, and the experience of navigators) that the earth was flat like a trencher; and that a man might walk to the end of it.

But how was Jesus Christ to make any thing known to all nations? He could speak but one language, which was Hebrew; and there are in the world several hundred languages. Scarcely any two nations speak the same language, or understand each other; and as to translations, every man who knows any thing of languages, knows that it is impossible to translate from one language into another not only without losing a great part of the original, but frequently of mistaking the sense: and besides all this, the art of printing was wholly unknown at the time Christ lived.

It is always necessary that the means that are to accomplish any end, be equal to the accomplishment of that end, or the end cannot be accomplished. It is in this, that the difference between finite and infinite power and wisdom discovers itself. Man frequently fails in accomplishing his end, from a natural inability of the power to the purpose; and frequently from the want of wisdom to apply power properly. But it is impossible for infinite power and wisdom to fail as man faileth. The means it useth are always equal to the end: but human language, more especially as there is not an universal language, is incapable of being used as an universal means of unchangeable and uniform information; and therefore it is not the means that God useth in manifesting himself universally to man.

It is only in the CREATION that all our ideas and conceptions of a *word of God* can unite. The creation speaketh an universal language, independently of human speech or human language, multiplied and various as they be. It is an ever existing original, which every man can read. It cannot be forged; it cannot be counterfeited; it cannot be lost; it cannot be altered; it cannot be suppressed. It does not depend upon the will of man whether it shall be published or not: it publishes itself from one end of the earth to the other. It preaches to all nations and to all worlds: and this *word of God* reveals to man all that is necessary for man to know of God.

Do we want to contemplate his power? We see it in the immensity of the creation. Do we want to contemplate his wisdom? We see it in the unchangeable order by which the incomprehensible Whole is governed. Do we want to contemplate his munificence? We see it in the abundance with which he fills the earth. Do we want to contemplate his mercy? We see it in his not withholding that abundance even from the unthankful. In fine, do we want to know what God is? Search not the book called the scripture, which any human hand might make, but the scripture called the Creation.

The only idea man can affix to the name of God, is, that of a *first cause*, the cause of all things. And incomprehensibly difficult as it is for man to conceive what a first cause is, he arrives at the belief of it, from the tenfold greater difficulty of disbelieving it. It is difficult beyond description to conceive that space can have no end; but it is more difficult to conceive an end. It is difficult beyond the power of man to conceive an eternal duration of what we call time; but it is more impossible to conceive a time when there shall be no time. In like manner of reasoning, every thing we behold carries in itself the internal evidence that it did not make itself. Every man is an evidence to himself, that he did not make himself; neither could his father make himself, nor his grandfather, nor any of his race; neither could any tree, plant, or animal, make itself: and it is the conviction arising from this evidence, that carries us on, as it were, by necessity, to the belief of a first cause eternally existing, of a nature totally different to any material existence we know of, and by the power of which all things exist, and this first cause man calls God.

It is only by the exercise of reason, that man can discover God. Take away that reason, and he would be incapable of understanding any thing; and, in this case, it would be just as consistent to read even the book called the Bible, to a horse as to a man. How then is it that those people pretend to reject reason?

Almost the only parts in the book, called the Bible, that convey to us any idea of God, are some chapters in Job, and the 19th Psalm. I recollect no other. Those parts are true *deistical* compositions; for they treat of the *Deity* through his works. They take the book of Creation as the word of God; they refer to no other book; and all the inferences they make are drawn from that volume.

I insert, in this place, the 19th Psalm, as paraphrased into English verse, by Addison. I recollect not the prose, and where I write this I have not the opportunity of seeing it.

> The spacious firmament on high,
> With all the blue etherial sky,
> And spangled heavens, a shining frame,
> Their great original proclaim.
> The unwearied sun, from day to day,
> Does his Creator's power display,
> And publishes to every land,
> The work of an Almighty hand.
> Soon as the evening shades prevail,
> The moon takes up the wond'rous tale,
> And nightly to the list'ning earth
> Repeats the story of her birth.
> Whilst all the stars that round her burn,
> And all the planets in their turn,
> Confirm the tidings as they roll,
> And spread the truth from pole to pole.
> What tho' in solemn silence, all
> Move round this dark terrestrial ball,
> What tho' no real voice, nor sound,
> Amidst their radiant orbs be found,
> In reason's ear they all rejoice,
> And utter forth a glorious voice;
> For ever singing as they shine,
> THE HAND THAT MADE US IS DIVINE.

What more does man want to know than that the hand, or power, that made these things is divine, is omnipotent. Let him believe this, with the force it is impossible to repel if he permits his reason to act, and his rule of moral life will follow of course.

The allusions in Job have all of them the same tendency with this psalm: that of deducing or proving a truth, that would be otherwise unknown, from truths already known.

I recollect not enough of the passages in Job to insert them correctly: but there is one occurs to me that is applicable to the subject I am speaking upon. "Canst thou by searching find out God; canst thou find out the Almighty to perfection."

I know not how the printers have pointed this passage, for I keep no Bible;[6] but it contains two distinct questions that admits of distinct answers.

First, Canst thou by *searching* find out God? Yes. Because, in the first place, I know I did not make myself, and yet I have existence; and by *searching* into the nature of other things, I find that no other thing could make itself; and yet millions of other things exist; therefore it is, that I know, by positive conclusion resulting from this search, that there is a power superior to all those things, and that power is God.

Secondly, Canst thou find out the Almighty to *perfection?* No. Not only because the power and wisdom he has manifested in the structure of the creation that I behold, is to me incomprehensible; but because even this manifestation, great as it is, is probably but a small display of that immensity of power and wisdom, by which millions of other worlds, to me invisible by their distance, were created and continue to exist.

It is evident that both these questions were put to the reason of the person to whom they are supposed to have been addressed; and it is only by admitting the first question to be answered affirmatively, that the second could follow. It would have been unnecessary, and even absurd, to have put a second question more difficult than the first, if the first question had been answered negatively. The two questions have different objects, the first refers to the existence of God, the second to his attributes. Reason can discover the one, but it falls infinitely short in discovering the whole of the other.

I recollect not a single passage in all the writings ascribed to the men, called apostles, that convey any idea of what God is. Those writings are chiefly controversial; and the gloominess of the subject they dwell upon, that of a man dying in agony on a cross, is better suited to the gloomy genius of a monk in a cell, by whom it is not impossible they were written, than to any man breathing the open air of the creation. The only passage that occurs to me, that has any reference to the works of God, by which only his power and wisdom can be known, is related to have been spoken by Jesus Christ, as a remedy against distrustful care. "Behold the lilies of the field, they toil not, neither do they spin." This, however, is far inferior to the allusions in Job, and in the nineteenth psalm; but it is similar in idea, and the modesty of the imagery is correspondent to the modesty of the man.

As to the Christian system of faith, it appears to me as a species of atheism; a sort of religious denial of God. It professes to believe in a man rather than in God. It is a compound made up chiefly of manism with but little deism, and is as near to atheism as twilight is to darkness. It introduces between man and his Maker an opaque body which it calls a redeemer; as the moon introduces her opaque self between the earth and the sun, and it produces by this means a religious or an irreligious eclipse of light. It has put the whole orbit of reason into shade.

The effect of this obscurity has been that of turning every thing upside down, and representing it in reverse; and among the revolutions it has thus magically produced, it has made a revolution in Theology.

That which is now called natural philosophy, embracing the whole circle of science, of which astronomy occupies the chief place, is the study of the works of God, and of the power and wisdom of God in his works, and is the true theology.

As to the theology that is now studied in its place, it is the study of human opinions and of human fancies *concerning* God. It is not the study of God himself in the works that he has made, but in the works or writings that man has made; and it is not among the least of the mischiefs that the Christian system has done to the world, that it has abandoned the original and beautiful system of theology, like a beautiful innocent to distress and reproach, to make room for the hag of superstition.

The book of Job, and the 19th psalm, which even the church admits to be more ancient than the chronological order in which they stand in the book called the Bible, are theological orations conformable to the original system of theology. The internal evidence of those orations proves to a demonstration, that the study and contemplation of the works of creation, and of the power and wisdom of God revealed and manifested in those works, made a great part of the religious devotion of the times in which they were written; and it was this devotional study and contemplation that led to the discovery of the principles upon which, what are now called Sciences, are established; and it is to the discovery of these principles that almost all the Arts that contribute to the convenience of human life, owe their existence. Every principal art has some science for its parent, though the person who mechanically performs the work does not always, and but very seldom, perceive the connection.

It is a fraud of the christian system to call the sciences *human inventions;* it is only the application of them that is human. Every science has for its basis a system of principles as fixed and unalterable as those by which the universe is regulated and governed. Man cannot make principles; he can only discover them:

For example. Every person who looks at an almanack sees an account when an eclipse will take place, and he sees also that it never fails to take place according to the account there given. This shews that man is acquainted with the laws by which the heavenly bodies move. But it would be something worse than ignorance, were any church on earth to say, that those laws are an human invention.

It would also be ignorance, or something worse, to say, that the scientific principles, by the aid of which man is enabled to calculate and fore-know when an eclipse will take place, are an human invention. Man cannot invent any thing that is eternal and immutable; and the scientific principles he employs for this purpose must, and are, of necessity, as eternal and immutable as the laws by which the heavenly bodies move, or they could not be used as they are, to ascertain the time when, and the manner how, an eclipse will take place.

The scientific principles that man employs to obtain the fore-knowledge of an eclipse, or of any thing else relating to the motion of the heavenly bodies, are contained chiefly in that part of science that is called trigonometry, or the properties of a triangle, which, when applied to the study of the heavenly bodies, is called astronomy; when applied to direct the course of a ship on the ocean, it is called navigation; when applied to the construction of figures drawn by a rule and compass, it is called geometry; when applied to the construction of plans of edifices, it is called architecture; when applied to the measurement of any portion of the surface of the earth, it is called land-surveying. In fine, it is the soul of science. It is an eternal truth: it contains the *mathematical demonstration* of which man speaks, and the extent of its uses are unknown.

It may be said, that man can make or draw a triangle, and therefore a triangle is an human invention.

But the triangle, when drawn, is no other than the image of the principle: it is a delineation to the eye, and from thence to the mind, of a principle that would otherwise be imperceptible. The triangle does not make the principle, any more than a candle taken into a room that was dark, makes the chairs and tables that before were invisible. All the properties of a triangle exist independently of the figure, and existed before any triangle was drawn or thought of by man. Man had no more to do in the formation of those properties, or principles, than he had to do in making the laws by which the heavenly bodies move; and therefore the one must have the same divine origin as the other.

In the same manner as it may be said, that man can make a triangle, so also may it be said, he can make the mechanical instrument, called a leaver. But the principle by which the leaver acts, is a thing distinct from the instrument, and would exist if the instrument did not: it attaches itself to the instrument after it is made; the instrument therefore can act no otherwise than it does act; neither can all the effort of human invention make it act otherwise. That which, in all such cases, man calls the *effect*, is no other than the principle itself rendered perceptible to the senses.

Since then man cannot make principles, from whence did he gain a knowledge of them, so as to be able to apply them, not only to things on earth, but to ascertain the motion of bodies so immensely distant from him as all the heavenly bodies are? From whence, I ask, *could* he gain that knowledge, but from the study of the true theology?

It is the structure of the universe that has taught this knowledge to man. That structure is an ever-existing exhibition of every principle upon which every part of mathematical science is founded. The offspring of this science is mechanics; for mechanics is no other than the principles of science applied practically. The man who proportions the several parts of a mill, uses the same scientific principles, as if he had the power of constructing an universe: but as he cannot give to matter that invisible agency, by which all the component parts of the immense machine of the universe have influence upon each other, and act in motional unison together without any apparent contact, and to which man has given the name of attraction, gravitation, and repulsion, he supplies the place of that agency by the humble imitation of teeth and cogs. All the parts of man's microcosm must visibly touch. But could he gain a knowledge of that agency, so as to be able to apply it in practice, we might then say, that another *canonical book* of the word of God had been discovered.

If man could alter the properties of the lever, so also could he alter the properties of the triangle: for a lever (taking that sort of lever, which is called a steel-yard, for the sake of explanation) forms, when in motion, a triangle. The line it descends from, (one point of that line being in the fulcrum) the line it descends to, and the chord of the arc, which the end of the leaver describes in the air, are the three sides of a triangle. The other arm of the lever describes also a triangle; and the corresponding sides of those two triangles, calculated scientifically, or measured gometrically; and also the sines, tangents, and secants generated from the angles, and geometrically measured, have the same proportions to each other, as the different weights have that will balance each other on the lever, leaving the weight of the leaver out of the case.

It may also be said, that man can make a wheel and axis, that he can put wheels of different magnitudes together, and produce a mill. Still the case comes back to the same point, which is, that he did not make the principle that gives the wheels those powers. That principle is as unalterable as in the former cases, or rather it is the same principle under a different appearance to the eye.

The power that two wheels, of different magnitudes, have upon each other, is in the same proportion as if the semi-diameter of the two wheels were joined together and made into that kind of lever I have described, suspended at the part where the semi-diameters join; for the two wheels, scientifically considered, are no other than the two circles generated by the motion of the compound lever.

It is from the study of the true theology that all our knowledge of science is derived, and it is from that knowledge that all the arts have originated.

The Almighty lecturer, by displaying the principles of science in the structure of the universe, has invited man to study and to imitation. It is as if he had said to the inhabitants of this globe that we call ours, "I have made an earth for man to dwell upon, and I have rendered the starry heavens visible, to teach him science and the arts. He can now provide for his own comfort, AND LEARN FROM MY MUNIFICENCE TO ALL, TO BE KIND TO EACH OTHER."

Of what use is it, unless it be to teach man something, that his eye is endowed with the power of beholding, to an incomprehensible distance, an immensity of worlds revolving in the ocean of space? Or of what use is it that this immensity of worlds is visible to man? What has man to do with the Pleiades, with Orion, with Sirius, with the star he calls the north star, with the moving orbs he has named Saturn, Jupiter, Mars, Venus, and Mercury, if no uses are to follow from their being visible? A less power of vision would have been sufficient for man, if the immensity he now possesses were given only to waste itself, as it were, on an immense desert of space glittering with shows.

It is only by contemplating what he calls the starry heavens, as the book and school of science, that he discovers any use in their being visible to him, or any advantage resulting from his immensity of vision. But when he contemplates the subject in this light, he sees an additional motive for saying that *nothing was made in vain;* for in vain would be this power of vision if it taught man nothing.

As the Christian system of faith has made a revolution in theology, so also has it made revolution in the state of learning. That which is now called learning was not learning originally. Learning does not consist, as the schools now make it consist, in the knowledge of languages, but in the knowledge of things to which language gives names.

The Greeks were a learned people; but learning with them, did not consist in speaking Greek, any more than in a Roman's speaking Latin, or a Frenchman's speaking French, or an Englishman's speaking English. From what we know of the Greeks, it does not appear that they knew or studied any language but their own; and this was one cause of their becoming so learned; it afforded them more time to apply themselves to better studies. The schools of the Greeks were schools of science and philosophy, and not of languages: and it is in the knowledge of the things that science and philosophy teach, that learning consists.

Almost all the scientific learning that now exists, came to us from the Greeks, or the people who spoke the Greek language. It therefore became necessary to the people of other nations, who spoke a different language, that some among them should learn the Greek language, in order that the learning the Greeks had, might be made known in those nations, by translating the Greek books of science and philosophy into the mother tongue of each nation.

The study therefore of the Greek language, (and in the same manner for the latin) was no other than the drudgery business of a linguist; and the language thus obtained, was no other than the means, as it were, the tools, employed to obtain the learning the Greeks had. It made no part of the learning itself; and was so distinct from it, as to make it exceeding probable, that the persons who had studied Greek sufficiently to translate those works, such, for instance, as Euclid's Elements, did not understand any of the learning the works contained.

As there is now nothing new to be learned from the dead languages,[7] all the useful books being already translated, the languages are become useless, and the time expended in teaching and in learning them is wasted. So far as the study of languages may contribute to the progress and communication of knowledge (for it has nothing to do with the *creation* of knowledge) it is only in the living languages that new knowledge is to be found: and certain it is, that, in general, a youth will learn more of a living language in one year, than of a dead language in seven; and it is but seldom that the teacher knows much of it himself. The difficulty of learning the dead languages does not arise from any superior abstruseness in the languages themselves, but in their *being dead,* and the pronunciation entirely lost. It would be the same thing with any other language when it becomes dead. The best Greek linguist, that now exists, does not understand Greek so well as a Grecian plowman did, or a Grecian milkmaid: and the same for the Latin, compared with a plowman or a milkmaid of the Romans; and with respect to pronunciation, and idiom, not so well as the cows that she milked. It would therefore be advantageous to the state of learning, to abolish the study of the dead languages, and to make learning consist, as it originally did, in scientific knowledge.

The apology that is sometimes made for continuing to teach the dead languages is, that they are taught at a time when a child is not capable of exerting any other mental faculty than that of memory. But this is altogether erroneous. The human mind has a natural disposition to scientific knowledge, and to the things connected with it. The first and favourite amusement of a child, even before it begins to play, is that of imitating the works of man. It builds houses with cards or sticks; it navigates the little ocean of a bowl of water with a paper boat; or dams the stream of a gutter, and contrives something which it calls a mill; and it interests itself in the fate of its works with a care that resembles affection. It afterwards goes to school, where its genius is killed by the barren study of a dead language, and the philosopher is lost in the linguist.

But the apology that is now made for continuing to teach the dead languages, could not be the cause at first of cutting down learning to the narrow and humble sphere of linguistry; the cause, therefore, must be sought for elsewhere. In all researches of this kind, the best evidence that can be produced, is the internal evidence the thing carries with itself, and the evidence of circumstances that unites with it, both of which, in this case, are not difficult to be discovered.

Putting them aside, as matter of distinct consideration, the outrage offered to the moral justice of God, by supposing him to make the innocent suffer for the guilty, and also the loose morality and low contrivance of supposing him to change himself into the shape of a man, in order to make an excuse to himself for not executing his supposed sentence upon Adam; putting, I say, those things aside, as matter of distinct consideration, it is certain, that what is called the christian system of faith, including in it the whimsical account of the creation; the strange story of Eve, the snake, and the apple; the amphibious idea of a man-god; the corporeal idea of the death of a god; the mythological idea of a family of gods; and the christian system of arithmetic, that three are one, and one is three, are all irreconcileable, not only to the divine gift of reason that God has given to man, but to the knowledge that man gains of the power and wisdom of God, by the aid of the sciences, and by studying the structure of the universe that God has made.

The setters up, therefore, and the advocates of the christian system of faith, could not but foresee that the continually progressive knowledge that man would gain by the aid of science, of the power and wisdom of God, manifested in the structure of the universe, and in all the works of creation, would militate against, and call into question, the truth of their system of faith; and therefore it became necessary to their purpose to cut learning down to a size less dangerous to their project, and this they effected by restricting the idea of learning to the dead study of dead languages.

They not only rejected the study of science out of the christian schools, but they persecuted it; and it is only within about the last two centuries that the study has been revived. So late as 1610 Galileo, a Florentine, discovered and introduced the use of telescopes, and by applying them to observe the motions and appearances of the heavenly bodies, afforded additional means for ascertaining the true structure of the universe. Instead of being esteemed for these discoveries, he was sentenced to renounce them, or the opinions resulting from them, as a damnable heresy. And prior to that time Vigilius[8] was condemned to be burned for asserting the antipodes, or in other words, that the earth was a globe, and habitable in every part where there was land; yet the truth of this is now too well known even to be told.

If the belief of errors not morally bad did no mischief, it would make no part of the moral duty of man to oppose and remove them. There was no moral ill in believing the earth was flat like a trencher, any more than there was moral virtue in believing it was round like a globe; neither was there any moral ill in believing that the Creator made no other world than this, any more than there was moral virtue in believing that he made millions, and that the infinity of space is filled with worlds. But when a system of religion is made to grow out of a supposed system of creation that is not true, and to unite itself therewith in a manner almost inseparable therefrom, the case assumes an entirely different ground. It is then that errors, not morally bad, become fraught with the same mischiefs as if they were. It is then that the truth, though otherwise indifferent itself, becomes an essential, by becoming the criterion, that either confirms by corresponding evidence, or denies by contradictory evidence, the reality of the religion itself. In this view of the case it is the moral duty of man to obtain every possible evidence, that the structure of the heavens, or any other part of creation affords, with respect to systems of religion. But this, the supporters or partizans of the christian system, as if dreading the result, incessantly opposed, and not only rejected the sciences, but persecuted the professors. Had Newton or Descartes lived three or four hundred years ago, and pursued their studies as they did, it is most probable they would not have lived to finish them; and had Franklin drawn lightning from the clouds at the same time, it would have been at the hazard of expiring for it in flames.

Latter times have laid all the blame upon the Goths and Vandals, but, however unwilling the partizans of the Christian system may be to believe or to acknowledge it, it is nevertheless true, that the age of ignorance commenced with the Christian system. There was more knowledge in the world before that period than for many centuries afterwards; and as to religious knowledge, the Christian system, as already said, was only another species of mythology; and the mythology to which it succeeded, was a corruption of an ancient system of theism.*

It is owing to this long interregnum of science, *and to no other cause,* that we have now to look back through a vast chasm of many hundred years to the respectable characters we call the ancients. Had the progression of knowledge gone on proportionably with the stock that before existed, that chasm would have been filled up with characters rising superior in knowledge to each other; and those ancients, we now so much admire, would have appeared respectably in the back ground of the scene. But the christian system laid all waste; and if we take our stand about the beginning of the sixteenth century, we look back through that long chasm, to the times of the ancients, as over a vast sandy desert, in which not a shrub appears to intercept the vision to the fertile hills beyond.

It is an inconsistency, scarcely possible to be credited, that any thing should exist under the name of a *religion,* that held it to be *irreligious* to study and contemplate the structure of the universe that God had made. But the fact is too well established to be denied. The event that served more than any other, to break the first link in this long chain of

---

* It is impossible for us now to know at what time the heathen mythology began; but it is certain, from the internal evidence that it carries, that it did not begin in the same state or condition in which it ended. All the gods of that mythology, except Saturn, were of modern invention. The supposed reign of Saturn was prior to that which is called the heathen mythology, and was so far a species of theism, that it admitted the belief of only one God. Saturn is supposed to have abdicated the government in favour of his three sons and one daughter, Jupiter, Pluto, Neptune and Juno: after this, thousands of other gods and demigods were imaginarily created, and the calendar of gods increased as fast as the calendar of saints, and the calendar of courts have increased since.

All the corruptions that have taken place in theology, and in religion, have been produced by admitting of what man calls *revealed religion.* The mythologists pretended to more revealed religion than the christians do. They had their oracles and their priests, who were supposed to receive and deliver the word of God verbally on almost all occasions.

Since then all corruptions, down from Moloch to modern predestinarianism, and the human sacrifices of the heathens to the christian sacrifice of the Creator, have been produced by admitting what is called *revealed religion,* the most effectual means to prevent all such evils and impositions, and is not to admit of any other revelation than that which is manifested in the book of Creation; and to contemplate the Creation, as the only true and real word of God that ever did or ever will exist, and that every thing else, called the word of God is fable and imposition.

despotic ignorance, is that known by the name of the reformation by Luther. From that time, though it does not appear to have made any part of the intention of Luther, or of those who are called reformers, the Sciences began to revive, and Liberality, their natural associate, began to appear. This was the only public good the reformation did; for with respect to religious good, it might as well not have taken place. The mythology still continued the same; and a multiplicity of national popes grew out of the downfall of the Pope of Christendom.

Having thus shewn, from the internal evidence of things, the cause that produced a change in the state of learning, and the motive for substituting the study of the dead languages in the place of the Sciences, I proceed, in addition to the several observations already made in the former part of this work, to compare, or rather to confront, the evidence that the structure of the universe affords, with the Christian system of religion. But as I cannot begin this part better than by referring to the ideas that occurred to me at an early part of life, and which I doubt not have occured in some degree to almost every other person at one time or other, I shall state what those ideas were, and add thereto such other matter as shall arise out of the subject, given to the whole, by way of preface, a short introduction.

My father being of the quaker profession,[9] it was my good fortune to have an exceedingly good moral education, and a tolerable stock of useful learning. Though I went to the grammar school,*[10] I did not learn Latin, not only because I had no inclination to learn languages, but because of the objection the quakers have against the books in which the language is taught. But this did not prevent me from being acquainted with the subjects of all the Latin books used in the school.

The natural bent of my mind was to science. I had some turn, and I believe some talent for poetry; but this I rather repressed than encouraged, as leading too much into the field of imagination. As soon as I was able I purchased a pair of globes, and attended the philosophical lectures of Martin and Ferguson,[11] and became afterwards acquainted with Dr. Bevis,[12] of the society, called the Royal Society,[13] then living in the Temple, and an excellent astronomer.

I had no disposition for what was called politics. It presented to my

---

*The same school, Thetford in Norfolk, that the present counsellor Mingay[14] went to, and under the same master.

mind no other idea than is contained in the word Jockeyship. When, therefore, I turned my thoughts towards matters of government, I had to form a system for myself, that accorded with the moral and philosophic principles in which I had been educated. I saw, or at least I thought I saw, a vast scene opening itself to the world in the affairs of America; and it appeared to me, that unless the Americans changed the plan they were then pursuing, with respect to the government of England, and declare themselves independent, they would not only involve themselves in a multiplicity of new difficulties, but shut out the prospect that was then offering itself to mankind through their means. It was from these motives that I published the work known by the name of *Common Sense,* which is the first work I ever did publish: and so far as I can judge of myself, I believe I never should have been known in the world as an author on any subject whatever, had it not been for the affairs of America. I wrote *Common Sense* the latter end of the year 1775, and published it the first of January 1776. Independence was declared the fourth of July following.

Any person who has made observations on the state and progress of the human mind, by observing his own, cannot but have observed, that there are two distinct classes of what are called Thoughts: those that we produce in ourselves by reflection and the act of thinking, and those that bolt into the mind of their own accord. I have always made it a rule to treat those voluntary visitors with civility, taking care to examine, as well as I was able, if they were worth entertaining; and it is from them I have acquired almost all the knowledge that I have. As to the learning that any person gains from school education, it serves only, like a small capital, to put him in the way of beginning learning for himself afterwards. Every person of learning is finally his own teacher; the reason of which is, that principles, being of a distinct quality of circumstances, cannot be impressed upon the memory. Their place of mental residence is the understanding, and they are never so lasting as when they begin by conception. Thus much for the introductory part.

From the time I was capable of conceiving an idea, and acting upon it by reflection, I either doubted the truth of the christian system, or thought it to be a strange affair; I scarcely knew which it was: but I well remember, when about seven or eight years of age, hearing a sermon read by a relation of mine, who was a great devotee of the church, upon the subject of what is called *Redemption by the death of the Son of God.*

After the sermon was ended I went into the garden, and as I was going down the garden steps (for I perfectly recollect the spot) I revolted at the recollection of what I had heard, and thought to myself that it was making God Almighty act like a passionate man that killed his son when he could not revenge himself any other way; and as I was sure a man would be hanged that did such a thing, I could not see for what purpose they preached such sermons. This was not one of those kind of thoughts that had any thing in it of childish levity; it was to me a serious reflection arising from the idea I had, that God was too good to do such an action, and also too almighty to be under any necessity of doing it. I believe in the same manner to this moment; and I moreover believe, that any system of religion that has any thing in it that shocks the mind of a child, cannot be a true system.

It seems as if parents of the christian profession were ashamed to tell their children any thing about the principles of their religion. They sometimes instruct them in morals, and talk to them of the goodness of what they call Providence; for the christian mythology has five deities: there is God the Father, God the Son, God the Holy Ghost, the God Providence, and the Goddess Nature. But the christian story of God the Father putting his son to death, or employing people to do it (for that is the plain language of the story), cannot be told by a parent to a child: and to tell him that it was done to make mankind happier and better is making the story still worse, as if mankind could be improved by the example of murder; and to tell him that all this is a mystery, is only making an excuse for the incredibility of it.

How different is this to the pure and simple profession of Deism! The true deist has but one Deity; and his religion consists in contemplating the power, wisdom, and benignity of the Deity in his works, and in endeavouring to imitate him in every thing moral, scientifical, and mechanical.

The religion that approaches the nearest of all others to true deism, in the moral and benign part thereof, is that professed by the Quakers, but they have contracted themselves too much by leaving the works of God out of their system. Though I reverence their philanthropy, I cannot help smiling at the conceit, that if the taste of a quaker could have been consulted at the creation, what a silent and drab-coloured creation it would have been![15] Not a flower would have blossomed its gaieties, nor a bird been permitted to sing.

Quitting these reflections, I proceed to other matters. After I had made myself master of the use of the globes, and of the orrery*, and conceived an idea of the infinity of space, and of the eternal divisibility of matter, and obtained, at least, a general knowledge of what is called natural philosophy,[16] I began to compare, or, as I have before said, to confront, the internal evidence those things afford with the christian system of faith.

Though it is not a direct article of the christian system that this world that we inhabit is the whole of the habitable creation, yet it is so worked up therewith, from what is called the Mosaic account of the creation, the story of Eve and the apple, and the counterpart of that story, the death of the Son of God, that to believe otherwise, that is, to believe that God created a plurality of worlds, at least as numerous as what we call stars, renders the christian system of faith at once little and ridiculous; and scatters it in the mind like feathers in the air. The two beliefs cannot be held together in the same mind; and he who thinks that he believes both, has thought but little of either.

Though the belief of a plurality of worlds was familiar to the ancients, it is only within the last three centuries that the extent and dimensions of this globe that we inhabit, have been ascertained. Several vessels, following the tract of the ocean, have sailed entirely round the world, as a man may march in a circle, and come round by the contrary side of the circle to the spot he set out from. The circular dimensions of our world in the widest part, as a man would measure the widest round of an apple or a ball, is only twenty-five thousand and twenty English miles, reckoning sixty-nine miles and an half to an equatorial degree, and may be sailed round in the space of about three years†.

A world of this extent may, at first thought, appear to us to be great;

---

* As this book may fall into the hands of persons who do not know what an orrery is, it is for their information I add this note, as the name gives no idea of the uses of the thing. The orrery has its name from the person who invented it. It is a machinery of clock-work representing the universe in miniature; and in which the revolution of the earth round itself and round the sun, the revolution of the moon round the earth, the revolution of the planets round the sun, their relative distances from the sun, as the center of the whole system, their relative distances from each other, and their different magnitudes, are represented as they really exist in what we call the heavens.

† Allowing a ship to sail, on an average, three miles in an hour, she would sail entirely round the world in less than one year, if she could sail in a direct circle; but she is obliged to follow the course of the ocean.

but if we compare it with the immensity of space in which it is suspended, like a bubble or a balloon in the air, it is infinitely less in proportion than the smallest grain of sand is to the size of the world, or the finest particle of dew to the whole ocean; and is therefore but small; and, as will be hereafter shewn, is only *one* of a system of worlds, of which the universal creation is composed.

It is not difficult to gain some faint idea of the immensity of space in which this and all the other worlds are suspended, if we follow a progression of ideas. When we think of the size or dimensions of a room, our ideas limit themselves to the walls, and there they stop. But when our eye, or our imagination, darts into space, that is, when it looks upward into what we call the open air, we cannot conceive any walls or boundaries it can have; and if, for the sake of resting our ideas, we suppose a boundary, the question immediately renews itself, and asks, what is beyond that boundary? and in the same manner, what is beyond the next boundary; and so on, till the fatigued imagination returns and says, *there is no end.* Certainly, then, the Creator was not pent for room when he made this world no larger than it is, and we have to seek the reason in something else.

If we take a survey of our own world, or rather of this, of which the Creator has given us the use, as our portion in the immense system of creation, we find every part of it, the earth, the waters, and the air that surround it, filled, and, as it were, crouded with life, down from the largest animals that we know of, to the smallest insects the naked eye can behold, and from thence to others still smaller, and totally invisible without the assistance of the microscope. Every tree, every plant, every leaf, serves not only as an habitation, but as a world to some numerous race, till animal existence becomes so exceedingly refined, that the effluvia of a blade of grass would be food for thousands.

Since then no part of our earth is left unoccupied, why is it to be supposed, that the immensity of space is a naked void, lying in eternal waste. There is room for millions of worlds as large or larger than ours, and each of them millions of miles apart from each other.

Having now arrived at this point, if we carry our ideas only one thought further, we shall see, perhaps, the true reason, at least a very good reason for our happiness, why the Creator, instead of making one immense world, extending over an immense quantity of space, has preferred dividing that quantity of matter into several distinct and separate worlds, which we call planets, of which our earth is one. But before I explain my ideas upon this subject, it is necessary (not for the sake of those that already know, but for those who do not) to shew what the system of the universe is.

That part of the universe, that is called the solar system (meaning the system of worlds to which our earth belongs, and of which Sol, or in English language the Sun, is the center) consists, besides the Sun, of six distinct orbs, or planets,[17] or worlds, besides the secondary bodies, called the satellites, or moons, of which our earth has one that attends her in her annual revolution round the sun, in like manner as the other satellites, or moons, attend the planets, or worlds, to which they severally belong, as may be seen by the assistance of the telescope.

The Sun is the center, round which those six worlds, or planets, revolve at different distances therefrom, and in circles concentric to each other. Each world keeps constantly in nearly the same tract round the Sun, and continues, at the same time, turning round itself, in nearly an upright position, as a top turns round itself when it is spinning on the ground, and leans a little sideways.

It is this leaning of the earth, (23½ degrees) that occasions summer and winter, and the different length of days and nights. If the earth turned round itself in a position perpendicular to the plane or level of the circle it moves in round the Sun, as a top turns round when it stands erect on the ground, the days and nights would be always of the same length, twelve hours day, and twelve hours night, and the season would be uniformly the same throughout the year.

Every time that a planet (our earth for example) turns round itself, it makes what we call day and night; and every time it goes entirely round the Sun, it makes what we call a year, consequently our world turns three hundred and sixty-five times round itself, in going once round the Sun.*

The names that the ancients gave to those six worlds, and which are still called by the same names, are Mercury, Venus, this world that we call ours, Mars, Jupiter, and Saturn. They appear larger to the eye than the stars, being many million miles nearer to our earth than any of the stars are. The planet Venus is that which is called the evening star, and

---

* Those who supposed that the Sun went round the earth every twenty-four hours, made the same mistake in idea, that a cook would do in fact, that should make the fire go round the meat, instead of the meat turning round itself towards the fire.

sometimes the morning star, as she happens to set after, or rise before the Sun, which, in either case, is never more than three hours.

The Sun, as before said, being the center, the planet, or world, nearest the Sun, is Mercury; his distance from the Sun is thirty-four million miles, and he moves round in a circle always at that distance from the Sun, as a top may be supposed to spin round in the tract in which a horse goes in a mill. The second world is Venus: she is fifty-seven million miles distant from the Sun, and consequently moves round in a circle much greater than that of Mercury. The third world is this that we inhabit, and which is eighty-eight million miles distant from the Sun, and consequently moves round in a circle greater than that of Venus. The fourth world is Mars; he is distant from the Sun one hundred and thirty-four million miles, and consequently moves round in a circle greater than that of our earth. The fifth is Jupiter; he is distant from the Sun five hundred and fifty-seven million miles, and consequently moves round in a circle greater than that of Mars. The sixth world is Saturn; he is distant from the Sun seven hundred and sixty-three million miles, and consequently moves round in a circle that surrounds the circles or orbits of all the other worlds or planets.

The space, therefore, in the air, or in the immensity of space, that our solar system takes up for the several worlds to perform their revolutions in round the sun, is of the extent in a strait line of the whole diameter of the orbit or circle, in which Saturn moves round the Sun, which being double his distance from the Sun, is fifteen hundred and twenty-six million miles; and its circular extent is nearly five thousand million, and its globical content is almost three thousand five hundred million times three thousand five hundred million square miles.*

---

* If it should be asked, how can man know these things? I have one plain answer to give, which is, that man knows how to calculate an eclipse, and also how to calculate, to a minute of time, when the planet Venus, in making her revolutions round the Sun, will come in a strait line between our earth, and the Sun, and will appear to us about the size of a large pea passing across the face of the Sun. This happens but twice in about an hundred years, at the distance of about eight years from each other, and has happened twice in our time, both of which were foreknown by calculation. It can also be known when they will happen again for a thousand years to come, or to any other portion of time. As, therefore, man could not be able to do those things if he did not understand the solar system, and the manner in which the revolutions of the several planets or worlds are performed, the fact of calculating an eclipse or a transit of Venus, is a proof in point that the knowledge exists; and as to a few thousand, or even a few million miles more or less, it makes scarcely any sensible difference in such immense distances.

But this, immense as it is, is only one system of worlds. Beyond this, at a vast distance into space, far beyond all power of calculation, are the stars called the fixed stars. They are called fixed, because they have no revolutionary motion as the six worlds or planets have that I have been describing. Those fixed stars continue always at the same distance from each other, and always in the same place, as the Sun does in the center of our system. The probability therefore is, that each of those fixed stars is also a Sun, round which another system of worlds or planets, though too remote for us to discover, performs its revolutions, as our system of worlds does round our central Sun.

By this easy progression of ideas, the immensity of space will appear to us to be filled with systems of worlds; and that no part of space lies at waste, any more than any part of our globe of earth and water is left unoccupied.

Having thus endeavoured to convey, in a familiar and easy manner, some idea of the structure of the universe, I return to explain what I before alluded to, namely, the great benefits arising to a man in consequence of the Creator having made a *plurality* of worlds, such as our system is, consisting of a central Sun and six worlds, besides satellites, in preference to that of creating one world only of a vast extent.

It is an idea I have never lost sight of, that all our knowledge of science is derived from the revolutions (exhibited to our eye, and from thence to our understanding) which those several planets, or worlds, of which our system is composed, make in their circuit round the Sun.

Had then the quantity of matter which these six worlds contain been blended into one solitary globe, the consequence to us would have been, that either no revolutionary motion would have existed, or not a sufficiency of it, to give us the ideas and the knowledge of science we now have; and it is from the sciences that all the mechanical arts that contribute so much to our earthly felicity and comfort are derived.

As therefore the Creator made nothing in vain, so also must it be believed that he organized the structure of the universe in the most advantageous manner for the benefit of man; and as we see, and from experience feel, the benefits we derive from the structure of the universe, formed as it is, which benefits we should not have had the opportunity of enjoying, if the structure, so far as relates to our system, had been a solitary globe, we can discover, at least, one reason why a *plurality* of worlds has been made, and that reason calls forth the devotional gratitude of man, as well as his admiration.

But it is not to us, the inhabitants of this globe, only, that the benefits arising from a plurality of the worlds are limited. The inhabitants of each of the worlds, of which our system is composed, enjoy the same opportunities of knowledge as we do. They behold the revolutionary motions of our earth, as we behold theirs. All the planets revolve in sight of each other; and therefore the same universal school of science presents itself to all.

Neither does the knowledge stop here. The system of worlds, next to us, exhibits in its revolutions, the same principles and school of science, to the inhabitants of their system, as our system does to us, and in like manner throughout the immensity of space.

Our ideas, not only of the almightiness of the Creator, but of his wisdom and his beneficence, become enlarged in proportion as we contemplate the extent and the structure of the universe. The solitary idea of a solitary world rolling, or at rest, in the immense ocean of space, gives place to the chearful idea of a society of worlds, so happily contrived, as to administer, even by their motion, instruction to man. We see our own earth filled with abundance; but we forget to consider how much of that abundance is owing to the scientific knowledge the vast machinery of the universe has unfolded.

But, in the midst of those reflections, what are we to think of the christian system of faith that forms itself upon the idea of only one world, and that of no greater extent, as is before shewn, than twenty-five thousand miles. An extent, which a man walking at the rate of three miles an hour, for twelve hours in the day, could he keep on in a circular direction, would walk entirely round in less than two years. Alas! what is this to the mighty ocean of space, and the almighty power of the Creator!

From whence then could arise the solitary and strange conceit that the Almighty, who had millions of worlds equally dependent on his protection, should quit the care of all the rest, and come to die in our world, because, they say, one man and one woman had eaten an apple. And, on the other hand, are we to suppose that every world, in the boundless creation, had an Eve, an apple, a serpent, and a redeemer. In this case, the person who is irreverently called the Son of God, and sometimes God himself, would have nothing else to do than to travel from world to world, in an endless succession of death, with scarcely a momentary interval of life.

It has been, by rejecting the evidence, that the word, or works of God in the creation, affords to our senses, and the action of our reason upon that evidence, that so many wild and whimsical systems of faith, and of religion, have been fabricated and set up. There may be many systems of religion, that so far from being morally bad, are in many respects morally good: but there can be but ONE that is true; and that one, necessarily must, as it ever will, be in all things consistent with the ever-existing word of God that we behold in his works. But such is the strange construction of the Christian system of faith, that every evidence the Heavens affords to man, either directly contradicts it, or renders it absurd.

It is possible to believe, and I always feel pleasure in encouraging myself to believe it, that there have been men in the world who persuaded themselves that, what is called *a pious fraud,* might, at least under particular circumstances, be productive of some good. But the fraud being once established, could not afterwards be explained; for it is with a pious fraud, as with a bad action, it begets a calamitous necessity of going on.

The persons who first preached the christian system of faith, and in some measure combined with it the morality preached by Jesus Christ, might persuade themselves that it was better than the heathen mythology that then prevailed. From the first preachers, the fraud went on to the second, and to the third, till the idea of its being a pious fraud became lost in the belief of its being true; and that belief came again encouraged by the interest of those who made a livelihood by preaching it.

But though such a belief might, by such means, be rendered almost general among the laity, it is next to impossible to account for the continual persecution carried on by the church, for several hundred years, against the sciences and against the professors of science, if the church had not some record or some tradition, that it was originally no other than a pious fraud, or did not foresee, that it could not be maintained against the evidence that the structure of the universe afforded.

Having thus shewn the irreconcileable inconsistencies between the real word of God existing in the universe, and that which is called *the word of God,* as shewn to us in a printed book, that any man might make,

I proceed to speak of the three principal means that have been employed in all ages, and perhaps in all countries, to impose upon mankind.

Those three means are, Mystery, Miracle, and Prophesy. The two first are incompatible with true religion, and the third ought always to be suspected.

With respect to mystery, every thing we behold is, in one sense, a mystery to us. Our own existence is a mystery: the whole vegetable world is a mystery. We cannot account how it is that an acorn, when put into the ground, is made to develope itself, and become an oak. We know not how it is that the seed we sow unfolds and multiplies itself, and returns to us such an abundant interest for so small a capital.

The fact, however, as distinct from the operating cause, is not a mystery because we see it; and we know also the means we are to use, which is no other than putting the seed in the ground. We know therefore as much as is necessary for us to know; and that part of the operation that we do not know, and which if we did, we could not perform, the Creator takes upon himself and performs it for us. We are therefore better off than if we had been let into the secret, and left to do it for ourselves.

But though every created thing is in this sense a mystery, the word mystery cannot be applied to *moral truth*, any more than obscurity can be applied to light. The God in whom we believe is a God of moral truth, and not a God of mystery or obscurity. Mystery is the antagonist of truth. It is a fog of human invention, that obscures truth and represents it in distortion. Truth never invelops *itself* in mystery; and the mystery in which it is at any time enveloped, is the work of its antagonist, and never of itself.

Religion, therefore, being the belief of a God, and the practice of moral truth, cannot have connection with mystery. The belief of a God, so far from having any thing of mystery in it, is of all beliefs the most easy, because it arises to us, as is before observed, out of necessity. And the practice of moral truth, or in other words, a practical imitation of the moral goodness of God, is no other than our acting towards each other, as he acts benignly towards all. We cannot *serve* God in the manner we serve those who cannot do without such service; and, therefore, the only idea we can have of serving God, is that of contributing to the happiness of the living creation that God has made. This cannot be done by retiring ourselves from the society of the world, and spending a recluse life in selfish devotion.

The very nature and design of religion, if I may so express it, prove even to demonstration, that it must be free from every thing of mystery, and unincumbered with every thing that is mysterious. Religion, considered as a duty, is incumbent upon every living soul alike, and therefore must be on a level to the understanding and comprehension of all. Man does not learn religion as he learns the secrets and mysteries of a trade. He learns the theory of religion by reflection. It arises out of the action of his own mind upon the things which he sees, or upon what he may happen to hear or to read, and the practice joins itself thereto.

When men, whether from policy or pious fraud, set up systems of religion incompatible with the word or works of God in the creation, and not only above but repugnant to human comprehension, they were under the necessity of inventing, or adopting, a word that should serve as a bar to all questions, inquiries, and speculations. The word *mystery* answered this purpose; and thus it has happened, that religion, which, in itself, is without mystery, has been corrupted into a fog of mysteries.

As *mystery* answered all general purposes, *miracle* followed as an occasional auxiliary. The former served to bewilder the mind, the latter to puzzle the senses. The one was the lingo; the other the legerdemain.

But before going further into this subject, it will be proper to inquire what is to be understood by a miracle.

In the same sense that every thing may be said to be a mystery, so also may it be said, that every thing is a miracle, and that no one thing is a greater miracle than another. The elephant, though larger, is not a greater miracle than a mite; nor a mountain a greater miracle than an atom. To an almighty power, it is no more difficult to make the one than the other, and no more difficult to make a million of worlds than to make one. Every thing therefore is a miracle in one sense; whilst, in the other sense, there is no such thing as a miracle. It is a miracle when compared to our power, and to our comprehension. It is not a miracle compared to the power that performs it. But as nothing in this description conveys the idea that is affixed to the word miracle, it is necessary to carry the inquiry further.

Mankind have conceived to themselves certain laws by which, what they call, nature, is supposed to act; and that a miracle is something contrary to the operation and effect of those laws. But unless we know the whole extent of those laws, and of what are commonly called, the powers of nature, we are not able to judge whether any thing that may appear to us wonderful, or miraculous, be within, or be beyond, or be contrary to, her natural power of acting.

The ascension of a man several miles high into the air, would have every thing in it that constitutes the idea of a miracle, if it were not known that a species of air can be generated several times lighter than the common atmospheric air, and yet possess elasticity enough to prevent the balloon,[18] in which that light air is inclosed, from being compressed into as many times less bulk, by the common air that surrounds it. In like manner, extracting flashes or sparks of fire from the human body as visible as from a steel struck with a flint, and causing iron or steel to move without any visible agent, would also give the idea of a miracle, if we were not acquainted with electricity and magnetism: so also would many other experiments in natural philosophy, to those who are not acquainted with the subject. The restoring persons to life, who are to appearance dead, as is practised upon drowned persons, would also be a miracle, if it were not known that animation is capable of being suspended without being extinct.

Besides these, there are performances by slight of hand, and by persons acting in concert, that have a miraculous appearance, which, when known, are thought nothing of. And besides these, there are mechanical and optical deceptions. There is now an exhibition in Paris of ghosts and spectres, which, though it is not imposed upon the spectators as a fact, has an astonishing appearance. As therefore we know not the extent to which either nature or art can go, there is no positive criterion to determine what a miracle is; and mankind, in giving credit to appearances, under the idea of their being miracles, are subject to be continually imposed upon.

Since then appearances are so capable of deceiving, and things not real have a strong resemblance to things that are, nothing can be more inconsistent, than to suppose, that the Almighty would make use of means, such as are called miracles, that would subject the person who performed them to the suspicion of being an impostor, and the person who related them to be suspected of lying, and the doctrine intended to be supported thereby, to be suspected as a fabulous invention.

Of all the modes of evidence that ever were invented to obtain belief to any system or opinion, to which the name of religion has been given, that of *miracle,* however successful the imposition may have been, is the most inconsistent. For, in the first place, whenever recourse is had to show, for the purpose of procuring that belief (for a miracle, under any idea of the word, is a show) it implies a lameness or weakness in the doctrine that is preached. And, in the second place, it is degrading the Almighty into the character of a show-man, playing tricks to amuse and make the people stare and wonder. It is also the most equivocal sort of evidence that can be set up; for the belief is not to depend upon the thing called a miracle, but upon the credit of the reporter, who says that he saw it; and therefore the thing, were it true, would have no better chance of being believed than if it were a lie.

Suppose I were to say, that when I sat down to write this book, a hand presented itself in the air, took up the pen, and wrote every word that is herein written; would any body believe me? certainly they would not. Would they believe me a whit the more if the thing had been a fact? certainly they would not. Since then, a real miracle, were it to happen, would be subject to the same fate as the falsehood, the inconsistency becomes the greater, of supposing the Almighty would make use of means that would not answer the purpose for which they were intended, even if they were real.

If we are to suppose a miracle to be something so entirely out of the course of what is called nature, that she must go out of that course to accomplish it; and we see an account given of such miracle by the person who said he saw it, it raises a question in the mind very easily decided, which is, Is it more probable that nature should go out of her course, or that a man should tell a lie? We have never seen, in our time, nature go out of her course, but we have good reason to believe that millions of lies have been told in the same time; it is therefore at least millions to one, that the reporter of a miracle tells a lie.

The story of the whale swallowing Jonah, though a whale is large enough to do it, borders greatly on the marvellous; but it would have approached nearer to the idea of a miracle, if Jonah had swallowed the whale. In this, which may serve for all cases of miracles, the matter would decide itself as before stated, namely, Is it more probable that a man should have swallowed a whale, or told a lie?

But supposing that Jonah had really swallowed the whale, and gone with it in his belly to Nineveh, and to convince the people that it was true, have cast it up in their sight of the full length and size of a whale, would they not have believed him to have been the devil instead of a prophet? or, if the whale had carried Jonah to Nineveh, and cast him up in the same public manner, would they not have believed the whale to have been the devil, and Jonah one of his imps?

The most extraordinary of all the things called miracles, related in the New Testament, is that of the devil flying away with Jesus Christ, and carrying him to the top of a high mountain; and to the top of the highest pinnacle of the temple, and showing him, and promising to him *all the kingdoms of the world*. How happened it that he did not discover America? or is it only with *kingdoms* that his sooty highness has any interest?

I have too much respect for the moral character of Christ, to believe that he told this whale of a miracle himself; neither is it easy to account for what purpose it could have been fabricated, unless it were to impose upon the connoisseurs of miracles, as is sometimes practised upon the connoisseurs of Queen Anne's farthings, and collectors of relics and antiquities; or to render the belief of miracles ridiculous, by outdoing miracle, as Don Quixote outdid chivalry; or to embarrass the belief of miracles by making it doubtful by what power, whether of God, or of the devil, any thing called a miracle was performed. It requires, however, a great deal of faith in the devil to believe this miracle.

In every point of view, in which those things called miracles can be placed and considered, the reality of them is improbable, and their existence unnecessary. They would not, as before observed, answer any useful purpose, even if they were true; for it is more difficult to obtain belief to a miracle, than to a principle evidently moral, without any miracle. Moral principle speaks universally for itself. Miracle could be but a thing of the moment, and seen but by a few; after this, it requires a transfer of faith, from God to man, to believe a miracle upon man's report. Instead therefore of admitting the recitals of miracles, as evidence of any system of religion being true, they ought to be considered as symptoms of its being fabulous. It is necessary to the full and upright character of truth, that it rejects the crutch; and it is consistent with the character of fable, to seek the aid that truth rejects. Thus much for mystery and miracle.

As mystery and miracle took charge of the past and the present, prophesy took charge of the future, and rounded the tenses of faith. It was not sufficient to know what had been done, but what would be done. The supposed prophet was the supposed historian of times to come; and if he happened, in shooting with a long bow of a thousand years, to strike within a thousand miles of a mark, the ingenuity of posterity could make it point-blank; and if he happened to be directly wrong, it was only to suppose, as in the case of Jonah and Nineveh, that God had repented himself, and changed his mind. What a fool do fabulous systems make of man!

It has been shewn in a former part of this work, that the original meaning of the words *prophet* and *prophesying,* has been changed, and that a prophet, in the sense the word is now used, is a creature of modern invention; and it is owing to this change in the meaning of the words, that the flights and metaphors of the Jewish poets, and phrases and expressions now rendered obscure by our not being acquainted with the local circumstances to which they applied at the time they were used, have been erected into prophecies, and made to bend to explanations at the will and whimsical conceits of sectaries, expounders, and commentators. Every thing unintelligible was prophetical, and every thing insignificant was typical. A blunder would have served for a prophesy; and a dish-clout for a type.

If by a prophet we are to suppose a man, to whom the Almighty communicated some event that would take place in future, either there were such men, or there were not. If there were, it is consistent to believe that the event, so communicated, would be told in terms that could be understood; and not related in such a loose and obscure manner as to be out of the comprehension of those that heard it, and so equivocal as to fit almost any circumstance that might happen afterwards. It is conceiving very irreverently of the Almighty to suppose he would deal in this jesting manner with mankind: yet all the things called prophecies, in the book called the Bible, come under this description.

But it is with prophecy, as it is with miracle. It could not answer the purpose even if it were real. Those to whom a prophecy should be told, could not tell whether the man prophesied or lied, or whether it had been revealed to him, or whether he conceited it: and if the thing that he prophesied, or pretended to prophesy, should happen, or something like it among the multitude of things that are daily happening, nobody could again know whether he foreknew it, or guessed at it, or whether it was accidental. A prophet, therefore, is a character useless and unnecessary; and the safe side of the case is, to guard against being imposed upon by not giving credit to such relations.

Upon the whole, mystery, miracle, and prophecy, are appendages that belong to fabulous and not to true religion. They are the means by which so many *Lo heres!* and *Lo theres!* have been spread about the world, and religion been made into a trade. The success of one impostor gave encouragement to another, and the quieting salvo of doing *some good* by keeping up a *pious fraud,* protected them from remorse.

Having now extended the subject to a greater length than I first intended, I shall bring it to a close by abstracting a summary from the whole.

First, That the idea or belief of a word of God existing in print, or in writing, or in speech, is inconsistent in itself for the reasons already assigned. These reasons, among many others, are the want of an universal language; the mutability of language; the errors to which translations are subject; the possibility of totally suppressing such a word; the probability of altering it, or of fabricating the whole, the imposing it upon the world.

Secondly, That the creation we behold is the real and ever existing word of God, in which we cannot be deceived. It proclaimeth his power, it demonstrates his wisdom, it manifests his goodness and beneficence.

Thirdly, That the moral duty of man consists in imitating the moral goodness and beneficence of God manifested in the creation towards all his creatures. That seeing, as we daily do, the goodness of God to all men, it is an example calling upon all men to practise the same towards each other; and consequently that every thing of persecution and revenge between man and man, and every thing of cruelty to animals is a violation of moral duty.

I trouble not myself about the manner of future existence. I content myself with believing, even to positive conviction, that the power that gave me existence is able to continue it, in any form and manner he pleases, either with or without this body; and it appears more probable to me that I shall continue to exist hereafter, than that I should have had existence, as I now have, before that existence began.

It is certain that, in one point, all nations of the earth, and all religions agree. All believe in a God. The things in which they disagree, are the redundancies annexed to that belief; and therefore, if ever an universal religion should prevail, it will not be believing any thing new, but in getting rid of redundancies, and believing as man believed at first. Adam, if ever there was such a man, was created a Deist; but in the mean time let every man follow, as he has a right to do, the religion and the worship he prefers.

———

Thus far I had written on the 28th of December, 1793. In the evening I went to the Hotel Philadelphia (formerly White's Hotel)[19] passage des Petits Pères, where I lodged when I came to Paris, in consequence of being elected a member of the Convention, but had left the lodging about nine months, and taken lodgings in the Rue Fauxbourg St. Denis, for the sake of being more retired than I could be in the middle of the town.

Meeting with a company of Americans at the Hotel Philadelphia, I agreed to spend the evening with them, and, as my lodging was distant about a mile and half, I bespoke a bed at the hotel. The company broke up about twelve o'clock, and I went directly to bed. About four in the morning I was awakened by a rapping at my chamber door: when I opened it, I saw a guard, and the master of the hotel with them. The guard told me they came to put me under arrestation, and to demand the key of my papers. I desired them to walk in, and I would dress myself, and go with them immediately.

It happened that Achilles Audibert, of Calais,[20] was then in the hotel; and I desired to be conducted into his room. When we came there, I told the guard that I had only lodged at the hotel for that night:—that I was printing a work, and that part of that work was at the Maison Bretagne, Rue Jacob; and desired they would take me there first, which they did.

The printing office, at which the work was printing, was near to the Maison Bretagne, where Colonel Blackden and Joel Barlow,[21] of the United States of America, lodged; and I had desired Joel Barlow to compare the proof sheets with the copy, as they came from the press. The remainder of the manuscript, from page 32 to 76,[22] was at my lodging. But besides the necessity of my collecting all the parts of the work together, that the publication might not be interrupted by my imprisonment, or by any event that might happen to me, it was highly proper that I should have a fellow citizen of America with me during the examination of my papers, as I had letters of correspondence in my possession of the President of congress General Washington; the minister of foreign affairs to congress Mr. Jefferson; and the late Benjamin Franklin; and it might be necessary for me to make a proces verbal to send to congress.

It happened that Joel Barlow had received only one proof sheet of the work, which he had compared with the copy, and sent it back to the printing-office.

We then went, in company with Joel Barlow, to my lodging; and the guard, or commissaires, took with them the interpreter to the committee of surety general. It was satisfactory to me, that they went through the examination of my papers with the strictness they did; and it is but justice that I say, they did it not only with civility, but with tokens of respect to my character.

I shewed them the remainder of the manuscript of the foregoing work. The interpreter examined it, and returned it to me, saying, "*it is an interesting work; it will do much good*." I also shewed him another manuscript, which I had intended for the committee of public safety: It is intitled, "Observations on the Commerce between the United States of America and France."

After the examination of my papers was finished, the guard conducted me to the prison of the Luxembourg, where they left me as they would a man whose undeserved fate they regretted. I offered to write under the proces-verbal they had made, that they had executed their orders with civility, but they declined it.

THOMAS PAINE

A Citizen of America
to the Citizens of Europe.

18th Year of Independence

Understanding that a proposal is intended to be made at the ensuing meeting of the Congress of the United States of America "to send commissioners to Europe to confer with the Ministers of all the Neutral Powers for the purpose of negotiating preliminaries of peace," I address this letter to you on that subject, and on the several matters connected therewith.

In order to discuss this subject through all its circumstances, it will be necessary to take a review of the state of Europe, prior to the French revolution. It will from thence appear, that the powers leagued against France are fighting to attain an object, which, were it possible to be attained, would be injurious to themselves.

This is not an uncommon error in the history of wars and governments, of which the conduct of the English government in the war against America is a striking instance. She commenced that war for the avowed purpose of subjugating America; and after wasting upwards of one hundred millions sterling, and then abandoning the object, she discovered, in the course of three or four years, that the prosperity of England was increased, instead of being diminished, by the independence of America. In short, every circumstance is pregnant with some natural effect, upon which intentions and opinions have no influence; and the political error lies in misjudging what the effect will be. England misjudged it in the American war, and the reasons I shall now offer will shew, that she misjudges it in the present war. In discussing this subject, I leave out of the question everything respecting forms and systems of government; for as all the governments of Europe differ from each other, there is no reason that the government of France should not differ from the rest.

The clamors continually raised in all the countries of Europe were, that the family of the Bourbons was become too powerful; that the intrigues of the court of France endangered the peace of Europe. Austria saw with a jealous eye the connection of France with Prussia; and Prussia, in her turn became jealous of the connection of France with Austria; England had wasted millions unsuccessfully in attempting to prevent the family compact with Spain; Russia disliked the alliance between France and Turkey; and Turkey became apprehensive of the inclination of France towards an alliance with Russia. Sometimes the quadruple alliance alarmed some of the powers, and at other times a contrary system alarmed others, and in all those cases the charge was always made against the intrigues of the Bourbons.

Admitting those matters to be true, the only thing that could have

quieted the apprehensions of all those powers with respect to the interference of France, would have been her entire NEUTRALITY in Europe;
but this was impossible to be obtained, or if obtained was impossible to
be secured, because the genius of her government was repugnant to all
such restrictions.

It now happens that by entirely changing the genius of her government, which France has done for herself, this neutrality, which neither
wars could accomplish nor treaties secure, arises naturally of itself, and
becomes the ground upon which the war should terminate. It is the
thing that approaches the nearest of all others to what ought to be
the political views of all the European powers; and there is nothing
that can so effectually secure this neutrality, as that the genius of the
French government should be different from the rest of Europe.

But if their object is to restore the Bourbons and monarchy together, they will unavoidably restore with it all the evils of which they
have complained; and the first question of discord will be, whose ally
is that monarchy to be?

Will England agree to the restoration of the family compact against
which she has been fighting and scheming ever since it existed? Will
Prussia agree to restore the alliance between France and Austria, or
will Austria agree to restore the former connection between France
and Prussia, formed on purpose to oppose herself; or will Spain or Russia, or any of the maritime powers, agree that France and her navy
should be allied to England? In fine, will any of the powers agree to
strengthen the hands of the other against itself? Yet all these cases involve themselves in the original question of the restoration of the
Bourbons; and on the other hand, all of them disappear by the neutrality of France.

If their object is not to restore the Bourbons, it must be the impracticable project of a partition of the country. The Bourbons will then be
out of the question, or, more properly speaking, they will be put in a
worse condition; for as the preservation of the Bourbons made a part
of the first object, the extirpation of them makes a part of the second.
Their pretended friends will then become interested in their destruction, because it is favourable to the purpose of partition that none of
the nominal claimants should be left in existence.

But however the project of a partition may at first blind the eyes of
the confederacy, or however each of them may hope to outwit the

other in the progress or in the end, the embarrassments that will arise are insurmountable. But even were the object attainable, it would not be of such general advantage to the parties as the neutrality of France, which costs them nothing, and to obtain which they would formerly have gone to war.

OF THE PRESENT STATE OF EUROPE,
AND THE CONFEDERACY

In the first place the confederacy is not of that kind that forms itself originally by concert and consent. It has been forced together by chance—a heterogeneous mass, held only by the accident of the moment; and the instant that accident ceases to operate, the parties will retire to their former rivalships.

I will now, independently of the impracticability of a partition project, trace out some of the embarrassments which will arise among the confederated parties; for it is contrary to the interest of a majority of them that such a project should succeed.

To understand this part of the subject it is necessary, in the first place, to cast an eye over the map of Europe, and observe the geographical situation of the several parts of the confederacy; for however strongly the passionate politics of the moment may operate, the politics that arise from geographical situation are the most certain, and will in all cases finally prevail.

The world has been long amused with what is called the "*balance of power.*" But it is not upon armies only that this balance depends. Armies have but a small circle of action. Their progress is slow and limited. But when we take maritime power into the calculation, the scale extends universally. It comprehends all the interests connected with commerce.

The two great maritime powers are England and France. Destroy either of those, and the balance of naval power is destroyed. The whole world of commerce that passes on the Ocean would then lie at the mercy of the other, and the ports of any nation in Europe might be blocked up.

The geographical situation of those two maritime powers comes next under consideration. Each of them occupies one entire side of the channel from the straits of Dover and Calais to the opening into the Atlantic. The commerce of all the northern nations, from Holland to Russia, must pass the straits of Dover and Calais, and along the Channel, to arrive at the Atlantic.

This being the case, the systematical politics of all the nations, northward of the straits of Dover and Calais, can be ascertained from their geographical situation; for it is necessary to the safety of their commerce that the two sides of the Channel, either in whole or in part, should not be in the possession either of England or France. While one nation possesses the whole of one side, and the other nation the other side, the northern nations cannot help seeing that in any situation of things their commerce will always find protection on one side or the other. It may sometimes be that of England and sometimes that of France.

Again, while the English navy continues in its present condition, it is necessary that another navy should exist to controul the universal sway the former would otherwise have over the commerce of all nations. France is the only nation in Europe where this balance can be placed. The navies of the North, were they sufficiently powerful, could not be sufficiently operative. They are blocked up by the ice six months in the year. Spain lies too remote; besides which, it is only for the sake of her American mines that she keeps up her navy.

Applying these cases to the project of a partition of France, it will appear, that the project involves with it a DESTRUCTION OF THE BALANCE OF MARITIME POWER; because it is only by keeping France entire and indivisible that the balance can be kept up. This is a case that at first sight lies remote and almost hidden. But it interests all the maritime and commercial nations in Europe in as great a degree as any case that has ever come before them.—In short, it is with war as it is with law. In law, the first merits of the case become lost in the multitude of arguments; and in war they become lost in the variety of events. New objects arise that take the lead of all that went before, and everything assumes a new aspect. This was the case in the last great confederacy in what is called the succession war, and most probably will be the case in the present.

I have now thrown together such thoughts as occurred to me on the several subjects connected with the confederacy against France, and interwoven with the interest of the neutral powers. Should a conference of the neutral powers take place, these observations will, at least, serve to generate others. The whole matter will then undergo a more extensive investigation than it is in my power to give; and the evils attending upon either of the projects, that of restoring the Bourbons, or of attempting a partition of France, will have the calm opportunity of being fully discussed.

On the part of England, it is very extraordinary that she should have engaged in a former confederacy, and a long expensive war, to *prevent* the family compact, and now engage in another confederacy to *preserve* it. And on the part of the other powers, it is as inconsistent that they should engage in a partition project, which, could it be executed, would immediately destroy the balance of maritime power in Europe, and would probably produce a second war, to remedy the political errors of the first.

A CITIZEN OF THE
UNITED STATES OF AMERICA

NOTES

1. *Government, like dress, is the badge of lost innocence:* This statement refers to the passage, in the biblical book of Genesis, in which Adam and Eve discover they are naked after succumbing to Satan's temptation. Paine, though not religious himself, used many biblical allusions throughout his published writings as a means to engage his readers.

2. *the so much boasted constitution of England:* Here Paine attacks England's unwritten constitution for the first time, beginning a theme that will continue in his writings for decades to come. The English Constitution is not a single written document or collection of documents, but a collection of laws and traditions. The modern concept of a constitution grew out of the American Revolution and the subsequent state and national governments' written constitutions.

3. *a felo de se:* A self-murderer, or suicide. English common law held strict punishments for those found certain to have willfully committed suicide, including burial outside of the common customs of the community, and forfeiture of all properties to the crown.

4. *giver of places and pensions:* One of the most controversial actions of the British government was the distribution of offices and pensions as political rewards or weapons.

5. *Charles the First:* Charles I of England (1600–1649) ruled from 1625 until his execution by act of Parliament on January 30, 1629. The memory of Charles's rule, and the fear that his pro-Catholic policies inspired in Protestants in England and America, made him a frequent target of critics of Britain and its king in the Revolutionary era.

6. *Turkey:* Turkey was frequently held up as an example of unrestricted despotic rule by Anglo-American writers of the seventeenth and eighteenth centuries.

7. *Holland without a king:* The Dutch Republic was formed in the late sixteenth century, consisting of the states of Holland, Zeeland, Utrecht, Gelderland, Overijssel, Friesland, and Gronigen. Following the republic's invasion by

France in 1747, the house of Orange was restored to the monarchy, under the rule of William IV. Holland's history was often used by Anglo-American liberals, as Paine uses it here, as a morality tale that power is constantly attempting to corrupt liberty.

8. *For monarchy in every instance is the Popery of government:* Paine's anti-Catholicism, and particularly his hatred of the pope, was typical of many eighteenth-century English Protestants, and an effective method to rouse the hatred of his readers. Anti-Catholic rituals, such as burning an effigy of the pope on Guy Fawkes Day, continued into the American Revolution.

9. *William the Conquerer:* William I of England (ca. 1027–1087), duke of Normandy who led the conquest of England in 1066.

10. *York and Lancaster:* Again, Paine is using the history of England's monarchy, and particularly the chaos of the Wars of the Roses (1455–85), to arouse opposition to the monarchy.

11. *Sir William Meredith:* English parliamentarian and privy councillor (d. 1790).

12. *the late Mr. Pelham:* Henry Pelham (ca. 1695–1754), younger brother of the Duke of Newcastle, was a leading parliamentarian of the mid-eighteenth century.

13. *the nineteenth of April:* The date of the battles of Lexington and Concord, in Massachusetts.

14. *The miseries of Hanover last war:* The Seven Years' War, or French and Indian War.

15. Paine was accurate in his assessment of colonial American demographics. Large numbers of immigrants had arrived from the German states, Ireland, and Scotland, many of whom came fleeing religious persecution in the Old World. In addition, numerous Africans had reached American shores in chains, not fleeing oppression in their native lands but facing it as slaves in the New World. Scholars now estimate that about 40 percent of white Americans were of English descent by 1790.

16. *the trade of America goes to ruin, because of her connection with Britain:* England had been at war repeatedly since the accession of William and Mary during the Glorious Revolution of 1688, and the American colonies had frequently suffered economic downturn during these wars.

17. *the reformation:* The sixteenth-century transformation of Christianity in Western Europe begun by Martin Luther, through his challenge to practices of the Catholic Church in 1517. Many of the settlers in colonial America were from religious groups who traced their beginnings to the Reformation in their home countries.

18. *Interested men:* As Paine uses the term here, interested men are those who have a personal financial stake in governmental acts or practices.

19. *redemption:* Release from imprisonment or captivity.

20. *Milton wisely expresses, "never can true reconcilement grow where wounds of deadly hate have pierced so deep."* From Book IV, lines 98–99 of *Paradise Lost*, by John Milton (1608–1674), English Puritan writer. *Paradise Lost* was widely read in colonial America.

21. *Denmark and Sweden:* Both countries were absolute monarchies during the eighteenth century, though both underwent a series of reforms at about the same time as the American Revolution.

22. *stamp-act:* Taxation act passed by Britain's House of Commons on February 27, 1765 and the House of Lords on March 8. The first direct tax on the American colonies, the act created widespread anger and hostility throughout British North America. Parliament repealed the act on March 18, 1766.

23. *pay a Bunker-hill price:* The Battle of Bunker Hill, in Massachusetts, took place June 17, 1775, and is considered the first major battle of the Revolutionary War. The Americans lost about 440 men during the conflict, and 30 were captured by the British, contributing to the American defeat.

24. *a youth of twenty-one:* George III of England (1738–1820), who was 21 years old at the time of his accession to the throne in 1760.

25. DRAGONETTI ON VIRTUE AND REWARDS: Paine quotes Giacinto Dragonetti's (1738–1818) "On Virtues and Rewards."

26. *stirred up the Indians and Negroes to destroy us:* One of the most controversial actions carried out by a British official in the period immediately before the Revolution was the plan devised by Virginia governor John Murray, Lord Dunmore, who announced in 1775 that he would emancipate any able-bodied black slave who took up arms with the British army against rebellious masters. That action thrilled enslaved men wanting their freedom, but outraged many Virginia planters who felt that the government was willing to overthrow their social system.

27. *A national debt is a national bond:* Throughout his political writings, Paine considered a strong economy as integral to the nation's strength. His stand on this issue would eventually lead him into alliance with men such as financier Robert Morris of Pennsylvania, who agreed with Paine on little else.

28. Entic's naval history: John Entick was author of *A New Naval History; or, Compleat View of the British Marine* (1757).

29. *The Terrible privateer, Captain Death:* Captain William Death commanded the privateer *Death* in a naval battle against the French ship *Vengeance* at the western edge of the English Channel on September 27, 1756, in which he was fatally wounded.

30. *Associators petition:* The Associators were a militia group created by Benjamin Franklin in 1747, without the support of the pacifist Quaker-

dominated Pennsylvania Assembly, to defend the colony in case of French attack. In October 1775, members of the Associators presented two petitions to the Assembly, requesting that all freemen give military service or pay fines, and that Quakers would have to pay these fines, despite their conviction against military service. The 14–14 split was decided by the lieutenant governor of Pennsylvania, who cast the deciding vote.

31. *Mr. Cornwall . . . with contempt:* Charles Cornwall (1735–1789) was a member of the House of Commons and a junior lord of the treasury. The petition was a measure passed by the New York assembly in 1775 condemning Britain's actions in the Declaratory, Coercive, and Quebec acts.

32. *Burgh's political Disquisitions:* Written by James Burgh (1714–1775), this three-volume critique of Britain's governmental structure was, according to historian Bernard Bailyn, "the key book of this generation."

33. *the King's Speech:* George III opened Parliament on October 25, 1775; copies of his speech arrived in Philadelphia on January 10, 1776.

34. *Sir John Dalrymple:* John Dalrymple (1726–1810), earl of Cranstoun, wrote this pamphlet in 1775.

35. *Marquis of Rockingham's:* Charles Watson-Wentworth (1730–1782), second marquis of Rockingham, was premier of the coalition ministry in July 1765, and outraged George III by his repeal of the Stamp Act. He was dismissed from office in July 1766, and favored granting independence to the colonies as a member of the opposition party in parliament. He became prime minister in 1782.

36. *on the footing we were on in sixty-three:* Returning to the political situation of 1763, at the end of the Seven Years' War.

37. *Our burnt and destroyed towns:* On January 1, 1775, a British warship bombarded Norfolk, Virginia in part due to George III's August 23 proclamation that the colonies were in open rebellion.

38. *"The Rubicon is passed":* The reference is to Julius Caesar's crossing of this small stream to challenge Pompey in 49 B.C., in defiance of the Roman Senate's order. The expression came to mean taking any irrevocable step.

39. THE ANCIENT TESTIMONY AND PRINCIPLES . . . : A pamphlet published by the Quaker Monthly Meeting of Philadelphia on January 20, 1776.

40. *at St. James's:* The royal palace at St. James's, constructed by Henry VIII, was the official London residence of the monarch, and still gives its name to the British court.

41. Barclay: Robert Barclay (1648–1690), a seventeenth-century English Quaker, who in his address called upon King Charles II to accept Quaker beliefs in the personal, spiritual piety of the inner light. Paine here is using the memory of Barclay, who addressed Charles as a man and not a king, to undermine the monarch's elevated status.

42. *The principles of Quakerism have a direct tendency to make a man the quiet and in-offensive subject of any, and every government* which is set over him: The principles of Quakerism call for personal modesty, but Paine, a birthright Quaker, was underestimating Friends' political actions somewhat here to support his point. Quakers had, for many years, "spoken truth to power" and critiqued government leaders in both the old world and the new. Politics in the Quaker-dominated colony of Pennsylvania was often heated and contentious.

43. OLIVER CROMWELL: English parliamentarian (1599–1658) who served as Lord Protector of England after the execution of Charles II in 1629.

FOUR LETTERS ON INTERESTING SUBJECTS

1. *The Proprietary party:* The political supporters of the proprietors of Pennsylvania, who were by this time William Penn's son Thomas and grandsons John and Richard. The opposition party was known as the Quaker Party, though the name is somewhat misleading, since Quakers eventually constituted a minority of its membership.

2. *Mr. Grenville:* George Grenville (1712–1770), first lord of the treasury and chancellor of Britain's exchequer. He created the Stamp Act (1765).

3. *Lord North's:* Frederick North, second Earl of Guilford (1732–1792), first lord of the treasury and prime minister, 1767–1782.

4. *General Gage:* Thomas Gage (ca. 1719–1787) was military governor of Massachusetts Bay and commander-in-chief of the British forces in North America at the outbreak of the revolution.

5. *non-importation agreement:* The agreement was passed by the First Continental Congress meeting at Philadelphia in the fall of 1774.

6. *The Charter, called, the Royal Charter for this province:* The charter was granted by King Charles II to William Penn in 1681. An often-repeated myth of Pennsylvania's founding was that Charles granted Penn his charter in order to pay off a debt that the crown had incurred to Penn's father, Admiral Sir William Penn (1621–1670). That is not quite accurate. Admiral Penn had been supportive—both militarily and financially—to the restored monarchy, but the crown could not have been prosecuted for debts. While the younger Penn's conversion to Quakerism did cause some problems for King Charles and his younger brother James, Duke of York, the three men did share a close relationship and both looked favorably on him. That favor would cause Penn some trouble when James was overthrown in the Glorious Revolution.

7. William Penn, *by entering into treaty with the Indians:* William Penn's treaty with the Native Americans of Pennsylvania in 1682 was, by the 1770s, already a much-mythologized event. The French *philosophe* Voltaire had

heralded Penn's treaty (probably a meeting or agreement, not a formal document) as the only treaty that was ever carried out between settlers and Indians that did not require a sworn oath (one would have gone against Quaker beliefs) and was never broken. The American-born painter Benjamin West created a much-copied work that depicted the Treaty of Shackamaxon. While Paine may be overstating Penn's beliefs here, the founder did certainly feel that treating Native Americans with justice and respect was crucial to his plans for the colony.

8. *he gave, contrary to his principles, an oblique approbation of war, and exhibited a striking instance of convenient conscience:* Here, Paine is playing on the irony that the pacifist founder of Pennsylvania only received his grant because of the actions of his father, one of mid-seventeenth-century England's most celebrated military men. Admiral Sir William Penn conquered Jamaica for England in 1655, and was a leading naval figure in the era of the English civil war and Restoration.

9. *like the vicar of Bray:* "The Vicar of Bray" (a parish in Berkshire, England) was a popular ballad of the early eighteenth century that described the religious convictions of the vicar, which changed every time the monarchy's preference did, from Protestant to Catholic.

10. The Charter of privileges: The act, granted by William Penn on November 8, 1701, that guaranteed religious toleration and other privileges to Pennsylvania's colonists. By the mid-eighteenth century, the charter was hailed by many as the foundation of Pennsylvania's prosperity and population growth. A commonly held belief is that the Pennsylvania Assembly ordered the Liberty Bell, with its passage from the book of Leviticus to "Proclaim Liberty through all the Land," to commemorate the Charter.

11. *deputy-governor Morris's:* The Penns, as proprietors, always held the title of governor within the family. Robert Hunter Morris was appointed Lieutenant Governor in 1754 and served until 1756.

12. *its power resembling that of an hermaphrodite:* As Paine is using the term, a hermaphrodite is anything composed of two contradictory parts.

13. *Queen Ann:* Anne (1665–1714) was the daughter of James II and younger sister of Mary II. She reigned from 1702 to 1714.

14. *Lord Bathurst:* Allen Bathurst (1684–1775) was a Tory member of Parliament who was given a peerage in 1712. His son, Henry Bathurst, was serving as lord chancellor (1771–1778) at the time Paine was writing. He was made Baron Apsley in 1771.

15. *Lord Mansfield's:* William Murray, first earl of Mansfield (1705–1793), was a leading jurist and politician in Britain from the 1740s until the end of his life. He was widely regarded for his decision commuting the sentence

of John Wilkes to a fine and imprisonment on the grounds of a technical flaw.

16. *Lord Camden:* Sir Charles Pratt, first Earl Camden (1714–1794), a British jurist who gained fame in the 1763 John Wilkes trial, in which he ruled that general warrants were illegal. As a Whig member of Parliament, he argued against policies on the American colonies and declared the Stamp Act unconstitutional.

THE AMERICAN CRISES

1. *Britain, with an army to enforce her tyranny, has declared:* Upon rescinding the Stamp Act in 1766, Parliament also passed the Declaratory Act. Viewed by many as a face-saving measure passed in response to having to give in to popular colonial sentiment, the act outraged Paine and others who shared his perspective, as potentially far more detrimental to American freedom.

2. *Major General Green:* Nathaniel Greene (1742–1786), a native of Rhode Island, commanded American troops at Boston, in New York, and in New Jersey. He commanded one of the two columns attacking Trenton, and was at the Battle of Brandywine in September 1777. Washington appointed him commander of American operations in the south in 1780. Paine served as his aide-de-camp at Fort Lee, New Jersey, in the fall of 1776.

3. *New-England is not infested with Tories, and we are:* Exact numbers of American Loyalists are difficult to ascertain, but percentages of Tories were especially high in the middle colonies of New York, New Jersey, and Pennsylvania.

4. *on this city:* Philadelphia.

5. *what rank of life you hold:* Rank, as Paine uses the term here, implies the station or social class one held within society.

6. *she has gained an Ally:* The treaties of alliance and treaty of amity and commerce with France were approved in Paris on February 6, 1778, and ratified by the Congress on May 4.

7. *The states of Holland are an unfortunate instance of the effects of individual sovereignty:* The former Dutch Republic had returned to being a monarchy with the assumption of Stadtholder William IV in 1747.

LETTER TO THE ABBÉ RAYNAL

1. *an original work in France, by the Abbé Raynal:* Raynal's work was *Revolution d'Amerique,* a supplement to his *L'Histoire philosophique et politique des êtablissements et du commerce des Europeans dans les deux Indies.*

2. *Declaratory Act:* Passed by Parliament at the time of the repeal of the Stamp Act, the Declaratory Act stated that Parliament had the right "to bind

America in all cases whatsoever." For radicals like Paine, this act, far more than any taxation legislation, was a sign of Britain's oppression of the colonies.

3. *tax on tea:* A revenue act passed by Parliament in 1773 that led to the Boston Tea Party of December 16, 1773. Tea was first taxed as part of the Townshend Duties in 1767, and remained taxed after the other duties were repealed. Hoping to shore up the failing British East India Company, the British government granted it special terms to import taxed tea to America in 1773, infuriating merchants and others.

4. *the reviving an obsolete act of the reign of Henry VIII:* Passed by Parliament on February 9, 1769, the statute allowed trials without juries for provincials, to be held in London.

5. *the massacre of the inhabitants of Boston:* The Boston Massacre occurred on March 5, 1770, when British troops guarding the Boston Custom House were surrounded by a mob, and fired into the crowd, killing five.

6. *the Treaty of Alliance between France and the United States:* Signed on February 6, 1778, at Paris, the treaty recognized American independence.

7. *The countries had been enemies, not properly of themselves, but through the medium of England:* Here, perhaps, Paine was oversimplifying the political and cultural situation between American colonists and their French neighbors to the north, in Canada. Colonial Americans, especially New Englanders, held deep-seated hatred of Roman Catholics and resentment against their Catholic alliances with Native Americans during the several wars that had taken place over the preceding century. Despite that deeply felt animosity, however, American leaders immediately strove to get along with their new allies.

8. *the change in the British Ministry:* Lord North resigned as British prime minister on March 20, 1782. Seven days later, George III accepted the coalition ministry headed by the Marquis of Rockingham, who served until his death on July 1. Britain's government, led by the Earl of Shelburne, acknowledged American independence September 27.

9. *bills of mortality:* Published annual accounts of the dead in a community; these often included places of burial or causes of death.

10. *Chatham:* William Pitt (1708–1778), English parliamentarian and statesman, made first Earl of Chatham by George III in 1766. He was noted for his support for the American cause in the 1760s.

11. *universal citizen:* The concept of the citizen of the world intrigued Paine from the 1770s through his death.

12. *Rodney:* George Brydges (1719–1792), English admiral and first baron Rodney.

RIGHTS OF MAN, PART THE SECOND

1. *Archimedes:* Greek mathematician and physicist (287–212 B.C.E.).

2. *riots of 1780:* Here Paine refers to the Gordon "no popery" riots, which took place in May 1740.

3. *Abbé Sieyes:* Emmanuel Joseph Sieyes (1748–1836), a clergyman prior to the French Revolution, was a revolutionary and statesman who helped write the Declaration of the Rights of Man and the constitution of 1781 while a member of the States-General during the Third Estate.

4. *Those of 1715 and 1745:* This refers to the two major uprisings by Jacobites, supporters of the Roman Catholic House of Stuart, in England. The Protestant succession to the throne was viewed as a key issue for English liberty after the deposition of King James II in 1688. His heirs James Frances Edward and Charles Edward Stuart kept the Jacobites' hopes alive. The 1745 Battle of Culloden was the last major stand of the Jacobites, but pro-Stuart sentiment existed throughout the century, and Protestants frequently used the image of the Stuarts and their Jacobite supporters as a political tool.

5. *The succession war for the crown of Spain:* The War of Spanish Succession, also known as Queen Anne's War (1702–1713). One of the wars of empire between European powers that occurred between 1789 and 1812, it arose over the issue of the king of France claiming the throne of Spain for his grandson. England, Holland, Sweden, and the Holy Roman Empire fought Spain and France. Peace was concluded with the Treaty of Utrecht in 1713.

6. *the republic of letters:* This was a central concept of enlightened thinkers in the eighteenth century. Its supporters believed in a citizenry who shared their ideas regardless of national lines. The realm of print, and the possibility of expressing ideas in it that could be anonymous and therefore stand only on their own merit, was integral to this idea.

7. *the civil list:* The annual tax-supported monetary payment made to the reigning monarch to support the royal household and its members.

8. *to meet in convention at Philadelphia, with powers to form a constitution:* The Pennsylvania Constitutional Convention wrote this document, considered the most radical of the new state constitutions, during the summer of 1776.

9. *the act of confederation:* The Articles of Confederation were approved by the Continental Congress meeting at York, Pennsylvania, on November 15, 1777, and finally ratified on March 1, 1781.

10. *a deputation from five or six of the state assemblies met at Anapolis:* The 1786 meeting in Annapolis, Maryland, to discuss trade issues and other govern-

mental problems under the Articles of Confederation led to the call for the Constitutional Convention in Philadelphia the following May.

11. *He delivered up his commission when the war ended:* George Washington's resignation of his military commission was considered by contemporaries to be one of the most significant acts of his career. Returning power to the elected government at the height of his power, Washington appeared to be exemplary of the republican principles of the American Revolution. When told by the American-born painter Benjamin West that he believed Washington would do so at the end of the war, King George III stated, "Then he will be the greatest man of his age."

12. *for a Dutch Stadtholder, or a German Elector:* Paine is referring to William III, a Dutch Stadtholder who became king of England in 1789 and co-ruled with his wife, Queen Mary II; and to George I, elector of Hanover, who became king following the death of Mary's younger sister, Queen Anne, in 1714. Both events—the Glorious Revolution and the Hanoverian succession—were celebrated for excluding Roman Catholics from the throne and were widely believed to be integral to the history of English liberty by many who celebrated England's constitution. Paine, however, saw them as representative of the general problems of a monarchy that ignored the ideas and needs of the people.

13. *Dr. Johnson:* Samuel Johnson (1709–1784), English author and lexicographer.

14. *Magna Charta:* Considered the most important document in the English constitution, it was issued by King John at Runnymede in 1215.

15. *their fate is well known:* King Charles I was executed by act of Parliament during the English Civil War in 1649. His younger son, James II, was deposed during the Glorious Revolution of 1688.

16. *the convention parliament:* The Convention Parliament met on January 22, 1689, at the request of William, Duke of Orange. (Parliament can only come into meeting at the request of the reigning monarch, and with the departure of James II, England did not have one.) On February 12, the convention offered the throne conditionally to William and Mary, and on February 23 William—now king—gave his assent that the convention was a legitimate parliament.

17. *red book of France: Le Livre Rouge, or Red Book: Being a List of Secret Pensions Paid out of the Public Treasure of France, and Containing Characters of the Persons Pensioned, Anecdotes of Their Lives, an Account of Their Services, and Observations Tending to Shew the Reasons for Which the Pensions Were Granted* (London: G. Kearsley, 1790) was a translation of the *Livre rouge,* published in Paris by the National Assembly.

18. *Canada constitution bill:* A bill proposed by the Pitt ministry in 1791.

19. *John Bull:* Common term to refer to the people of England.
20. *the only office from which a foreigner is excluded:* Article 2, Section 1 of the U.S. Constitution requires that the president be a natural-born citizen.
21. *Alliances, contrary to all former systems:* Here Paine refers to the reactions in the courts of Europe regarding the French Revolution. Initially bringing together Prussia and Austria, after the execution of Louis XVI the First Coalition grew to include Great Britain, Holland, and Spain against France.
22. *House of Peers:* The House of Lords of Great Britain.
23. *a rotten borough:* One of the causes of anger that American patriots felt about the English electoral system. Rotten boroughs were allowed to elect members to Parliament, despite the fact that they might have little or no population remaining, while new, large cities might have little or no representation.
24. *Sir John Sinclair's History of the Revenue: History of the Public Revenues of the British Empire,* by Sir John Sinclair, published 1785–1790.
25. *Chelsea College pensioners:* Those treated at the Royal Hospital for veteran soldiers, built 1682–1692.
26. *parks and chases:* The area surrounding English manors; a chase was land not necessarily owned by the landholder, but through which he was allowed to hunt game.
27. *want of firmness in Mr. Fox:* Charles James Fox served briefly as British Foreign Secretary in 1782 during the debates over ending the war with America. He took office March 27, resigned July 11.

THE AGE OF REASON, PART ONE

1. *the total abolition of the whole national order of priesthood:* Paine refers to the disestablishment of the special rights and privileges of Roman Catholic priests at the start of the French Revolution. In 1790, the Civil Constitution of the clergy required all priests and bishops to swear a loyalty oath to the new French government. Many refused to do so, and they drew support to the old guard, giving the anti-Revolution cause a religious tone.
2. *Diana of Ephesus:* Diana was the Roman goddess of childbearing, whose cult was centered at Ephesus in Asia Minor.
3. *the Apocraphy:* The Apocrypha was the collection of books kept out of the Authorized (King James) Bible.
4. *he was the son of God in like manner that every other person is:* Here, Paine the deist is revealing an idea than many early, radical Quakers held.
5. *invention of a purgatory:* Purgatory, in Roman Catholic teachings, is the state between life and paradise for those who are destined for heaven, but not ready to enter it. Medieval Catholicism adopted the idea as a means of

drawing the faithful to pray for the souls of the dead and to carry out acts to assist their souls in this cleansing period. By the sixteenth century, however, the church was using the idea of purgatory as a fund-raising method, selling indulgences to get loved ones out of purgatory. This became a central issue in Martin Luther's break from the Catholic Church and the Reformation.

6. *I keep no Bible:* Paine claimed that he had no Bible with him when he wrote *The Age of Reason.* He obviously did know the texts of the Bible well, though, and frequently used allusions from it to support his writings.

7. *As there is now nothing new to be learned from the dead languages:* The teaching of ancient languages had become a frequent class-based theme of debate by the late eighteenth century. Paine's friend Benjamin Franklin wanted to keep it out of the curriculum of the Academy of Philadelphia (now the University of Pennsylvania), but lost the argument. Classical languages were one of the most telling ways by which Anglo-Americans attempted to identify themselves as a member of the gentry.

8. *Vigilius:* Irish abbot (d. 784), Bishop of Salzburg; canonized in 1233.

9. *My father being of the quaker profession:* Joseph Pain, a staymaker, was a member of the Society of Friends in Thetford, England. Paine's mother, Frances, was a member of the established Church of England, and was both married in that church and had her son confirmed in it.

10. *grammar school:* Public schools in Britain were first created in the sixteenth century.

11. *the philosophical lectures of Martin and Ferguson:* Philosophy, as used here, was the pursuit of any field of scholarly inquiry. Frequently, natural philosophers traveled, giving lectures to support themselves and presenting contemporary ideas to wide audiences. Benjamin Martin (1704–1782) was a mathematician and lecturer; James Ferguson (1710–1776) was a noted astronomer.

12. *Dr. Bevis:* John Bevis (1693–1771), noted British astronomer and student of medical science.

13. *Royal Society:* The Royal Society of London for Improving Natural Knowledge was founded in 1660 and incorporated two years later. Still in existence, it promotes scientific inquiry and research. In the eighteenth century, it welcomed many colonials to its discussions, including Franklin.

14. *counsellor Mingay:* James Mingay, British jurist.

15. *what a silent and drab-coloured creation it would have been:* Here Paine is referring to the plain style followed by some Quakers of his time. Many Quaker meetings enforced the practice that members could not wear bright colors or have sumptuous possessions. In colonial Pennsylvania, this increasingly enforced policy drove many wealthy Friends to convert to other religions.

Others, who stayed in the meeting, adopted personal policies that allowed them to buy goods "of the best sort, but plain."

16. *natural philosophy:* The study of the natural world and related sciences was just beginning to make inroads into schools' curricula in the mid-eighteenth century. Most scientific discovery was pursued by interested amateurs, many of whom shared their ideas in public lectures or by carrying out correspondence with others through the republic of letters.

17. *six distinct òrbs, or planets:* Paine was writing prior to the discoveries of Uranus, Neptune, and Pluto.

18. *balloon:* The first balloon flight was carried out by J.A.C. Charles and the Robert brothers, in France, in December 1783. Numerous other public displays of balloon ascents intrigued enlightened minds in the eighteenth century. After watching one in Philadelphia in 1793, Thomas Jefferson wrote of his longing to own one, to cut the travel time between his home, Monticello, and the nation's capital.

19. *Hotel Philadelphia (formerly White's Hotel)* Parisian hotel near the Church of the Little Fathers, popular with Americans visiting the city.

20. *Achilles Audibert, of Calais:* Achille Audibert, revolutionary French politician who traveled from Calais to London to inform Paine that he had been chosen to serve in the National Assembly. He became Paine's friend, and pled for his release from prison after the death of Robespierre.

21. *Colonel Blackden and Joel Barlow:* Samuel Blackden was a veteran of the American Revolution who pursued business interests in France. He corresponded with Thomas Jefferson, including relating information about French affairs after Jefferson had returned to America in 1789. Joel Barlow (1754–1812), a Connecticut native and one of early America's preeminent men of letters, was in France conducting business affairs at this time. Eventually, he would be one of federal America's leading diplomats, including serving as minister to Algiers in 1796.

22. Page numbers refer to Paine's original manuscript, thus do not correspond to any subsequent printed edition.

BIBLIOGRAPHY

Aldridge, A. Owen. *Man of Reason: The Life of Thomas Paine.* Philadelphia: J. B. Lippincott Company, 1959.

———. *Thomas Paine's American Ideology.* Newark: University of Delaware Press, 1984.

Bailyn, Bernard. *Ideological Origins of the American Revolution.* Cambridge, Mass.: Harvard University Press, 1967.

Foner, Eric. *Tom Paine and Revolutionary America.* New York: Oxford University Press, 1976.

Foner, Philip S., editor. *The Complete Writings of Thomas Paine,* 2 vols. New York: The Citadel Press, 1945.

Fruchtman, Jack, Jr. *Thomas Paine: Apostle of Freedom.* New York/London: Four Walls Eight Windows, 1994.

Gimble, Richard. *Thomas Paine: A Bibliographical Check List of* Common Sense *with an Account of Its Publication.* New Haven: Yale University Press, 1956.

Keane, John. *Tom Paine: A Political Life.* Boston: Little, Brown, and Company, 1995.

Stephans, Hildegard. *The Thomas Paine Collection of Richard Gimble in the Library of the American Philosophical Society.* Wilmington, Del.: Scholarly Resources, 1976.

Wood, Gordon S. *The Creation of the American Republic, 1776–1787.* Chapel Hill: University of North Carolina Press, 1969.

———. *The Radicalism of the American Revolution.* New York: Alfred A. Knopf, 1992.

A NOTE ON THE TYPE

The principal text of this Modern Library edition
was set in a digitized version of Janson, a typeface that
dates from about 1690 and was cut by Nicholas Kis,
a Hungarian working in Amsterdam. The original matrices have
survived and are held by the Stempel foundry in Germany.
Hermann Zapf redesigned some of the weights and sizes for
Stempel, basing his revisions on the original design.

Modern Library is online at
www.modernlibrary.com

MODERN LIBRARY ONLINE IS YOUR GUIDE TO CLASSIC LITERATURE ON THE WEB

THE MODERN LIBRARY E-NEWSLETTER

Our free e-mail newsletter is sent to subscribers, and features sample chapters, interviews with and essays by our authors, upcoming books, special promotions, announcements, and news.

To subscribe to the Modern Library e-newsletter, send a blank e-mail to: sub_modernlibrary@info.randomhouse.com or visit www.modernlibrary.com

THE MODERN LIBRARY WEBSITE

Check out the Modern Library website at
www.modernlibrary.com for:

- The Modern Library e-newsletter
- A list of our current and upcoming titles and series
- Reading Group Guides and exclusive author spotlights
- Special features with information on the classics and other paperback series
- Excerpts from new releases and other titles
- A list of our e-books and information on where to buy them
- The Modern Library Editorial Board's 100 Best Novels and 100 Best Nonfiction Books of the Twentieth Century written in the English language
- News and announcements

Questions? E-mail us at modernlibrary@randomhouse.com.
For questions about examination or desk copies, please visit
the Random House Academic Resources site at
www.randomhouse.com/academic